ICONS OF AMERICAN PROTESTANTISM

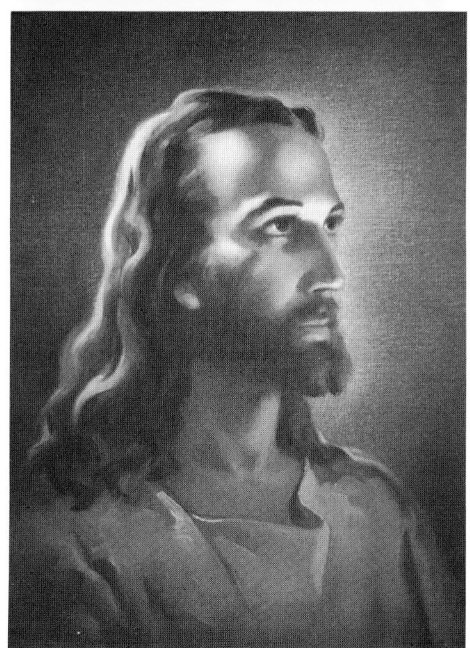

Icons of American Protestantism

THE ART OF WARNER SALLMAN

Edited by David Morgan

Yale University Press   New Haven and London

Published with assistance from the Lilly Endowment, Inc.

Designed by Sonia L. Scanlon.
Set in Bembo type with Optima display by
The Composing Room of Michigan, Inc., Grand Rapids, Michigan.
Printed in the United States of America by
Thomson-Shore, Inc., Dexter, Michigan.

Library of Congress Cataloging-in-Publication Data

Icons of American Protestantism : the art of Warner Sallman /
edited by David Morgan.
p.   cm.
Includes bibliographical references and index.
ISBN 0-300-06342-3 (hardcover : alk. paper)
1. Sallman, Warner, 1892–1968—Criticism and
interpretation.   2. Protestantism in art.   3. Popular culture—
United States.
I. Morgan, David, 1957–
N6537.S29I3   1996
759.13—dc20   95-35800
CIP

A catalogue record for this book is available from
the British Library.
The paper in this book meets the guidelines for permanence
and durability of the Committee on Production Guidelines for
Book Longevity of the Council on Library Resources.

10 9 8 7 6 5 4 3 2 1

Contents

4
The Ministry of Christian Art:
Evangelicals and the Art of Warner Sallman, 1942–1960   123
BETTY A. DEBERG

5
Interchangeable Art:
Warner Sallman and the Critics of Mass Culture   148
SALLY M. PROMEY

6
"Would Jesus Have Sat for a Portrait?"
The Likeness of Christ in the Popular Reception of Sallman's Art   181
DAVID MORGAN

Notes   207

List of Contributors   241

Index   243

Credits for Chapter-Opening Illustrations   247

Color plates follow page 188.

Foreword

N E I L   H A R R I S

This book, or more properly the essays composing it, constitute something of a departure in the study of American religious art. They take, in the religious art of Warner Sallman, what had previously been a marginalized subject and place it solidly and irretrievably within the mainstream of American thought and culture. These scholars give due acknowledgment to the power and pervasiveness of this set of images and the difficult, indeed, the often angry reactions the images aroused. But even more than that, the story they tell reflects the special stresses of American civilization in the mid-twentieth century and reveals several of the fault lines that define and divide our social structure, our religious community, and our intellectual world.

Summary is difficult. But it is necessary before commenting on some of the implications raised by the essays. Several questions seem to dominate the investigation: How were Warner Sallman's images produced and marketed? Where did they come from? Why did so many people consume the art? And what kinds of intellectual issues were raised by its popularity, among both the evangelicals who endorsed it and the liberal Protestants who were more skeptical about its value?

What do we learn from the authors? First, that Sallman's art fits within a long history of Protestant art production in America, whose vigor and variety challenge many popular beliefs. The nineteenth-century origins of his work, or at least its nineteenth-century analogues, centered on a vision of domestic Christian nurture, a physical environment meant to surround the family with reminders of its creed and to announce itself, to others, through its commitments. In itself, as Colleen McDannell points out, the Sallman industry represented a specialized religious-industrial phase of what had once been a secular commerce, and it was built with particular effectiveness, apparently, on wartime distribution. Ingenious and adaptive in its product lines, Gospel Trumpet, later Warner Press, successfully married traditional and modern. When, in the 1960s and 1970s, a new and expansive era in Christian object production and consumption began, more complex destinies awaited the Sallman image, now seen variously in condescending and nostalgic modes, a classic inheritance popular enough for secular companies to profit from it, and making, according to some, an impressive comeback.

Where did the images come from? David Morgan (Chapter 1) and McDannell point to a stock of chromolithographs and engravings by nineteenth-century European painters, a body of work widely distributed in devotional literature, in popular art books, and by such religious presses as the Gospel Trumpet Company. But these were not the only sources of Sallman's imagery. Examining the artist's training and early commercial work, Erika Doss explores the secular visual culture that helped shape him and his religious public. Doss demonstrates that secular commerce and religious piety intermingle in the age of the modern advertising agency. As a prominent advocate of this merger, Bruce Barton fashioned Jesus into a first-rate sales representative whose product had an unlimited market. As Doss shows, Sallman's publishers followed Barton in moving Christianity from "its nineteenth-century feminine and private domination," orienting it "toward a more masculinized public sphere, where audiences were promised . . . self-realization through consumption."

Why have so many found the Sallman images appealing? For any number of reasons, Morgan tells us, based on the varied responses to a survey that he conducted and on his review of the written reactions (Chapter 6). But he wrestles these responses to earth in three large categories having to do with literalism, transformation into presence, and corroboration of ideological expectation: Jesus as he actually was, as he can be seen, and as he is expected or needed to be. Sallman appealed across denominations and income levels, although the images did not fare well among those who found them offensive for reasons of theology, race, or gender. Underlying these generalizations is Morgan's admission that the same face inspires diametrically opposite reactions in viewers, an observation with portentous consequences for any larger analysis. And finally, Morgan suggests that this kind of popular art is essentially corroborative and discursive, fulfilling promises that are based on the life histories, religious beliefs, and cultural values of its audiences, reinforcing their sense of things rather than challenging or extending it. In confirming attitudes, identities, and aspirations rather than provoking, modifying, or transforming them, the Sallman art must be understood as embedded within a set of cultural practices. These are in effect social events and can be interpreted only within the context of the cultural system they help support.

How did evangelical intellectuals and liberal Protestants view these images? Betty DeBerg defines the "neo-evangelical" position in the 1940s and 1950s as a deviation from the hard line of 1920s fundamentalism. A new generation of well-educated conservatives sought a positive basis for faith in the historicity of biblical facts as the only effective way to battle the "ongoing spread of humanistic skepticism and atheism" undermining the historical Jesus. Avoiding crude anti-intellectualism and separatist rhetoric, these neo-evangelicals sought to build consensus among conservative Christians around "sound scholarship, academic credentials, social responsibility, and cultural refinement." Christian art became a desideratum for this group, expressing an evangelical understanding of Christ in ways that stood opposed to the interpretations mandated by the secular art world.

Sally Promey considers how liberal Protestant intellectuals coped with the same art. For them, Sallman's popularity typified an ongoing crisis, his images symbolizing broader trends in culture and politics that they abhorred even more than the portraiture itself. The liberal clergy found Sallman's art, Promey argues, so standardized, sentimentalized, and homogenized—above all, so apparently popular— that it soon stood for a mass culture that threatened cultural and religious authority. Its power and impersonal, predigested conformity suggested a threat to political democracy. These critics claimed that the passive absorption inspired by the art carried over into the political sphere, endangering the critical spirit. Kitsch, dishonest beautifying naturalism, was the curse of contemporary taste.

The liberal clergy, in attacking Sallman's art, forged something of an alliance with such modernist champions as Alfred Barr of the Museum of Modern Art. Modernism's victimization, by both bourgeois critics and totalitarian authorities, gave it a new legitimacy in the eyes of this group, transforming it into an asylum for individuality, independence, vigor, idiosyncrasy, and courageous resistance to mass conformism. Labeling popular religious art effeminate, they dismissed a mass culture that denied the value and the appeal of a masculinized modernism. In effect, the *Head of Christ* was demonized by liberal Christians as they sought their own rapprochement with high culture.

The chapters of this book disclose a story featuring high drama, bitter contest, and a conjunction of many of the great forces traditionally presented as endemic to American history: religious mission, commercial enterprise, aggressive popularization, and the tensions between a taste-defying majority and a resistant saving remnant. Some themes, however, have emerged more recently. These involve an awareness that this art, like many others, is largely defined by its audience and its specific cultural setting. As Morgan argues, the "image of Christ thus inevitably becomes like those whose faith it is appropriated to assist"; it is "part of a cultural system that has shaped Protestant devotion" (Chapter 6). We need, inevitably, more guidance on the cultural conventions governing this image distribution. Textual analysis here points, inexorably, toward contextual reconstruction and a willingness to blur some of the lines between the religious and the secular worlds of display. Precedents, values, and practices can help us move closer to the significance of the Sallman phenomenon.

The success that Sallman enjoyed occurred within a culture flooded by commoditized images designed to enhance personality by stimulating intense emotions and new loyalties in a heterogeneous mass public. Lionizing visions of various kinds, deliberately conceived to nurture hero worship among different kinds of people, must have been absorbed both by Sallman and his audiences: Sallman's popularity was in part a tribute to his successful absorption and translation of existing visual conventions and distributive practices.

What were these conventions? Among them was the legacy of personal promotion and facial display that was current in American life from the second and third decades of the twentieth century until the 1940s and 1950s, the years that saw the production, refinement, and distribution of the Sallman images. By the 1940s and the wartime popularization of Sallman, Americans had two generations of intensive, literally naturalistic and well-prepared facial display behind them, thanks to the combined efforts of commercial advertisers, Hollywood filmmakers, patriotic propaganda, and news reporting. The ingredients of Sallman's most famous image—the uplifted face, the half-turned studio posture, the artist's sketch of head, shoulders, and upper body, the dramatic lighting—as well as some of the specific features and, for other images, the superimposition of epic scenes, could be found in those redefinitions of male and female visual appeal and celebrity that had been conventions of posters, photographs, and magazine covers for decades. Fan magazines and such news magazines as *Time, Life,* and *Fortune;* photo montages, which were particularly popular in wartime; billboard displays; and political campaigns had habituated the mass public to colossal images of heads and shoulders, floodlit, often but not always lithographically enhanced or in technicolor, projecting a golden glow of inspiration, heroism, or simple celebrity. Each clearly represented a cause, an emotion, a state of being. In talking about Sallman and his iconography of the face, we should acknowledge not only Heinrich Hofmann, Léon Lhermitte, and Bernhard Plockhorst but also J. C. Leyendecker, Edward Penfield, Haddon Sundbloom, Norman Rockwell, Batiste Maddalena, Dean Cornwall, and dozens of other commercial artists. The faces and the features varied, of course, but these artists confronted the challenge of designing countenances that simultaneously reassured audiences, meeting their standardized expectations of appropriateness, and provided room for personal construction and interpretation.

All this may or may not have been achieved by commercial photographic portraiture, whose resemblance to Sallman's Christ is pointed out by David Morgan. But it was certainly the task of Yosouf Karsh, Edward Steichen, Alfred Eisenstaedt, and other portrait photographers of the middle third of the twentieth century, Sallman's contemporaries, who worked for mass-circulation magazines and strived to confirm their famous subjects' heroism and yet capture their personal vulnerability. Henry Luce may have been the most effective opponent of

Protestant iconoclasm in the twentieth century, for his publications un-
leashed an epidemic of visual celebrity worship that, in different media
translations, we still live with.

Even more significant, in their own way, were the Hollywood
portrait photographers, artists like George Hurrell, hard at work in the
1930s and 1940s, projecting personalities for those walking brand names,
the stars being worshiped in their own special national cults. These
brilliant planned photographs, sometimes signed and mailed to eager
fans, sometimes just cut out of fan magazines, set the standards for
personal persuasiveness, concentrating in a single likeness a world of
transformation and even of sacrament that lay beyond likeness. "They
had faces then"—the words that have supplied at least one book title—
referred to an extraordinary moment in the history of portraiture. I feel
convinced that Sallman's relation to such images was not a casual one. He
was one of a public that consumed them on a daily basis. The Hollywood
closeups and publicity stills, carefully posed and theatrically lit, were
absorbed by anyone concerned with the business of marketing images.
They were linked to many things in the 1930s and formed a strange
counterpoint to the powerful work of such Farm Security Administra-
tion photographers as Dorothea Lange. The camera narratized even
the unfamiliar faces and demonstrated that they, too, had the power
to move.

Individual stars also played a part in preparing the public for
certain kinds of religious imagery. I think particularly of the long-
haired and bearded Errol Flynn, who, in *Adventures of Robin Hood,* modeled a masculinity that was, to his admirers, appropriately virile and
romantically gentle. Indeed, one might argue that the faces of stars like
Leslie Howard, Flynn, Douglas Fairbanks, and others of this group—
slender, delicate, even, to some, effeminate—paralleled the Sallman
Christ, whom some critics viewed as insufficiently masculine. The
swashbucklers were permitted to redeem their manhood in scenes of
hand-to-hand combat and personal bravery, and perhaps such scenes
were necessary for their reputations.

In any event, the slickly finished pinups produced in the millions
during the 1930s and 1940s entered the personal art collections of hundreds of thousands of people; they were taped to cockpits and foxholes as
well as bedroom walls, and some of them appeared capable of transfer-

ring power, fortune, and inspiration. The worshiped image in mid-century America was not confined to traditional religion.

In certain Protestant households religious images enjoyed respectful shelter. But which households? Who, in the end, displayed religious art in mid-century America? Until recently this question would have been difficult to answer. But the literature of household analysis and inventory is beginning to pile up. It goes back at least as far as Herbert Gans's classic 1962 study *The Urban Villagers* and continues through work done by other social scientists like Edward Laumann and Mihaly Csikszentmihalyi at the University of Chicago. And the publication of David Halle's *Inside Culture* begins to give us even more precise information about American taste for art objects of various kinds, including abstractions, landscape, and religious art.

Whatever generalizations can be made, it seems clear that most of these analyses make structural categories vital. Significantly enough, Halle subtitles his text *Art and Class in the American Home*. Leaving his conclusions aside for the moment (and it seems to me that some of them would be seriously amended by several of the chapters in this book), we would do well, in analyzing the consumption of religious images, to scrutinize the hidden injuries of class. To account for patterns of image display, gender and denomination must be supplemented by class and family structure. Halle argues that the disappearance of renditions of the *Last Supper* from dining room walls has something to do with emerging gender identities, waning notions of women cooking for and waiting on a group of men and then disappearing from sight. Modern medicine and the growth of bureaucracy have both contributed to the decline of saint displays. Truncated Madonnas, in glass, porcelain, and plaster, as well as in paintings and sculpture, reflect new attitudes to virginity. Halle's concern with households divided by class affiliation attempts to get at the audience's construction of venerated images and its tolerance for their display. One might ask whether the same principles apply to political images. Is one likely to find, in the living rooms of well-to-do, upper-middle-class households, magazine photographs of political personalities like the Kennedys or Martin Luther King?

In our culture, image worship is even more closely correlated with age groups than with class membership. The child or adolescent is permitted unadulterated displays of hero worship that would be found unacceptable in adults. Generally these are secular figures—athletes, musicians, movie stars. Their quantity—along with pennants, medals, cups, signs, mottoes, postcards, photos—evokes cohorts of youngsters whose loyalties are intense but changeable and multiple. These children's rooms are display arenas for the proclamation of emotions. Their adult counterparts are dens and rec rooms, often filled with trophies of personal accomplishments or family pictures. These displays are better controlled, more handsomely mounted, more distanced than those of the youths. But they are part of a system of familial presentation. And, in one way or another, religious images in Protestant America coexist with them. To understand the appeal, we must understand more about such settings and the functions they serve in American domestic life.

And, to move to the final point I wish to make here: what is happening now? I believe we must place contemporary interest in religious objects and images in relation to two powerful sensibilities: one, the systematic collection and cataloguing of memorabilia; the other, the growing taste for what could be called distanced or demeaned display, the taste for game playing, burlesque, and sermonizing through slogans, ornaments, and costume. In the first case, the prevailing tone would appear to be nostalgic and elegiac; in the other, ironic. But together both patterns present new issues. The immediate future of the Sallman art is not clear to me. It may be in process of replacement by "Victorian angels and decorative crosses," to use Colleen McDannell's words, or it may be entering a new phase of life, but I would like to speculate on these two additional trends.

First, the breadth of the passion for collecting is rather remarkable. Religious and secular objects alike, of almost any period and character, are pursued by millions of enthusiasts in a highly organized and carefully plotted manner. Flea markets, newsletters, specialized journals, catalogues, electronic mailing lists, and clubs characterize a vast array of collectibles, which acquire commoditized and reliquary value in addition to the semi-utilitarian, affiliative, and expressive purposes that their display and possession served their original consumers. In 1994 the *Chicago Tribune* described contemporary collectors of American religious art, in one of dozens of articles on the subject that the two local newspapers produce annually, along with weekly calendars of fairs and exhibitions.

The impact of the collecting sensibility on the urge to display is complex. For as yesterday's discards become today's trophies and tomorrow's treasures, owners can redefine their relation to art and religious objects. They are custodians and conservators both, amateur scholars and archivists whose purchase of older objects can have an evocative as well as a devotional purpose. What McDannell calls the commercial religious economy includes antique stores as well as Christian bookshops. It also includes scholars who study kitsch, and who form one of the more powerful elements of the collecting culture. As mass culture was once demonized by an intellectual elite, it is now being rescued by another elite, intent on penetrating its codes and sometimes valorizing its status. The symbiosis between the analysts of popular culture and its merchandisers can be as close as that between the dealers and connoisseur-scholars of high culture.

The second contemporary tradition—that of producing, wearing, and displaying objects in an ironic, deprecatory, or critical manner, best expressed, perhaps, through those many T-shirts and bumper stickers that offer improbable invitations or make statements of dubious propriety—suggests how carefully one must look at specific display rituals. The political arena, in the post-Vietnam era, is especially rich here. Coincident with the rise of radical protest, pop art, and the development of the playful, punning, one-line or parody landscape, with its unexpected monuments and commercial preservationism, we find complex systems of provocative transgressions. In the most venerated and contested symbol of nationhood (and an acceptable relic for even the most iconoclastically pious), the American flag, we have seen elaborate and complex modulations, provoking outspoken responses. The flag can be carried or worn in ways suggesting a wide range of positions and emotions on large issues. Once, sacred icons were exploited mainly by commercial interests; now they become available for personal and ideological purposes. A culture simultaneously absorbed by and critical of image worship discloses some older religious biases in the punctuating successions of parade and parody. The market for these commodities is defined by audiences large enough to have frequent changes of attitudes and casts of characters produced for it.

The current taste for religious images, then, rests partly on a longing to restore an older relation between signifier and signified, to return emblematic badges to a place of honor, to announce church affiliation in an unambiguously positive manner. Awarded legitimacy by scholarship (both professional and amateur) and reanimated by a response to parodic defilement, religious objects and images have been given a new centrality. The commercializing forces that theorists of mass culture feared would irrevocably taint religious expression have served instead to highlight it.

Specific judgments aside, we readers can be grateful to the authors of this book for provoking us to think about important things. They remind us of the seamlessness of popular display practices, the variety of their origins, the intimacy of the connections between the sacred and the profane, and above all the need to learn much more about what is going on in the world of image consumption.

Acknowledgments

This book is the culmination of a research project first conceived of in the fall of 1990, when Jason Knapp showed me the collection of original works by Warner Sallman at Anderson University. Supported by seed money from Valparaiso University and the thoughtful assistance of Jason Knapp, I examined the collection in much greater detail in the summer of 1991 and wrote an initial grant proposal. Dorothy Bass encouraged me to submit this to the Louisville Institute for the Study of Protestantism and American Culture, which provided Anderson University with funds as a planning grant. With Jason Knapp, I then submitted a much larger proposal to the Louisville Institute and its parent, the Lilly Endowment. This grant enabled me to gather a team of scholars. Jason Knapp served throughout as an indispensable administrator of the grant and a troubleshooter extraordinaire in a project that configured the interactions of numerous institutions and individuals over the next three years. He ably coordinated and installed the exhibition of Sallman's work at conferences at the University of Chicago's Divinity School and Yale University's Institute of Sacred Music. My debt to him is enormous.

I should like to thank a long list of individuals and institutions. Valparaiso University and Anderson University provided encouragement, resources, and financial support from the inception of the project. The Louisville Institute and the Lilly Endowment were enthusiastically supportive from the beginning. My colleagues at Valparaiso have been of great assistance: Dorothy Bass, Mark Schwehn, and Richard Baepler provided early support and read proposals; Paul Contino, Jim Champion, and the faculty of Christ College contributed constant conversation; Richard Brauer organized a splendid symposium on Sallman at Valparaiso; and Gail Eifrig supplied editorial assistance in the production of the exhibition catalogue. Clark Gilpin and Elena Vassallo at the Divinity School, University of Chicago, were wonderful hosts and planners for the conference there. Peter Hawkins and Dianne Witte hosted a delightful exhibition and conference at Yale. A number of other individuals involved in the planning stage or the conferences should be mentioned as friends of this enterprise: Martin Marty, Robert Orsi, Sue Taylor, Neil Harris, Leonard Sweet, and James Lewis. Several friends and family members of Warner Sallman provided, during the course of research, information and material that have formed the Sallman Archives at Anderson University: Charles Bates, Howard Ellis, Jack Lundbom, and Mr. and Mrs. Richard Sallman. Jim and Gene Sallman deserve special thanks.

Finally, I would like to thank my co-authors for the enthusiasm, creativity, patience, and care that it has taken to complete this project. Their work and collegiality have been inspiring. Conversation with each of them enriched this book immeasurably.

Portions of this book have appeared elsewhere in altered form. Sections of Chapter 1 were published in the exhibition catalogue *Icons of American Protestantism,* a special issue of Valparaiso University's *Cresset.* A much-abridged version of Chapter 6 appeared in the University of Chicago Divinity School's *Criterion.* Chapter 3, by Colleen McDannell, also appears in her book *Material Christianity,* published by Yale University Press.

ICONS OF AMERICAN PROTESTANTISM

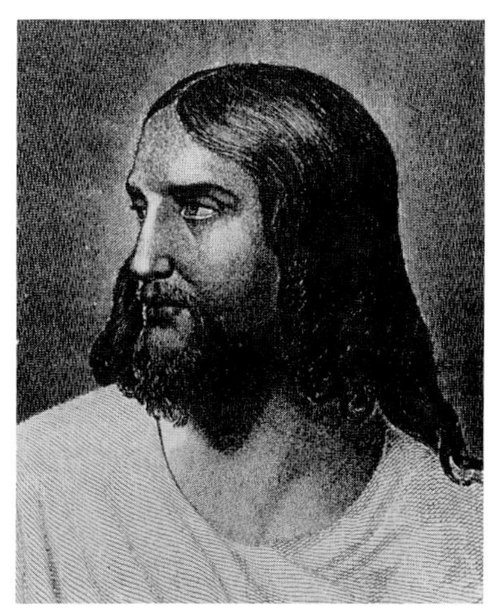

Introduction

DAVID MORGAN

In the age of modern mass culture the sheer volume of production statistics defies comprehension. It is befuddling to contemplate the number of soft drink containers, hamburgers, baseball caps, and crucifixes that are manufactured, bought, and discarded each day. Yet what we can learn from these patterns of popular consumption is rich indeed, and scholars of popular culture have not balked at scrutinizing sales records, consumer response, production figures, marketing strategies, and distribution methods—in short, the vast infrastructure of mass consumption that does more to shape daily life than many care to acknowledge.[1]

Although scholars have produced important work analyzing fast food, popular music, and sports, the popular visual culture of religion has not received as much attention.[2] Perhaps this is because popular religious culture suffers from the double fate of belonging to mass culture and to what academics and intellectuals since the Enlightenment have considered the problematic mentality of religious belief. This book, however, foregrounds the inexpensive, often ephemeral material culture of everyday Christianity by examining the history of the production and reception of the work of arguably the most widely reproduced religious artist in the twentieth century, Warner Sallman (1892–1968). Each of the essays included here explores the production of, use of, or response to Sallman's images within the context of North American Protestantism since the 1920s. Instead of reducing such images to illustrations of theological ideas or "bad art for bad faith" (as theologians and denominational church historians have tended to do) or dismissing them as third-rate art rooted in a mass culture of tastelessness (as cultural critics and art historians might be inclined to do),[3] the scholars in this project have preferred to see Sallman's imagery and its wide dissemination as a crucial part of a cultural system that has shaped religious piety and social identity among millions of American Protestants. We undertake neither a defense nor a critique of religion but a historical analysis of its overlooked visual culture, with the intention of learning more about the role that images have played in twentieth-century Protestantism.

THE VISUAL CULTURE OF PROTESTANTISM

In the long wake of the Reformation, many have claimed that Protestantism, particularly its radical and evangelical varieties, is aniconic—that images have played no important part in, indeed have been explicitly proscribed from, worship and devotional life.[4] Many Protestants regard the notion of a Protestant icon as problematic, even as a contradiction in terms. Yet the popular reception of Warner Sallman's *Head of Christ* (pl. I), painted in 1940, shows that in many instances Protestants have experienced images in ways traditionally associated with Roman Catholicism and Eastern Orthodoxy (see Chapter 6). For generations of Christians since World War II, the *Head of Christ* has represented the authentic portrait of Jesus. But—as articles in devotional magazines and correspondence sent to Sallman, his publishers, and the authors of this volume indicate—the response to this image varies considerably. Those who admire the picture and others by Sallman find in his works the mores, theology, social agenda, and ecclesiology they profess. Millions of believers claim to see in Sallman's art a compelling visualization of the values and devotional and religious ideals that they hold dearest. The imagery acts as a window onto the world as it ought to be. In this manner, Sallman's pictures serve as icons for large numbers of American Protestants.

Contradicting the cliché that Protestants have no truck with images, the popularity of Sallman's picture should encourage scholars of American visual culture to assess the role that Sallman's images have played in popular piety. This book aims to do just that. But expanding the range of American historiography will not suffice, because an even broader prejudice holds that Protestantism from its beginning was inimical toward images and has never afforded any important place to the visual. That this claim is alive in the twentieth century was made plain by the influential Swiss theologian Karl Barth, who reiterated the Reformed position on images in a 1956 essay in which he announced that "there is no theological visual art. Since it is an event, the humanity of God does not permit itself to be fixed in an image." The "fundamental form of theology," Barth insisted, "is the prayer and the sermon."[5] In the early 1520s this view flared into the spectacle of iconoclasm, which, in the minds of the iconoclasts, ushered the Reformation into reality. A history of polemics between Protestant and Catholic ecclesiasts and scholars ensued, which enshrined the destruction of images—from one perspective the cleansing of the church, from another, the wanton destruction of tradition—as a potent symbol of a tenacious cultural divide.

Protestantism, however, in one form or another has always enjoyed a living visual culture, though not always at the level of "high" art. Putting aside such artists of recognized stature as Lucas Cranach the Elder, Rembrandt van Rijn, or William Blake, a long line of popular imagery stretches back from present-day Protestant piety to the earliest days of the Reformation in Europe. The character of Sallman's art—both in its subject matter and in the commercial and mass-produced nature of its production and use—owes much to the history of Protestant image making.

The leaders of the Reformation on the Continent and later in Britain were of several minds regarding images. Martin Luther opposed only those images, located largely in pilgrimage churches, that invited the confusion of image and referent; he considered them idols.[6] He desired that these images, often of the Virgin, be removed from churches in an orderly and officially conducted manner. Luther's position was in stark contrast to that of his former colleague at Wittenberg, Andreas Karlstadt, who wrote vehemently against images in churches as symbols of the papacy and idols inviting worship. Luther maintained that images, once separated from idolatrous abuse in the heart, had an important pedagogical value. Although he appears to have cultivated no taste for painting as a fine art, he welcomed abundant illustrations, including as many as twenty in the first edition of his translation of the New Testament.[7] Subsequent editions carried many more. He encouraged the wealthy to paint Bible stories on their homes for the public good, and he dismissed as bad exegesis the radical Protestant reading of the second commandment as a flat proscription of all images.[8]

Like Calvin after him but in contrast with Luther, the Swiss reformer Ulrich Zwingli set up a fundamental distinction between hearing and seeing: the former symbolizes true faith, the latter false belief.[9] As Charles Garside, Jr., has argued, Zwingli sought to overturn the late medieval emphasis on the material nature of the sacred in the mass, the cult of saints and their relics, and particularly the use of images.[10] Here Zwingli, who argued against Luther's belief in the real presence of the body and blood of Jesus in the sacrament of the altar, joined with Calvin to embrace a rationalism that distinguished the mind from the body as the appropriate medium of communication with the deity. The Bible, according to Zwingli, spoke in comprehensible words that were assembled in the mind to inform human understanding. "Faith," Zwingli wrote, "is from the invisible God and it tends toward the invisible God, and is something completely apart from all that is sensible. Anything that was body, anything that was of the senses, could not be an object of faith."[11] Garside points out that Zwingli's focus on the Word of Scripture was so intense that he often stressed the divine aspect of Christ's two natures "to the point . . . of depreciating His humanity."[12] No images of any kind were to be tolerated in Zurich's churches, not even figurative pew carvings. All were summarily removed in the summer of 1524. The barren walls were then whitewashed to conceal the traces.

John Calvin interpreted Exodus 20:4–5 as an injunction against any image of God, including Jesus, and regarded such pictures as an affront to God's sovereignty, a blatant exercise of human vanity.[13] Images had no place in churches, according to Calvin, and "everything respecting God which is learned from images is futile and false."[14] God was a "Divine energy" who could not be expressed corporeally, a lofty deity, untouchable, incomprehensible, invisible, disembodied, a God whose majesty would not tolerate likeness.[15] The theocentrism of Zwingli and Calvin understood the corporeality of Jesus in strictly historical terms: he was God incarnate, who had died, was resurrected, and ascended to heaven, where he remained corporeally and could not therefore be identified ontologically with any phenomenon here below. To depict the incarnation artistically was, in effect, to deny Christ's post-resurrection spiritual unity with God the Father. Because Christ was in heaven, anything on earth, such as the Eucharist, was only a sign that marked his absence. Images sought to make Jesus present and incarnate, and were therefore, in Zwingli's and Calvin's spiritualistic view, inclined to idolatrous abuse.

Yet neither Calvin nor Zwingli wished to proscribe images in toto. Zwingli repeatedly noted that he enjoyed sculpture and painting, and Calvin assured readers of the *Institutes of the Christian Religion* (1536) that painting for instruction and amusement, insofar as it did not purport to predicate anything of God, was acceptable. By contrast, however, those images displayed in churches that "exhibit bodily shapes and figures" were chosen from a "foolish and inconsiderate longing."[16] Calvin wanted them kept out of the church. In this wish he recalls another well-known iconoclast. In the tenth book of the *Republic* Plato contrasted artistic representations—from poetry to scene painting—which play on feelings (the lower part of the soul), with measurement—measuring, counting, weighing—which appeals to the rational, higher aspect of the soul. *Logos* (thought or word) was able to temper *eros* (longing, or the energies of embodiment) and propel the soul upward and away from preoccupation with the passions.[17] For Calvin, the republic was the church, and images were properly banned because they were reminders of the unruly body. Imaging God meant to "reduce the immense and incomprehensible Deity to the stature of a few feet."[18] Images, in other words, embodied God—or presumed to do so, Calvin asserted, in a vain act that offended a divinity who was unlike any form that the human mind might conceive in its desire to "imagine a god suited to its own capacity."[19] God chose to reveal himself in his *words* recorded in Scripture, disembodied signifiers that spoke not to the imagination and its carnal proclivities but to the mind.

Art historian Hans Belting has pointed out that the sixteenth-century iconoclastic reformers in Switzerland and Germany regarded the destruction of images as the appropriate symbol of the Reformation.[20] Storming churches and removing their images were seen as the equivalent of Christ's cleansing the temple of merchants plying the trade of atonement. The reformers sought to purge the church of its medieval commerce with the transcendent, which they felt commodified the spiritual goods of faith as the material capital of relics and images. What the reformers accomplished in short order was the substitution of one economy for another. By privatizing capital, by dismantling the caste of priests to found a priesthood of believers empowered by the mass production of Bibles and pamphlets, the reformers shifted intercourse with the divine from the image to the word. Fueled by the printing press and the rise of literacy, partisans of the Reformation privileged the word as the basis of divine communication. The economy of indulgences was replaced by the "metaphysical" economy of substitutionary atonement. Images were put to the new task of selling the Reformation, which often meant representing Luther in an appealing way. Artists in the Reformation party hastened to respond to the new paradigm in the hope of preserving their livelihood. Thus, in 1525, Albrecht Dürer presented to the Lutheran city of Nuremberg his portraits of four New Testament authors and included passages from their writings taken from Luther's German translation of the New Testament. As Belting has discussed, Lucas Cranach the Elder worked with Luther to create a Reformation iconography for a new didactic imagery that conveyed law and gospel, the doctrinal formula of Lutheran theology.[21]

Popular response to the Reformers' views on images varied, but

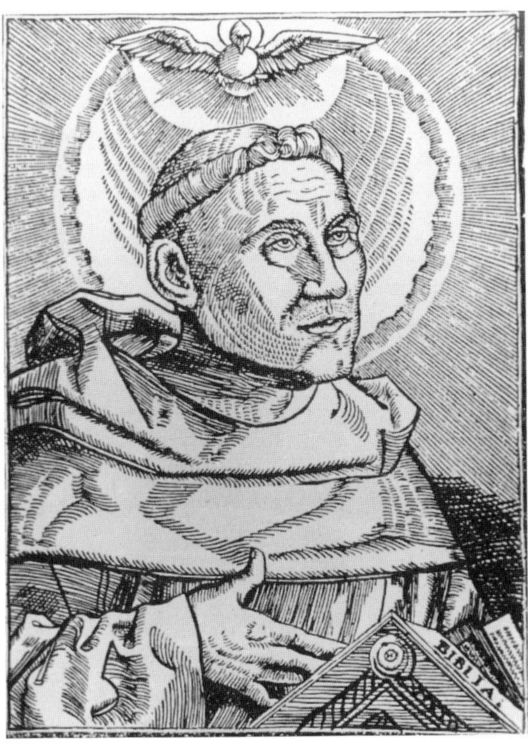

i.1. Hans Baldung Grien, *Luther as Monk with
Dove and Nimbus*, 1521, woodcut. From *Im
Morgenrot der Reformation,* ed. Julius von Pflugk-
Hartung (Lorrach: A. Rhode, 1924), 405.

the taste for images did not subside.[22] The new print technology provided inexpensive images for a Protestant market in Northern Europe in
the sixteenth century.[23] Lucas Cranach the Elder provided woodcuts for
Luther's translation of the Bible and illustrated title pages of pamphlets
by the reformer.[24] Cranach, his son, and their workshop of painters and
printers supplied this market with numerous portraits of Luther: Luther
as Doctor, Monk, Husband, Preacher, Reformer, and Evangelist.[25]
Prints of the reformer could be displayed in the home and public house,
exchanged as gifts, handed down as heirlooms, and afforded by those not
in the position to commission oil paintings. Hans Baldung Grien portrayed Luther in a woodcut of 1521 as a faithful monk whose study of and
appeal to the Bible were genuine and inspired by the Holy Spirit (fig. 1 of
the introduction, hereafter referred to as i.1). Luther appears in monastic

vestments and tonsured; the Bible is unambiguously labeled, and the nimbus of the symbolic dove radiates to form a halo about the monk.

What is most striking in the image in light of the subsequent history of Protestant image making, however, is the three-quarters head-and-shoulders format and the steadfast gaze. The same format appears in Rembrandt's well-known oil studies of Christ (see fig. 2.1). In the modern period, it appears in the frontispiece of *Cobbin's Commentary on the Bible* (1876), entitled *Our Savior* (fig. i.2), and in extracts of Christ's portrait from larger works by Heinrich Hofmann (fig. i.3) and Mihaly Munkácsy (see fig. 2.3). Sallman then excerpted Christ's image from Léon Lhermitte's 1892 *The Friend of the Humble* (figs. i.4 and i.5) to create *Son of Man* in 1924 (fig. i.6) and *Head of Christ* (pl. I). The iconography of

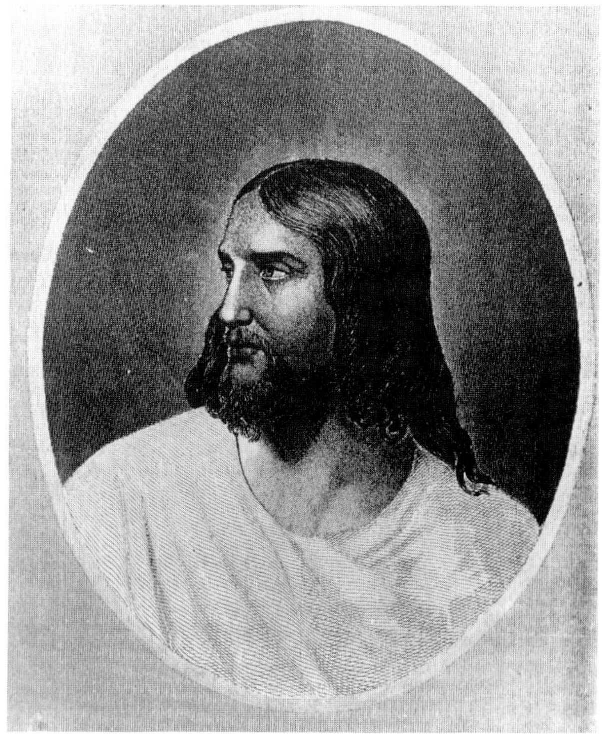

i.2. Original painting by Paul Delaroche, engraved
by John G. MacRae, *Our Savior*. From Rev. Ingram
Cobbin, *Cobbin's Commentary on the Bible for
Young and Old*, ed. Rev. E. J. Goodspeed (New
York: Selmar Press, 1876), vol. 1, frontispiece.

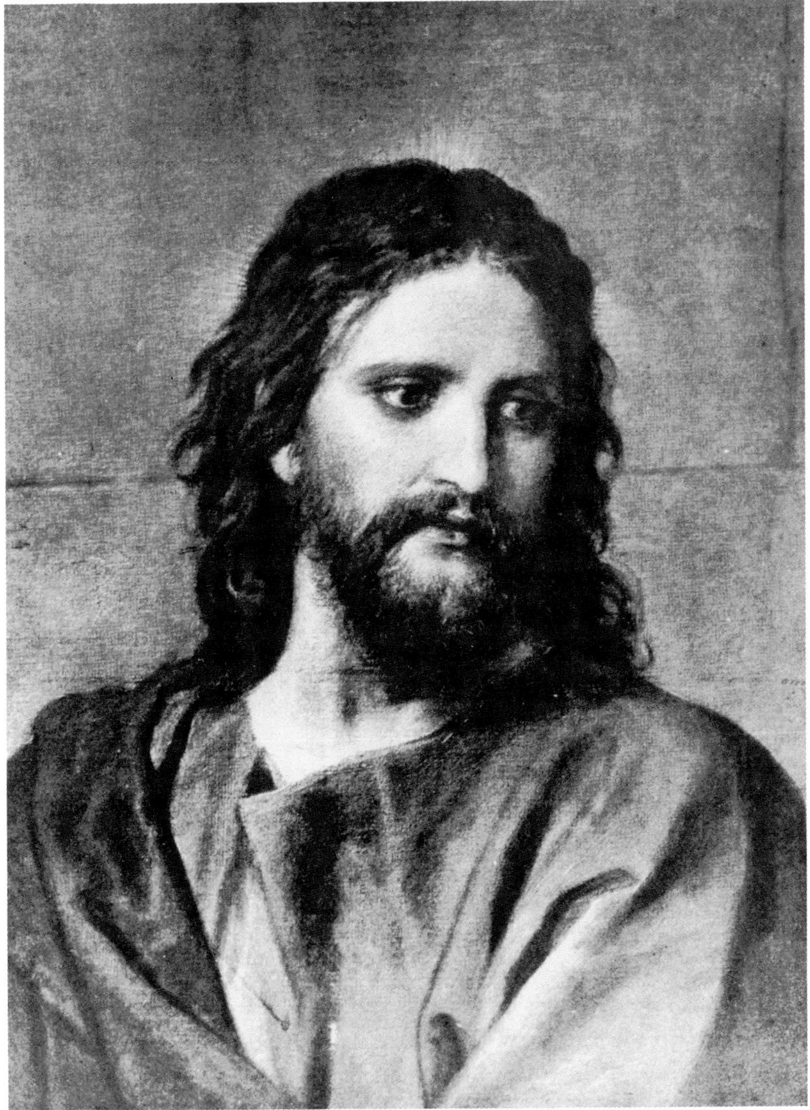

i.3. Heinrich Hofmann, *Christ and the Rich Young Ruler,* 1899, detail, oil on canvas.
Courtesy Riverside Church, New York.

Christ's face can be traced back to sixth-century Byzantine icons. Hans Belting has tracked the movement of the portrait from the Eastern icon to its introduction in late medieval Europe in the form of the devotional image portraying Christ's passion.[26] Such imagery provides a close focus

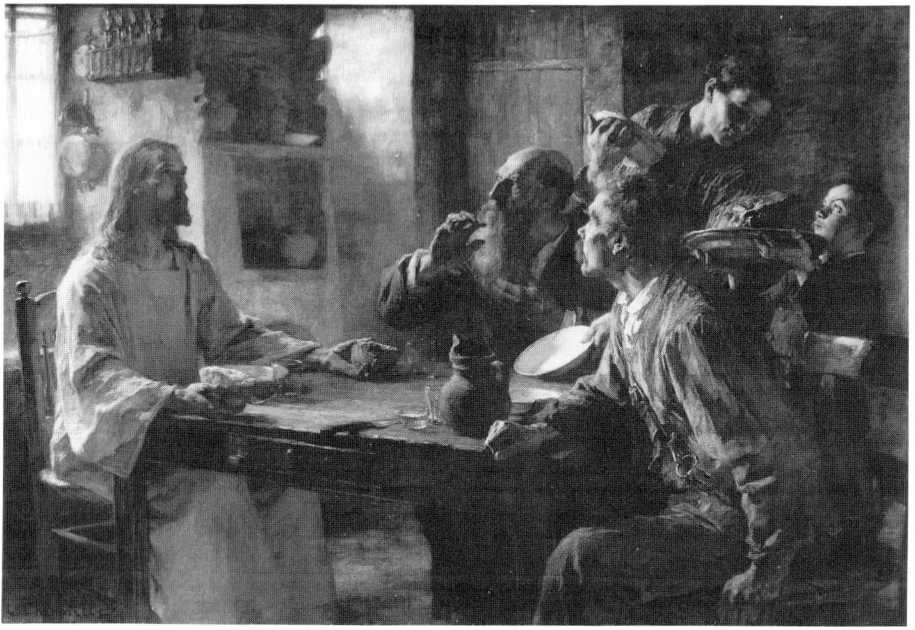

i.4. Léon Lhermitte, *The Friend of the Humble*, 1892, oil on canvas, 61¼ × 87¾". Gift of
J. Randolph Coolidge, courtesy Museum of Fine Arts, Boston.

on the head, shoulders, and upper torso of Christ to create an intimate
encounter with the savior, in whose pain and torment the devout viewer
was invited to participate empathically. All its historical particularities
notwithstanding, however, the head-and-shoulder format has consistently signified immediacy and intimacy and has engaged the viewer in a
contemplative gaze popular among the devotional cults of Christianity
and (as Neil Harris suggests in the Foreword) among the personality
cults of modern celebrities, whose glossy photographs (signed in order
to compound their authenticity—the medieval equivalent would have
been the relics of the pictured saint) are avidly collected by devoted fans
and displayed reverently in the home. Although such images may represent the secularization of religious iconography, they reflect Protestants'
inclination to identify with the hero of faith, to take part in the hero's
experience, and to understand redemption as a direct appeal to the savior,
which is experienced as an intimate relation—as personal knowledge of
the savior's life. The image is the material means for realizing this relation. Whether the knowledge is expressed as a daily reading of the life of

Christ in the Gospels, memorization of the decisive dates in the career of Martin Luther (fig. i.7), or familiarity with the favorite sport, favorite color, model of car, and current lover of a movie star, the image mediates between the hero figure and the devotee, imaginatively embodying the knowledge.

The Reformation in England and its legacy enforced a rejection of anything resembling the religious icon or the votive portraiture of the saints, Mary, and Christ, although secular portraiture thrived like no other pictorial genre. But contrary to the notion that English Protestants repudiated all images, Tessa Watt has pointed to the wide use of emblem books among artisans in the early seventeenth century and the fact that embroidery pattern books included "scenes of Adam and Eve, the pelican in her piety, and even the crucifixion."[27] Watt argues persuasively that word and image were engaged in conflict with one another during

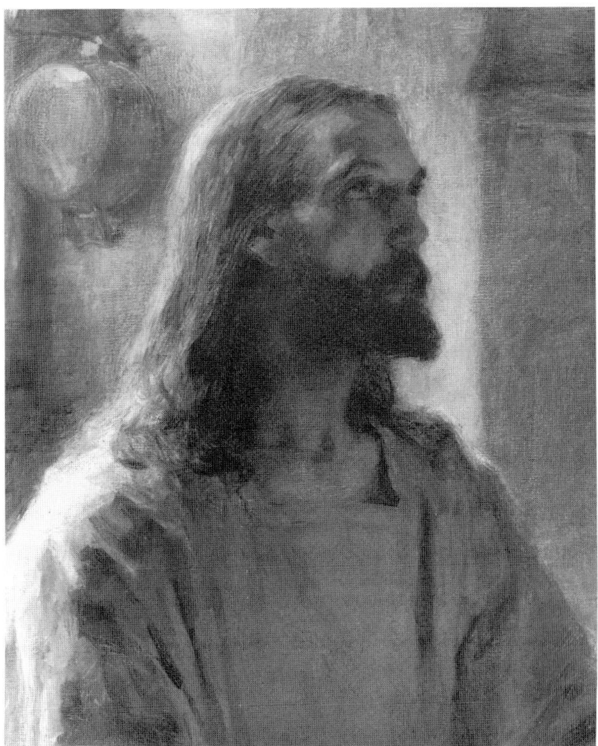

i.5. Léon Lhermitte, *The Friend of the Humble*, 1892, detail. Gift of J. Randolph Coolidge, courtesy Museum of Fine Arts, Boston.

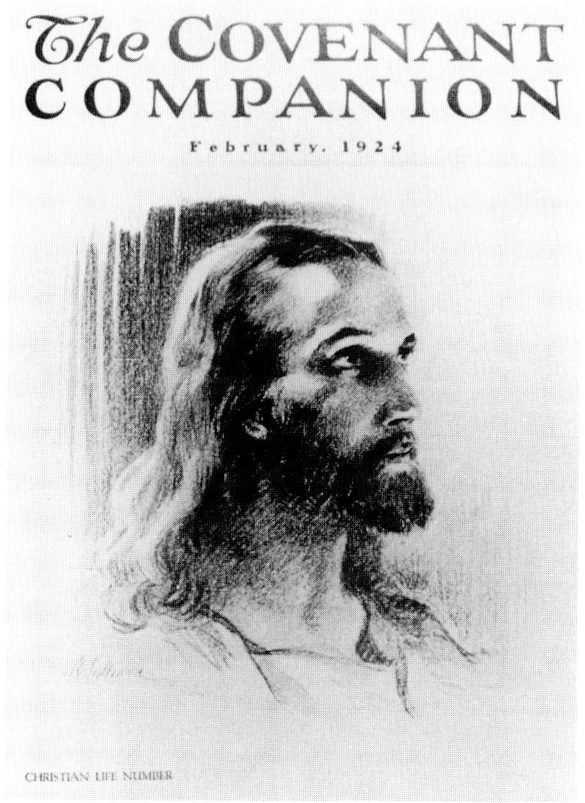

i.6. Warner Sallman, *Son of Man*, 1924. From *Covenant Companion*
(February 1924), cover. Collection of James B. Sallman; Covenant
Publications, 5101 N. Francisco, Chicago, IL 60625.

and after the English Reformation but that neither one ever triumphed
over the other. Text and image intermingled in the fascinating visual
culture of broadsides, frontispieces, and illustrated pamphlets. Prayers,
Bible verses, songs, and didactic inscriptions were arranged around images in woodcut prints that Protestants attached directly to walls in their
homes or to painted cloths hung on the wall. "A Meditation on the
Passion" (1630) contained text in the shape of three crosses, thereby
visualizing text in a manner that must have seemed acceptable to English
iconophobes who followed Zwingli and Calvin on the preeminence of
the word.[28]

Seventeenth-century book illustration also included the development of an elaborate schematic iconography in millennialist Joseph

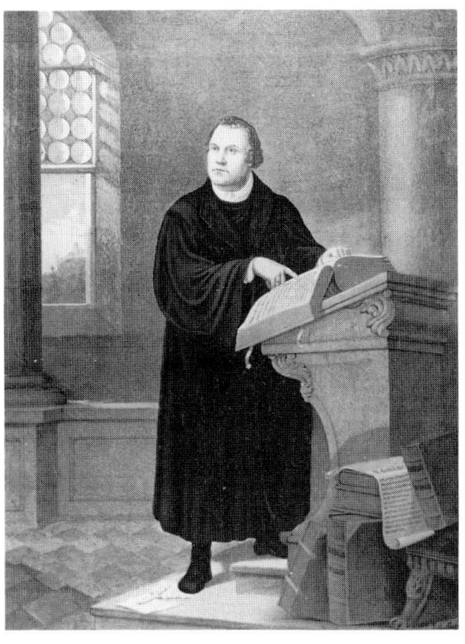

i.7. F. W. Wehle, *Dr. Martin Luther,* 1882,
lithograph. Milwaukee Litho and
Engraving Company.

Mede's 1643 *Key to the Revelation* (fig. i.8).[29] This kind of chart, representing a chronological interpretation of the Bible's prophecies, appeared in
many eighteenth- and nineteenth-century expositions as a frontispiece or
insert and became a lithographed poster among the American Millerite
group in the early 1840s. The Millerites also published a variety of prophetic charts and images in their newspapers and pamphlets for the
purpose of mass distribution on the eve of the apocalypse.[30] This imagery integrated word and image into a single graphic scheme that charted
time encoded in biblical symbols of prophecy. Although the Millerites
expressed antagonism toward realistic pictorial portrayals of Christ's
second coming, the highly symbolic representation of the event in schematic diagrams was not only acceptable but also a favored means among
the Millerites for spreading the word and teaching both children and
adults.[31]

Why would mass-produced images be acceptable to otherwise
iconophobic Protestants? Such images were often riveted to words that,
Protestants no doubt felt, exhausted the meaning of the image.[32] With no
surplus of meaning, the image remained a controlled sign, a denotation
that only reinforced the accompanying text. Seventeenth-century German woodcuts often carried as headings such phrases as *warhafttige Ab-
contrafeyung* (truthful counterfeit), *wahre Abcontrafactur* (real facsimile), or

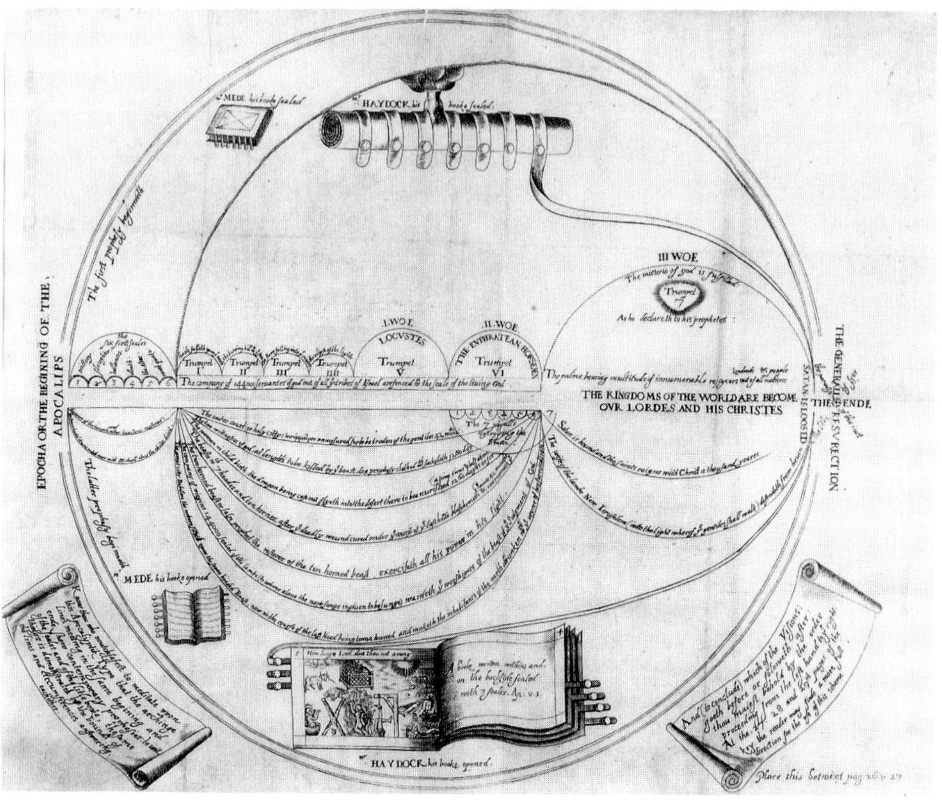

i.8. *The Apocalyptic Type*, engraving. From Joseph Mede, *The Key of the Revelation* (London, 1643), facing p. 27. Courtesy Department of Special Collections, University of Chicago Library.

eigentliche Abbildung (actual illustration).[33] Such oxymorons signified a mechanical duplication, which underscored the ontological distinction between the original and the copy while authenticating the image as a "faithful copy." The mass-produced image was not easily confused with its original because the image was generally (though not always) inexpensive and was composed of an ephemeral medium. Further, because the woodcut was not a precious object (unlike a painting or the work of a silversmith or jeweler) and was widely used as a vehicle of information, iconophobic Protestants in the Netherlands, England, and elsewhere may not have considered it a signifier of the body and its passions or a mark of vanity and self-importance. As a popular medium of information about such things as ominous celestial events, the execution of notorious murderers, natural wonders and oddities, and extraordinary

medical abnormalities, the woodcut belonged to a visual culture of reportage, documentation, novel information, and human interest.[34] As
such, the print image did not call attention to itself but gestured toward
historical referents and wove itself into the fabric of textual discourse that
accompanied every description of a comet, strange heavenly appearance,
flood, miraculous animal, beached whale, or execution. Typically such
reportage carried a moral purpose, such as a divine message or legal
retribution for misdeeds. So the print medium channeled to the public
morally useful information behind which the medium safely concealed
itself, a real counterfeit of something else.

Use of the print medium exploded in the eighteenth and nineteenth centuries under the auspices of the encyclopedia, which continued
to use the print illustration as a principal form of information, and of such
periodicals as annual almanacs, quarterly journals, monthly magazines,
and, eventually, daily newspapers. Many publishers in nineteenth-century
Europe and North America determined that the Protestant market could
bear almost countless ventures in illustrated Bible publication. An exhaustive list would be long indeed, and the range in quality quite broad.[35]
The well-known Bible by artist Julius Schnorr von Carolsfeld, patterned
after the late medieval *Biblia pauperum,* was nothing but images portraying crucial moments from Genesis to Revelation in Schnorr's academic
style (fig. i.9).[36] His plates were often appropriated and reused in other
contexts, as were the widely disseminated images of Gustave Doré (see
fig. 2.4).[37] Bibles illustrated by artists who, like Doré, provided imagery
for other great works of literature sold well. Consumers came to expect
illustrations in novels, epics, and the Bible. Religious publishing firms
produced Bibles aimed at families and children, such as Cassell's Illustrated Family Bible (4 volumes, 1859–63), published by John Cassell,
British Methodist and advocate of temperance.[38] Cassell also published
the English-language version of Doré's Bible, around 1866. A wide array
of illustrated biblical commentaries and books depicting the life of Christ
appeared in the last decades of the nineteenth century, among them
Cobbin's Commentary on the Bible for Young and Old (1876; see fig. i.2) and
Edward Eggleston's *Christ in Art* (1875), which showcased the well-
known illustrations of Alexandre Bida.[39]

The history of nineteenth- and twentieth-century Protestant visual culture is largely one of mechanically reproduced images linked in
some way to a text—whether printed or memorized—and used as a

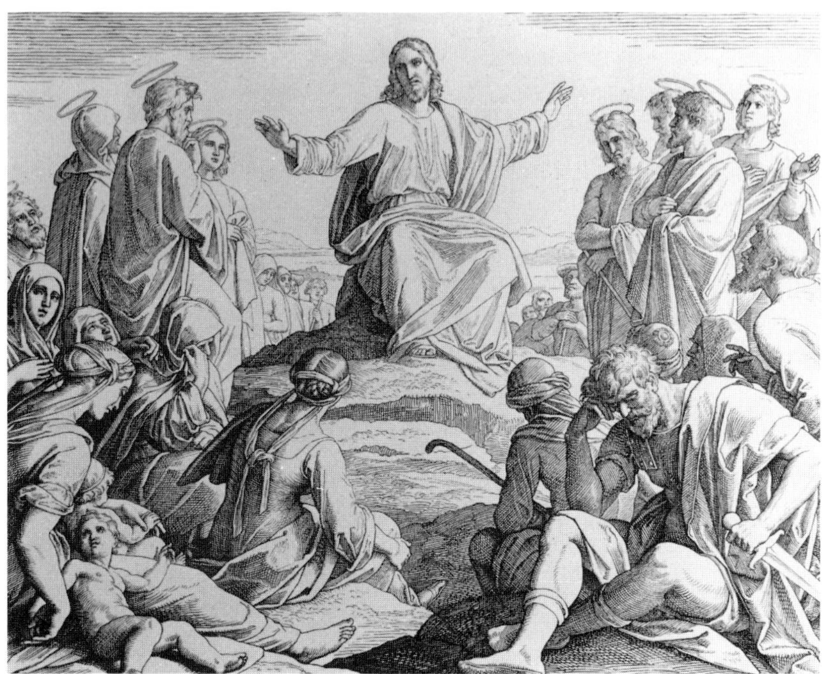

i.9. Julius Schnorr von Carolsfeld, *Sermon on the Mount,* woodcut. From *Die Bibel in Bildern*
(Leipzig: Georg Wigland Verlag, [1870?]), pl. 186.

means of teaching a particular biblical doctrine or interpretation, or of
remembering either a historical event or one from the life of the individual who received the image as a commemorative gift. Religious publishing houses produced a wide variety of both expensive and inexpensive
gifts to mark birthdays, baptisms, confirmations, weddings, and anniversaries. These greeting cards, mottoes, Bibles, or certificates typically
displayed scriptural texts. The result was a material and graphic isolation
of the word to be placed in the home or office in order to remind the
owner or family members or announce to visitors what Protestants considered the essential form of truth: the scriptural word.

This cultural obsession with the word is further evident in the
sometimes excessive concern for the legibility of images in the history of
Protestant visual culture. From the altar paintings by Cranach, which
carry captions of scriptural text, to visual narratives from Rembrandt's
etchings of biblical subjects to William Hogarth's moralizing serials to
Blake's illustrated poetry, images depicted by Protestant artists have

often been narrative or allegorical and densely encoded with references to literary discourse. The image has often not been allowed to stand alone: its function has been not to draw attention to itself but to act as a sign that tells a story. Were the image left to its own devices, its meaning would be subject to autonomous interpretation or might be understood to function independent of any text. The presence of biblical text in mottoes or captions, and the use of a conventional code of gestures, symbols, or subjects, all served to anchor the signification of the image. Combining word and image clarified meaning: the image invited explicit interpretation, and the text was naturalized—given a spatial and concretely historical referent. The image was made to speak, as it were; it was committed to a didactic purpose.

A nineteenth-century lithograph of Martin Luther (see fig. i.7) represents an obvious instance of this tradition of visual legibility. Produced by the Milwaukee Litho and Engraving Company in 1882 after a painting by F. W. Wehle, the image gathers together a host of references to the popular history of the career of Luther; indeed, an open scroll lists the principal dates from the reformer's life, ending in 1546 with "seliger Tod" (blessed death). Luther stands at a lectern, clothed in a doctoral robe, which underscores the academic title of "Dr." written in the margin beneath the image. Standing on a letter of indulgence (*Ablassbrief*), which he has decisively torn in two, Luther rests a clenched fist on the large Bible and gestures with the other hand to a legible passage, Romans 3:28, his finger pointing to the word *allein* (alone) from the phrase "by faith alone." This is, of course, a reference to justification by faith, which Luther put in the place of atonement by indulgence. He stands conspicuously, as if in reference to the famous announcement, "Here I stand, I can do no other." The Bible before which he stands is clearly his translation; on the floor beside the lectern, notably closed in contrast to the open German Bible, are the Vulgate and the Jewish Bible. The castle seen through the window may be the Wartburg, where Luther translated the Old and New Testaments. Light enters through the window, illuminating his translation or interpretation of Scripture, blessing his historical mission, and sanctioning his authority as the leader of the Reformation and the founder of the ecclesiastical tradition that followed, particularly among the German immigrant population in nineteenth-century America to which the Milwaukee firm directed its products. The image is so densely encoded with tropes and symbolic references—set within an otherwise empty and generic interior—that it appears almost to be a mnemonic device, a visual shorthand of the life of Luther.[40]

    The sale of this and many other kinds of items among devout Protestants exemplifies what Laurence Moore has discussed, namely, that piety and commerce in nineteenth- and twentieth-century America have become finely intermeshed.[41] Moore acknowledges that the two have always been linked in one way or another, but the mass production of religious material culture, particularly images, catered to the American demand for religious commodities in an economy that was already shifting from producer-based to consumer-based industries in the late nineteenth century.[42] Although clergy continued to believe that sermons, revivals, and personal appearances were important, radio, television, and the print media, all shaped by the marketplace and commodifying their religious message, became the preferred means of many religious leaders to affect public and private conduct. As Moore writes, "The technology and the distribution networks that made possible the creation of larger and larger reading audiences stimulated alert entrepreneurs who concluded that personal contact was neither necessary nor even particularly useful in efforts to affect people's behavior."[43] Religious and secular domains learned from one another. Gifts of religious images and objects, no matter how inexpensive and ephemeral, could convey what mattered.[44] The mass media were but an effective channel for communicating truth. Religious publishers turned out products for which their secular counterparts had found markets. Conversely, politicians and advertisers made extensive use of sacred imagery and language in merchandising their products. The packaging of information was the central concern of every cultural producer in the age of the mass media.

PRODUCTION AND RECEPTION AS A CULTURAL SYSTEM

The mistaken assumption that Protestantism lacks a significant visual practice has caused students of art and religion to overlook fruitful opportunities for investigating how religious communities understand themselves, how they convey their self-understandings, and how they practice their devotion in both private and public spheres. One of the most iconographically distinctive, and certainly the most ubiquitous, bodies of images deployed in Protestant communities (also widely used among Roman Catholics as well, though on a smaller scale) is the work of Warner Sallman. Sallman's publishers provided an image for every occasion in the daily lives of the devout: pictures by Sallman adorned bookmarks, calendars, prayer cards, tracts, Bibles, lamps, clocks, plates, buttons, stickers, and stationery. Promoters gave special attention to literature catering to youth in the church. Images by Sallman illustrated Sunday school materials, devotional services, and conferences for youth. Conservative Protestants undertook special initiatives during the postwar era to secure youth membership in the church, and Sallman's art played an important role in outreach. His pictures were immensely popular gifts on such occasions as baptisms, confirmations, marriages, birthdays, and anniversaries.

Zwingli had considered the word of God to be the privileged medium precisely because it made no appeal (in his view) to the sensuous domain of the body as constructed by sight. "Why," he asked rhetorically, "do we not send images to unbelievers so that they can learn belief from them?"[45] Why indeed, Sallman's publishers may well have asked, for they supplied a global market with images of Jesus, which church groups and religious organizations sent around the world during World War II and after. Yet, to take Zwingli's point, which was, in effect, substantially expanded and explored by Roland Barthes: the message of the photographic image is imbricated with the textual codes of discourse, which connote something other than what we see. But we naturalize the codes by taking the image to signify them.[46] This operation of connotation or imbrication is not limited to the photograph, however. Sallman's imagery naturalizes what his viewers think or have been told to think, and it is able to do so in no small way because of the massive dissemination of his work. People so often see it and have continually seen it since childhood in so many places that it acquires a kind of de facto normative stature. As many people say, it's what Jesus looks like.[47] By virtue of its ubiquity, Sallman's image has informed at least two generations of mid- to late-twentieth-century Christians in North America and abroad.

There are many ways to view images. We can see them as objects of beauty, as historical artifacts, as mementos, as articles of piety, or as propaganda in the service of a particular ideology. The images painted by Warner Sallman have been seen in each of these ways and many more. Scholars could certainly critique Sallman's art as a commercial phenomenon with no authentic spiritual content, but not without treading on the faith of millions and not without engaging in religious polemics. The authors of this book have sought to find more in the production and reception of the Sallman imagery than an excuse to attack what many regard simply as bad art. Recent scholarship in the humanities and social sciences has sought to de-center the study of culture from the traditional pivot of the individual creator: the genius, artistic or otherwise, who has served as the measure of cultural achievement since the Renaissance. The shift from "creation" to cultural "production" has refocused attention on the interacting processes that make up any cultural moment. Rather than creations, one speaks of the cultural work that fashions signs of prestige or worlds of meaning. But more than that, the signs themselves are understood as the products of a systemic action, a complex interplay of forces, interests, cultural rhetorics, and forms of representation that evoke diverse and often conflicting reactions. Many students of culture and society today understand the artist as a producer rather than a creator, that is, as someone who participates, knowingly or not, in a cultural system to which the artist contributes and by which he or she is variously shaped. Only the rashest critics are prepared to argue that the artist's work is strictly or totally determined by the marketplace, just as only the most reactionary will persist in claiming that true artists rise fully above the historically and socially rooted conditions of their lives.[48] A systemic approach to the study of visual culture argues neither for a totalizing theory of causation nor for a heroic one but, rather, configures a host of social realities in the production of a visual artifact.

Among the most instructive examinations of cultural categories and hierarchies is Lawrence Levine's *Highbrow Lowbrow,* which argues that "culture is a process, not a fixed condition; it is a product of unremitting interaction between the past and the present."[49] Rather than sacralize Shakespeare (or Spenser or Poussin) as an immortal jewel in the crown of Western culture, the historian should locate Shakespeare's works within the context of their production and reception—in the sixteenth century or anytime thereafter. Levine describes the process by which the popular American renditions of Shakespeare and Beethoven, interlarded with skits and ditties in the first half of the nineteenth century, were transformed over the next fifty years into the vaunted, purist, sacralized presentation of authentic works of genius.[50] The sacralization of art scorns the idea of rendition or interpretation in performance and holds devoutly to the notion of an artwork's original purity. This attitude, as Levine documents, regards the artist and the work of art as a standard to which the audience must conform its taste in order to become elevated.[51] Such condescension deliberately undermines the capacity of a director, conductor, or performer to change the "authoritative" text of the composer or playwright. Popular enjoyment is subordinated to critical response. The work of art exists as a direct communication between a prophetic artistic genius and the faithful few who are uplifted by a revelatory experience.

This understanding of art has led many to ignore Sallman's art or to condemn it as religious kitsch. But in its zeal to make certain works of art transcendent, the sacralized view of art conceals the world of social relations that endow any image with its meanings, uses, and abuses. Following Clifford Geertz's cognitive theory that culture is a complex system of meaning-making activities, this book maps out and describes in detail the fundamental components of the cultural system that produced Sallman's images.[52] This system is composed of many fluctuating parts and cannot be understood as a simple mechanism or as a mere arithmetic equation showing, for example, that artist plus publisher plus marketplace equals imagery. The configuration of factors that shaped Sallman's art may be broadly organized into categories of production and reception, each of which was composed of several facets. We know, for instance, that Sallman, as a commercial artist, worked closely with Fred Bates, his publisher and de facto art director, in developing visual concepts. Sallman also listened closely to his consumers by receiving their mail, speaking with them at church, and interacting with audiences in his "chalk talks" in the 1940s, 1950s, and 1960s. Church groups commissioned him to create images for special occasions, campaigns, and mass rallies. Moreover, Sallman competed in a growing market of religious publishers plying the face of Jesus and the material culture of piety. Clearly, all parties within this network of exchange communicated with one another across the marketplace of religious supply and demand. On the side of production was the impetus of Sallman's publishers and the trade they knew, the history of Protestant image making, the conventions and practices of commercial art, and the artist's personal and religious commitments. On the side of reception were those factors that provided the market and use for Sallman's pictures: the practice of observing holidays and rites of passage with commemorative religious gifts, critical response to Sallman's imagery and its popularity, and the institutional uses of the imagery by religious groups. This array of cultural operations must be situated within such historical circumstances as World War II and the Cold War, which provided the occasion for Sallman's imagery to become so popular. These aspects constitute the shifting lineaments of a system, a changing configuration of forces and interests that are collectively responsible for the social fact of Sallman's art.

A few art historians studying "high" art have shown that a comparable approach can be taken in studying the museum piece.[53] Yet the study of popular culture may well take the lead in visual studies because the scholar is freed from traditional fine-art constraints, unhindered by disciplinary preoccupations with such hierarchical or evaluative categories as "masterpiece," "aesthetic quality," "genius," and the biography of the "great man." We would like to understand in Sallman's art and its popularity more about the use of religious images in twentieth-century everyday life. In so doing, we will neither ignore nor lament the fundamentally commercial character of Sallman's imagery, for we see work like Sallman's as part of the American marketplace of culture, where piety has embraced commerce not merely to survive but to flourish. To give the *Head of Christ* as a gift is both to commodify religious practice and to transmit piety, establishing a symbolic continuity between the past and the present. Holding both a material and a symbolic place within the system of social relations that makes up the practice of belief, Sallman's picture must be understood as the product of a marketplace in which belief is not subverted but promoted by consumption.

The chapters in this book situate production and reception within a single cultural system because the authors seek to move beyond understanding an image as only an artistic intention or only a market strategy or only a religious fetish or only an object of discourse. An image is never simply what an artist says it is but is also what the artist's training, publisher, dealer, market, audience, and critics say it is. The ontology of a work of art is restricted neither to the artist's intention nor to the formalist view of the image as some sort of irreducible thing in itself. An art object is a complex and ongoing social event composed of many cultural practices, which should be analyzed in terms of their social and historical relations to one another. Created in a studio, manufactured in a printing factory, sold in stores, installed in homes and churches, exchanged as gifts, and cherished as mementos, Sallman's mass-produced images belong to a cultural economy in which the inexpensive image is charged with crucial significance. It is this entire cultural system that has characterized the practice of what one might call the visual piety of twentieth-century American Christianity in general, and conservative Protestantism in particular.

In Chapter 1, I provide an analysis of Sallman's art in terms of its production and reception, intended to introduce the reader to the range of Sallman's imagery, its themes, and a host of issues that have occupied the investigation. Essays by Erika Doss (Chapter 2) and Colleen McDannell (Chapter 3) focus on issues of production. In addition to providing biographical background on Sallman, Doss examines the relation between the artist's early secular illustration practice and his subsequent work as a religious image maker. McDannell conducts a study of the industry of religious material culture and Sallman's publishers in order to situate Sallman's career and the consumption of his work within the historical patterns of nineteenth- and early twentieth-century religious merchandising and production. Betty A. DeBerg (Chapter 4) provides the necessary theological context by discussing American evangelicals during the 1940s and 1950s and exploring their concerns about the role that imagery might play in the evangelical effort. Sally M. Promey (Chapter 5) studies the critical reception of Sallman's art among the liberal Protestant intelligentsia, whose volatile rejection of the imagery was rooted in aspirations for cultural legitimacy in postwar America. In the final chapter, I focus on the popular reception of Sallman's art, by drawing on 531 letters received in response to an ad that I placed in numerous religious magazines to solicit reactions to Sallman's work.

Together, these chapters locate Sallman's work within a cultural system of production and reception. The devotional use of the images combined what Sallman produced with what the publisher promoted and supplied and what the believer needed psychologically and was predisposed by popular discourse to expect. Public, publisher, artist, marketplace, and ecclesiastical institutions together constitute a cultural matrix that shaped the visual piety of mid-twentieth-century conservative American Protestantism. Any attempt at understanding Sallman's pictures that does not consider all these factors seems destined to provide an incomplete account, and probably one committed to the polemical task of either denouncing or defending the work. If we are to grasp the abundant and hitherto overlooked historical significance of the Sallman corpus, we must place the images within the full context of their production and consumption.

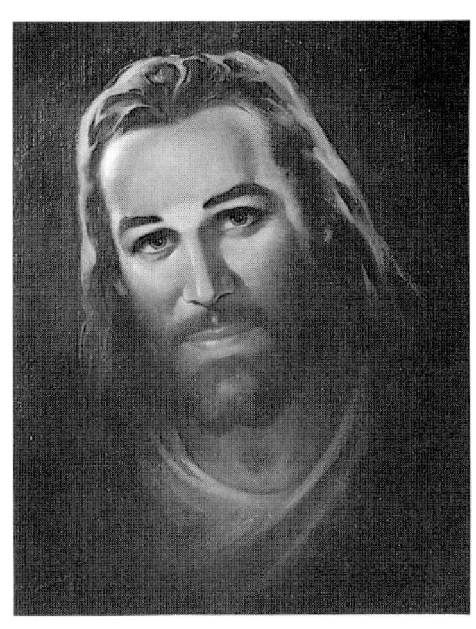

Warner Sallman and the

Visual Culture of American Protestantism

DAVID MORGAN

1

Because of mass advertising, Warner Sallman's *Head of Christ* (pl. I) is found nearly everywhere. More than anywhere else, however, this cardboard icon hangs poised on the boundaries of consciousness. When we have seen something often and in many places, we dismiss it from the visual field. Ubiquity transfigures a commercial product into the signage of the unconscious, which is, perhaps, just where producers and vendors want it, in order to prompt and guide consumption. The art of Warner Sallman, precisely because of the way it fuses commerce and piety and because of its widespread dissemination, presents scholars with the opportunity to investigate how the trade in inexpensive religious images shapes the visual practice of popular Christian piety. And the commercial stature of Sallman's picture is mind-boggling. His original publisher, Kriebel and Bates, estimated in 1984 that the *Head of Christ,* the artist's most familiar image, had by then been reproduced more than 500 million times and distributed around the world.[1] Further tallies indicate that the remaining well-known images by Sallman have also been reproduced 500 million times.[2] Since 1941, churches, religious youth groups, missionary leagues, and a host of private organizations and individuals thus have placed into global circulation more than 1 billion reproductions of Sallman's devotional art.

THE FACE OF JESUS: PRODUCTION AND RECEPTION

Through an arrangement with publishers Anthony Kriebel and Fred Bates in 1941, Chicago Offset Printing Company printed the *Head of Christ* in a six-color separation lithographic process that preserved what many admirers consider unique about the picture: its radiant glow. During World War II, one press at Chicago Offset continuously printed the *Head of Christ* under the operation of two shifts of laborers.[3] In a document written in 1945, the publishers indicated that 14 million pictures had been printed by 1944.[4] One run of the image, which required three to four weeks to complete, consisted of five thousand sheets and included reproductions of the *Head of Christ* in a variety of dimensions, usually ranging from $3\frac{1}{2} \times 2\frac{1}{2}$ inches to 20×16 inches. Several runs were completed in 1941. By 1944 the market supported increasing the size of individual prints to 40×30 inches for images to be used in such public spaces as churches.

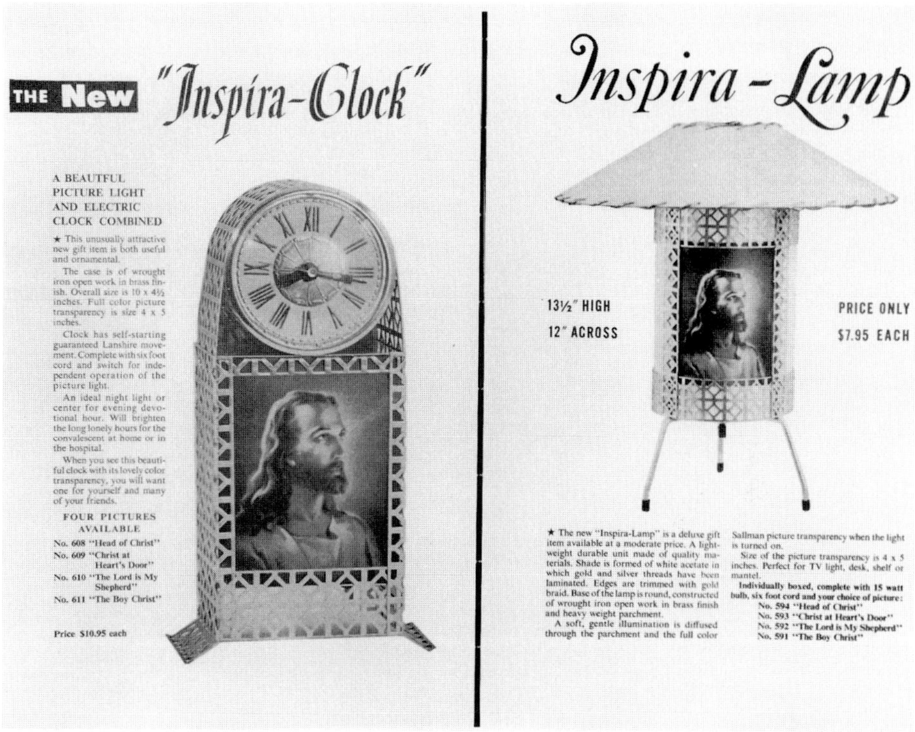

1.1. Kriebel and Bates, Inspira-Clock and Inspira-Lamp ads, c. 1957. Courtesy Jessie C. Wilson Galleries, Anderson University.

Kriebel and Bates marketed the image in an inexpensive frame; as cards bearing devotional texts; and on greeting cards, church bulletins, clocks, lamps, buttons, and funeral announcements, to name only a few examples (figs. 1.1 and 1.2). Sales catalogues and promotional literature advertised Sallman's principal paintings each year. The *Head of Christ* became the virtual trademark of the company and found public acceptance so quickly that the publishers encouraged Sallman to use the *Head* as frequently as possible in his depictions of the life of Christ.[5] The artist complied by duplicating the head in other images (pls. IX and XI), rotating it to reveal more of the face (pls. V and X), and reversing it, as in *Christ Our Pilot* (pl. VII).

Perhaps the most frequently cited feature of Sallman's *Head of Christ* is its radiance, which many people see as evidence of Christ's

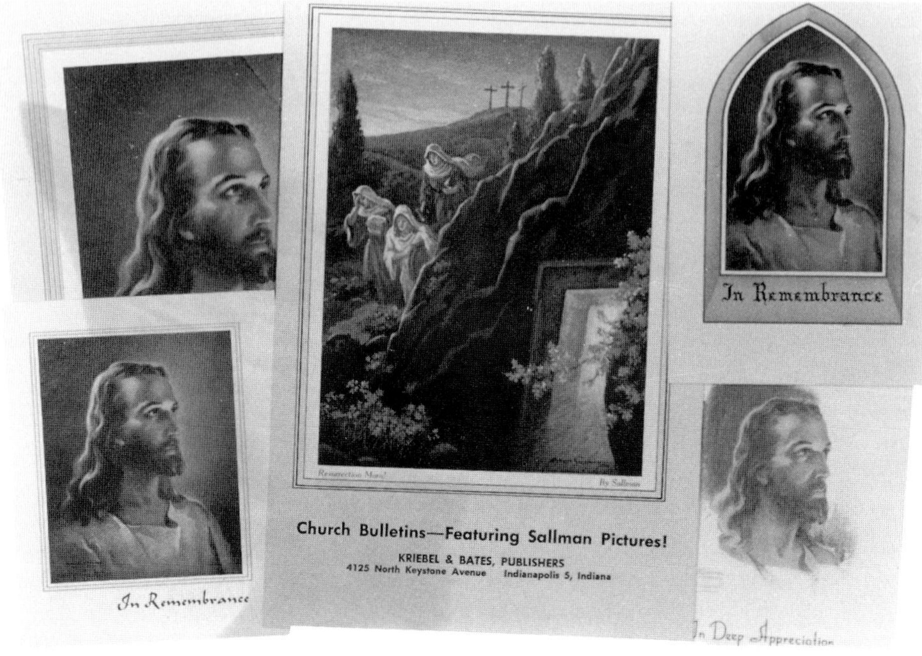

1.2. Kriebel and Bates, funeral cards and church bulletins, n.d. Courtesy Jessie C. Wilson Galleries, Anderson University.

divinity and juxtapose with the obedience and humility of his human gaze. One admirer of the *Head of Christ* writes, "There is something more about Warner Sallman's pictures that makes me feel . . . when I see them that this artist had felt Christ's presence when he made the images . . . and you can feel Christ's presence . . . conveyed . . . to you through his images. . . . From the way the hair in the image is highlighted in the back and highlights around the front of the head and face there seems to be a Holy radiance emitted from the image, depicting the qualities mentioned above."[6]

The radiance of the face is the subject of the church bulletin cover *Let's Go to Church* (pl. VI), in which members of a congregation file past a luminous stained glass window of the *Head of Christ* miraculously come to life. The lead veining has vanished from Christ's face, and the radiance, which some of the churchgoers notice, reverses the passage of sunlight and becomes the light of Christ's divinity beckoning the faithful to worship. The image itself acquires generative power to illuminate faith. This "real presence" experienced in the image challenges traditional notions of Protestant iconoclasm.

The picture has even appeared to some to come literally to life. Sallman's *Head of Christ* (and other images like it) has repeatedly offered Protestants the power of making the supernatural present, making the invisible visible. In 1958 one admirer of Sallman's picture wrote a letter to the editor of the widely read conservative Protestant magazine *Christianity Today,* in objection to the vociferous claim of a seminary professor that Sallman's image was a "pretty picture of a woman with a curling beard . . . [and not] the Lord who died and rose again!"[7] The letter writer replied that Sallman's work was "very evangelical Christian art. I have had visions of our Lord Jesus Christ and his painting is a very close resemblance." Such testimony is not uncommon. Sallman received several letters reporting mystical visions and experiences of a Christ who resembled his picture. On July 6, 1955, in her Clinton, Iowa, living room, a Protestant woman experienced the image "turn from paper to living flesh," as she put it in a letter to Sallman two years later.[8] And in 1979 an image of the *Head of Christ* is on record as having bled. At approximately 1:30 P.M. on May 25, according to a story printed in the *National Enquirer,* a drop of blood appeared under the right eye of a wallet-sized picture of Sallman's *Head of Christ,* encased in plastic and owned by an elderly Protestant woman in Roswell, New Mexico (fig. 1.3).[9] According to the *Enquirer,* a local hospital technician performed tests which proved that the substance was in fact human blood. A family member reported that thousands of people came to see the tiny icon, many of whom fell to their knees and wept. Local Protestant clergy vouched for the sincerity of the family, and one minister concluded, "I am convinced it is a miracle and a thing of God."

Such instances are exceptional, however. The popularity of the face no doubt owes less to miracles than to the material and historical circumstances of its marketing and the appeal of its visual properties within a particular cultural context. Aside from the radiance, which Sallman accentuated in the 1940 oil version of the *Head,* the basic features of the oil portrait were established in the original drawing, which served as the model for the painted version. The 1924 charcoal drawing entitled *Son of Man* appeared on the cover of the *Covenant Companion* (see fig. i.6), the official magazine of Sallman's own Evangelical Covenant Church. As art director of the *Companion,* Sallman was responsible for arranging

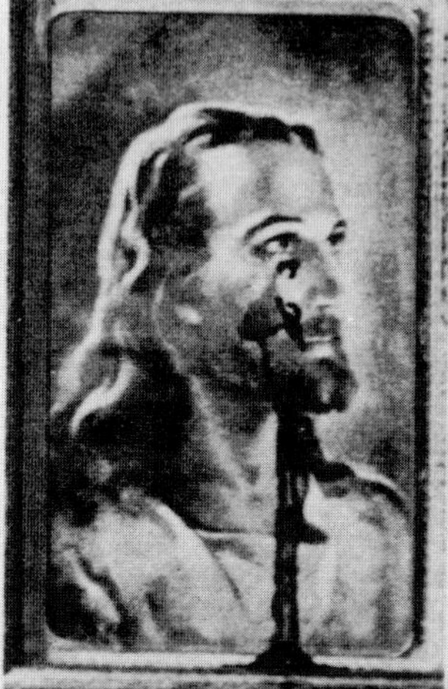

Tiny Picture of Christ Weeps Tears of Blood

Thousands of people are flocking to a small town in New Mexico to gaze in awe at a wallet-sized picture of Christ that has wept tears of blood, according to witnesses.

Four members of the family of Willie Mae Seymore, of Roswell, N. Mex., say they've seen the blood seep from the eye of the tiny, plastic-encased portrait — and a hospital's chief medical technologist has confirmed it actually is human blood.

"I was tremendously shocked, but I knew immediately that I was seeing a beautiful miracle," said Kathy Malott, 28, granddaughter of Seymore.

Kathy's husband Zach, a soft-spoken electrician who describes himself as "a common man," told The ENQUIRER: "I've always been a facts-and-figures man, a skeptical person. And when I first saw this it shocked me.

"But you either have to go crazy or accept something like this when you see it with your own eyes. Think about it!

"To see blood flow from a plastic picture of Jesus, to watch it flow, knowing there could be no other explanation but supernatural power causing it, is a tremendous shock to the nervous system."

Kathy, a registered nurse, had given the wallet-sized portrait of Christ — which measures 4¼x2¼ inches — to her grandmother seven years ago. She bought it at a drugstore for 35 cents.

Her grandmother had placed it in the lower corner of a larger-framed picture hanging in her living room.

About 1:30 p.m. May 25, while Zach and Kathy were visiting her grandmother, Zach glanced at the picture and noticed a drop of red under the right eye. Puzzled, he called his wife and her grandmother over to look at it.

"Kathy said: 'It looks like blood to me!' " Zach recalled.

"Well, it shook us up but I thought something had splashed on it, or something of that nature."

Kathy, however, was so excited that she phoned her mother, Charline Spidahl, who lives a half-mile away. A little later, when the blood began oozing from the eye again,

A MIRACLE: Close-up of plastic-encased portrait of Christ was taken by a reporter about 20 minutes after the flow of blood stopped. "The blood was still wet," he says.

Zach left the house and picked up his mother-in-law and drove her back to the Seymore house.

"I saw the blood on the picture," Spidahl told The ENQUIRER. "It was very, very dark red . . . very thick. It seemed to be coming from the right eye — it came right on out-side of the plastic. It just seemed to come from nowhere.

"I couldn't believe it. I really felt that it was a miracle!"

Again at 3 p.m. the blood began to ooze out of the portrait, for a period of about 10 to 15 minutes.

Finally, Seymore called the local newspaper, and a reporter, Al Gibes, arrived around 3:45 p.m.

"I looked at the picture and I could see that the blood was still wet," Gibes said. "Everybody is believing this to a certain degree. It would have been really hard for anyone to tamper with the picture. I believe the family didn't tamper with it. It would be real tough to fake it."

The following day Gibes brought the chief medical technologist from a local hospital to the house.

He took a sample of the red substance from the picture, tested it, and confirmed it was human blood.

"The test did turn out positive," he said. "All I can say is that it is blood.

"This is honest-to-gosh, bona fide human blood."

The story of the miraculous appearance of the bloody tears appeared in a local newspaper a day later and people began flocking to see the mysterious portrait of Jesus for themselves.

Lines formed down the block.

So many came — from hundreds of miles away — that Zach moved the picture from the wall and hung it in a front window for easier viewing by the throngs.

"People were falling to their knees and crying," he said.

Rev. Harold Burnside, pastor of a non-denominational Protestant church in Roswell, told The ENQUIRER: "As soon as I saw the picture, I knew it was genuine. I'm sure there is no way it could have been rigged."

Another Protestant clergyman, Rev. Randall W. Grill, agreed: "The Malotts in every way appear to be honest, sincere people. For them, it is definitely a miracle.

"I am convinced it is a miracle and a thing of God."

— TOM SMITH

1.3. "Tiny Picture of Christ Weeps Tears of Blood," *National Enquirer* (August 21, 1979), 29. Courtesy *National Enquirer*.

for cover art. For the special youth issue of February 1924 he provided his image of Jesus. After the 1940 oil painting of the *Head of Christ* gained wide recognition, Sallman undertook a ministry of visiting congregations and church groups to reproduce the image in chalk (fig. 1.4) and to share his testimony concerning its miraculous origin—a narrative that exists in several versions (see Chapters 2 and 6).

The image that Sallman drew closely resembles the face of Christ in a painting of 1892, *The Friend of the Humble,* by Frenchman Léon Lhermitte (1844–1925; see figs. i.4 and i.5), reproduced in the December 1922 issue of the *Ladies' Home Journal.*[10] In an article of 1961, Sallman acknowledged that he had seen the Lhermitte reproduction, cut

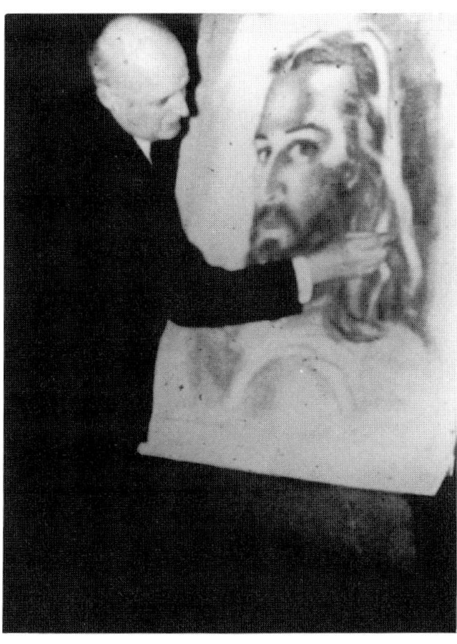

1.4. Sallman at a chalk talk, 1950s. Courtesy Jessie
C. Wilson Galleries, Anderson University.

it out, and framed it as a gift for his mother.[11] The resemblance is undeniable and marks one of many instances in which Sallman borrowed an
image and reworked it in a new context. His use of the French painting,
however, is reappropriation rather than plagiarism. He replaced the
rough facture of Lhermitte's painting with what became a characteristic
softness. Mollifying surfaces and contours, and adding the familiar radiance and immediate focus on the head, Sallman achieved an intimacy that
became his trademark.

When lifted from Lhermitte's picture and isolated in the head-
and-shoulders format, the profile of Christ conforms to the standards of
popular commercial portrait photography. This association is enhanced
by the elimination of the historical particularity of Lhermitte's image and
the use of a simple screen reminiscent of the studio backdrop used by
photographers. As a film of Sallman at work during a "chalk talk" demonstrates, he paid special attention to the eyes and lips of Jesus.[12] His
careful delineation of these features in the *Head of Christ* resembles re-
touched photographic portraits designed to present the sitter to best
advantage. Sallman approximated the oval format and tonal vignetting
of photographic portraiture in the *Son of Man*, leaving the bottom of the
portrait unfinished and contrasting the background in light and dark on
either side of the face. Both the pose and the lighting of the *Head of Christ*

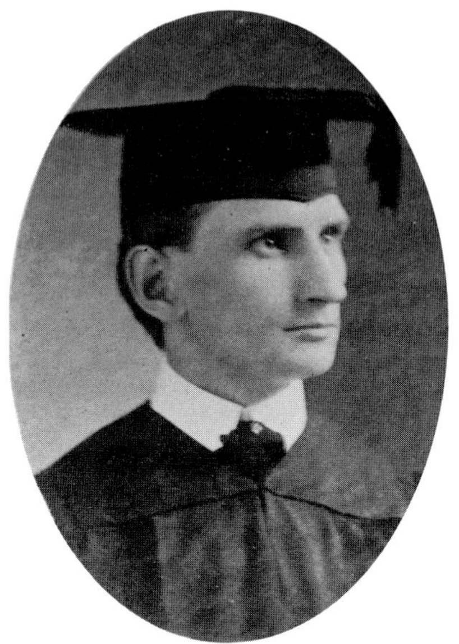

1.5. Science graduate class photograph, 1905,
Valparaiso University. Courtesy Valparaiso
University Archives.

recall such commemorative commercial photography as graduation portraits from the turn of the century to the 1920s (figs. 1.5 and 1.6). In these
pictures a solemn occasion and rite of passage are also marked by a three-
quarter profile gazing steadily ahead, illuminated by a primary and
secondary source, seen in a head-and-shoulders format. In a device con-
ventionalized by nineteenth-century photographers for commercial portraiture, Sallman surrounded Jesus with a vignette of light that fades
quickly into shadows at the edges of the image. The same device is also
found in the repertoire of contemporary commercial photographers (fig.
1.7).

Sallman thus transformed Lhermitte's painting of Jesus by sub-
mitting it to the conventions of studio photography. To these he added
the smooth complexion, the dark linear clarity of features, and the warm
color of advertising imagery, like the imagery he had created years earlier
in advertisements for Chicago vendors and newspapers (see fig. 2.6).
The photographic rhetoric of his image—which extended so far that
people gave reproductions of the pocket-sized version of the *Head of
Christ* as gifts, recalling the practice of exchanging small photographic
portraits for the wallet, album, or desktop—accounts in part for its
popularity; several people who responded to a query in religious periodicals cited the portrait realism of the image as appealing, stating that they

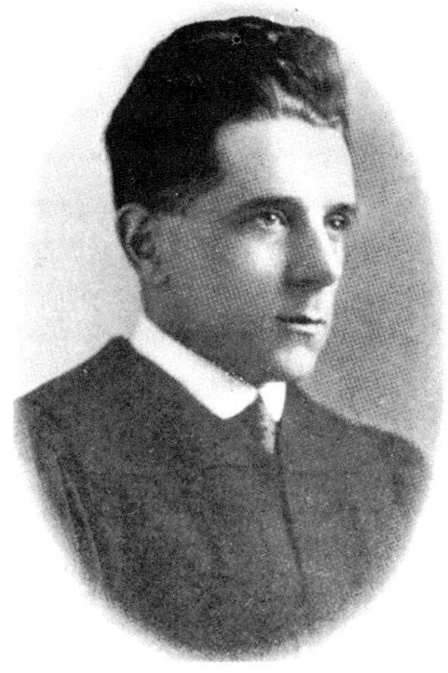

1.6. Head of College of Civil Engineering, *1921 University Annual,* Valparaiso University. Courtesy Valparaiso University Archives.

felt that it bore an exact likeness to Jesus. One person even called the image a "true photo of Jesus" (292).

Sallman produced more than a dozen variations of his original Jesus. *Portrait of Jesus* (pl. XII) was his last version of the portrait style. The head-and-shoulders format proved very successful, prompting

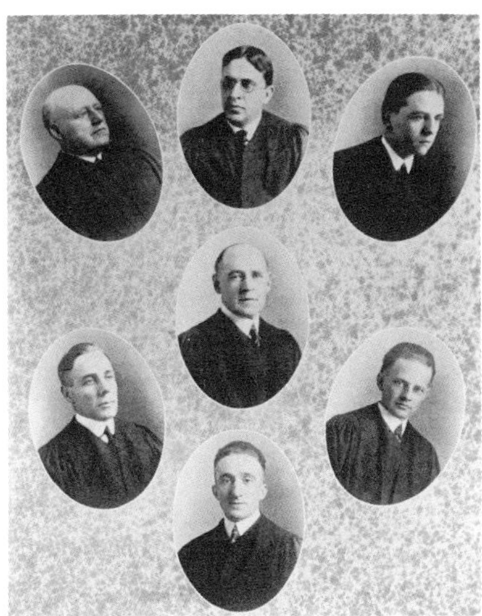

1.7. Faculty, *1921 University Annual,* Valparaiso University. Courtesy Valparaiso University Archives.

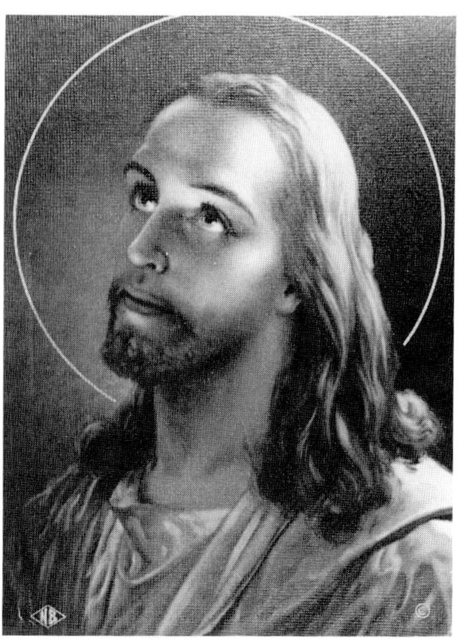

1.8. Louis Jambor, *Head of Christ*, n.d., 7 × 5",
reproduction. Copyright Basevi, 1945.

other painters and publishers to produce rival images, such as Louis
Jambor's head of Christ, copyrighted in 1945 (fig. 1.8). Another similar
portrait by Jambor (fig. 1.9) was copyrighted in 1949 by Augsburg
Publishing House in Minneapolis, one of Kriebel and Bates's most challenging competitors. Jambor not only appropriated Sallman's picture of

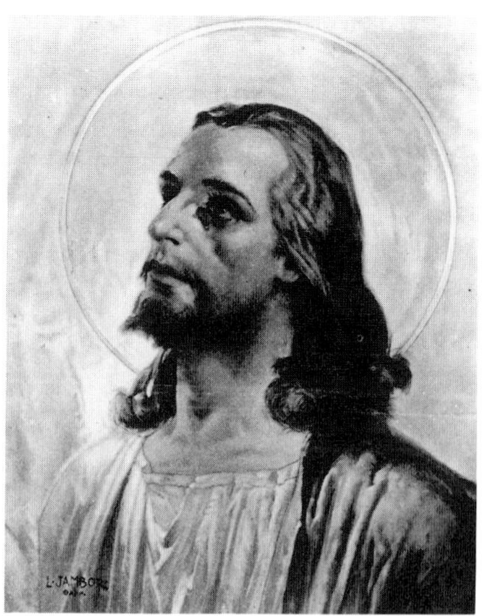

1.9. Louis Jambor, *Jesus of Nazareth,* 1949.
Copyright © Augsburg Publishing House. Reprinted
by permission of Augsburg Fortress.

Jesus but even borrowed the gendered popular discourse that accompanied Sallman's portrayal of Christ. Jambor is quoted in 1949 as stating that he had sought to represent in his most recent image (see fig. 1.9) his subject's "spiritual greatness and physical strength." He observed that "people wanted to see stronger interpretations of Christ than the paintings many artists have produced—paintings in which spirituality is diluted with too much sweetness. I tried to develop the face to show the strength His manual labor wrought."[13] The same objective had been attributed to Sallman as early as 1943.

By the late 1950s and early 1960s, Sallman and his publishers found it necessary to modify the smooth and quiescent features of the *Head of Christ* absorbed in obedient submission to his Father's will. Several critics of Sallman's *Christ* had derided what they considered its effeminate character. Augsburg and Concordia publishing houses marketed their own portraits of Jesus, following Sallman's original formula but portraying a younger, more vigorous Christ, such as Richard Hook's *Head of Christ* (fig. 1.10). In these images Christ faces the viewer in an informal manner that a younger generation found more appealing. Hook's *Christ,* copyrighted by Concordia Publishing House in 1964, presents a huskier Jesus, rendered more roughly as a sketch. The soft sheen of Sallman's 1940s style was replaced by a broken, less-resolved brush stroke. Hook left the hair uncombed and showed the beard as close-cropped, eliminating the fine and flowing texture of the beard of Sallman's Jesus, which had been singled out for criticism by his detractors. A slight tilt of the head combined with eyes that gaze directly at the viewer gave Hook's portrait an immediacy that seemed to outmode Sallman's suddenly Victorian picture.

Documents from Sallman's publishers indicate the kinds of changes deemed necessary. One version of Christ under production in 1962 (fig. 1.11) carried instructions to the artist or printer to roughen the texture of the hair, whose waviness seemed "feminine." *Portrait of Jesus* (pl. XII) appears to have been influenced by Hook's painting: the tilted head and the frontal aspect address the viewer directly. The face emerges from deep brown shadow and exhibits greater color (including clear blue eyes) and more loosely painted hair than Sallman's earlier work. The sensation of untrammeled encounter was deliberate, but neither Sallman nor his publishers abandoned the tie to the 1940 original. As the caption in a sales catalogue suggests, "It is as if the profile from his original 'Head

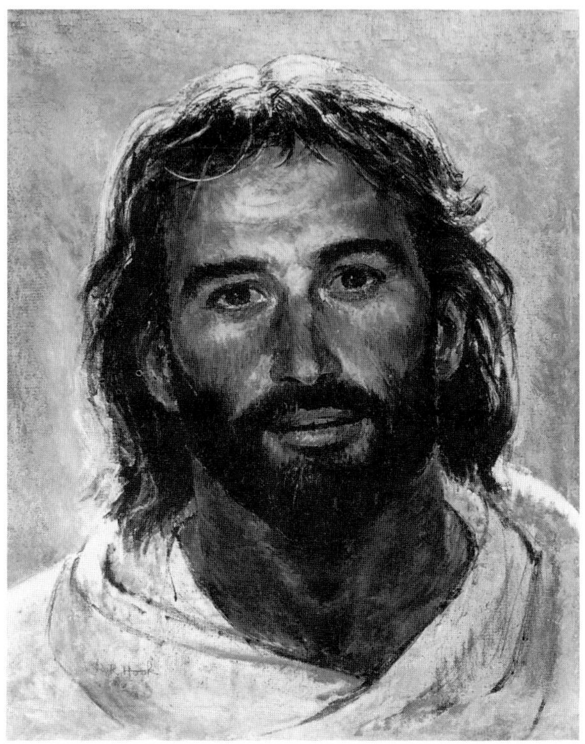

1.10. Richard Hook, *Head of Christ,* 1964, oil on board, 24 × 20″.
Copyright Concordia Publishing House. Reprinted by permission.

of Christ' has turned to a full face view, allowing the eyes to follow the observer from every angle."[14] In fact, many viewers refer to this feature of the portrait with fond approval, as visual proof of God's benevolent omnipresence: the eyes, they say, follow you everywhere.[15]

In *Portrait of Jesus* Sallman updated the photographic rhetoric of the 1940 picture. Graduation portraits from the turn of the century through World War II consistently posed the sitter with the head on the same vertical axis as the spine, with the head at an angle of ten to twenty-five degrees from the picture plane.[16] The sitter appeared solemn, gazing soberly out and slightly upward. Smiles were infrequent. The *Head of Christ* reflects these practices. Beginning in the 1950s, however, the head in annual class portraits was tilted, the shoulders began to parallel the picture plane, smiles appeared more often, and the gaze fixed more frequently on the viewer. The sitter was meant to address the viewer

more directly. This trend developed further in the 1960s, as hair length-
ened and the degree of formality lessened. Almost everyone smiled in
1960s school annuals, and heads tilted as if to resist the more rigid presentation of portraiture from previous decades, in which the sitters appeared
to pose for the purpose of being viewed. In the 1960s, by contrast, sitters
appear to pose for the purpose of addressing the viewer more directly.

Certainly this is the sense of Sallman's 1966 *Portrait of Jesus.*
Compare it, for instance, with a photograph portrait of a midwest university president produced by a New York commercial firm (Blackstone
Studios) about 1957 (fig. 1.12). The image was originally a half-length
pose but was cropped for use in a 1967 university yearbook, where it
appeared as reproduced here. Both Sallman and the portrait photogra-
pher have tilted their subject's head several degrees, oriented the body to

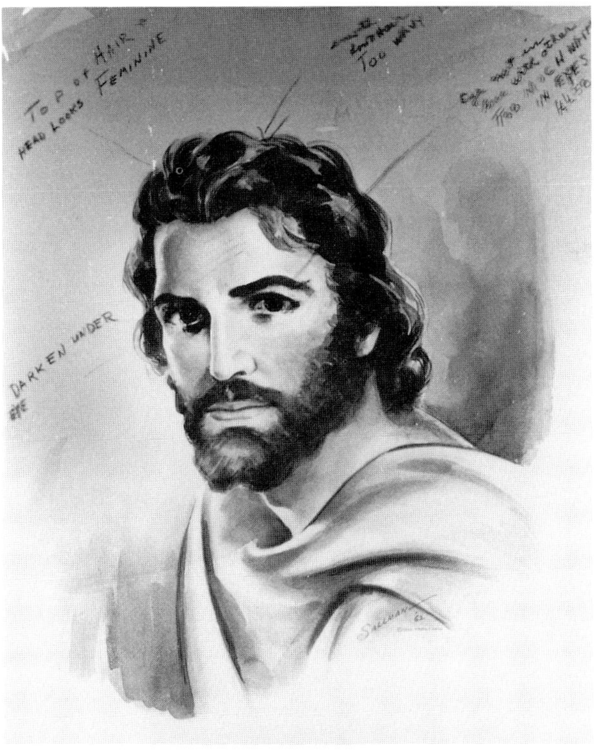

1.11. Warner Sallman, untitled (Head of Christ), 1962, watercolor on
paper with transparency and charcoal, 30 × 24". Courtesy Jessie C.
Wilson Galleries, Anderson University.

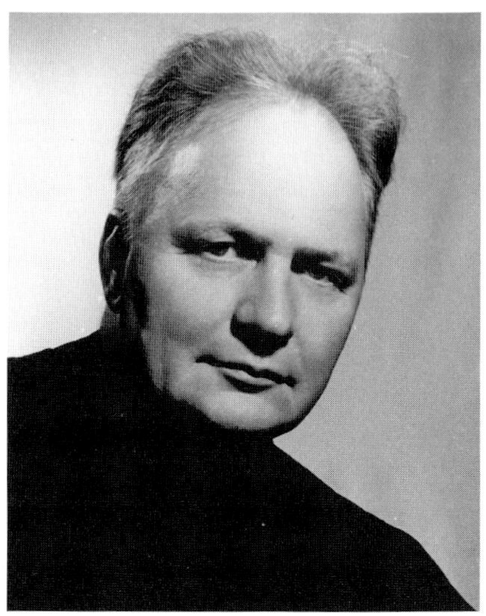

1.12. O. P. Kretzmann, president, Valparaiso University, *1967 Valparaiso University Annual.* Courtesy Valparaiso University Archives.

be nearly parallel to the picture plane, positioned the gaze of the sitter directly at the viewer, and silhouetted the face by highlighting it against a dark ground. The president's oval head was anchored above the dark form of his body and encircled by darker tones. The prominently lit forehead and the vignetting effect were anachronisms, the first a feature of portrait photography and hairstyle from the first several decades of the twentieth century, the second a pictorialist device that recalls the interaction between the formal portraiture of painting and photography in the late nineteenth and early twentieth centuries.[17] In the 1960s Sallman and some photographers used these devices to lend an air of ritualized formality and dignity to the commemoration of college graduation or to adorn the face of president, dean, or divinity with the visual imprimatur of authority.

SALLMAN AND THE TRADITION
OF POPULAR RELIGIOUS ART

Many of Sallman's well-known pictures suggest debts to religious paintings by other artists. Sallman found ample material to consider in devotional magazines, popular Bible literature, and a host of books on Christian art and the life of Christ, illustrated by the work of artists from the nineteenth and twentieth centuries. An associate described him as an avid collector of such images and noted that he gathered them in his studio.[18] Some have accused Sallman of plagiarism.[19] But artists of all times have borrowed from their predecessors, and Sallman never simply reproduced the work of another to be marketed as his own. Most interesting from the perspective of this book are the sorts of selections Sallman made and the impact of his modifications on the reception of his images.

Christ in Gethsemane (pl. II) derives from the painting of Christ at prayer by Heinrich Hofmann (1824–1911; fig. 1.13). Hofmann's *Jesus in the Garden of Gethsemane,* painted in 1890, often appeared in devotional magazines, and many have compared it to Sallman's art. Hofmann's image was frequently the subject of stained glass windows and of murals painted in church sanctuaries throughout the Midwest from 1900

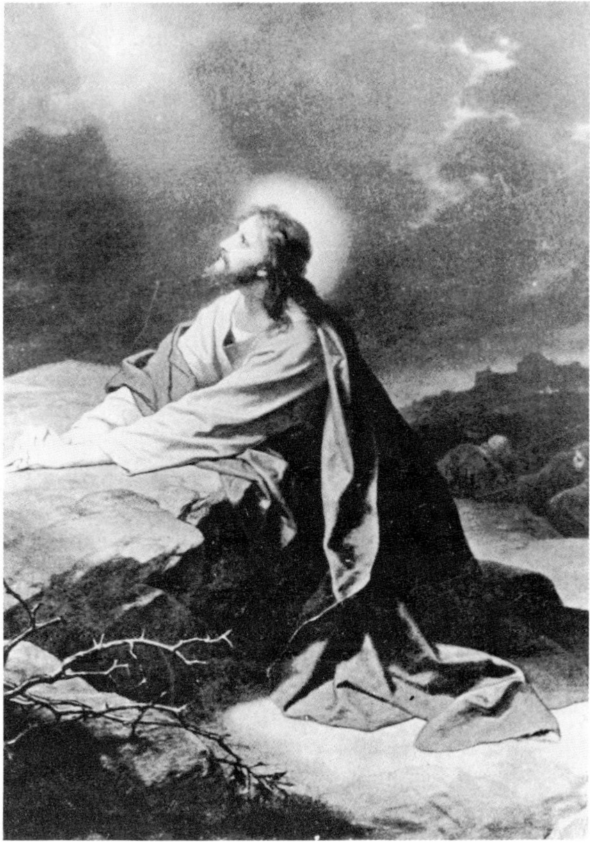

1.13. Heinrich Hofmann, *Jesus in the Garden of Gethsemane,* 1890, oil on canvas, size unknown. Courtesy The Riverside Church, New York.

through the 1940s, including at least three versions by Sallman, painted before he produced his own version of *Gethsemane* in 1941.[20]

Sallman modified the German picture in obvious and subtle ways. Both artists constructed their pictures on the basis of a diagonal. Hofmann aligned a ray of heavenly light, falling from the upper left, with the angle of Christ's back. In the center of Hofmann's picture a halo shines about Christ's head. Sallman reversed the German composition and substituted a dark diagonal of rock that parallels the kneeling Christ and silhouettes his glowing tunic, providing part of what a sales catalogue described as a "quiet and natural background." Christ's face, a reiteration of the *Head of Christ,* bisects the stone slope at a right angle, serving to arrest the viewer's eye once again at the center of the picture. Sallman exchanged Hofmann's Italianate chiaroscuro for bright and broadly brushed colors. Christ was not placed in the middle distance but was pulled closer to the picture plane and situated in something of an alcove, a partial enclosure that reinforced both his isolation from the sleeping disciples in the distance and his intimate proximity to the viewer. The alcove, a gardenlike feature furnished with the stone slab or altar at which Jesus prays, connotes the picturesque silence of the Garden of Gethsemane, where the Christian savior addresses himself to the divinity in a final moment of privacy before public humiliation and execution. Both artists conveyed the nature of Christ's suffering with a thorn bush, but Sallman supplemented the legibility of this suggestion by linking the thorny growth to a shadowy cruciform that is scarcely concealed in the rock backdrop in the upper right. Sallman also heightened the emotional state of Jesus by clasping his hands in prayer and deeply furrowing his brow. Although Hofmann's Christ calmly resigns himself to his fate, Sallman's assumes a beseeching posture.

This distinction, in addition to the bright colors and the isolation of Christ in the foreground, may help account for the popularity of Sallman's image. Sallman's *Gethsemane* has served many as a devotional aid in prayer. One writer recalled receiving inspiration as a teenager whenever she looked on her picture and prayed (317). An Iowa woman wrote that the large stained glass version of the image in her church helped to "comfort me and preserve my inner peace" (397). Several people who responded to my call for letters reported that Sallman's picture was hanging in their bedrooms, where it inspired pathos and prayer. One woman recalled the effect of the image during her college years: "Whenever I felt lonely or afraid or overwhelmed by the chaos of a twisted world, I would look up at that picture and be overcome by a deep sense of peace and comfort" (421). Another woman, widowed after forty-five years of marriage, wrote that the "sight of the Lonely Savior, pouring out his heart in prayer to His Father, has inspired me through many hard and lonely problems. My pain and sorrow could never compare with the extreme suffering He endured for our sake" (431).

Such response indicates a contemplative encounter with the image that was encouraged by the composition of the picture. Like several of Sallman's most popular images (*Christ at Heart's Door,* pl. III; *Christ Our Pilot,* pl. VII; *He Careth for You,* pl. X; and *Teach Me Thy Way,* pl. VIII), *Christ in Gethsemane* placed Christ in the center foreground of the image, enclosed or embraced in some way by his immediate surroundings. The visual result was an isolation of the figure of Jesus, which enshrined him with an intimacy and privacy that may have appealed to Protestant piety's Christology of friendship: the conception of Christ as a personal friend who remained true throughout the hardships of life. Christ was made available for personal communion, a partner whose quiet proximity in devotion was an assurance of his benevolent presence in all aspects of life.

Kriebel and Bates promoted this response to Sallman's imagery. In a pamphlet issued to accompany the commercial debut of Sallman's *Teach Me Thy Way* (pl. VIII) in 1952, Sylvia Peterson offered a narrative that focused on the relation between Jesus and the boy. Jesus, we read, "had found a brief respite from the throngs in this lovely spot." Seclusion from the masses in a private enclosure provided the setting for the encounter. Jesus invited the boy to join him in conversation, but the disciples rebuked Jesus: "'Why bother with the child? You are much too tired. Why not rest?' 'Rest?' Jesus must have answered. 'Wist ye not that I must be about my Father's business?'" Jesus, the pamphlet continues, then considered the slowness of his disciples to grasp his teachings and recalled such proclamations as the one not to forbid children, "for of such is the kingdom of God," and "except ye be converted, and become as little children, ye shall not enter the kingdom of heaven." Sallman's picture envisioned for Peterson and others the intimacy of the believer with Christ. This paternal relation is mirrored in Christ's own relationship with his Father. The faithful are called to Christ's bosom to be as children. The boy asks, "How can I become like Jesus?" then exclaims,

"Teach me thy way!" According to Peterson—a devout member of Sallman's denomination (Evangelical Covenant) and a friend of the artist—a childlike faith in Christ was "fundamental to Christlike character."[21] For personal Protestantism, God was to be embraced in the intimate space of a face-to-face encounter, within the relationship of a child to a parent, which applied to children and adults, women and men.

From this perspective, authentic faith was personal faith, evidenced for many conservative Protestants by private response to God's call. No iconographic motif in evangelical Christianity indexes this aspect of personal call and response like the oft-repeated theme of Christ at the door of the individual soul. In the letters that the research project received from readers of popular religious magazines, *Christ at Heart's Door* (pl. III) was the second most frequently cited image. A tradition of British and German paintings and prints from the nineteenth century depicting Christ knocking at the door of a home inspired it.[22] The images by Karl Schönherr (1824–1906; fig. 1.14) and Hofmann (fig. 1.15) join several others (most important is William Holman Hunt's *The Light of the World,* the first version of which was completed in 1853; a second hangs today in Keble College, Oxford) as Sallman's sources. Sallman could have found these images reproduced in popular books on Christian

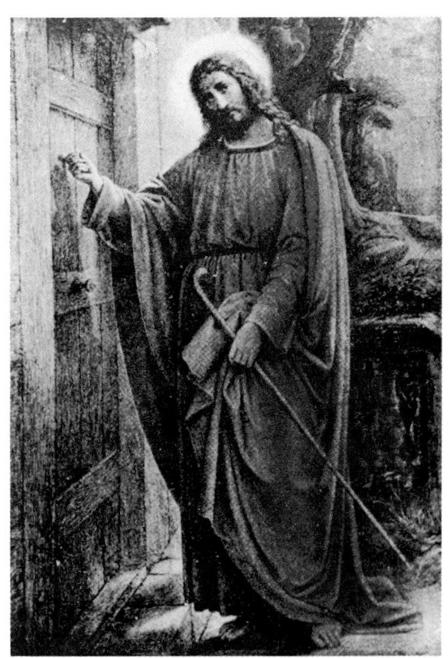

1.14. Karl Schönherr, *The Savior,* date unknown, medium unknown, size unknown, location unknown. Reproduced in *The Light of the World or Our Saviour in Art,* ed. Abram P. Elder (Chicago: Elder, 1896), pl. 129 (wrongly attributed to Bernhard Plockhorst).

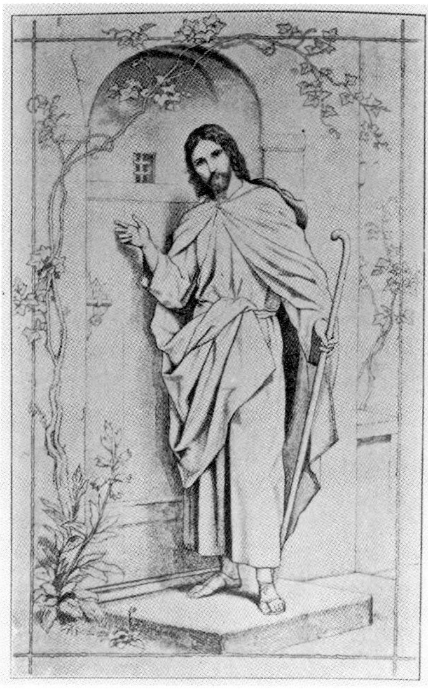

1.15. Heinrich Hofmann, *I Stand at the Door and Knock,* date unknown, chalk on paper, size unknown, location unknown. Reproduced in William Dallmann, *Jesus, His Words and His Works* (Milwaukee: Northwestern Publishing House, 1914), frontispiece.

art and iconography.[23] He adopted and extended the overt allegorizing evident in such European versions of the subject as Hunt's. Viewers appreciate the unambiguous legibility of Sallman's picture, whose subject is Revelation 3:20: "Behold, I stand at the door, and knock." The barely concealed heart produced by the luminous Christ and the frame of the doorway conveys the savior's call to the soul ensnared in thistles of sin and the darkness of ignorance and willfulness. Yet, as promotional literature points out, "all is not hopeless, for there is an opening of grillwork in the door 'revealing the darkness within,' so that the individual may see who is at the door, and see that He is good and kind."[24] For evangelical Protestants whose spirituality was premised on the acceptance of a call, a "born again" experience, and subsequent testimony to that experience, this image represented a central theological principle and served to commemorate such experiences (259 and 473). For others, the image offered assurance of Christ's benevolent yet persistent love. Still others interpreted the image in terms of the freedom of will. A Lutheran clergyman admired the painting "because the absence of any outside knob or latch on the door indicates that one must open one's heart to Christ from within—He will not force His way inside" (331). In either case, the highly symbolic character of the image invited the personal and theological narratives of conservative Protestant piety.

PROTESTANT VISUAL CULTURE
AND THE APPEAL TO YOUTH

One of the most important uses of Sallman's imagery corresponds to a major aspect of the conservative Protestant agenda in the postwar period: ministry to youth. Sunday school focused on the education and nurturing of youth, and several youth organizations in evangelical and mainline Protestantism sought to appeal to adolescent Christian youth.[25] Among them was Youth for Christ, founded in 1945, which employed the young Billy Graham as its first full-time evangelist. Sallman's *Head of Christ* served as the backdrop to the speaker's platform at an early rally, which featured the Chicago evangelist Torrey Johnson striking a Billy Sunday pose (fig. 1.16). The evangelical initiative to mobilize youth and family contributed to the broader political end of transforming the military conflict of the war into the moral and spiritual conflict of the Cold War.

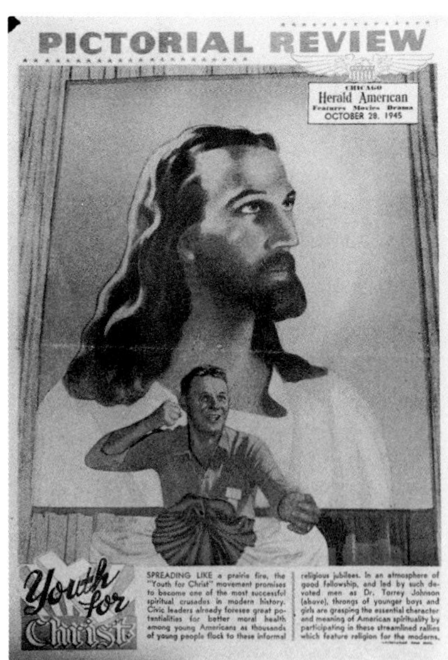

1.16. "Dr. Torrey Johnson Speaking at Youth for Christ Rally," *Chicago Herald American* (October 28, 1945), 8.

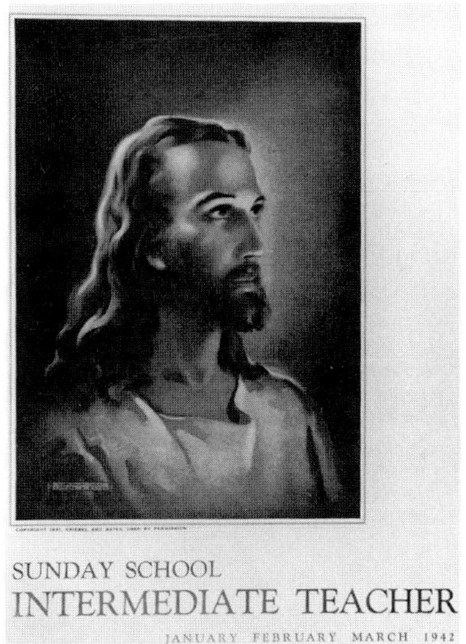

1.17. *Sunday School Intermediate Teacher* 3, no. 1 (January–March 1942), cover.

The Methodist Church (Epworth League), Missouri Synod Lutherans (Walther League), and both Northern Baptists and the Southern Baptist Convention used Sallman's art extensively in connection with youth groups and Sunday school programs. Within less than a year of its appearance, Sallman's painting appeared on the cover of a new Southern Baptist quarterly for Sunday school instructors (fig. 1.17). The marketing of the image by religious bookstores and such church supply firms as, in the South, the Baptist Bookstore targeted teachers and their pupils. The back cover of the winter 1942 issue of the *Sunday School Intermediate Teacher* carried an ad for the *Head of Christ* to be purchased through the mail from Baptist Bookstores from New Mexico to North Carolina. Pocket versions measuring $3^{1}/_{2} \times 2^{1}/_{2}$ inches sold for fifty cents per dozen in 1942 and were often gifts from teacher to student. Frequently placed in Sunday school classrooms, the largest version of the *Head of Christ* promoted in this ad (20×16 inches) sold for $1.50. Teachers of intermediate Sunday school students (twelve to fourteen years of age), students whom the author of the lessons in this issue characterized as "builders of air castles and dreamers of dreams," made extensive use of visual imagery and metaphor.[26] Lessons and essays were entitled "The Synoptic Picture of Jesus," "Three Pictures of the Life of Christ," "Picturing Truth," and

"Vision and Duty." The author suggested in one lesson that instructors encourage students to bring to class copies of their favorite pictures of Jesus. The author referred readers to Sallman's image on the cover in case they were familiar with no others.

In its appeal to youth, Sallman's art constructs an ideal of obedience and gentleness. For instance, a favorite image to place in the bedroom and Sunday school classroom, *The Lord Is My Shepherd* (pl. V), visualized the pastoral image of Psalm 23, but without the dark side of the ancient verse. Indeed, this may explain the attraction of Sallman's rendition: there was not a hint of the "valley of the shadow of death" here, only a tranquil vision of "still waters" and "green pastures." The small, plump sheep inhabited a peaceable utopian garden landscape. Christ was as gentle as the creatures in his charge, with whom he was identified by the color and softness of his robe. In the heart of the quiet flock, Christ doted on the lamb, symbol of his concern for children. Even the little black sheep followed his lead. According to promotional literature, this animal was a "symbol of the wayward sheep who have been restored again to the fold."[27] Although Sallman's imagery might be dismissed for its sentimentality, it is clear from such details as this and from the overall composition of *The Lord Is My Shepherd* that he was able to create pictures that conveyed the feeling that mattered to his appreciative public. In this painting, for instance, Christ and his flock nestle into a brightly painted landscape. Framed by the diagonal creek in the lower left, the sheep are surrounded by the hatched movement of the verdure and the diagonal shore of the river to the upper right. The tree in the upper left echoes Christ's gesture and helps construct a balanced and centered composition that conveys the serenity which Sallman and his audience considered the ideal of the pious life. One mother, for whom the *Head of Christ* symbolized stability and peace during a childhood plagued by an alcoholic parent, displayed *The Lord Is My Shepherd* in her bedroom when she was raising her own children. She referred to Christ "holding the lamb with the mother sheep looking on with concern" and drew great relief from the relationship between savior, lamb, and ewe: "What solace to know who held them [her children] as they began to go out on their own" (342).

Sallman found the idea for this painting in Plockhorst's portrayal of the subject (fig. 1.18), which shows the mother sheep craning her neck upward toward the lamb in Christ's arms. In his version, Sall-

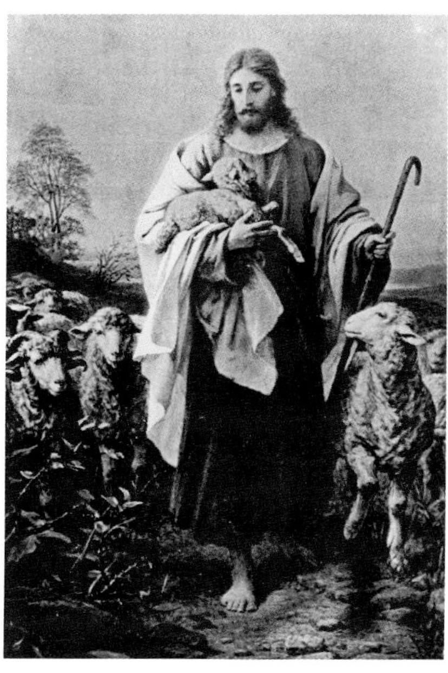

1.18. Bernhard Plockhorst, *The Good Shepherd*, date unknown, oil on canvas, size unknown, location unknown. Reproduced in *The Light of the World or Our Saviour in Art*, ed. Abram P. Elder (Chicago: Elder, 1896), pl. 101.

man elevated the viewer, to accentuate the intimate grouping of savior and sheep and to introduce the colorful landscape. Yet in adjusting the perspective of the landscape and sheep, he did not reduce the height of Christ, who towers above the flock gathering about his knees. This characteristic diminution of subject matter may be an important element in the appeal of Sallman's work: by making the sheep doll-like, Sallman enhanced their dependence on the paternal savior and gave them a charm that corresponds to the cherubic cuteness of children in such images as *He Careth for You* (pl. X).

The protection of children and the preservation of their purity and innocence were vital to Christians during and after World War II. Sallman responded by modifying the iconography of an anonymous wartime poster published in Chicago (fig. 1.19) for his 1950 painting *Christ Our Pilot* (pl. VII). He exchanged the flatness of the poster's design—the layered frontal arrangement of the figures against a plain ground—for the stormy seascape and the diagonal of the boat (which bears no perspectival relation to the wheel, helmsman, or pilot). Instead of depicting the dramatic moment of the poster, in which Christ supports the sailor and lends a firm hand to the wheel, Sallman's Christ provides only guidance. The stern, frontal view of Jesus in the poster is

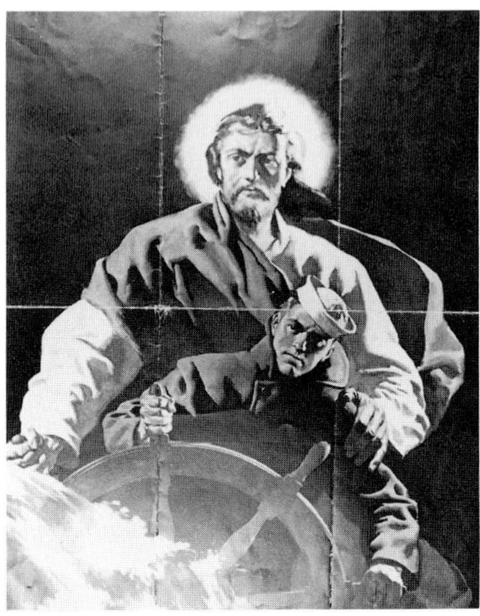

1.19. Anonymous, untitled (Christ with Sailor), 1944, 14⅞ × 11¾″. Copyright by Extension, Chicago. Courtesy Jessie C. Wilson Galleries, Anderson University.

without parallel in Sallman's art. His pilot seems to hover as a spiritual presence, a moral assurance rather than the towering corporeal authority of the earlier work. Sallman transfigured the literal participation of the wartime Christ intervening on America's behalf into an allegorical voice of comfort and conscience. As a sales catalogue indicated, the publishers intended this Christ to aid all who "steer the proper course of our lives . . . [to] land us safely in a peaceful harbor."[28] Sallman generalized the specificity of the military Christ into a moralizing allegory of everyday life. In this image the benevolent guidance of a higher power, personally interested in the welfare of youth, offered assistance in negotiating life's critical junctures. Sallman directed his message to the parent giving the picture as a gift, and to the child receiving it; both derived comfort from its content. The parent–child bond remained the central concern for Sallman's art; the devout discerned in this human relationship the nature of their own relationship with God.

Christ Our Pilot visualized the rite of passage into male adulthood and became a favorite gift to boys and young men for display in the bedroom. (A counterpart to this image for girls was *Madonna and Christ Child* [fig. 1.20].) The male rite of passage had been a crucial concern for parents during the war, as hundreds of thousands of young men left the security of home for the chaos far away. This moment of transition in the lives of young men continued to be a concern in regard to the problems

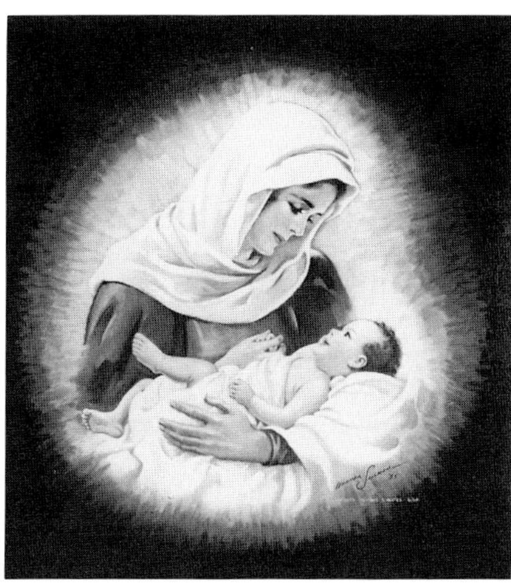

1.20. Warner Sallman, *Madonna and Christ Child,*
1955, oil on board, 22 × 20″. Courtesy Jessie C.
Wilson Galleries, Anderson University.

of raising children in a postwar society that bore less and less resemblance to the childhood of postwar parents. *A Series of Interpretations of the Sallman Religious Masterpieces,* a pamphlet published in about 1955 (part of a kit for part-time salespersons working for Kriebel and Bates), included an account of *Christ Our Pilot.* The narrative recalls the nineteenth-century literary tradition of painting, in which features of the landscape carried crucial aspects of the moralizing story of a soul's journey. In his transformation of the martial poster, Sallman changed the pose of Christ and his relation to the young man by removing Christ's firm grip on the helm and directing his gaze away from the viewer. Jesus rests a paternal hand on the boy's shoulder and points out safe passage. "We note that the Pilot does not take the wheel. He leaves this responsibility to the helmsman. He never removes from him the task of making his own decisions and steering his own vessel."[29]

Some viewers have claimed to see in the clouds directly to the left of Christ's face the profile of a roaring lion, possibly a reference to 1 Peter 5:8: "Your adversary the devil, as a roaring lion, walketh about, seeking whom he may devour." Whether Sallman included this image intentionally or not, he did use concealed imagery in other works (such as the heart in *Christ at Heart's Door,* pl. III), and many have discerned additional hidden images in a number of paintings, most notably a chalice and wafer on the temple and forehead of the *Head of Christ* (pl. I).[30] In any case, the lion underscores how *Christ Our Pilot* visualized the difficulties of coming of age and how conservative Protestants conceptualized and negotiated this threat. With Christ as pilot, Satan's wrath was safely avoided, life's storms successfully navigated, and the purity of youth and the freedom of the will securely preserved.

Perhaps no image by Sallman conveys the conservative Protestant ideal of childhood and its association with the unspoiled space of fantasized memories of an age of innocence as well as *He Careth for You* (pl. X), also a product of the postwar period. This painting seems to envision a bourgeois parable of the ideal faith. The *Series of Interpretations* describes this picture's "soft fleecy clouds," "majestic mountains," and "fertile fields" and points to the "peaceful little town" nestled among trees at the "foot of the mountains." The town "reminds us of the love and security of the home and of the family." This country idyll and its publisher's interpretation portrayed a paternalistic idea of security that was rooted in traditional notions of gender. Three young children have brought a wounded sparrow to the savior. On the viewer's left stand two quiet girls. The smaller of the two is enrapt by the countenance of Jesus, the larger gazes silently on the young boy, who narrates the sparrow's mishap. Appearing almost as a photomontage, Jesus stares beyond the boy in a portrait nearly identical to the 1940 *Head of Christ*. The young girls assume a passive role in the composition. Encompassed by Christ's body, they direct the viewer's gaze toward Jesus and the boy. The oldest girl embraces the younger, who in turn hugs a doll dressed as a nurse. The *Series of Interpretations* provides the following characterization of the two girls: "The oldest girl displays the big sister traits, she has a protective arm about the younger child, but is concentrating on her brother and his problems, while the little girl clings to her doll and leans close to Jesus and looks up into his face with frank and admiring acceptance." The boy, in contrast, stands out from Christ's contour in his role of active explanation. The lamb, who also participates in the network of gazes, may be the children's playmate in the countryside, but it also serves as an emblem of innocence—the innocence of childhood that was so often adduced by evangelicals as the ideal model of faith. The lamb reinforces the cute, cuddly, doll-like character of the children, whom the savior gently embraces. This lamb, no longer the traditional symbol of paschal sacrifice— that is, of a bloody, substitutionary death—but a residue of Victorian art and children's tales, represents the security that children (and adult believers) enjoyed in Christ, the benevolent shepherd.

The binary opposition of male and female is also particularly apparent in *Ready to Go—Ready to Stay!* (pl. IX), an oil painting probably intended for the bulletin of a special youth service or program initiative. The young man and woman are distinguished from one another in height, shape, color, and gesture—all the traditional markers signifying sexual difference. The young woman, seen in profile, rests her folded hands on the young man's shoulder and is fully framed within Christ's body, while her companion gestures, speaks, and holds the Bible, symbol of authority, and extends beyond the enclosure of Christ's contour. Jesus towers above the two and sanctions their differences. Sallman and his appreciative public construed the woman as a homemaker, child-bearer, and caregiver—the one who is ready to stay, not to go. The artist consistently portrayed young girls and women in enclosed forms, passively submissive to active boys and men (see also *He Careth for You,* pl. X).

MASS MEDIA AND MERCHANDISING

The unprecedented dissemination of the Sallman corpus resulted directly from its mass merchandising and the effective use of inexpensive mass production. If we are to understand why Sallman's images of Jesus have achieved such popularity, we must explore the material means by which they were produced and marketed and the historical circumstances of their production and consumption. How were the images packaged and promoted, and to whom? Where and when did this marketing phenomenon occur? Colleen McDannell examines the historical and economic conditions of Sallman's production in detail and places the Sallman line of products at Kriebel and Bates within a long history of religious commerce (see Chapter 3). My purpose here is to provide an introduction to the visual forms and conditions of Sallman's mass-produced imagery, by exploring the circumstances attending the appearance of the *Head of Christ,* its market audiences, the mechanisms of distribution, and the ideological apparatus that shaped the image's reception as a commercial, mass-produced product.

Several charcoal and pastel versions of the head of Jesus circulated on calendars, on stationery, and in framed reproductions under various copyrights before the appearance in 1941 of the oil painting known as the *Head of Christ*.[31] But none enjoyed the reception of the *Head of Christ,* which certainly owed its initial success to mass distribution during World War II.

Sallman's image of Jesus was most widely circulated on pocket-sized prayer cards. On the reverse Kriebel and Bates printed a variety of texts. The diversity of these texts—which included the Mysteries of the Holy Rosary, the Beatitudes, the Ten Commandments, and the Seven Last Words of Christ—suggests the confessional range of Kriebel and Bates's clientele. The earliest versions of the wallet image carried the anonymous text "One Solitary Life" (fig. 1.21). Millions of cards with these words were distributed through the United Service Organizations (USO) by the Salvation Army and the Young Men's Christian Association (YMCA) beginning in 1942 to U.S. soldiers in Europe and later in the Pacific. Parents and churches also made gifts of these cards to young men departing for the front. Fascinating accounts of the effect of the pocket icon tell of the picture's power to provide refuge from battle or even to unite Japanese and American soldiers who were Christians.[32] One Indiana businessman with three sons and many fellow church members in the war initiated a campaign of sending wallet-sized reproductions of Sallman's picture to Americans in the service. With the pictures, he included a letter: "Keep these handy in your purses where you see them

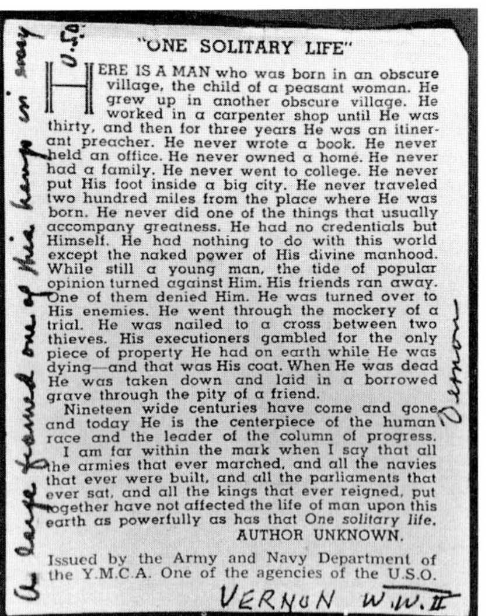

"ONE SOLITARY LIFE"

HERE IS A MAN who was born in an obscure village, the child of a peasant woman. He grew up in another obscure village. He worked in a carpenter shop until He was thirty, and then for three years He was an itinerant preacher. He never wrote a book. He never held an office. He never owned a home. He never had a family. He never went to college. He never put His foot inside a big city. He never traveled two hundred miles from the place where He was born. He never did one of the things that usually accompany greatness. He had no credentials but Himself. He had nothing to do with this world except the naked power of His divine manhood. While still a young man, the tide of popular opinion turned against Him. His friends ran away. One of them denied Him. He was turned over to His enemies. He went through the mockery of a trial. He was nailed to a cross between two thieves. His executioners gambled for the only piece of property He had on earth while He was dying—and that was His coat. When He was dead He was taken down and laid in a borrowed grave through the pity of a friend.

Nineteen wide centuries have come and gone, and today He is the centerpiece of the human race and the leader of the column of progress.

I am far within the mark when I say that all the armies that ever marched, and all the navies that ever were built, and all the parliaments that ever sat, and all the kings that ever reigned, put together have not affected the life of man upon this earth as powerfully as has that *One solitary life.*
AUTHOR UNKNOWN.

Issued by the Army and Navy Department of the Y.M.C.A. One of the agencies of the U.S.O.

1.21. Anonymous, "One Solitary Life," c. 1943, printed on verso of the *Head of Christ*, 2¾ × 3½". Letter 269, Sallman Archives, Jessie C. Wilson Galleries, Anderson University.

most frequently. If and when the going gets tough, it will help you in your thinking, always reminding you of his presence."[33]

By the end of 1942, when Sallman produced a cover for the Salvation Army's Christmas issue of the *War Cry* (pl. IV), American men and women had been mobilized for military action.[34] Parents faced the terrible task of giving up their sons to the slaughter of combat. One response to this ordeal among Christians was the use of images that preserved ties to religious faith as a means of comfort and protection. In an image that mingles patriotism and religion, Sallman merged the Nativity and the American flag as the content of a spiritual meditation of a young soldier, far from home, reading an unambiguously labeled copy of the New Testament. Sallman had published work in the *War Cry* since the 1930s, and it was the Salvation Army that was partially responsible for distributing pocket-sized reproductions of the *Head of Christ* to GIs during the war.

The war and Christmas provided the strongest possible combination of occasions for giving Sallman's images as gifts. As William Waits has shown, gift giving in the history of Christmas in North America symbolizes the relationship between giver and receiver.[35] The exchange of cards and such imagery as Sallman's became one of the most common forms of observing holidays and nurturing the network of familial and social relations that formed the extended community of modern life. But we can also speak of the gift's capacity to signify during rites of passage (such as leaving for the war) the continuity of the worldview that the recipient is in danger of losing. The same holds in a less dramatic way for the use of imagery to mark birthdays, confirmations, and so forth. In either case, the assumption appears to be that in the absence from loved ones (either by physical distance or a change in social hierarchy, for example, the passage from boyhood to manhood) the apotropaic power of the image consists of its ability to re-present the world of values that will keep the individual safe. Scores of letters from those who possess Sallman's pictures indicate that the images were gifts received on the occasion of a wedding, confirmation, religious conversion, birthday, anniversary, or departure. These are each (or can be) moments of loss and rebirth during which the individual's fate and relation to the past and to the family and religious community come into jeopardy. The gift image is meant to conduct the initiate through the time of passage. The aim is not so much a fleeing of linear time, as Waits suggests, as a fixing of certain relations among family or friends as linear time proceeds.[36] The rite of passage acknowledges change but attempts to control it, to shape it toward a particular end. The image is meant to secure constancy in the face of inexorable change, allowing the linearity of the rite of passage to unfold successfully. The act of giving an image of Jesus (particularly the pocket-sized devotional image of the *Head of Christ,* which could be carried about on one's person and therefore make Jesus always present, or such imagery as *Christ Our Pilot* [pl. VII], which visualizes the moment of passage) helps ensure the individual's safe negotiation of the critical juncture. The images bridge the gap opened by such radical social change as war, birth, marriage, or death by reminding the itinerant initiate of his or her past. Moreover, the image, unlike a parent or lost friend, remains with the initiate. Indeed, letters indicate that whatever the occasion, the gift images have often been kept and displayed in the home in order to commemorate the ritual passage and the relationship between giver and receiver that was reconfigured as a result of the passage. The fondness that many correspondents expressed for the *Head of Christ,* and their statements that they have seen the image frequently and in diverse places, suggest that its appearance in the material culture of piety (greeting cards, Bibles, pictures, bookmarks, and so on) effectively communicated the significance of the occasion, indeed, acted as a kind of imprimatur for its ritual authenticity. The uniformity and ubiquity of Sallman's pictures of Jesus were an essential part of their power as gifts: the same image was found in one's church, home, and the homes of one's relatives and friends. Giving and receiving it reaffirmed a unity and permanence even as life submitted to difference and change. Clearly, in this regard, the commerce and mass production of devotional images as gifts were a characteristic and constructive element of Protestant piety.

In addition to such inexpensive paper products as Sunday bulletins, funeral announcements, prayer cards, and greeting cards, Kriebel and Bates experimented with such household commodities as the Inspira-Clock and Inspira-Lamp (see fig. 1.1). These small and affordable items designed for bedroom tables literally exhibited the radiance that so many admired in the *Head of Christ.* Each item included a light bulb within it to provide an incandescent glow to the face of Jesus. Sallman's imagery also hangs on living room, dining room, and bedroom walls. Many letter writers commented that hanging the *Head of*

Christ in the home proclaims Jesus to be the head of the household. The home constitutes the most sacred site in the faith of many Protestants, because it is the seat of the marriage and the place where children are raised and where relatives and friends are entertained. The home is also the public measure of personal success and divine favor in American life. The images on the walls, and on the clocks and lamps on the mantel, table, or shelf, are thought to be shapers of positive behavior. They are generative forces in the spiritual formation of children and in family life. Sallman's images often serve as the centerpiece of a room and the focal point for family devotions and prayer. Further, owners become so attached to the images they received as confirmation, wedding, and anniversary gifts that the pictures subsequently accompany them from home to home and into retirement. Not infrequently, the images pass from generation to generation. Kriebel and Bates anticipated this attachment to their commodities and sought to present the Inspira-Clock accordingly. The ad copy for this "attractive new gift item" reads, "An ideal night light or center for evening devotional hour. Will brighten the long lonely hours for the convalescent at home or in the hospital."

Kriebel and Bates tried many different products and marketing techniques. Although this book focuses on the Protestant marketing and reception of Sallman's art, his work was also well received among Roman Catholic believers. Sales records from Kriebel and Bates in 1968, the last year of Sallman's life, show that sales to Protestant vendors (for resale) exceeded those to Catholic buyers by roughly a factor of seven to one. Yet the cover illustration of *COR* (fig. 1.22), a magazine published by the Congregation of the Priests of the Sacred Heart at Sacred Heart Monastery in Hales Corner, Wisconsin, documents the appeal of Sallman's imagery to non-Protestants. An editorial note in this issue provided the following explanation of Sallman's image: "We see here depicted a strong masculine face and firm, capable hands and eyes near tears as Christ pleads with His Heavenly Father for His disciples. June is the Month of the Sacred Heart. Jesus, His Sacred Heart on fire with love for us, is constantly pleading for us before the throne of His Heavenly Father, always begging for new graces to add to the superabundance of graces which He has showered upon us already. He pleads with us, too, asking us to draw close to His Sacred Heart in all trials and difficulties with trust, unwavering trust, in His infinite goodness and mercy."[37] In 1962 Sallman painted an image virtually identical to *Head of Christ* in

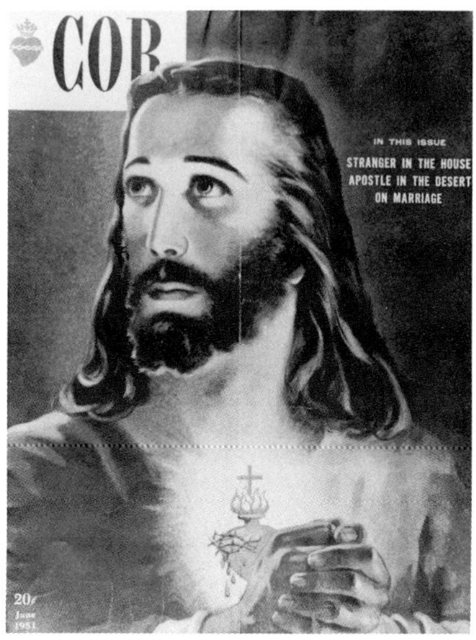

1.22. Warner Sallman, *Sacred Heart of Jesus*. From *COR* 23, no. 6 (June 1951), cover. Reprinted by permission of the Priests of the Sacred Heart.

pose, entitled *Pledging Savior*. He also produced a few other images intended for a specifically Roman Catholic market, such as *Mary, Mother of Christ* (fig. 1.23).

One of the primary strategies of Kriebel and Bates was to offer suites of Sallman's most recognized images to customers, inserting new

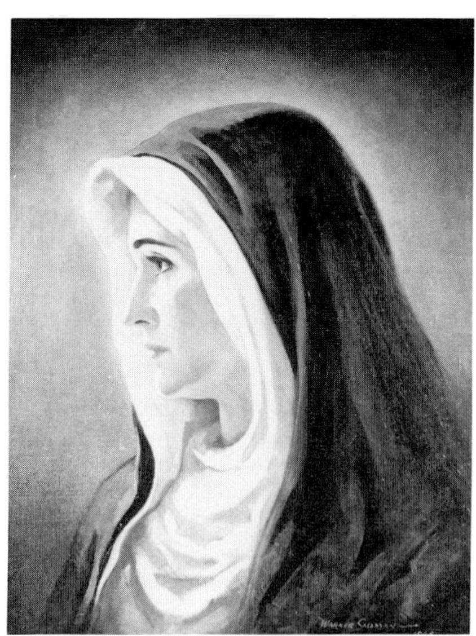

1.23. Warner Sallman, *Mary, Mother of Christ*, 1948, oil on canvas, 28 × 22⅛″. Courtesy Jessie C. Wilson Galleries, Anderson University.

images when they appeared in order to identify them with the growing corpus and the authorizing prototype, the *Head of Christ*. In 1946 Sallman undertook a project of reproducing five of his previously marketed images of Jesus as ink drawings executed to resemble prints: *The Boy Christ, Christ at Dawn, Christ at Heart's Door, Christ in Gethsemane*, and *The Lord Is My Shepherd*. Marketing materials and copyright documents refer to the images as etchings, but none were etched, and some simulate engravings more than etchings (fig. 1.24). In 1944, the *Head of Christ* had been issued in a "special etching style" and was marketed in catalogues of the Gospel Trumpet Company. The 1946 project recalls traditional print media and the format of suites of prints produced by such familiar artists as Albrecht Dürer, Gustave Doré, and Julius Schnorr von Carolsfeld, whose enormously popular nineteenth-century Picture Bible (see fig. i.9) is discussed in the Introduction. Gathered into inexpensive volumes published by commercial presses in the United States, prints by Schnorr von Carolsfeld and works by countless other artists—including Doré (see fig. 2.4), whose work Sallman knew well and admired—had been the most important source of religious iconography for popular audiences since the nineteenth century. Collections of such imagery were available for Sunday school instruction and were also gathered into Bibles to serve as confirmation and marriage gifts. Sallman's successfully

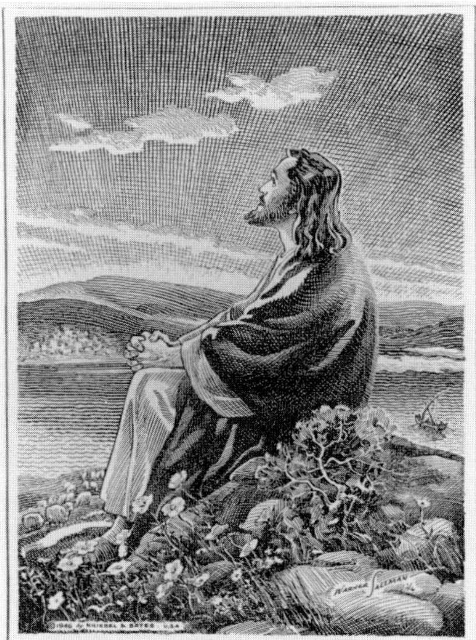

1.24. Warner Sallman, *Christ at Dawn*, 1946, ink on paper, 10 × 7¼". Courtesy Jessie C. Wilson Galleries, Anderson University.

simulated technique certainly evokes this long-established tradition of printed imagery. This genre was the only continuous form of visual culture in Protestantism dating from the Reformation, when Luther followed medieval tradition by illustrating the first edition of his translation of the New Testament with woodcuts. Yet Sallman was not satisfied with the flatness of the patterned gravure, so he introduced whiting on stat photo reproductions of some of the ink drawings. By this means he enhanced the three-dimensional illusion of the image as well as the radiance of Christ, a prominent feature of the painted version of *Christ at Heart's Door* (pl. III).[38]

A final promotional device that proved effective for at least a dozen years was the informative booklet issued concurrently with the appearance of each new painting by Sallman. Kriebel and Bates published several of these pamphlets between 1944 and 1956 (fig. 1.25). The first ones were written by Howard Ellis or Sylvia Peterson, both of whom were personally acquainted with Sallman, and the later ones were written by Fred Bates, the publisher. These booklets were a primary source of information about the subject matter, symbolism, and theology of Sallman's images for generations of viewers. Patterns of popular reception can be traced to these texts, particularly to Howard Ellis' pamphlet of 1944 on the *Head of Christ* and to a widely reprinted article by

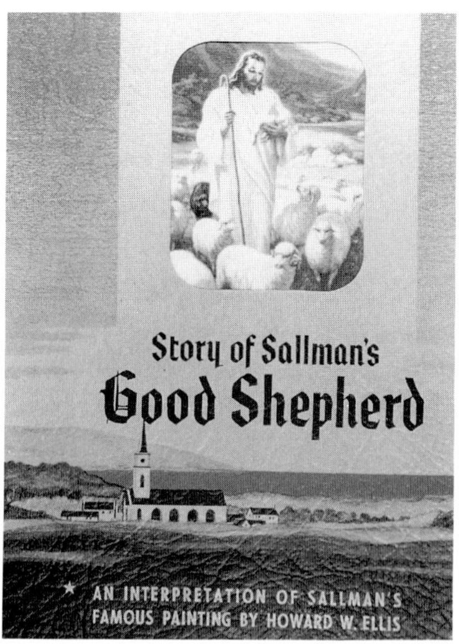

1.25. Howard W. Ellis, *Story of Sallman's "Good Shepherd,"* 1944, pamphlet. Reproduced by permission of Warner Press.

Sylvia Peterson called "The Ministry of Christian Art," which first appeared in the *Lutheran Companion* in 1947.[39] Fred Bates, the active member of the publishing partnership, always edited the pamphlets and items.[40] Peterson has indicated that she discussed each image with Sallman before writing her interpretations, and allowed him to read them before publication.[41]

In his text on *The Lord Is My Shepherd,* Howard Ellis dwelled on the topography of the Judean landscape and the vocation of the Palestinian shepherd in a manner that recalls myriad accounts in biblical travel literature popularized since the nineteenth century.[42] The prose is full of pastoral imagery and intends in its idyllic, moralizing ekphrasis to create a picturesque sense of the Holy Land. Both image and literary account present a paternalistic vision of a devoted and protective shepherd overseeing his flock, which follows him in complete trust. Whereas Sallman alluded to nothing dark in his picture (the delicate crook that Christ holds seems of little value as a weapon), Ellis claimed to discern the danger and threat of the *real* valley of the shadow of death, which he located "six miles northwest of Jerusalem." Other promotional materials situated the scene in Galilee, the district where Jesus grew up,[43] but in his emulation of the "historical authenticity" of Holy Land literature, Ellis linked the painting to the historical site of the valley, in Judea. In such a valley, Ellis claimed, the sheep follow their shepherd along a "gloomy pathway," through ravines in which "lurk marauding robbers and wild beasts of prey."[44]

The discourse of the didactic travelogue through the Holy Land shaped popular response to Sallman's picture along two lines. First, Ellis followed an ancient practice of allegorizing the landscape: "In this picture Mr. Sallman is telling [us] that there is no path in life too rough and long for us to travel, if we are convinced of Christ's leadership."[45] Second, the author produced a narrative that often contradicted the image's appearance, but in so doing linked it to an overarching theme in twentieth-century conservative Protestantism: the masculinity of Christ. The Palestinian shepherd possessed a crook, the "emblem of his vocation," as the means of protecting his sheep from predators. His devotion to the flock was selfless and his battle against wild beasts unceasing. "His is a man's task calling for genuine courage, physical strength, and a kindly concern for the flock. Sallman's shepherd is as rugged as the staff he carries."[46] This final judgment seems as dubious as the often repeated assertion that the *Head of Christ* portrays Jesus as manly and rugged.[47] By the time Sallman enrolled in the Moody Bible Institute in 1914, the institute had become involved with the Men and Religion Forward Movement, which was sweeping the nation.[48] Sallman was confronted with two rhetorics: the manly Christ and the tender Jesus. The second was closer to his heart, although he recalled a conversation with a Moody professor who encouraged him to create a distinctly masculine image of Christ.[49] I believe that for Sallman, however, this memory rarely proved more than an accommodation to a prevalent rhetoric. Sallman and millions of Christians like him may have thought they saw a man's man in the *Head of Christ,* but as Ellis' contradictory remarks indicate, the discourse about Christ's manliness was so dominant that many Protestants saw what the rhetoric told them to see. Like Ellis, they simply ignored the appearance of the imagery—or perhaps they privately embraced what they publicly concealed. Popular art—but not just *popular* art—seems to thrive on visualizing what an audience is predisposed to see. The intermingling of image and discourse has always been a concern for Protestant image making, which has joined image and text in order to secure the transmission of information and naturalize theological discourse (see the Introduction). Popular art also camouflages or mediates contradictions within the field of cultural production. Many people needed a gentle, intercessory, motherly God, so they found one in Sallman's image of Jesus. They also, however, were told to want and came to want a he-man God, so they saw him, or at least they *say* that they saw him, in Sallman's picture. In the marketplace of religious culture, such a product was bound to sell.

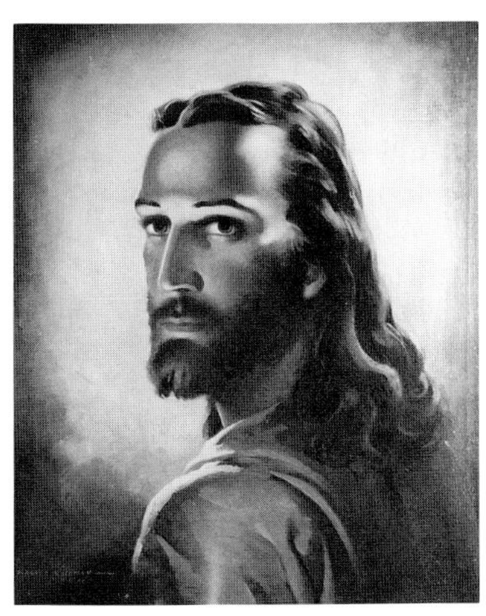

Making a "Virile, Manly Christ"

The Cultural Origins and Meanings of Warner Sallman's Religious Imagery

ERIKA DOSS

2

In 1914 Warner Sallman enrolled in a night class on Scripture at the Moody Bible Institute in Chicago. According to an often repeated story, one faculty member, after hearing that Sallman was an artist, advised, "Good. Keep right at it. We need Christian artists. And I hope sometime you give us your conception of Christ. Most of the pictures I have seen are too effeminate. I hope you'll picture a virile, manly Christ!"[1] A decade later, Sallman sketched the *Son of Man,* the charcoal drawing that eventually inspired his most popular picture, perhaps the most popular picture ever made: the *Head of Christ,* which he painted in 1940 (see fig. i.6 and pl. I).

Sallman drew on a two-thousand-year tradition of painting the historical Jesus when he made his portrait of Christ, but he added decidedly contemporary features. Captured against a bare wall in a head-and-shoulders pose common to high school yearbooks, Sallman's Jesus can be recognized by his pseudo-biblical robes, his wavy hair cascading just below his shoulders, his neat beard, and the golden light shining halo-like around his head. Painted in soft browns and yellows in a touch-up technique reminiscent of hand-painted studio photography (indeed, Sallman simply painted over a black-and-white reproduction of the *Son of Man* to make at least one version of the *Head of Christ*), Sallman's steadfast Jesus gazes quietly off to the side, lifting his eyes slightly upward.[2] Sallman's *Head of Christ,* an obviously Northern European Jesus with blue eyes, auburn hair, and pale skin, is a far cry from the dark-skinned Jewish Jesus painted by Rembrandt (fig. 2.1). Nor does it have much in common with popular nineteenth-century representations of Christ, such as the sweet and ethereal Jesus painted by Fritz von Uhde (fig. 2.2) or the stern and shadowy patriarch of Mihaly Munkácsy's 1881 oil, *Christ Before Pilate* (fig. 2.3).

Neither frail nor authoritarian, Sallman's Christ is unambiguously masculine and yet so enigmatic as to evoke a wide variety of responses, as the letters solicited by David Morgan reveal. Morgan explains that for many Christians during the Cold War Sallman's portrait did symbolize a virile, manly Christ, while for others it embodied a more intimate and nurturing Jesus, a personal savior for modern times (see Chapter 1). One writer remarks that "copies of Warner Sallman's *Head of Christ,* sold through religious outlets and catalogs, saturate the American Christian public; in fact, Sallman's is the dominant contemporary image of Jesus."[3] The key to the *Head of Christ*'s popular reception is its mercu-

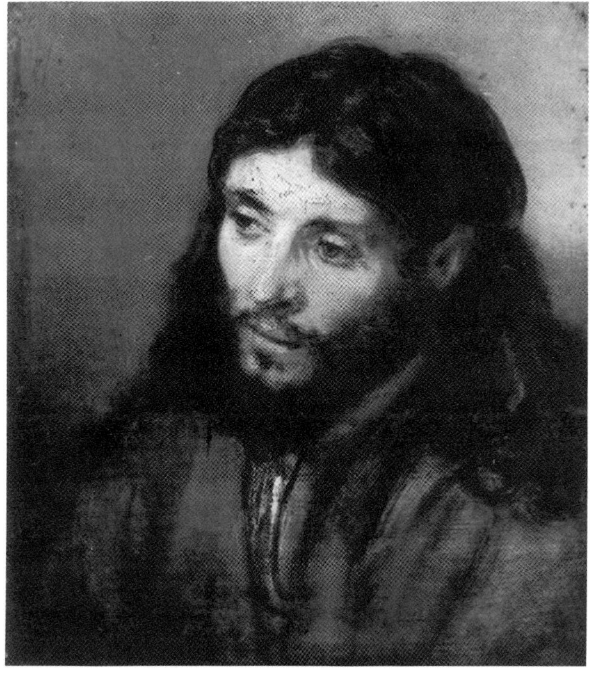

2.1. Rembrandt van Rijn, *Head of Christ,* ca. 1650, oil on wood panel,
10 × 12″. Gemäldegalerie, Dahlem Museum, Berlin.

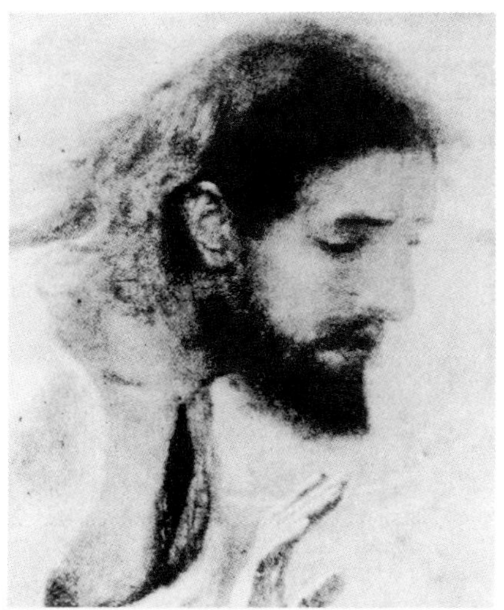

2.2. Fritz von Uhde, *Head of Christ,* n.d., size
unknown, location unknown.

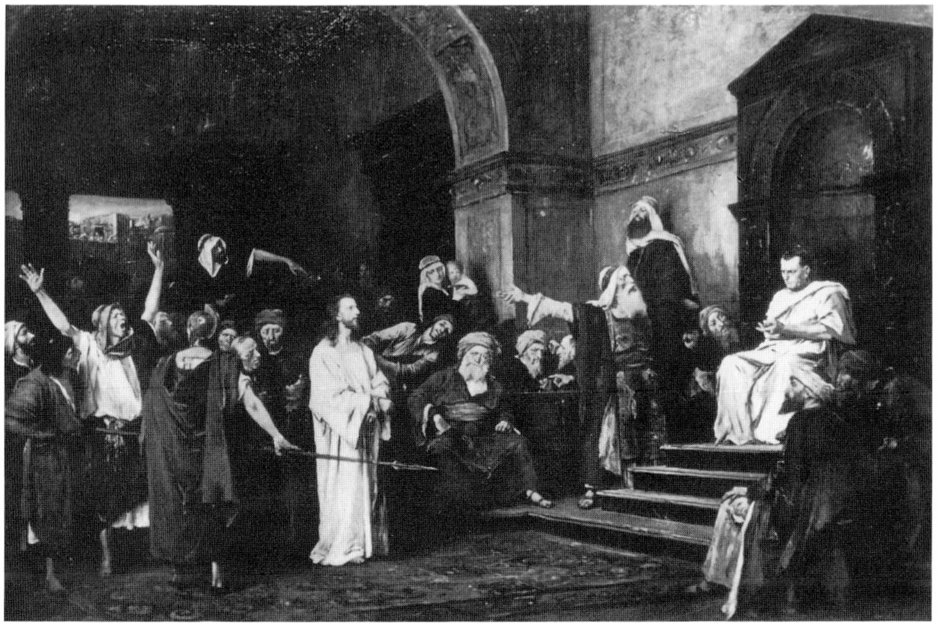

2.3. Mihaly Munkácsy, *Christ Before Pilate*, 1880–81, oil on canvas, 54³/₈ × 78³/₄". Magyar
Nemzeti Galeria, Hungarian National Gallery, Budapest.

rial quality: each viewer is allowed, and indeed encouraged, to find in it,
as Morgan writes in the Introduction, the "mores, theology, social
agenda, and ecclesiology" that he or she desires. Sallman constructed a
"manly" portrait of Christ that was so versatile that it could easily be
adapted within a modern cultural system of consumer capitalism that is
itself constantly in flux.

That Warner Sallman should have produced such a versatile icon
is not surprising in view of his career in the advertising industry. Trained
as a commercial illustrator, Sallman was active as an advertising artist in
some of Chicago's top agencies for most of his adult life. In his work as
an adman, he was clearly attentive to popular taste. In the *Head of Christ*
and the many other popular Christian images that he painted from the
1920s through the postwar era, Sallman transferred his sense of what
sells, and what the public will buy, into the religious realm. Setting out,
like advertising mogul Bruce Barton, to "give Christ a new image,"
Sallman refashioned Christ for the modern age, linking, as Jackson Lears
has written, "therapeutic religiosity with an ideology of consumption."[4]

In so doing, he joined others in wresting Christianity away from its nineteenth-century feminine and private domination and toward a more masculinized public sphere, where audiences were promised personal salvation and self-realization through consumption—through buying and praying to a reproduction of the *Head of Christ,* for example. If the emphasis of early twentieth-century Protestantism on manliness helped inform the artistic style of the *Head of Christ* and the reception of Sallman's painting, it also explains why, in an increasingly feminist and multicultural America, this image no longer holds such widespread appeal. Sallman's religious images, shaped from popular taste and for broad consumption, have been subjected to the vagaries of contemporary consumerism. Analyzing the components of this consumerism will further our understanding of how mass culture functions and gives meaning to religious icons.

Sallman always insisted that his initial sketch of Jesus was the result of a spiritual "picturization," a miraculous vision that he received late one night.[5] "The answer came at 2 A.M., January 1924," he wrote. "It came as a vision in response to my prayer to God in a despairing situation." The situation was a deadline: Sallman had been commissioned to paint the February cover for the *Covenant Companion,* the monthly magazine of the Evangelical Covenant Church, and he had had artist's block for weeks. The February issue was focusing on Christian youth, and Sallman's assignment was to provide an inspirational image of Christ that would "challenge our young people." "I mused over it for a long time in prayer and meditation," Sallman recalled, "seeking for something which would catch the eye and convey the message of the Christian gospel on the cover." He continued,

> Finally, the day before the deadline arrived and nothing had materialized. After an exhaustive and anxious six hours alone at my drawing board without satisfactory results, I retired at midnight. . . . All during the previous days and the long evening, my mind was dwelling on some complex type of composition involving the many shining facets of the Christian life. After retiring, within two sleepless hours, the glorious appearing shown [*sic*] about in the darkened room and instantly impressed on my mind that that is what I should do on the morrow. After

the vision vanished, I went up to my studio and made a
memory thumbnail sketch to help me make the charcoal
drawing the next day in time for the engraver's deadline
for the February issue. This experience has pointed out to
me that often we endeavor to serve our Lord with all kinds
of complicated devices, where just the simple, sincere presentation and witness for Him is more effective and fruitful.[6]

Spiritual receivership aside, Sallman's 1924 drawing of Christ
bears an uncanny resemblance to the Jesus depicted in French artist Léon
Lhermitte's 1892 painting *The Friend of the Humble* (see fig. i.4 and Chapter 1). Sallman, however, dehistoricized Lhermitte's depiction of Christ
among the peasant poor of some premodern era and reclaimed Jesus in an
open and ambivalent setting that allowed for unlimited responses—and
future artistic renderings. Moreover, Sallman's description of how and
why the *Son of Man* was made in 1924 suggests that the origins for the
Head of Christ lay as much in the style and substance of modern advertising as in revelatory experience. Deadlines, drawing boards, and thumbnail sketches are not, after all, the stuff of aesthetic visionaries but that of
commercial illustrators. Nor do most independent artists approach their
easels aiming to "catch the eye and convey the message"—these are the
sorts of ambitions usually associated with people in public relations and
ad agents.

Sallman followed a procedure typical of advertising artists by
making a small preliminary pencil sketch, enlarging it to a larger charcoal
drawing, and finally (some sixteen years later) tracing the master sketch
onto canvas and adding colors, to produce the *Head of Christ*. His acute
anxiety about the assignment was a fairly common psychological reaction in the high-pressure world of advertising, where nervous professionals struggled every day to meet deadlines with satisfactory designs.
As one ad agency veteran remarked, "If you have never wrapped a cold
towel around your head at three o'clock in the morning in an effort to get
a piece of copy ready for delivery before nine, you have never given it
your all." Sallman, to package a hard sell in a "simple, sincere presentation," searched for a visual hook that would catch the eye of the consumer. Aiming to fulfill the main objective of modern advertising—to
"move merchandise" to as many consumers as possible—Sallman pared

the complexity of the "many shining facets of the Christian life" into the bare essentials of a single face, and wound up producing the dominant twentieth-century image of Jesus Christ.[7]

The competing versions of the *Head of Christ*'s origins—the inspiration versus the construction of a religious advertisement aimed at a youthful audience—suggest the picture's multiple sources. Sallman's faith led him to the *Son of Man,* but so too did his savvy about what kind of Christ and what kind of face would most appeal to a large and diverse audience of twentieth-century consumers. Moreover, his anxiety about creating an icon that would spiritually satisfy the modern masses paralleled that of the American Protestant church in the 1920s, which was preoccupied with sustaining its religious authority in an era of vanishing devotionalism.

Sallman's search for an appropriately modern image of Jesus, and the formation of his commercial art style, began while he was still a child. Born in 1892 in a Chicago suburb to extremely pious Northern European immigrants, Sallman was encouraged from boyhood to combine a nascent talent for drawing with a commitment to Christ. "From earliest childhood I have loved Jesus Christ and wanted to serve Him," Sallman recalled. "At first I dreamed of becoming a doctor; then my interest turned to preaching, but I became an artist."[8] His father, a former Finnish seaman who worked as a craftsman and carpenter and often spent weekends sketching at nearby Lake Michigan, guided Sallman's interest in the visual arts and set up an attic studio in the family home, where he taught his son to paint in oils and watercolors.

Sallman's postwar biographers credited his Christian upbringing and youthful study of Gilded Age biblical illustrations with his eventual development of the *Head of Christ* and hundreds of other New Testament scenes, which, if they depicted Christ, usually featured an exact duplicate of his most famous face. In an article commissioned in 1947 by Kriebel and Bates, Sallman's publishers and agents, Sylvia E. Peterson suggested that Sallman's adult art was directly shaped by pictures of Jesus that he saw in Sunday school classes, especially Munkácsy's *Christ Before Pilate* (see fig. 2.3).[9] The young Sallman probably studied other nineteenth-century religious scenes, painted by such popular artists as Alexandre Bida, Heinrich Hofmann, Holman Hunt, Lhermitte, Will H. Low, Bernhard Plockhorst, Ottilie Roederstein, Herbert Schmalz, Frederick Stackpoole, James Tissot, and Uhde, all of whose paintings, draw-

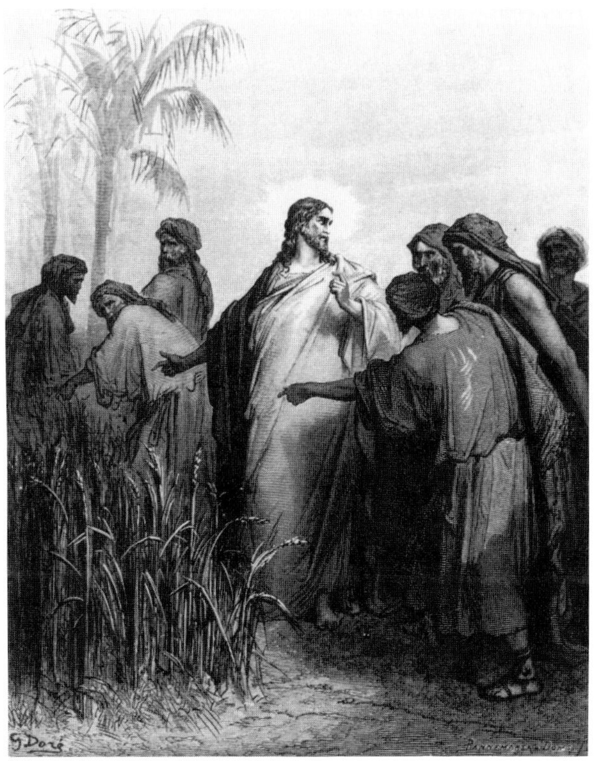

2.4. Gustave Doré, *The Disciples Plucking Corn on the Sabbath*,
c. 1865, engraving. From Gustave Doré, *The Bible in Pictures* (New York:
Dover Publications, 1974), 176. Reproduced by permission of
Dover Publications, Inc.

ings, and prints were easily found in the plentifully illustrated Bibles and
religious tracts produced during Sallman's youth. A two-volume set of
Gustave Doré's biblical illustrations made a particularly lasting impression on Sallman, Peterson remarked: "Hour upon hour he would peruse
these books while stretched out in real boyish fashion on the floor" (fig.
2.4). Sallman concurred: "I believe this [Doré's religious imagery] has
been the strongest and greatest individual influence in my life, not only
when it came to drawing and painting, but also in that it brought about
an early conviction regarding the reality of God."[10]

It is not surprising that postwar religious writers (especially
Sallman's own merchandisers) and even Sallman himself maintained that
his New Testament images were inspired in part by the popular Chris-

tian art of the late nineteenth century. Such ties linked Sallman's art with traditional religious imagery and affirmed his status as a modern-day Christian iconographer on par with previously popular artists. But the Christian images that Sallman grew up with are substantially different from those he wound up painting. In contrast with Sallman's snapshot format for the *Head of Christ,* Doré and Munkácsy, like Hofmann and Plockhorst, most often depicted scenes of a full-bodied Jesus preaching to the multitudes or standing before Pilate. Whereas Doré's and Munkácsy's representations of Christ varied somewhat from scene to scene, Sallman's image was always the same—often he simply pasted a reproduction of the *Head of Christ* onto a fresh canvas when preparing a new picture. Further, Sallman painted neither a suffering nor a sweet Christ but an earnest and accessible Jesus. Certainly, he copied the subjects and poses he recalled from pictures by Gilded Age Christian artists (like Lhermitte), but the style of his religious imagery was more the result of his keen attention to *modern* taste than of a retention of Gilded Age sentimentality. Nineteenth-century art had convinced him during his childhood of the reality of God, but as an adult artist Sallman incorporated his version of a contemporary aesthetic to evoke a sense of faith and salvation.

His Swedish-born mother showed him how to draw simple figures but was more influential as Sallman's spiritual guide: "From early childhood, my mother taught us our prayers before meals and at bedtime such as '*Fader var, som ar i himmelen*' and '*Gud, som haver barnen kar, se till mig som liten ar.*' By these instructions and devotional attitudes she inculcated in me a deep respect for God and the spiritual life."[11] Sallman's parents were devout members of the Swedish Evangelical Covenant Church, which both had joined in the 1880s. A part of the Swedish Pietist movement, the Evangelical Covenant Church was a revival movement that migrated to America in the mid-nineteenth century and organized its own synods. By 1910, there were some four hundred Covenant churches in the United States, mostly located among the substantial Swedish populations of the Midwest in Chicago and Minneapolis, with a few churches situated on the East Coast. The straitlaced Covenant church frowned on drinking, smoking, dancing, and card playing and encouraged its members, called Mission Friends, to lead devout lives of churchgoing, hymn singing, and proselytizing. The Covenant church, a noncreedal denomination that is essentially Lutheran, accepts "as Biblical truth the life and significance of Christ and a relationship with him by faith"; the Bible is the "only and the sufficient rule for faith and conduct." At outdoor summertime mission meetings in the early twentieth century, Covenanters were exhorted to be "born again unto a living hope" and help the church grow "in faith" by converting new members.[12] Accompanying his parents to the Lakeview Swedish Evangelical Mission Covenant Church each week, Sallman dutifully attended the three requisite Sunday services, plus Sunday school, and often went to Wednesday evening church meetings as well. Services were in Swedish, the only language Sallman spoke until he began attending Chicago public schools at the age of eight.

Sallman's own conversion took place in a Congregationalist church, however. Learning English and befriending children from Methodist and Congregationalist backgrounds led him to break away from the Covenanters when he was about ten years old. A few years after completing eighth grade (the extent of his public education), Sallman attended Waveland Avenue Congregational Church, located on Chicago's North Side. In memoirs written decades later, Sallman recalled the "pivotal crisis" in his life that led to his conversion: "As I grew older and came in contact with others at school and play, I began having problems of proper conduct. As teenage years approached, there were added the powerful surges of coming manhood with their attendant complications. My conscience was often disturbed as I found myself in circumstances beyond my control or resulting from weakness of character on my part."[13]

Like thousands of other Protestants in the early twentieth century, Sallman became obsessed with the "problem of drinking" and joined various Prohibition campaigns. He designed anti-alcohol parade banners and attended "booze sermons" by some of the leading urban evangelists of the day, including J. Wilbur Chapman, Billy Sunday's mentor (fig. 2.5). In 1908, while listening to a preacher on tour with the Chapman-Alexander Evangelistic Campaign, Sallman "came under strong conviction, repentance, and commitment to Christ." Experiencing "God's redeeming grace," Sallman promised to dedicate his "artistic bent" to making Christian religious imagery.[14] Soon thereafter he began to sing in the Chapman-Alexander Choir at the Waveland Avenue church. He remained in the congregation until the day a play was presented in the sanctuary. Shocked at what he considered a secular viola-

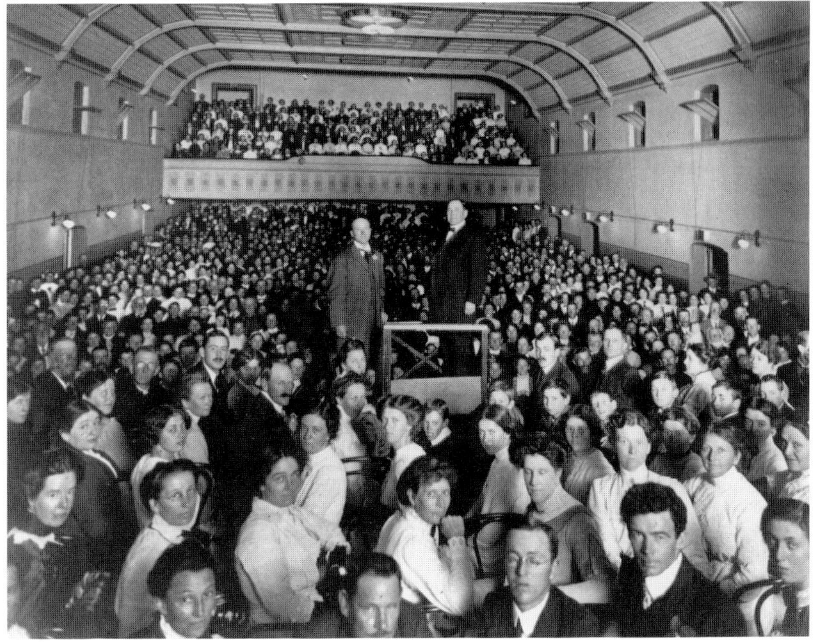

2.5. Photo of urban revival led by J. Wilbur Chapman, c. 1910. Courtesy
The Billy Graham Center Museum.

tion of sacred space, Sallman returned to the Protestant denomination of
his upbringing, joining the Edgewater Mission Covenant Church in
1911.[15] His anxiety about sustaining his evangelical Protestant piety
amid the temptations of twentieth-century consumerism continued,
however, especially in the fast-paced world of advertising in which he
made his career.

After completing public school, Sallman shopped around for a
job in commercial art. Arming himself with a portfolio of designs and
drawings and with the names of firms found in the phone book, he
applied at various Chicago area advertising agencies. Eventually, in
1910, he landed a job with Meyer–Both Studios, then one of Chicago's
largest agencies, where he and some eighty-five other illustrators prepared advertising copy for men's and ladies' fashions (fig. 2.6). Sallman
stayed with Meyer–Both until 1918, eventually receiving the munificent
salary of five dollars per week. He once left Chicago to pursue a job in a
Madison Avenue agency (and was offered a job in a London branch), but
his father convinced him to return home and Meyer–Both promised to

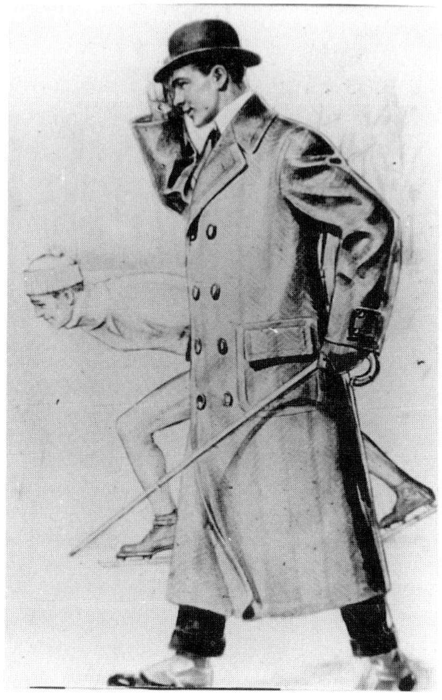

2.6. Warner Sallman, men's fashion illustration, c. 1910–18, chalk on paper, location unknown. Photograph courtesy Jessie C. Wilson Galleries, Anderson University.

double his salary. From 1918 through the early 1930s, Sallman worked with several Chicago ad firms, including Sidney B. Egan, Kling-Gibson, and Olsen-Schmid Art Studios. In 1932 he started taking advertising assignments on commission and working out of his own home studio on the North Side of Chicago (in North Park).[16]

Sallman's choice of career was perfect not only for his artistic talents but for his faith. More than a few prominent ad industry figures, including Francis Wayland Ayer (founder of N. W. Ayer and Son) and Bruce Barton (head of Barton, Durstine, and Osborn), were devout Christians whose evangelical zeal spilled into their professional lives. Ayer, a Baptist, Sunday school teacher, and uncompromising teetotaler, apparently directed his firm to investigate church and YMCA affiliations among potential employees and openly expressed an interest in hiring people with Christian leanings. Barton, the son of a Congregational preacher in Oak Park, Illinois, was drawn to the ministry but chose to work in the more lucrative field of advertising—where he applied the form and style of "his father's business" to consumer culture. In such books as the best-seller *The Man Nobody Knows: A Discovery of the Real Jesus* (first published in 1924), Barton helped publicize a new image of

Christ as a muscular, outdoorsy man who was the model of a modern businessman. Both Ayer and Barton saw little or no difference between the commercial and Christian spheres and emphasized that the essential goal of American business, and hence American advertising, was to carry on the "unfinished task of creation."[17]

Sallman could not have escaped the advertising industry's assertions about Christ's modern, masculine image. In fact, his religious anxieties about consumer culture may have been somewhat tempered by his work with and around other Christian advertising professionals who, as Sallman's biographers noted, became his mentors. At Meyer-Both, for instance, Sallman "met an older artist, a sincere and devout Christian, named U. S. Abel, who took a special interest in Warner and greatly encouraged him in his studies, especially in his dream to become some day a painter of religious pictures."[18] The evangelical mindset and mentoring that Sallman discovered in the world of commercial art no doubt helped profoundly to sustain his religiosity. In the *Head of Christ,* he would eventually supply the iconic image that embodied his sense of Christian identity and catered to the ad industry's revitalization of Christ as Protestantism's premier businessman.

In spite of a deep-seated desire—and personal commitment—to tithe his talents to religious art, Sallman supported his wife (Ruth Anderson, whom he married in 1916) and three sons by sketching innumerable ads for products ranging from men's fashions and trucks to toothpaste and pianos (fig. 2.7). His drawings were done mainly for regional newspapers and advertising supplements—the Chicago *Tribune, Daily News, Herald-American, Sun Times,* and *Downtown Shopping News*—and, late in the second decade of the twentieth century, he produced nationally distributed posters for the U.S. war effort (fig. 2.8). Samples of Sallman's advertising copy from 1910 through 1930 show a tightly controlled pen-and-ink style resembling that of Charles Dana Gibson (1867–1944) and James Montgomery Flagg (1877–1960), deans of American commercial illustration around the turn of the century.[19] Like most advertising designers of the era, Sallman adopted a human-interest approach that emphasized the benefit of the product more than the product alone. His advertisements for musical instruments, for example, focused on happy families or exuberant teenagers gathered around their new Martin Brothers Baby Grand or Cable Midget Upright in a spacious living room—usually with no one actually playing the piano. A 1925 ad for an

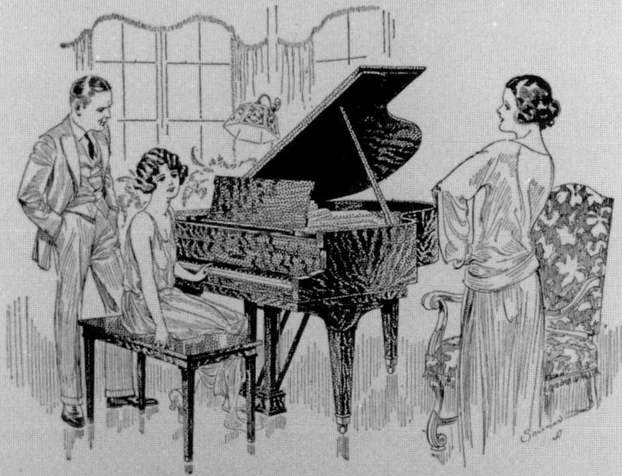

2.7. Warner Sallman, Martin Brothers Piano Company advertisement, c. 1922–24. Courtesy Sallman Archives, Jessie C. Wilson Galleries, Anderson University.

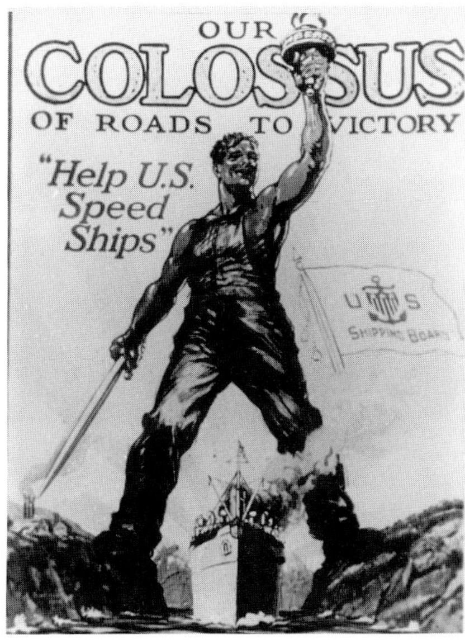

2.8. Warner Sallman, *Our Colossus*, 1916, poster
for U.S. Shipping Board, location unknown.
Photograph courtesy Jessie C. Wilson Galleries,
Anderson University.

Ampico Player Piano featured wispy portraits of Rachmaninoff and other composers as the "spirits of great musicians" that the buyer would hear "simply by pressing a concealed button" (fig. 2.9).

Sallman's ads, engaging consumers' desire for family togetherness or instant melody, thus helped encourage consumption of a product only remotely linked to the thing being sold—pianos do not, after all, guarantee either family or musical harmony. His advertisements were not particularly moderne—Sallman rarely employed the montage or off-center styles of other contemporary advertising artists—but they did play to the emotions and desires of the buying public.[20] Coupled with copy probably written by another agency staffer, Sallman's ads encouraged twentieth-century Americans to live the experience promised by purchasing the product, to "realize" themselves through consumption. He produced these ads during a period of dramatic cultural transformation, when a nineteenth-century "bourgeois ethos [that] had enjoined perpetual work, compulsive saving, civic responsibility, and a rigid morality of self-denial" gave way to a "new set of values sanctioning periodic leisure, compulsive spending, apolitical passivity" and a "morality of individual fulfillment."[21] Sallman's advertisements encouraged twentieth-century Americans to imagine the personal, therapeutic possibilities of the burgeoning consumer culture. Although he had strong

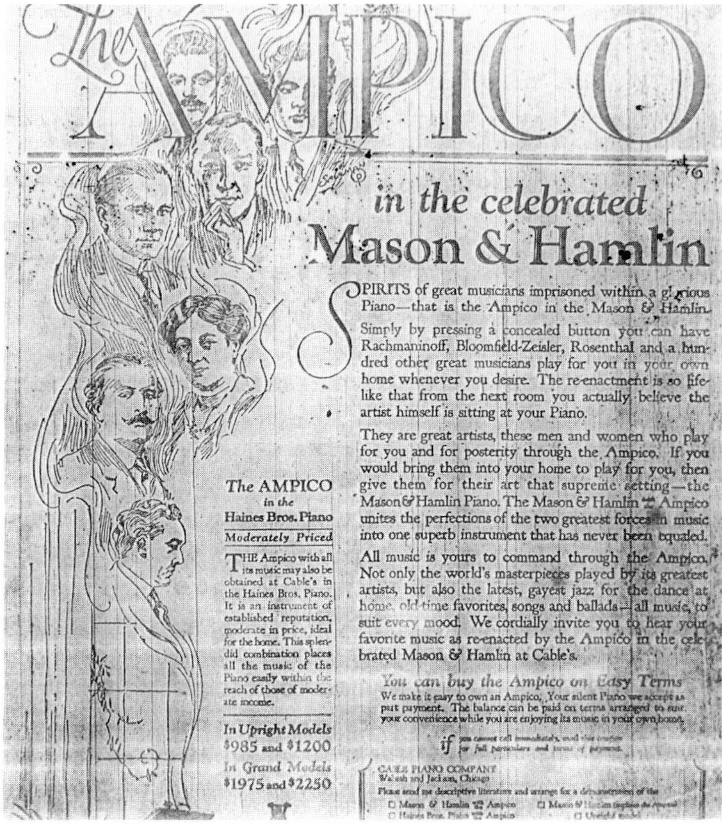

2.9. Warner Sallman, Ampico, Mason and Hamlin Piano Company advertisement. From *Chicago Sunday Tribune*, part 1 (January 4, 1925), 4.

religious convictions about the dangers of such consumer habits as drinking alcohol, Sallman made a career out of creating the advertising images that encouraged habits of mass consumption.

Sallman entered the world of advertising in a particularly fortuitous period. In the years just before World War I, and especially in the boom years of the 1920s, advertising experienced an unprecedented explosion in copy, campaigns, and budgets; one estimate shows total U.S. advertising volume increasing from $682 million in 1914 to $1,409 million in 1919 and to $2,987 million in 1929.[22] Modern businesses had come to recognize that ads not only sold products but shaped consumer consciousness, and they readily paid for more promotion. The advertising industry proliferated as accounts and personnel increased, salaries skyrocketed, and agencies opened in Chicago and elsewhere to challenge Madison Avenue's dominance of the field.

The status of advertising nevertheless remained suspect among most Americans, whose memories of snake-oil salesmen and P. T. Barnum hucksterism lingered well into the twentieth century. To challenge that image, in 1912 the industry launched a "truth in advertising" campaign to try to prove the scientific and social merit of the trade. During the Progressive Era and World War I, the industry sought to redefine itself as a powerful new tool for social betterment, and commercial art firms eagerly supplied various government agencies with the cultural and civic publicity they needed in posters for everything from public health programs to military propaganda (see, for example, Sallman's U.S. Shipping Board poster, fig. 2.8). In the pro-business climate of the roaring twenties the industry sought to be both an advocate of consumers and an ally of business. "Both the ambiguities and the hubris of such a position," remarked historian Roland Marchand, are characterized in this in-house ad agency offprint from the early 1920s: "The product of advertising is something . . . powerful and commanding—it is *public opinion;* and in a democracy public opinion is the uncrowned king. It is the advertising agency's business to write the speeches from the throne of that king; to help his subjects decide what they should eat and wear; how they should invest their savings; by what courses they can improve their minds; and even—for so far has advertising advanced— what laws they should make, and by what faith they may be saved."[23] As the ad industry searched for a more authoritative and professional image, declarations like these about advertising's power over consumer desire— and faith—became commonplace and probably did not escape the attention of young advertising professionals like Warner Sallman.

In the 1920s, the ad industry became particularly interested in the "age factor in selling and advertising." A "scientific analysis" of department store sales conducted by Barton, Durstine, and Osborn in 1922 showed that people between the ages of eighteen and thirty were the primary purchasers of merchandise ranging from wearing apparel and household furnishings to musical instruments. "Whoever would introduce the new in frocks or frying pans, motor cars or magazines, must first sell it to his fellow-pioneers—the new generation," the study concluded. Barton's findings were collected in a short (fifty-five-page) text aimed at advertising executives and published by the Chicago-based

Photoplay magazine. Emphasizing the essential "impressionability of Youth," Barton's copywriters instructed others in the industry on how to manipulate youthful desires profitably. Copywriters and artists were especially urged to focus on the "preoccupation of Youth with personal appearance" and to realize that young consumers were "comparatively cold to considerations of the practical; of utility and price, of durability and healthfulness, or moral and ethical qualities."[24]

The key to the youth market, then, was to emphasize a personal relationship between the consumer and the thing to be bought. In his advertisements from the 1920s, such as the ads for musical instruments (see fig. 2.7), Sallman succeeded in this task by depicting teens and other "impressionable Youth" enjoying themselves around their new pianos. Indeed, his pen-and-ink drawings were remarkably like the photos supplied in Barton's 1922 book (fig. 2.10). In 1924, as Sallman anxiously

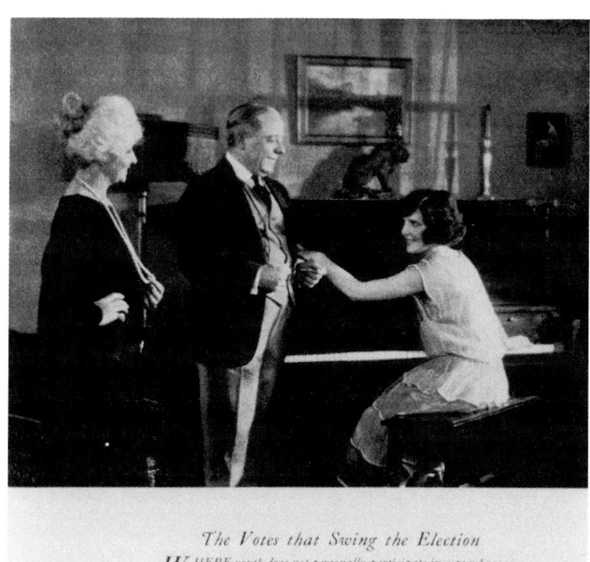

2.10. Photograph illustrating "votes that swing the election." From
*The Age Factor in Selling and Advertising: A Study in a New Phase of
Advertising* (Chicago: *Photoplay* Magazine, 1922). Survey conducted
by Barton, Durstine, and Osborn.

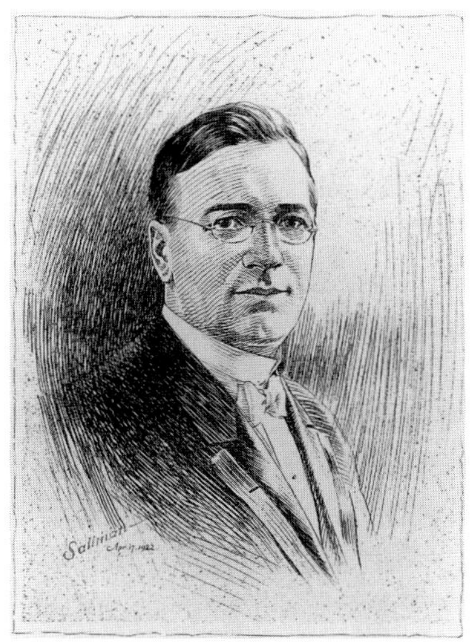

2.11. Warner Sallman, *Portrait of F. O. Kling,* 1922, pen on paper, 8 × 5¾". Courtesy Covenant Archives and Historical Library, Chicago.

struggled to produce a portrait of Christ that would also speak directly to young people (the Protestant church, too, knew that the youth market was essential to its modern survival), it is not surprising that he relied on a format that embodied the sort of intimacy that Barton's firm advised.

Like many artists, Sallman saw his stint in advertising as a way station on the road to making "real" art like the *Son of Man* and the *Head of Christ*. Such artists as Edward Hopper and such writers as Sherwood Anderson deeply resented that they had to turn to commercial illustration or copywriting to make a living. Sallman seems to have been more ambivalent about the commercialization of his creativity, as the presence of his signature suggests. With equal aplomb he signed his ads, his secular portraits (see fig. 2.11), and the left side of his famous portrait of Jesus, which suggests that Sallman saw his advertising copy, his art, and his religious iconography all on the same level.[25] He was anxious about his work in advertising less because he was suppressing his creativity than because he had dedicated himself to religious art but had yet to succeed in that arena. He had learned the power of advertising to influence consumer taste—and faith—but was still unclear about the particular form of persuasion his religious art should take.

To become better prepared for what he believed was his Christian lifework, Sallman took evening classes at the School of the Art Institute in Chicago from 1909 to 1913 and at the Moody Bible Institute from 1914 to 1917. At the Art Institute, Sallman studied the technical points of graphic design. In the fall of 1913, for instance, he took a class taught by Walter Clute, a popular illustrator who had made his reputation with a series of drawings of the Spanish-American War that were widely published in U.S. newspapers. At the Moody Bible Institute, a four-year training school for Protestant evangelicals located in downtown Chicago, Sallman learned more about religious subjects and stories. It was there, while taking a class with E. O. Sellers (director of night classes at Moody), that Sallman received the providential advice that he paint a virile, manly Christ. As recounted in a 1943 issue of the *Evangelical Beacon,* Sellers encouraged Sallman to "make Him a real man! Make Him rugged, not effeminate. Make Him strong and masculine, not weak, so people will see in His face that He slept under the stars, drove the money changers out of the temple, and faced Calvary in triumph."[26] Armed with the ideas about mass communication that he had learned in advertising, and with a style of commercial illustration refined at the Art Institute, Sallman set out to do exactly as Sellers suggested.

In late 1923, Sallman became art director for the *Covenant Companion,* a publication of the Evangelical Covenant Church. During the 1920s, the Covenant Church, like most Protestant churches, experienced a crisis. Although membership continued to grow, attendance declined; as the culture shifted further toward consumerism, Christian commitment cooled and the overall authority of Protestantism eroded. Attempting to rectify this situation, ecclesiastical orders began to model themselves as contemporary commercial enterprises. Because the era was dominated by the spirit of business, mainline Protestantism decided that the business of the Lord should become similarly efficient, adaptable, and competitive in order to survive. President Calvin Coolidge's oft-repeated adages, like "the business of business is America" and "the man who builds a factory builds a temple," made him a favorite among 1920s business executives, who wanted all Americans to trust in the values and leadership of corporate capitalism—and as business went, so went much of American Protestantism. Notions of faith and piety became complicit with those of sales techniques and scientific management. One 1923 issue of the *Christian Herald* advised churches to become more "thoroughly modern, making use of all modern devices to attract, competing, but in a more dignified manner, with those commercialized entertainments that are said to be keeping many away."[27]

Protestant modernization took two forms. First, churches became increasingly interested in adopting modern business methods, and second, they began to develop a new look for Jesus. Sinclair Lewis satirized these new "salesmen of salvation" in such 1920s novels as *Babbitt* and *Elmer Gantry,* but his insights were not far off the mark. Historian Rolf Lundén writes that in the 1920s Protestant churches "became community-oriented service institutions, which deliberately employed secular methods to become acceptable to as many people as possible." From gyms and clinics to kindergartens, Bible schools that met daily during public school vacations, art galleries, reading rooms, weekly movies, musical performances, plays, pool rooms, bowling alleys, swimming pools, bingo halls, and Bible study classes, Protestant churches offered a variety of incentives for Americans to return to the fold. They also began to advertise themselves. By hiring publicity secretaries and ad agency experts, attending special seminars on ecclesiastical salesmanship, designing posters, billboards, subway cards, and logos, and buying ad space in newspapers, Protestant leaders set out to sell the church to modern consumers.[28]

The Evangelical Covenant Church was no exception, although as a conservative sect it did not embrace all the secular amusements that much of mainline Protestantism used to attract larger crowds of Christians. In its numerous magazines—including the *Covenant Weekly,* the *Covenant Companion,* the *Covenant Home Altar,* and the *Covenant Quarterly*—and in plentiful parish papers, the Covenant church advertised itself and what it could offer.[29] "Thank God for Our Home Missions, Foreign Missions, Churches, Schools, Hospitals, Children's, Old People's and Sailor's Homes, and Now, Our Gospel Radio Broadcasting," one 1929 ad declared in *Forbundets Veckotidining,* the Swedish-language version of the *Covenant Weekly* (fig. 2.12). KFLV Gospel Radio in Rockford, Illinois, a station founded in the mid-1920s "for the use of the Mission Covenant for the purpose of spreading the Gospel," asked the Federal Radio Commission to increase its power from five hundred to a thousand watts, thereby enabling it to reach not just residents of urban Chicago but a statewide (and multistate) audience. Appealing to Mission Friends for financial support, KFLV's ads asked Covenanters to "Help us send out the True Gospel in Sermon and Song to the Thousands of Our Countrymen hidden away in scattered communities where there are no Scandinavian Services."[30]

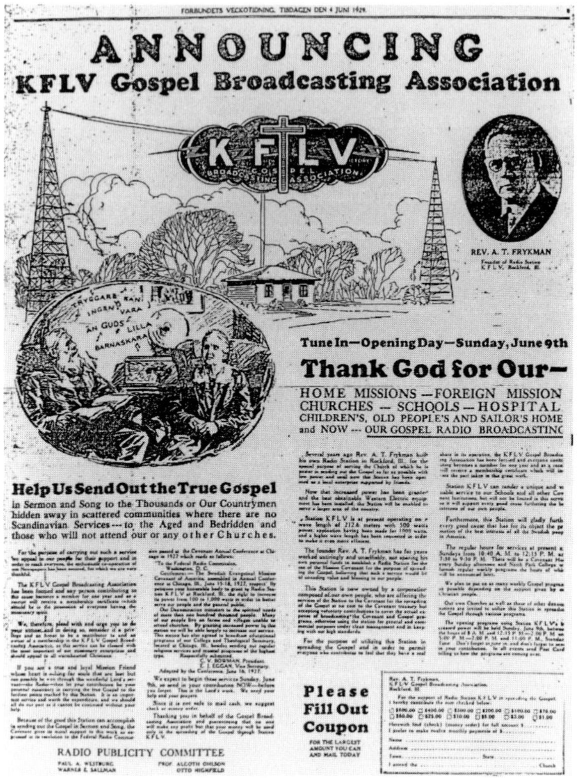

2.12. Warner Sallman, KFLV Gospel Broadcasting Association
advertisement. From *Forbundets Veckotidining* (*Covenant Companion*)
(June 4, 1929), 9. Copyright © Covenant Publications, 5101 N.
Francisco, Chicago, IL 60625.

In the 1920s, radio's promise of mass communication became
highly attractive to a Protestant church struggling for revitalization.
Before the emergence of national networks in the later years of the
decade, almost a sixth of the nation's radio stations were owned by
churches, and the airwaves were filled with the sermons of some of the
era's most prominent ministers, ranging from well-known social gospel
proponent Harry Emerson Fosdick, pastor at New York City's Riverside Church (an interdenominational Protestant church largely built
through the largesse of John D. Rockefeller, Jr.), to J. Frank Norris,
fundamentalist preacher of the Southern Baptist church in Fort Worth,
Texas. Many evangelists, including Aimee Semple McPherson, Norris,
and Paul Rader, had their own stations (the call letters of Rader's were

WJBT—Where Jesus Blesses Thousands). Radio, exclaimed Rev. Warren L. Rogers, dean of St. Paul's Episcopal Church in Detroit, "has enabled us here in the cathedral to embark upon a great missionary enterprise in the broadcasting of the Gospel of Jesus Christ, on a scale that would have astonished the old-time Apostles of our Lord." Radio was modern Protestantism's "dream medium of advertising," offering the "perfect blend of the public and private" by delivering a mass message of salvation to at-home Americans.[31] The possibility of reaching thousands of non-churchgoers, especially those who had no means to attend church services, made religious radio programming an especially attractive PR vehicle for modern Protestantism.

Sallman's church found radio ecumenism as attractive as other churches did. Sallman designed the previously discussed ad for KFLV (along with several other ads) and was also one of four members of the Radio Publicity Committee of the KFLV Gospel Radio Broadcasting Association, which was formed to advertise the station and solicit operating expenses. His ad featured a vignette of an older couple listening to a Swedish sermon, a portrait of the station's founder, and a sketch of the station building, its twin radio towers linked by a billowy cloud containing a cross and the letters K(nowledge), F(aith), L(ove), V(ictory) (see fig. 2.12).

Throughout the 1920s and well into the 1930s, Sallman put his knowledge of the power of mass communication to work, producing a variety of advertisements and other visual images for the numerous Covenant publications. At the *Covenant Companion* he concentrated those skills on the production of hundreds of cover illustrations and smaller drawings inside the magazine. In addition to the portrait of Christ that he sketched for the February 1924 cover (see fig. i.6), Sallman's covers ranged from a mural called *The Ascension of Christ* in 1926 to a scene titled *The Benediction of Christian Education* in 1929 and the drawing *Julottan* ("Christmas" in Swedish) in 1930.[32] Although his subjects and media varied from oil-on-canvas depictions of Christ's ascension to pen-and-ink sketches of Sunday school classes and Covenant Christmas services, the style of commercial illustration that he practiced in the advertising industry easily made its way into his religious art. Indeed, some compositions and figures closely resemble his advertising layouts: a 1935 illustration for the Covenant church's Golden Jubilee, for example, looks like the portrait collages he made for piano ads in the 1920s.

Occasionally he included drawings obviously made for other venues: a sketch of a gypsy girl in a 1933 issue of the *Covenant Companion* bears little resemblance to the character described in the story it was meant to illustrate. And sometimes Sallman featured his own nonreligious art in the magazine: one 1924 cover carried a reproduction of an oil painting he had done of a harvesting scene.[33] But by and large Sallman produced original sketches for the *Covenant Companion*. His stint as art director allowed him to practice putting Scripture into pictures that were consistently used as vehicles for Christian uplift and as advertisements for the ways and workings of the Covenant church.

Whereas mainline and more fundamentalist strains of American Protestantism may have enthusiastically and noncritically courted business in the 1920s, Sallman's sketches suggest that he was conflicted about relations between faith and finance. One 1923 drawing depicted Jesus sadly gazing at a robust, cigar-smoking merchant, who is carrying a cornucopia of moneybags and a miniature car but depositing mere pennies in a church offering box. Another, an Easter illustration, contrasted Christ's passion with two vignettes, one of a well-dressed family taking a stroll on Sunday morning and another of a family gathered together in Mission fellowship—reading the Bible and writing a check to the church.[34] Although Sallman was certainly not opposed to the commercial spirit that pervaded the era and, indeed, made his living advertising that spirit, his religious sketches from the 1920s implied that true Christians should invest in their personal relationship with Jesus, not simply in the stock market.

An outstanding example of Sallman's critique of the gospel of success is his cover for the November 1924 issue of the *Covenant Companion,* which shows a family of four praying at home—perhaps listening to the sermons and gospel music on KFLV (fig. 2.13). Sketched in the background are the skyscrapers of contemporary capitalism, and off to the right is a bannered portrait of Coolidge and one of his popular quotes: "The true civic center of our municipalities will be found not in some towering edifice with stately approaches, nor in broad avenues flanked with magnificent mansions, but around the family altar of the American home, the source of that strength which has marked our national character, where above all else is cherished a faith in the things not seen." A few years earlier, the *Christian Herald* had featured a sketch of the multistory Woolworth Tower, calling it a Cathedral of Commerce and noting that

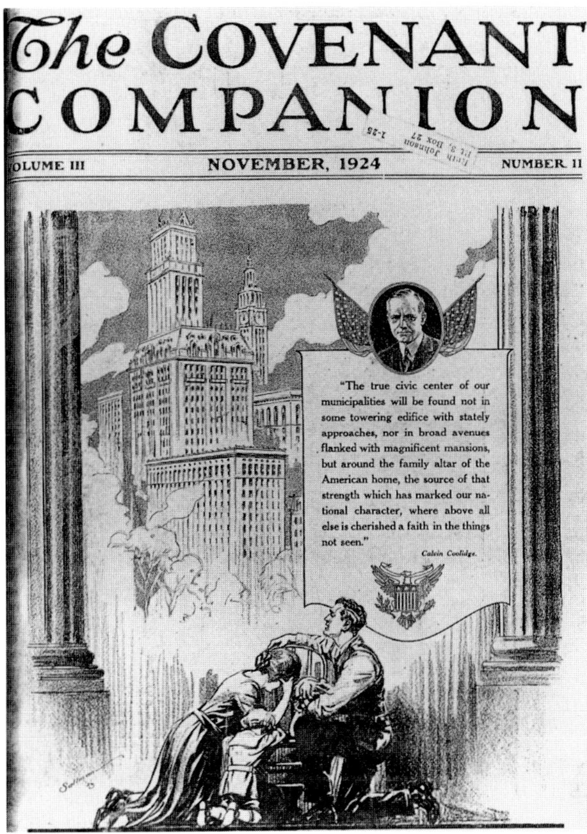

2.13. Warner Sallman, cover of the *Covenant Companion* (November 1924). Copyright © Covenant Publications, 5101 N. Francisco, Chicago, IL 60625.

"in such skyscrapers, our country has developed a form of architecture which does not suffer by comparison with the cathedrals which Europe built in that marvelous burst of energy which ushered in the modern era."[35] But Sallman's drawing emphasized that faith and fellowship lay with the family of true believers rather than solely in the business community. His response to the declining devotionalism that preoccupied American Protestantism in the 1920s was to create images that encouraged Christians to deepen their *personal* communion with God.

The possibility of personal communion lies at the heart of the *Head of Christ*'s extraordinary popularity—Sallman's famous face appeals to many because it means different things to different people. The need for broad appeal intensified Sallman's anxiety about the *Covenant Companion* cover assignment that led to the original sketch for the *Head of Christ:* Sallman was determined to produce a versatile image of Christ that would inspire many people and yet allow for a private, personal devotionalism. Such were the conflicted criteria of a consumer culture whose success depended on its ability to generate mass demand on the basis of individual desire. Sallman's task as an artist was to create an image of Christ that both spoke to the intimacy of personal salvation and cast that intimacy in terms that would appeal to masses.

The tensions of that responsibility were coupled with his anxiety about producing a virile image of Jesus. His keen attention to the modern masculine image of Christ mirrored the fears of impotency that racked Protestantism in the 1920s; his efforts to produce manly portraits of Christ were meant to assuage those fears and recall the authority of the Christian church. In addition to the *Son of Man* cover for February 1924, Sallman made several illustrations for the *Covenant Companion* that reflected prevalent Protestant anxieties about gender and power. One, a 1929 sketch showing Christ holding a man dressed in contemporary clothing (fig. 2.14), derived from an image by Plockhorst, displayed the poem "A Man":

> He breathed a prayer; he sang a song
> He helped a weary soul along;
> His life thus spent in kindly deeds.
> He had no time for warring creeds.
> A being built on God's own plan—
> The world could say, "Here was a man!"[36]

Sallman's depiction of an upright, broad-shouldered, square-jawed Jesus embracing a young man of the world was clearly aimed at convincing the Horatio Alger–type man of Christ's redemption *and* his masculinity. In *The Man Nobody Knows,* Bruce Barton similarly portrayed Christ as a vigorous, muscular, popular (especially with women), steely-nerved Babe Ruth of the Bible. Troubled by Christianity's apparent lack of significance among Americans, both Sallman and Barton were engaged in a cultural movement that sought to revitalize Protestantism by giving Jesus a new image.

Their anxiety about Christ's masculinity stemmed from what modern churchmen called the crisis of feminized American Protestant-

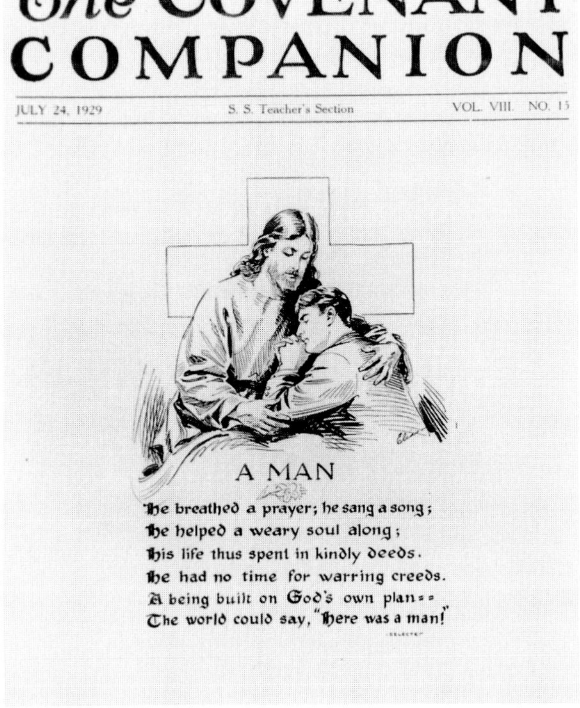

2.14. Warner Sallman, cover of the *Covenant Companion* (July 24, 1929). Copyright © Covenant Publications, 5101 N. Francisco, Chicago, IL 60625.

ism.[37] For well over two centuries an ideology of separate spheres relegated men to the marketplace and women to the domestic and moral fronts. Put simply, the competitive materialism of the individual male producer was made morally permissible by his marriage to a pious female; put generally, the rapacious self-interest of laissez-faire capitalism was balanced by its links to a feminized Protestantism. With the advent of suffrage, however, women extended themselves, and often their sense of moral housekeeping, into the public sphere of corporate capitalism, thereby threatening to upset the authority and male dominance of this burgeoning economic system. At the same time, a growing consumer culture worked to undermine rigid gender divisions and social gospel moralism, urging the end of Gilded Age habits of thrift and self-denial and promising the therapeutic possibilities of consumption to both men and women. Because feminized morality posed a problem for consumer-oriented corporate capitalism, easing divisions between business and religion became a necessity. Women were not, however, invited into the world of corporate capitalism; rather, men were recruited to seize control of Christianity.

The Protestant evangelism that Sallman subscribed to emerged as Gilded Age notions of gender roles and sexual mores gave way to suffrage and self-realization.[38] Disturbed by the dramatic social, economic, and cultural changes that occurred at the turn of the century, conservative Christians reacted by targeting feminized Protestantism. Alarmed by the authority that women demonstrated in church attendance (in 1905, the U.S. Census on Religion reported that mainline American Protestant churches were two-thirds female) and church work (by 1906, women comprised 90 percent of Sunday school teachers), they sought to assert male dominance in the church. As Betty DeBerg summarizes in her book on gender ideology and early twentieth-century Protestantism, "Fundamentalists rejected the feminized Jesus of Victorian evangelical piety and identified Jesus with traditional notions of masculinity."[39] Although religion had been the domain of women since the time of the founding of the republic, in the face of significant social and cultural changes that directly challenged traditional gender roles, many Christian ministers and laymen agitated for a more virile Protestantism.

Although these men sometimes had religious and political differences, their plan of attack was broad and direct. From 1900 to 1912, the Men and Religion Forward Movement spent hundreds of thousands of dollars on a campaign aimed at bringing men back to Christianity—"the only widespread religious revival in American history which explicitly excluded women."[40] Revival meetings of the sort that Sallman attended in Chicago featured such combative preachers as Billy Sunday, whose body language and "violent warrior" rhetoric extolled the virility of the new modern version of Christianity.[41] In addition to Barton's best-sellers, more than two hundred books and novels about the new muscular Christ appeared, with titles like *The Manhood of the Master* (written by Rev. Harry Emerson Fosdick in 1911) and *The Businessman of Syria* (written by Charles Francis Stocking in 1923). And, although it had been founded before the Civil War, the Young Men's Christian Association (YMCA) became an important sponsor of muscular Christianity, packaging its mode of strenuous evangelism in gyms and sports for young urban males. In the early 1920s, Sallman attended noontime Bible classes at the central Chicago YMCA, where lectures by Charles Ray Goff titled "The Essential Equipment for Work" apparently made a big impact: "The likable personality of the youthful teacher, his deep masculine voice, and the firm convictions which he expressed unflinchingly, made a forceful impression on the young artist. As the speaker portrayed Jesus as a strong man Sallman drew sketches and made mental notations of a picture which was forming in his mind."[42] From revivals and novels to sermons encouraging the visual construction of a manly Jesus, throughout the early twentieth century Protestantism was preoccupied with linking itself with masculinity and thereby reasserting its cultural and moral authority.

Both components of Protestant modernization—adopting procedures of the business world and establishing a new image of Jesus—can be seen as attempts to generate a specifically masculine authority for the church. The Protestant church modeled itself after modern business not only because it was the dominant spirit of the age but because it embodied masculine domination: corporate capitalism was the realm of powerful men, and assimilating its ideology might give the church the same cultural and social import. Likewise, creating a manly image of Christ was a way of distancing the old feminized Protestantism from the new muscular Christianity. Although Sallman may have criticized the dominance of a business world ethos in his sketches for the *Covenant Companion,* he nevertheless provided this muscular Protestantism with its most popular manly image of Christ.

As an artist, Sallman was no doubt attentive to the discussions about Christian and biblical imagery—and the worries about pictorial representations of an effeminate Christ—that filled the pages of the *Covenant Companion.* Twice a year, the magazine published special youth-oriented "teacher's companions," which suggested appropriate materials for Sunday school classrooms. In fall 1923 it featured an essay by Olga E. Lindborg, advising teachers about Bible pictures. Lindborg began with a short chronological history of Christian religious art and credited Léon Lhermitte with achieving a "spirituality in his paintings of scenes from the life of Christ, and interpreting the Christ-spirit in modern settings." Lhermitte's pictures were "truly wonderful and usable not only as works of distinctive art but as *illustrations* of Bible truths and Bible stories," she wrote, noting that *The Friend of the Humble* (see fig. i.4) was an especially "fine example of his art."[43]

Lindborg continued her essay by cautioning against the "highly fantastical" pictures by Roman Catholic artists ("the Protestant Church cannot use them as illustrations in its Bible instruction, no matter what admiration the instructor may have for the artist and his art"). She reserved her praise for pictures by Protestant artists that "give boys and girls true value in the sense of beauty, plus regard for fact, plus spirituality, as they help them visualize Jesus in His earthly associations." Such artists as W. L. Taylor, Harold Copping (an English illustrator), and O. A. Stemler (who illustrated the Primary Bible Story books of the Covenant Graded Lessons) were singled out for their modern and "factual" (rather than fantastic) pictures of Christ: "Jesus, to the modern illustrator of Bible stories, is not Italian, or Flemish, or Spanish, or French, or English. His physical type is the Semitic racial type, His costuming the dress of His contemporary Palestinites, while the portrayal of 'the light of His face' is as *universal* in its appeal as the intense longing in the human heart for truth and peace." Insisting on a blend of the "ideal and the practical," Lindborg encouraged Covenant teachers to choose (and Covenant artists to paint) "faithful" pictures of "Bible truths": no angels, no halos, no clouds, no "Roman type" depictions of an effeminate Christ. Although she generally liked Stemler's Bible pictures, Lindborg harangued him for his depiction of John the Evangelist as a "lily-like maiden of the mid-Victorian era," adding, "Why should we give the boys and girls, whom we wish to inspire by the *manliness* of these men who were the pillars of the first Christian Church, such ludicrous ideas as to their appearance?"[44] Published just months before Sallman began to agonize about his own youth-oriented image of Christ, Lindborg's arguments probably made quite an impact on his decision to create a portrait of Jesus that looked like Lhermitte's, focused on the light of Christ's face, and aspired to a universal sort of appeal.

Because such Covenant artists as Stemler failed to provide Lindborg with the specifically manly biblical imagery that she and many others called for, we need to ask where Warner Sallman derived his closeup, snapshot image of the Jesus that so many considered manly. He was certainly inspired by the Christian artists who preceded him—such as Lhermitte—and by the proponents of muscular Christianity who were his business world and religious world colleagues. But as an artist,

Sallman was undoubtedly also influenced by the plethora of masculine faces that made their marks on posters, in magazines, in advertisements, and in the movies in the early twentieth century.

Sallman appropriated only Lhermitte's head of Christ because he believed that it—and it alone—could carry the Protestant and popular appeal that he desired. How Sallman sensed that simply the face of Christ might be able to do this came from his experience in the world of advertising and his keen attention to the dynamics of consumerism. In her chapter on Christian retailing, Colleen McDannell notes that closeups of Jesus' face were already being marketed as early as the 1920s (see Chapter 3). As consumer fascination with celebrities escalated because of a deluge of star-filled motion pictures, photo magazines, and ads, it is not surprising that Christian artists were drawn to making *portraits* of Jesus, which conformed to this cultural obsession with personality. Much of early-twentieth-century modernity, historian Warren Susman argued, focused on the links between character (appearance, manners), self-consciousness, and well-being.[45] Images of ideal personalities—movie stars, athletes, celebrities—continue to play a huge role in this cult of personality by functioning as the key symbols, the role models, for self-realization.

Sallman never alluded to the influence that popular culture had on his religious images, to the ways in which cropped, three-quarter views of, for example, male movie stars in film stills, on magazine covers, and in contemporary advertisements influenced his own lionizing constructions of the *Son of Man* and the *Head of Christ*. Nor did he mention that the postwar popularity of the *Head of Christ* was due in part to its stylistic similarity to movie star pinups and celebrity face shots. But his new look for a more manly Jesus certainly stemmed as much from the style and substance of popular iconography and modern advertising as it did from the revelatory experience he claimed. Indeed, in response to queries about the similarities between his portrait of Christ and that by Lhermitte, Sallman replied, "I don't wonder that people say the Lhermitte painting influenced my drawing. Isn't everything we create a composite of what we have subconsciously stored through the years?"[46]

Son of Man, and by extension Sallman's *Head of Christ,* are the products of his "subconscious" attention to a huge variety of visual, religious, personal, and cultural sources. Admittedly, as a Protestant pietist, Sallman may not have gone much to the movies or professed as

　　　　　　　　　　　　　　　　　　　　　　　Erika Doss

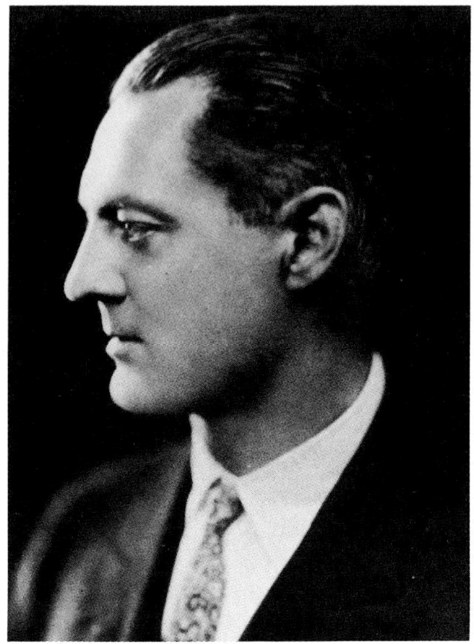

2.15. Movie studio head shot of Lionel Barrymore,
1923. From Daniel Blum, *A Pictorial History
of the Silent Screen* (New York:
G. P. Putnam's Sons, 1953).

much of an interest in celebrities and stars as other Americans. But, as an adman, he was certainly aware of the popular styles and fashionable poses that, especially in the age of personality, would most influence an audience. It is not surprising, as Neil Harris suggests, that Sallman's 1924 picture of Jesus follows a format used in countless movie studio head shots and publicity posters for silent film stars ranging from Tom Mix to Rudolph Valentino, Lionel Barrymore, John Garfield, Douglas Fairbanks, Wallace Beery, Warner Baxter, Adolphe Menjou, Ramon Novarro, Ronald Colman, Rod La Rocque, and many more (figs. 2.15 and 2.16). Nor is it a surprise that when the *Son of Man* was colorized in 1940 to become the *Head of Christ,* the yellow, green, and brown hues that Sallman relied on were exactly those most popularly used in contemporary commercial illustration. The millions of color reproductions that were subsequently made from Sallman's famous face displayed those hues, too, largely because of the color separation processes then used by printing houses.[47] But the fact that in 1940 Sallman copied those colors, and hence the look of a mass-produced image, in his initial, handmade painting of Christ suggests that he was readying the picture's popular appeal in advance—by painting it in colors that audiences would clearly recognize through their own subconscious attention to countless previously seen and similarly colored movie posters and advertisements.

Years of work as a designer had taught Sallman what to anticipate in terms of popular taste and preferences.

Having prepared his portrait of Christ for mass consumption, Sallman saw it used in that manner for the next several decades: as McDannell reveals in Chapter 3, Sallman's publishers, Kriebel and Bates (and by extension, Warner Press), were as canny as Sallman about the iconic preferences of the Protestant public. Carried in the wallets of World War II soldiers, displayed on buses and subway cars, hung in hospitals, schools, stores, churches, "huts and mansions," Sallman's portrait of Jesus was seen everywhere. Whether the *Head of Christ* was really any more manly and virile than previous pictures of Jesus is, of course, open to interpretation: notions of masculinity (like those of femininity) are cultural constructions rather than matters of fact. It comes as no surprise, then, that in postwar America, when anxiety about gender roles so completely affected everyday life, Sallman's 1940 picture was explicitly marketed and particularly understood as a "manly head of Christ."[48]

Just as Sallman's portrait replaced previously popular pictures by Hofmann, Hunt, Plockhorst, and Stemler, by the 1970s it too, it seems, had been replaced. Despite its recent rebirth as "third-degree kitsch," said critic Celeste Olalquiaga in 1992, Sallman's *Head of Christ* simply does not command the degree of popularity it did in the 1950s.[49]

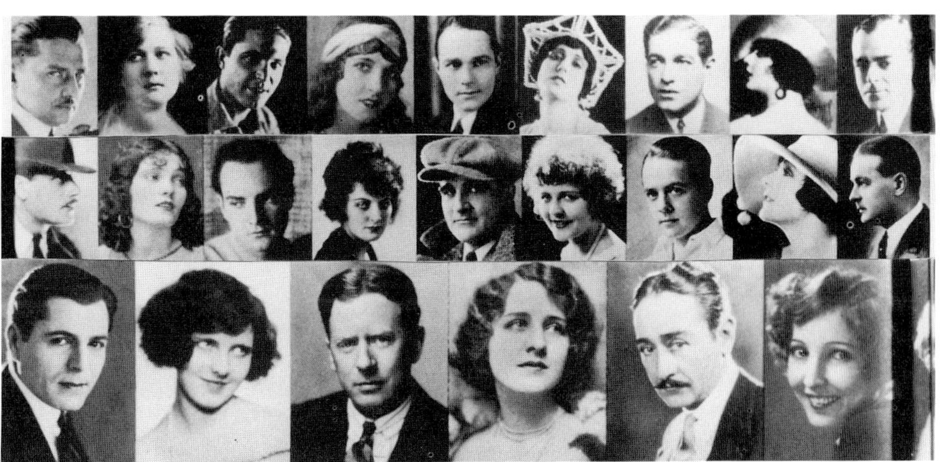

2.16. Varieties of movie studio head shots, 1923. From Daniel Blum, *A Pictorial History of the Silent Screen* (New York: G. P. Putnam's Sons, 1953).

Its decline is an economic tenet of consumer capitalism: having commodified Christ, Sallman saw his art subjected to the same inconstancies of consumer taste as any other image or product.[50] But the decline has not led to obsolescence. The imagery continued to sell, and Sallman received royalties until his death in 1968. Although he never became wealthy, sales provided him a comfortable income from the 1940s onward.

When I first began considering Sallman's *Head of Christ,* I was struck by this thought: "Yes, I know this image, I grew up with this image, but it seems to have disappeared." Certainly, its popular declension is bound up in the image itself: its Aryan (and supposedly masculine) assertiveness is no longer credible in a multicultural and feminist America. Clifford Geertz argues that incongruence between social and cultural systems provides the impetus for significant societal transformation when cultural forms no longer satisfy social demands.[51] This may account for the decline in the *Head of Christ*'s mass appeal. Christian individuals, sensing that they were being manipulated by religious, commercial, and political systems that used this image to their own advantage, and sensing that their own private appropriation of this image of Jesus no longer held sway, responded by evaluating, questioning, and challenging the image. Still searching for religious images that satisfy spiritual needs, today they turn to other images for devotion and display—images that, perhaps, embody less conflicted and more authentic notions of contemporary religiosity.

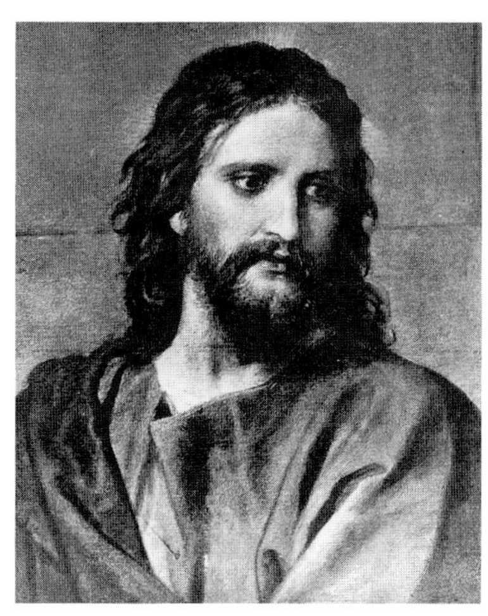

Marketing Jesus

Warner Press and the Art of Warner Sallman

COLLEEN MCDANNELL

3

To understand the popularity of the art of Warner E. Sallman, we must unwind the connections between the worlds of business, taste, piety, and domesticity. From its inception, Sallman's art was a commodity to be manipulated and traded. His images were sold as calendar art, pasted on Sunday school rewards, made into church bulletin covers, and even put on clocks. Sallman's art became ubiquitous in American Christianity because of the production and marketing of Gospel Trumpet Company, later called Warner Press (fig. 3.1). By the 1940s, Gospel Trumpet was a major force in Christian retailing. It produced inspirational mottoes and greeting cards and distributed a vast array of Sunday school rewards, books, and stationery. The commodification of Sallman's art was not a unique religious phenomenon but a part of the effort by Christians to provide visual and physical representations of their faith. The production, distribution, and use of religious goods are as much a part of the story of American Christianity as the evolution of theological debates, the biographies of noted ministers, or the history of social reform. Unfortunately, scholars have preferred not to examine this aspect of Protestant life. By privileging spirit over matter, text over image, and male over female, they have neglected a crucial aspect of American religious history: the intertwining of faith, family, and fashion.

The making, displaying, and exchanging of Christian merchandise —though highly dependent on secular fashion and production trends— have always been essentially religious activities. The people who made the merchandise, sold it door-to-door, bought it in bookstores, and mounted it on their living room walls all felt that they were involved in Christian endeavors. In this chapter I examine the ideological and institutional structures that made it possible for Christians to buy a Warner Sallman print for their homes.

Conservative Christians of the 1990s and evangelical Protestants of the 1890s share a preoccupation with the sacrality of the family. To understand the popularity of Sallman's art in both the 1940s and the 1990s, we must comprehend the importance of domestic Christianity in shaping religious life in America. Families bought, and still buy, Christian merchandise because they believed that their homes were sacred places and that the display of such goods helped inculcate religious values. This attitude was ubiquitous during the last half of the nineteenth century and continued among evangelical Christians throughout the twentieth century. It is domestic Christianity, which integrates faith,

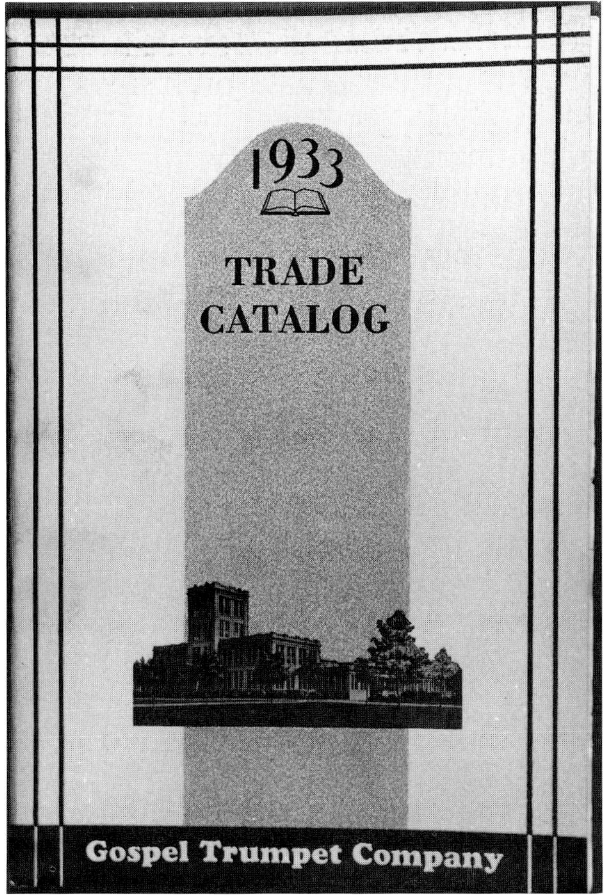

3.1. Gospel Trumpet Company, "1933 Trade Catalog," cover.
Reproduced by permission of Warner Press.

family, and environment, that provides the foundation on which the art of Warner Sallman could be marketed.

PARLOR PIETY AND MATERIAL CULTURE

The creators of Victorian American culture—ministers, reformers, novelists, and architects—saw the home as a vehicle for the promotion of values.[1] Like the church, the home as a physical space and a kinship structure was sacred. During the second half of the nineteenth century, Protestant Americans sought to make their domestic space holy by elaborating an ideology that placed the home, not the church, at the center of the creation of religious and civic values. The home was believed to be the nursery of both patriotism and piety. Life in the home taught that all people were mutually dependent and reciprocally responsible. The family connected the individual to the community and instilled notions of morality, order, stability, education, purity, refinement, and discipline. Although the church also played an important role in creating good Christians, the Victorians saw home life as the more crucial purveyor of ethics and piety. The clerical promotion of family worship also asserted the ability of the members of the family to aid each other in the mission of salvation. Although it is impossible to know just how many families really participated in this domestic Protestantism, ample evidence in the literature of material culture and advice suggests that "parlor piety" was a significant aspect of nineteenth-century American religious life.

The point was not merely that life in a family helped make good Christians—a notion as old as Martin Luther. Victorian writers emphasized that the house itself shaped the character of its inhabitants. Beginning with British art critic John Ruskin, Victorians came to believe that right states and moral feelings could be produced by good architecture. Architecture was not morally neutral, it actively created a productive or destructive society. Americans eagerly embraced the idea that good architecture produced good people and good people produced good architecture. "There is so intimate a connection between taste and morals, aesthetics and Christianity," architect William Ranlett wrote, "that they in each instance mutually modify each other."[2] Housing design, rather than being merely a matter of taste, provided the means for good family life. Physical space, as well as positive kinship relations, was believed to shape the moral outlook of Americans. Because Victorian sensibilities combined aesthetics with morality, an emotional or aesthetic response simultaneously evoked a moral or domestic response. "Our minds and morals are subject to constant influence and modification," explained architect Oliver Smith, "gradual yet lasting, by the inanimate walls with which we are surrounded."[3] The physical character of the house would uplift the spirituality of the family—even if unconsciously.

One particular style of design captured this close relation between space and religious sentiment. From 1840 to 1870 Gothic revival designs enlivened American ecclesiastical, commercial, and domestic architecture. Drawing its impetus from European Romanticism, Gothic revival emphasized the vertical over the horizontal, exploited medieval styles, and created a playful and dramatic domestic space. Gothic-style furniture, which looked like it belonged in an Anglican church, could be purchased by the well-to-do. A tea set with the twelve apostles in a Gothic revival style was registered by Charles Meigh of Hanley, Staffordshire, and later copied by a series of American companies, including the Jersey City Pottery Company. It was produced in large quantities and set the standard for relief-molded jugs.[4] No evidence suggests that companies considered Gothic furniture, jugs, or tea sets different from any of their other products. Biblical characters were acceptable images for fashionable Victorians. Likewise, ladies' fancywork books gave instructions for designing Gothic-style Bible holders and even constructing Protestant Marian shrines. Victorian Americans subscribed to both the ideology of sacred domesticity and the material culture that symbolized those commitments.

For those who had neither the money nor the inclination to indulge in Gothic fantasies, the production and display of explicitly religious art also created a sacred environment in the home. Too often American Protestantism is equated with a privatized, simple, and non-iconic religion best represented by the Puritans. Under the influence of Romanticism and the Victorian predilection for conspicuous consumption, Protestants departed from the Calvinist distrust of religious art. A mother's domestic sentiments, artistic accomplishments, and spiritual devotion (and through hers, the family's) came to be measured by her ability to decorate her home. Religious home decorations were nonsectarian and reflected popular taste. Articles like a leatherwork statue of Jesus and John the Baptist, or a wax cross, required time, skill, and patience to produce. Such goods were probably not used in family worship but served to evoke a general religious sentiment in the home. Bible sayings were stitched into samplers, embroidered on perforated cardboard and hung on walls, or made into bookmarkers. Fathers carved Noah's arks for their children, and by the end of the century religious games began to be sold.

The religious goods that Protestants put in their homes during the nineteenth century were not all carefully made by mother. Statues, pottery, paperweights, bread dishes, and glasses with Christian themes were all mass produced. Even the handiwork that women did was based on mass-produced patterns and advertised through popular magazines.

Consequently, the marketplace played an active role in shaping and reinforcing Protestant domestic piety as early as the 1840s. Throughout the second half of the nineteenth century, religious goods were not segregated from secular goods or sold by specifically Christian companies but were designed and sold by companies whose primary motivation was profit. These companies met the needs of Christian Americans. Although Protestant denominations produced books and tracts, it was not until the end of the nineteenth century that they produced other religious goods.

By the end of the century, sandwiched among velvet swags and gilded picture frames were the wax crosses, family Bible stands, and religious paintings of fashionable Protestants. In his 1880 article "The Ethics of Home-Decoration," Presbyterian J. R. Miller summarized the effects that such art had on the minds of the family. Although a country house with "neatly-painted palings . . . pleasant walks, lovely plants and beds of flowers" had a good moral influence, the "moral effect of interior home-decoration is still greater."[5] Merely believing was not enough; Christians had to visually demonstrate their piety. They had to make their homes sacred. Companies that made goods, or sold the materials to make crafts, happily provided the accoutrements that Victorians wanted in order to physically demonstrate their religious sensibilities. At the same time, the display of such objects reinforced the domestic ideology by making it both tangible and fashionable. Protestants did not invent "Jesus junk" during the twilight of the twentieth century, nor was the popularity of Warner Sallman's art unique. Victorian Protestantism already had established a strong connection between the American commercial economy, popular artistic fashion, and Christianity.

What separated the nineteenth century from the twentieth century in terms of Protestant material culture was the entrance of specifically Protestant businesses into the production and selling of Christian goods.[6] Secular companies marketed art or objects with religious themes only as long as it was fashionable. By World War I, the eclectic and cluttered Victorian style was giving way to more simple and abstract styles. In 1911 Elsie de Wolfe's influential *House in Good Taste* preached a gospel of simplicity, harmony, and unity in interior design. The Arts and Crafts movement, Colonial Revival, and the later, modern styles set the tone for fashionable Americans: clutter was out, restraint was in.[7] In particular, by presenting eighteenth-century America as the model of good taste, designers unconsciously promoted the Puritans' suspicious attitude toward religious art. Whereas an antique sampler might be acceptable, brightly colored prints and mottoes of biblical scenes did not harmonize with Colonial Revival design. It was the change in aesthetics, more than any change in American religious life, that motivated secular producers to stop making goods with religious themes. The figurative image, whether sentimental or religious, was being replaced by the abstract form. By the 1920s, style-conscious Protestants might still go to church on Sunday, but they did not display wax crosses in their modern living rooms. A child's bedroom could have a statuette of praying Samuel, but other religious knickknacks were relegated to the attic. Wherever the abstract was considered superior to the figurative, religious arts had a difficult time finding a place in twentieth-century homes.

Not all Americans wanted a home free from "superficial application of ornament."[8] Not all Americans had the economic power to first collect and display, then reject and simplify. As historian Lizabeth Cohen has pointed out, middle-class reformers failed to persuade immigrants and the working class to furnish their homes in the modern style.[9] Working-class aesthetics had little in common with middle-class notions of taste. In the mid-1920s, Robert and Helen Lynd did not mention religious art in the Middletown homes of the very poor or prosperous, but they did note pious mottoes in the homes of the "working man."[10] Not only was the working man financially incapable of buying the latest Colonial Revival furniture, but he was not willing to trade the figurative for the abstract. For some Protestants and Catholics, pictorial depictions of the Scriptures or saints reflected the historical reality of the sacred and the personal nature of faith. Evangelical piety thus supported a continuation of Victorian sentimental faith. This is not to say that evangelicals were not attuned to changing styles and fashions; just the opposite is the case. Not all twentieth-century Protestants, however, closed themselves off to religious material culture.

Secular companies that stopped selling religious art and objects to the growing American middle class left a vacuum that would be filled by explicitly religious companies with specific Christian commitments. Until the 1980s, not enough consumers were interested in Protestant material culture to sustain the production of goods with religious themes by nonreligious companies. Between 1900 and 1980, however, there were enough Christian consumers to warrant the establishment of small companies, which frequently had denominational affiliations. By the end of the nineteenth century, certain Protestants took on the responsibility of providing Christian goods for those consumers who continued to want them. Revivalism, tent camp meetings, Sundays schools, and sermons were not enough. Christian retailing and manufacturing developed in the late-nineteenth century because some Protestants continued to need physical reminders of their faith.

A CHRISTIAN MANUFACTURER: GOSPEL TRUMPET COMPANY

In 1877 Daniel Sydney Warner experienced sanctification, the realization that God had given him the gift of Christian perfection. From that point on, he understood that he would be free from all conscious or intentional sin. His desires and motives would be utterly pure. Warner had been caught up in the Holiness movement of the 1870s. His enthusiastic proclamation of his sanctification led to his expulsion from his church. Although Warner never wanted to establish another Holiness denomination, he did actively preach and publish. His activities as editor of a newspaper called *Gospel Trumpet* (founded in 1881) and author of religious books and tracts moved him out of the pulpit and into commerce. Slowly an organization (which would become known as the Church of God) emerged in Anderson, Indiana.[11] From the beginning the movement was held together not by a set of doctrines and rituals but by a publishing company.[12] Although many denominations have their own publishing houses, the Church of God is unique because its merchandising business, Gospel Trumpet Company, formed the core of its religious outreach. The publishing of *Gospel Trumpet,* along with the writings of Warner and his followers, eventually led to the marketing of tracts, stationery with scriptural sayings, motto cards, Christian postcards, and the distribution of other Christian merchandise. In the 1940s the business became known as Warner Press.[13] Its net sales now exceed $24 million.

The first Gospel Trumpet catalogue produced by workers in the Church of God is dated 1895. It contains descriptions of books, tracts, Bibles, and songbooks along with the message "We keep on hand an assortment of envelopes upon which are printed various mottoes and suitable scriptural texts with name and address."[14] Other denominational presses printed tracts and books, but Gospel Trumpet was the only one to produce motto cards. The company would buy prints and glue them onto boards on which pious sayings had been printed. Women were employed to do the repetitious handwork, while men did the printing. Initially, Gospel Trumpet goods were sold at camp meetings and through ads in *Gospel Trumpet*.

D. S. Warner intended Gospel Trumpet to be a Christian organization that reinforced what he perceived as authentic Christian truth. Between 1881 and 1915 company workers lived together and received no wages. Workers were converts to the movement, and each summer after the camp meeting one or more new workers would join the company.[15] "The entire force of workers," a leader of the community wrote, "were as one family in respect to their associations and manner of life. Until the size of the family would no longer permit, they all ate at one table, and participated in family worship together."[16] Men slept on one floor and women on another. They had their own library and reading rooms. Striving to be self-sufficient, the group raised animals for food. Gospel Trumpet also provided its live-in workers with the latest in domestic comforts: indoor toilets, electricity, and steam heat. Eventually an "Old Folks Home" and a cemetery were constructed. Members of the group shared a commitment to particular religious principles and a willingness to work to produce a Christian newspaper and merchandise. Working for Gospel Trumpet was thus more than just a job.

In its early years, Gospel Trumpet tried to combine its religious commitments with a strong desire to produce products in an efficient, rational, and technologically competent manner. The unification of faith and profit, however, was difficult to maintain. In 1917, the company changed its articles of incorporation to link church and company legally. The informal arrangement between business and faith was over. Profit from the company was to be used to support other aspects of the Church of God movement, especially its annual camp meetings. Other agencies in the denomination expected, and received, funds from the business. In 1926, for instance, the company had an operational profit of more than forty-five hundred dollars but, when expenses for the church were factored in, Gospel Trumpet was left with slightly more than forty-six dollars in surplus funds. In the early years this arrangement caused few problems, but eventually the close association between the church and the company weakened the company financially. Church of God historian Harold Phillips admitted that by the 1920s, "little by little the Company was being strangled" by church activities.[17] Church agencies also borrowed money using Gospel Trumpet machinery as collateral. Paying for the church college, Old Folks Home, and camp meetings meant that the business had no way to expand or even achieve a sense of financial stability.

At the same time, the enthusiasm of the workers for the Church of God movement was waning. Although workers still were members of the church, by World War I their needs had changed. Initially, converts were single men and women. Eventually, even the most committed of them married and started families. Communal living became less appealing. Gospel Trumpet tried to accommodate them by providing a wedding allowance of fifty dollars, housing, and furnishings, but the workers still were not satisfied. They wanted an increase in allowance from eight to thirteen dollars for babies, and they complained that workers in the Old Folks Home got no butter with their meals, and that families needed more money to clothe their children.[18]

Around 1915, Gospel Trumpet administrators made a decision that would be reiterated throughout the history of the company. Rather than stir up the religious sentiments of their workers by evoking God and self-sacrifice (making Gospel Trumpet more like a community of Shakers or Oneida Perfectionists), leaders opted to construct a more modern, businesslike environment at Anderson. It is not clear why the decision was made to privilege business over community. Perhaps leaders felt that more souls could be reached through the promotion of religious products than by maintaining a small Christian community. Perhaps they saw what happened to the Perfectionists and the Shakers. In any case, in 1917 cash payments to workers were introduced. The work force was cut by one-third, and only the most skillful employees were retained. Workers were given nine-hour work days, with Sunday and half of Saturday off. An Efficiency Committee was appointed. Gospel Trumpet was trying to follow the business standards of the time. In spite of such measures, in 1918 company debt was at an all-time high of $88,433.[19]

During the Depression, Gospel Trumpet laid off even more employees, causing unrest among workers. In 1931 half the composing room employees, members of the typographical union, left in protest over retrenchment. Union members picketed the company for more than a year and parodied the motto cards they had made by creating cards with anti-administration slogans. Gospel Trumpet, however, did not give in to their requests. A new general manager, who was thought to have more business experience than previous managers, was appointed to continue the company's professionalization. The new manager, A. T. Rowe, argued that if the company was to be run like a business, it had to get rid of the "excess baggage" of church organizations.[20] The baggage, however, did not move. Throughout the 1940s, Gospel Trumpet continued to supplement the church, and the chairman who succeeded Rowe after he retired in 1948 was a former pastor and executive with the Board of Church Extension and Home Missions. Not until the 1960s would Warner Press no longer be expected to fund various church agencies.

Nevertheless, Gospel Trumpet always considered itself to have a religious mission. It was never a "normal" twentieth-century business. The workers at Gospel Trumpet had commitments to both their unions and their religion. Company leaders did not want to deny the religious character of the organization but aimed to funnel their profits back into their business, an understandable goal. Warner Press still is a denominational press. Its mission statement explains that its primary reason for existence is to "serve the publishing needs of the Church of God" by providing "Christian Witness materials" in order to "fulfill its founding fathers' objectives of transcending denominational limitations, leading people to unity in Christ."[21] Now a successful and complex company, Warner Press continues its tradition of unifying faith, productivity, and profit.

CHRISTIAN MERCHANDISE BEFORE SALLMAN

During its first thirty years Gospel Trumpet's main products, in addition to the newspaper, were scriptural mottoes and religious stationery. "Art velvet" mottoes (lettering on a velvet-covered cardboard ground) were mass-produced versions of the embroidered texts that Victorian women sewed on perforated cardboard in colorful Berlin needlework.[22] Initially, the mottoes were simple: a floral design or nature scene (rarely a figure) accompanied a brief text (fig. 3.2). Of the twenty-four mottoes listed in the 1897–98 catalogue, many sounded a threatening note: Behold, Now Is the Day of Salvation, Prepare to Meet Thy God, Ye Must Be Born Again, Where Will You Spend Eternity? A few showed the leanings of the Church of God movement: antisectarianism (Be Ye All of One

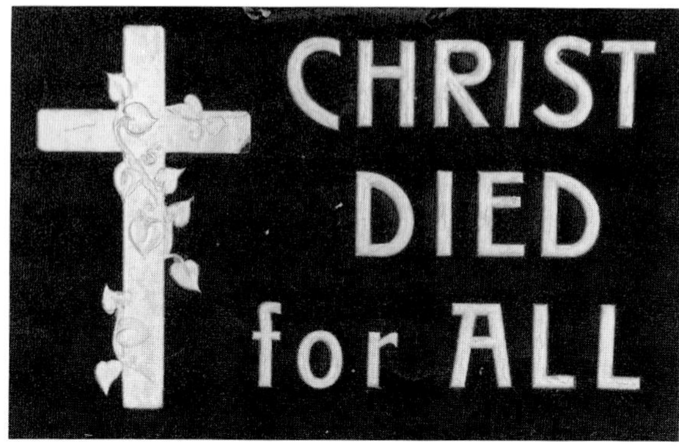

3.2. *Christ Died for All,* n.d., velvet motto, 4 × 6″,
produced by the Gospel Trumpet Company.
Reproduced by permission of Warner Press.

Mind), faith healing (Is Any Afflicted? Let Him Pray), and sanctification
(Without Holiness No Man Shall See the Lord). By 1909 the harsh tones
and sectarian sentiments had disappeared, and the mottoes contained
words of consolation and faith in English, French, and German: Prayer
Changes Things, Jesus Never Fails, Abide in Me. Gospel Trumpet had
discovered that buyers wanted inspirational words and straightforward
proclamations of belief. This language also supported the attitude of
Church of God leaders that sectarian division was un-Christian. Like
their Victorian predecessors, the paper mottoes preached a gentle Christianity that had no links to specific doctrinal controversies.

Producers of religious goods have always been keenly aware of
what is in and out of style, and they follow cultural fads just as other
companies do. In 1920 the first printed Christmas cards with general
pious sentiments were made, and two years later scriptural verses were
included in the Christmas greetings. Gospel Trumpet first merely
printed pious or scriptural sayings on prebought cards, but eventually all
the cards were printed on presses at Anderson. By 1923 Gospel Trumpet
sold boxed cards. Eventually cards for every occasion were sold, including ones for the newly created holiday of Mother's Day.[23] Although
velvet mottoes were still sold, by the late 1920s sales managers envisioned the end of the motto market and turned their attention to greeting
cards. In 1930 Anthony W. Kriebel (who would eventually hold partial
copyright to Warner Sallman's art) became sales manager of Gospel

Trumpet. Kriebel took charge of the scriptural greeting cards and developed that line into a major segment of the company. Gospel Trumpet became the country's leading producer of religious greeting cards under Kriebel's management.[24]

Gospel Trumpet not only tried to follow popular fads but also sought to present products that were in style. Advertisements in company catalogues consistently emphasized that the merchandise being sold was new and in good taste. In 1925–26 the Newart line of hand-painted mottoes were to "appeal to the taste of the tastiest. A motto that shows class and refinement throughout. The dainty designs of flowers, sprigs of blossoms, etc. are artistically arranged and show the taste of the artist. Much delicate color work brings out the delightful appearance. The beautiful sentiments and texts of Scripture will be appreciated by all."[25] Gospel Trumpet followed the trends set by more sophisticated producers and advertisers in urban centers. As historian Roland Marchand points out, advertisers were "apostles of modernity" who tried to combine an appeal to the new with a "buffer against the effects of modern impersonalities of scale."[26] By the 1920s, secular advertisers had introduced color into their copy in order to transform household objects into fashion goods. Gospel Trumpet also colored their catalogues and introduced new product designs. As with secular retailers, Gospel Trumpet embraced the call of the 1920s for advertising to "cast off its sober, utilitarian outlook in favor of a new, more pleasure-minded, consumption ethic."[27] Christians, like other Americans, wanted new and stylish decorations in addition to uplifting and comforting messages.

In pursuit of the new and stylish, Gospel Trumpet also developed an Art Deco motto: "Here is a beautiful combination of strong Christian verse and modern art. The soft, velvety backgrounds, as illustrated, are in different pleasing shades of grey, salmon, chestnut, black, green and beige." The mottoes reflected the geometrical moderne style that hit the American market between 1926 and the early 1930s. In 1929 Art Deco furniture and decorations were displayed in New York exhibitions, and Art Deco mottoes were advertised in Gospel Trumpet's 1930–31 catalogue.[28] Company designers probably saw advertisements in *Ladies' Home Journal* and the *Saturday Evening Post* that used modern art to sell everything from Chryslers to Johnson's baby powder.[29] Even in Anderson, Indiana, designers could see that American tastes were changing. Given the cost of introducing new designs and making production

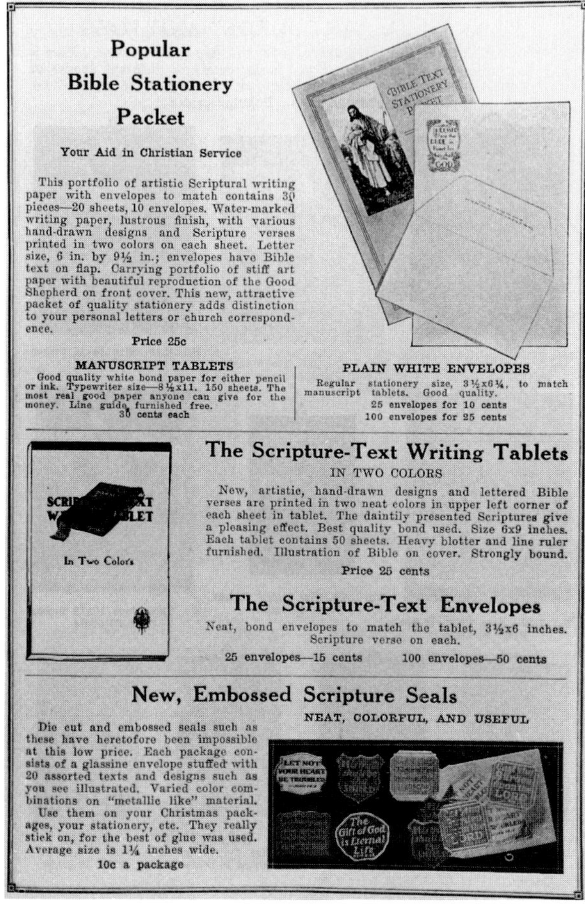

3.3. A page from a 1939 Gospel Trumpet Company sales catalogue.
Reproduced by permission of Warner Press.

changes, it is significant that Gospel Trumpet was willing to accommodate evolving taste in order to place its merchandise in people's homes. Thanks to advertising's promotion of the new and fashionable, even families of modest means wanted to feel that they had purchased religious goods that were modern, tasteful, and stylish (fig. 3.3).

Gospel Trumpet produced a steady line of religious paper products during the 1920s, but it was not until the 1930s that a full line of Christian products was marketed. Beginning in 1931, Gospel Trumpet began to link various objects with pious verses and pictures. Rather than make the items themselves, Gospel Trumpet contracted to buy goods from other manufacturers and place religious sayings and pictures on them. Mottoes were put on thermometers. Pictures of Jesus were placed on plaques made of "mountain Rhododendron." A Home Blessing table set, sold for a dollar, included "four beautiful heat-resisting and protecting mats—each with a Scripture text. This new item fills a definite need in the home. Hot dishes or pans can be safely rested now on table or buffet." Bookends were decorated with the Good Shepherd and Jesus praying at Gethsemane. In 1935 Jesus' image was put on a lamp: "These lovely lamps with inspiring Scripture texts and beautiful pictures of the Savior will help to bring into your home that something so essential and yet so easily forgotten today. Nothing more quickly adds a touch of freshness and charm to a room than a new lamp." Scriptures and mottoes were put on pencils, pencil clips, rulers, and the backs of mirrors. Chromium-silver key chains showing the head of Christ were sold as an "ideal gift for Juniors or older boys."[30] Few objects seemed incapable of sporting a religious saying or figure.

By the 1930s, Protestantism and secular advertising freely borrowed ideas from one another. Advertising designers tried to make their vacuum cleaners and refrigerators appear divine by visually emphasizing their size and numinous quality.[31] Churches tried to organize themselves around the principles of scientific management and even built "skyscraper churches."[32] Pastors devised sermons around advertising slogans.[33] Consequently, it is not surprising that Gospel Trumpet copied the gimmick of putting a company's name or logo on a pencil, calendar, or ruler, where it would be frequently seen. "Pencils are considered one of the best commercial advertising mediums," explained one Gospel Trumpet caption in 1937, "Why not spread the Gospel through the use of Scripture-text pencils?"[34] Consumers of the 1930s could choose from a seemingly endless variety of goods and services. Gospel Trumpet joined the competition and followed the path cut by secular businesses.

Religious goods were used for teaching, spiritual uplifting, and cementing bonds between people. David Morgan discusses how contemporary Christians use Warner Sallman's art (see Chapter 6), and Protestants of the 1920s and 1930s probably had similar uses for religious items. A 1922–23 catalogue, however, reveals that some Protestants during this period may have also used these goods for healing. "A short time ago a woman paralyzed from her waist down applied to her church for aid," read the citation under one art velvet motto advertisement. "It was refused. Not only to her own church people did she apply, but to others. In her room one day, sitting alone, tired out, discouraged, forsaken, her eyes by chance fell upon a motto. Through it her faith grasped the promises of God. She was instantly healed. Hundreds flocked to hear her tell her story." The advertisement concluded, "See what a simple motto performed—just a little Scripture verse. Catch the vision of what God would have you do."[35] Religious goods are thus a means of channeling the power of God directly to the individual. It is important to note that the church, the institutional expression of religion, failed the invalid. God could have just as easily healed her without the intercession of the motto, but it was via the visual reminder that she "grasped the promises of God." The ambiguities of the last sentences heighten the sense of the power of the motto. The text does not say, "See what God performed through the motto." The copywriter insinuates that the vision of what God wants us to do is best "seen" on objects.

Faith healing, which frequently included anointing the sick with oil, was part of the tradition of the Church of God and many other conservative Protestant churches during the pre–World War II period. A Church of God historian wrote that in 1901 more than six hundred anointed handkerchiefs were sent to those requesting prayers and healing.[36] Like Catholics, some Protestants placed symbols of miraculous healings in holy places. Within the building where Gospel Trumpet manufactured its goods was a prayer room. E. E. Byrum, an editor of the newspaper and important figure in the movement, is pictured in the prayer room, surrounded by crutches, medicine bottles, his own writings, and Gospel Trumpet mottoes. The crutches and medicine bottles were given to him by people who had been healed through his mediation. The prayer room thus contained objects that proved that God healed those who came to him in faith. Even if Church of God members denied that any superstitious power was present in the room, the room functioned visually as a shrine to the healing power of God and E. E. Byrum.

Like other advertisers and manufacturers of the 1920s and 1930s, Gospel Trumpet exploited the need for tradition, for the numinous, for self-sufficiency, and for personal intimacy in a changing society. Although Christian sentiments were eternal (a buffer against modernity), Christian products were mass produced in a businesslike manner and reflected contemporary aesthetic taste. Gospel Trumpet saw no inconsistency in making a motto that was both a decoration and a sermon. It could and did print mottoes with aesthetically pleasing flowers, a sorrowful Christ, and the text Even Christ Did Not Please Himself. The object thus denied and affirmed pleasure at the same time. Kenneth Ames, in his analysis of nineteenth-century religious mottoes, called the connection of fashion with faith an "uneasy union."[37] By the 1920s, however, this was a necessary union. Religious objects, like advertising, had therapeutic functions. Americans were told that they "could enjoy every modern artifact and style without losing the reassuring emotional bonds of the village community."[38] The type of piety placed on wall plaques, key chains, and lamps expressed the religion of the imagined village community. The style could be urbane, but the sentiment had to be eternal. Objects accompanied by religious texts, from stationery to home blessings, reassured their users that even in a threatening world the old truths of the Bible remained constant.

WARNER SALLMAN AND GOSPEL TRUMPET

By the end of the 1930s, Gospel Trumpet was vigorously selling a vast array of religious goods. Although some products might have been sold through bookstores and at camp meetings, most Gospel Trumpet products were distributed through independent agents. Not only was Gospel Trumpet a producer, it also ran a type of retail establishment through its traveling sales force. Advertisements in Christian newspapers and in Gospel Trumpet catalogues explained that the "business can be handled successfully by both male and female." With only a small investment, anyone can make "a success of it . . . if you push the work with a determination to win, and follow our instructions."[39] Agents carried sample cases containing Bibles, cards, books, mottoes, and other merchandise to show prospective customers. Once the goods were purchased, the agent could order more merchandise to sell, pocketing the profit. Church groups could also arrange to sell products and use the profits for their organizations. Anthony Kriebel, as sales manager, oversaw the activities of the independent agents.

Door-to-door agents continued the tradition of traveling Bible sales representatives.[40] Protestant magazines advertised for readers to sell everything from religious merchandise to Comer's all-weather coats.[41] During times of economic instability and unpredictability, such as the

Depression, door-to-door selling provided work with a modicum of independence and control for the unemployed. Although nonbelievers certainly may have sold Gospel Trumpet products, advertisements soliciting agents emphasized both the religious and financial nature of the work. For rural residents, the door-to-door agent functioned somewhat like a walking Sears and Roebuck's catalogue for Christian merchandise. By the 1940s, Gospel Trumpet employed only one full-time sales representative, who sold to Christian bookstores and publishing houses: Fred M. Bates, who would eventually join with sales manager Anthony Kriebel to market Warner Sallman's art.

In spite of its network of agents and its variety of goods, Gospel Trumpet still occupied a precarious financial position. Its business volume kept increasing ($328,000 in 1934; $543,476 in 1937), but the Church of God and *Gospel Trumpet* newspaper kept putting the company in the red. By the 1930s it was clear that the company was not going to rid itself of its church commitments. The only way to continue its mission to provide religious goods to Christian consumers and not go bankrupt was to keep up its sales. A major factor in Gospel Trumpet's ability to do this was its successful marketing of the art of Warner Sallman. In 1942, after the first of Sallman's art began to be sold, the company more than doubled its 1937 sales figure. Gospel Trumpet sold more than $1.2 million in goods but ended up with a deficit of more than $150,000 because of Church of God siphoning of company profits.[42] In 1944 the revenues almost doubled again, to more than $2.2 million. Sallman's popularity was obviously making a big impact on sales, but net profit was still nonexistent. Finally, in 1955, a business volume of $3.7 million resulted in an income for the company of more than $350,000. At that point, the Church of God began to allow the company to keep the profits it made. It is unclear why the church stopped tapping into company funds. Perhaps the church itself had become more financially stable, or perhaps leaders recognized that a religious goods company should be independent.

While Warner Press increased its sales because of Sallman's art, the popularity of Sallman's art was also highly dependent on the marketing history and infrastructure of Gospel Trumpet. Warner Press, the partnership of Kriebel and Bates, and the artist Warner Sallman had a symbiotic relationship. In the 1920s Sallman was a struggling commercial illustrator making art for various organizations, including religious ones.[43] In 1924 he made a charcoal sketch of a head of Christ for the

Covenant Companion (see fig. i.6). It is of no interest to us here whether he copied the head from a larger work by Léon Lhermitte that had been reprinted in the *Ladies' Home Journal,* or whether he knew of Heinrich Hofmann's *Christ,* or whether he was inspired by God, because the sketch did not sell. Sallman had prints of it made, and in the ensuing ten years he could barely give a thousand copies of them away.[44]

In the late 1930s, however, the drawing caught the eye of Anthony W. Kriebel and his only sales representative, Fred M. Bates. It is unclear whether Warner Sallman approached Kriebel and Bates or if the sales staff at Gospel Trumpet first contacted Sallman. Given the busy schedule of Kriebel and Bates and Sallman's desire to sell his art, I suspect that Sallman contacted Gospel Trumpet. In any case, Anthony Kriebel was always on the lookout for ways to improve the Gospel Trumpet line of goods. His colleagues remember his going to five and dime stores, seeing a clever knickknack, and bringing it back to ask them if they thought that a scriptural saying could be attached to it.[45] Both Kriebel and Bates traveled across the country, selling goods and attending merchandise conventions. Both men were also entrepreneurs who would have been interested in supplementing their Gospel Trumpet salaries.[46]

Sallman's art would have had immediate appeal to Kriebel and Bates. Here was an obscure, pious artist whose art already resembled that of the popular Hofmann and Bernhard Plockhorst. Gospel Trumpet was always looking to stay in fashion, so why not see if the 1924 charcoal drawing would sell? In 1938 Gospel Trumpet began to market Sallman's sepia print, entitled *Son of Man.* Because Gospel Trumpet did not object to their negotiations with Warner Sallman, Kriebel and Bates, seeing a business opportunity, cultivated their relationship with the artist. They encouraged Sallman to make color illustrations because the "masses preferred color in religious pictures."[47] When Sallman made the *Head of Christ* oil painting late in 1940, he agreed to sign over the copyright to Kriebel and Bates. He was paid one hundred dollars and given a royalty on the number of prints made from the painting. Over the next five years, Sallman was paid a total of almost five thousand dollars for five paintings and was given a royalty on their reproductions.[48]

Kriebel and Bates decided to let Gospel Trumpet's trade firm, Warner Press, sell and promote the prints. Early in 1941 the first run of lithographs was made by a Chicago firm and shipped directly to Anderson. Gospel Trumpet paid Kriebel and Bates for the prints. The 1942

Gospel Trumpet catalogue of home and church supplies included Sallman plaques, but the bookends, mottoes, and thermometers still displayed the art of Hofmann and Plockhorst. The outbreak of World War
II, however, shifted the attention from Victorian representations of
Christ to Warner Sallman's. In what would turn out to be a brilliant
marketing maneuver, small prints of Sallman's *Head of Christ* were sent
to members of the service stationed overseas. The original idea might
have come from individual members of the clergy, religious groups, or
people at Warner Press. Beginning in 1942 millions of cards were distributed through the USO by the Salvation Army and the YMCA. Parents and
church congregations also made gifts of the small cards to young men
departing for the front. Similar distribution occurred during the Korean
War. Soldiers facing death in war thus looked at Sallman's portrayal of
Christ. American men developed a personal connection to a particular
religious painting. For that generation of men, Sallman's image was
associated with the quintessential masculine activity of defending one's
country. Promoters of Warner Sallman could easily label the art of
Plockhorst and Hofmann as Sunday school art, redolent of childhood
and old women. Warner Sallman became the Christian artist of his age.
The *Head of Christ* had in effect become masculinized through its war
experience.

 In 1944 Kriebel and Bates set up an agreement with Warner Press
to divide the potential market for Sallman merchandise. Warner Press
would have the exclusive right to sell and distribute Sallman's pictures to
the Protestant denominational field, and Kriebel and Bates would sell
directly to the secular and Catholic field. Kriebel and Bates, for instance,
would sell the prints to companies who framed them and then sold the
framed copies. Warner Press, in contrast, would sell only to Protestant
bookstores or churches. Kriebel and Bates would also market any of
Sallman's art that Warner Press did not want to sell or distribute.[49]
Anthony Kriebel continued to work for Warner Press at its office in
Sacramento until he retired in the early 1950s. He was a silent partner in
the firm run by Fred Bates. As the partnership of Kriebel and Bates
gained momentum, Fred Bates quit Warner Press. In 1946 his two sons,
Roy A. Bates and Charles O. Bates, joined the partnership.

 From 1940 until 1947 Warner Sallman painted oils that replaced
the Victorian artwork sold by Warner Press (fig. 3.4). The close-up of
Christ's head from Heinrich Hofmann's *Christ and the Rich Young Man*

No. 250

No. 251

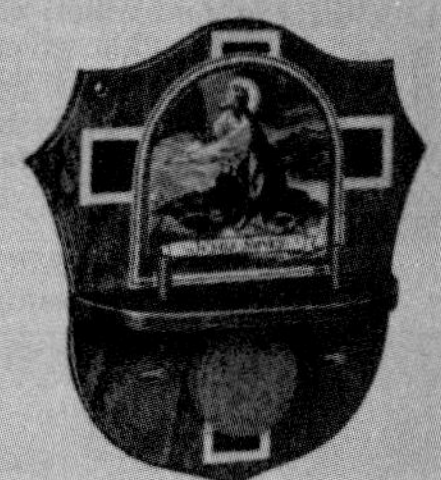

No. 252

No. 253

No. 351

No. 825

No. 826

Page 66

3.4. A page from a 1943 Gospel Trumpet Company sales catalogue. Reproduced by permission of Warner Press.

was replaced with Sallman's *Head of Christ*. Warner Press supplanted Hofmann's *Jesus in the Garden of Gethsemane* (1890) with Sallman's *Christ in Gethsemane* (1941). Sallman's *Christ at Heart's Door* (1942) took over for Hofmann's *I Stand at the Door and Knock* (no date), which itself had upstaged *The Light of the World,* by British artist William Holman Hunt (1853). Warner Press retired Plockhorst's *The Good Shepherd* (no date) and substituted Sallman's *The Lord Is My Shepherd* (1943). "The Child Christ," one print in a popular series reproduced by the Perry Picture Company (a close-up of Hofmann's *Christ among the Doctors*), was superseded by Sallman's *The Boy Christ* (1944). A scene of Christ looking out over Jerusalem (artist's name unavailable) was replaced by Sallman's *Christ at Dawn* (1945). Finally, Sallman painted *Jesus, the Children's Friend* (1947), which succeeded Plockhorst's *Christ Blessing Little Children*. By 1947 Warner Sallman's art had replaced every popular image in the Warner Press catalogue, with the exception of the Victorian guardian angel. Why Sallman never painted an angel remains a mystery. Perhaps managers at Warner Press felt that the Victorian angel was too dated to be renovated. Maybe Sallman's conservative religious commitments kept him from painting such a nonbiblical image. Eventually the angel disappeared from Warner Press's catalogue, although it currently is quite popular in Christian merchandise shops.

Between 1942 and the mid-1960s Warner Press bought reproductions of Sallman's art through Kriebel and Bates and had them placed on the same articles that had previously displayed Hofmann's and Plockhorst's art. Sallman also painted oils that Warner Press marketed as church bulletin covers and other denominational materials. Such Sunday school attendance awards as key chains now had Sallman's *Head of Christ* and *Gethsemane* on them. Bookends, rustic "art-wood" plaques, billfolds, calendars, Bibles, and crosses all displayed Sallman's art (fig. 3.5). In 1953, a Christian Art Lamp was marketed by Warner Press. Copywriters advertised that its "off-white translucent background will radiate an atmosphere of Christianity and reverence throughout the room." The lamp had a three-way switch and even came with a seven-watt bulb suitable as a "night light for a child's room."[50] The lamp, advertised in such Christian magazines as *Christian Life,* retailed for $7.95.

Although none of the responses to David Morgan's request for letters mention those lamps, a poignant letter discussed a Sallman nightlight.[51] According to the letter, around 1982 a family was having finan-

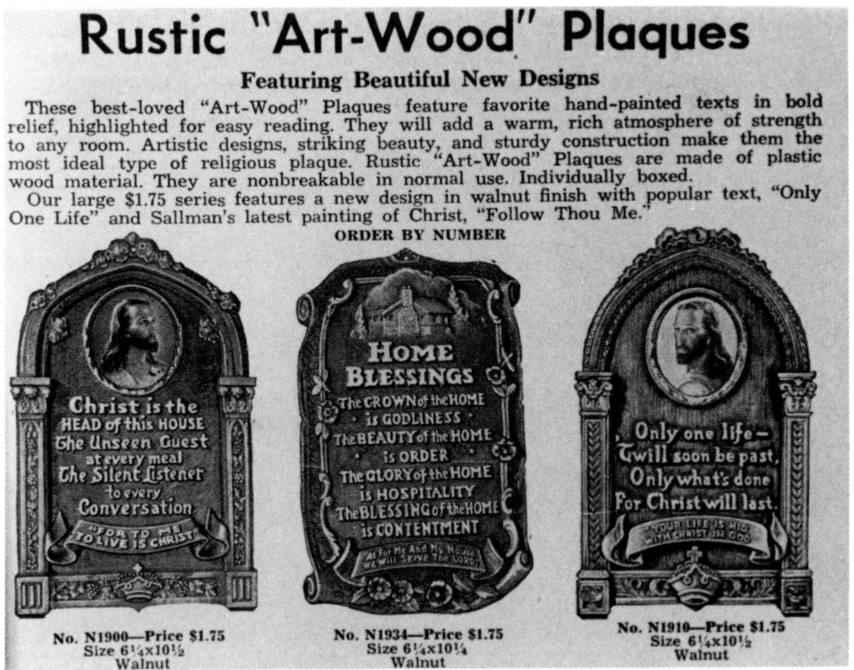

3.5. "Rustic 'Art-Wood' Plaques," 1950 Warner Press sales catalogue.
Reproduced by permission of Warner Press.

cial troubles and was on a strict budget. When the local Lutheran church had a Christmas bazaar, the mother of the family saw a "night light with an 8 × 10 picture of the 'Head of Christ,'" which she really wanted. The lamp was priced at five dollars. "It tore at my soul," the woman wrote, "the conflict of spending 2 days of food money on a secondhand night-light, against this incomprehensible desire." In order to resolve her dilemma, the woman prayed that if it was God's will for her to buy the light, it would still be there when she returned to the bazaar after lunch. If God did not intend for her to buy it, it would already be purchased. "When I went back to buy it," she recalled, "it was gone. I thanked God for not letting me squander my food money and praised Him for letting the right person get it." When Christmas came, however, her son presented her with the light. He had gotten one of the women from their church to buy it for her. "It is my most treasured possession," she wrote, "next to my wedding ring." For this woman, the night–light carried with it associations of hardships overcome, the triumph of family love, the charity of neighbors, and the bountiful nature of a caring God who answers prayers. Through the exchange of religious merchandise, social and religious bonds were strengthened.

The Sallman night-light became meaningful for this woman because she attached to it memories of suffering, love, and divine compassion. The promoters of Sallman's art also attached "memories" to his art in order to sell more products. Between 1944 and 1956 Kriebel and Bates issued a series of booklets that interpreted Sallman's art. Written by either Howard Ellis or Sylvia Peterson (both friends of Sallman's), the pamphlets were edited and sometimes written by Fred Bates. The booklets served not only to explain the subject matter, symbolism, and theology of Sallman's images but also to transform the art from a commodity into a sacred image. By clearly connecting the paintings to specific biblical scenes and delineating the more esoteric elements of the art, the booklets encouraged people to think of the art as more than just art. Interpretations permitted the commercial aspect of the exchange to recede into the background while the religious meaning of the art was highlighted. Although a complicated commercial establishment underlay the history, production, and marketing of Sallman's art, the interpretive booklets served to negate the profane aspect of the exchange. To sell Sallman's art meant, in effect, to negate the fact that it was sold.

The popularity and power of Sallman's art and merchandise were achieved through the combination of several factors. Domestic Christianity, which flourished in the United States during the nineteenth century, encouraged people to create a religious environment in their homes. That environment was produced through visual and tactile reminders of religious commitments, as well as through family worship and a generalized notion of Christian nurture. Christian nurture continued to be a part of twentieth-century American religious life, particularly among conservative Protestants. When secular companies no longer could make a profit by selling religious art and objects because of changing notions of domestic fashion, such religious businesses as Gospel Trumpet sold their own Christian merchandise. Consequently, by the 1940s Gospel Trumpet had developed a merchandise and marketing structure into which Sallman's art easily fit. Because in 1935 Gospel Trumpet had marketed lamps displaying Heinrich Hofmann's *Head of Christ,* people could accept similar lamps in 1953. Since the company's inception, the leaders of Warner Press had wanted to keep apace of new and stylish forms of religious merchandise. It made sense for them to update their product line in the 1940s, after a generation of selling familiar images. They knew, however, that modernization must not radically alter familiar forms. Warner Sallman, orchestrated by Kriebel and Bates, complied with that requirement. Once the *Head of Christ* became the religious icon of soldiers, it achieved a power that earlier images never had. Memories combined with marketing assured the popularity of all Sallman's art, as long as it did not stray too far from the standard of the *Head of Christ.*

A CHRISTIAN CLASSIC:

SALLMAN'S *HEAD OF CHRIST*

After World War II, social changes in the structure of American life made obsolete the door-to-door agent who sold religious merchandise. The number of people who lived on farms continued to decline, and new subdivisions of affordable housing appeared around cities. Churches focused on the family in the suburbs rather than in the city or on the farm. An expanded interstate highway system made transportation easier, and the postwar economic boom made it possible for even rural people to drive their own cars into town for shopping. While traveling Bible sales representatives continued to sell in the South, by the early 1950s only fundraisers peddled religious cards and novelties door-to-door. Enterprising Christians decided that it was time to set up their own stores and sell Bibles, books, stationery, and other merchandise.

Christian bookstores and their merchandise would have remained a minor aspect of American Protestant life if it had not been for the Jesus movement of the early 1970s. Curiously, it was the youth-focused and more expressive evangelism of the late 1960s and 1970s that instilled Christian merchandise with new meaning while threatening the popularity of Warner Sallman's art. The Jesus movement combined Protestant piety with the spirit of the 1960s counterculture to produce a new understanding of Christianity. Jesus people sought to experience the reality of Jesus outside of an institutionalized church structure. For them, the intense personal relationship they had achieved with Christ motivated them to redirect their lives. They turned from drugs and a meaningless existence and toward a life where every action should be shaped by faith and every question answered by the Bible. Like other members of the counterculture, they idealized a rural religious past, sought to separate themselves from mainstream society, and rejected the claims of science and technology. They felt that the end of the world was near. Christians from the 1970s on were following a general trend in postwar evangelism to stress the importance of living a holy life in accord with spiritual principles. These evangelicals claimed that Christianity was not merely a belief system but a lifestyle.[52]

In order to create a Christian way of life and a Christian culture, young evangelicals sought to replace "dead" Christian art with "living" Christian art. From an aesthetic perspective, they wanted to replace "bad" art with "good" art. Producers and bookstore owners proclaimed that a new era in Christian merchandising had begun. They disparaged previous generations of goods, which they felt were cheap, shoddy, and old-fashioned. "The young people are tired of an artificial world," reported the owner of a complex of artisan workshops and a bookstore in Orange County, California. "They are hungry to study the Bible and share God's love in every possible way. In their disdain of a superficial society, they have rejected the plastic trinkets of the religious market and have begun creating witness items more relevant to their needs."[53] And who was producing that "uninspired, unwanted" art, that "holy hardware" and those plastic trinkets? Companies run by their parents, companies like Warner Press. Jesus freaks who had never stared at Sallman's *Head of Christ* in a foxhole or received *Gethsemane* for a wedding present had no positive associations with his art. They saw Sallman's art in their churches (dull, dogmatic, and dead) and in their homes (run by "Sunday-only" Christian parents).

Some members of the Jesus movement tried to provide a viable Christian alternative to both the secular marketplace and traditional religious goods. Such companies as Bob Siemon's Designs gave established firms like Warner Press new competition. "'Christian junk' makes me sick," summarized Siemon in 1979. "I'm determined our jewelry will never be classified as cheap or gaudy. We hope to establish a standard that cannot be surpassed."[54] Older firms responded to this change in Christian consumerism. They not only updated their merchandise and eliminated many products but also marketed more contemporary art. Warner Press ran advertisements describing "'With it' Inspirational gifts for youth." A third generation of images of Christ appeared. In 1964 Concordia Publishing House copyrighted a head of Christ by Richard Hook (see fig. 1.10). Sallman painted *Portrait of Jesus,* showing Christ's eyes gazing out at the viewer like Hook's *Christ* (see pl. XII). During the 1970s, the market for Christian goods shifted from the Sunday school classroom and rural housewife to the under-thirty evangelical. Warner Press had to change its product line, and it was unclear what would happen to the art of Warner Sallman.

Warner Press continued to adjust its goods to meet Christian consumers' demand, a demand that was shaped equally by events in the religious world and in the secular world. Christian retailing, which included the sale of books, gifts, music, and church goods, experienced a constant growth during the postwar years. By the 1990s the sales of Christian products in bookstores exceeded $3 billion annually.[55] Warner Press reflects the growth of the Christian retailing industry. Its net sales doubled between 1971 and 1981, growing from more than $6 million to more than $13 million. In 1991 sales rose to more than $22 million. Statistics on profit are more difficult to come by. Profit in the 1980s reflected the national recession: in the early 1980s the net profit of Warner Press exceeded $450,000, but losses were experienced between 1985 and 1989. In 1990 profit gains were again achieved, and in 1992 Warner Press made a net profit of $154,000, down from $222,000 in 1991. Beginning in the 1980s, company leaders seriously deliberated about what kind of merchandise Warner Press would produce. According to Susan Hare, vice president for marketing and sales, it was decided that the company should no longer be in the novelty business.[56] The trinkets of the 1940s and 1950s—the Sunday school attendance awards, the lamps, the plaques—were no longer to be produced by Warner Press. Company leaders felt that they had a huge spread of product items with no focus. Looking at the aging population of Christians and at the company's history, Warner Press decided to produce only a high-quality line of "personal expressions," distribute church supplies, and publish books specifically geared for the members of the Church of God.

Warner Sallman's art was placed within the realm of personal expressions—which is what Warner Press called such paper products as stationery, note cards, wrapping paper, gift bags, posters, and bookmarkers. It also included small gift items, like coffee mugs or Christmas ornaments. By limiting its merchandise to paper products, Warner Press returned to its roots as a supplier of Christian cards and stationery. In 1987 Kriebel and Bates sold the copyright of the art of Warner Sallman to

Warner Press and liquidated the partnership. Now Warner Press may freely reproduce the Sallman paintings, but it does so selectively. The *Head of Christ* became a classic image of Christian merchandising when it weathered the changes of the 1960s and 1970s. As the Christian baby boomers aged, they rediscovered the images of their childhood. Nostalgia, rather than rebellion, now shapes their aesthetic taste. Victorian angels and decorative crosses have reemerged in Christian bookstores. The *Head of Christ* now appears on coffee mugs. Sallman's famous image now symbolizes old-time religion and the enduring faith of Christians.

The other paintings of Sallman, however, have not fared as well. Although they appear on a calendar of Sallman's art, they are not reproduced on Warner Press's cards, stationery, or posters. Small prints or prayer cards are sold of some of the paintings, but these are not made by Warner Press. Instead, Warner Press licenses other companies to produce paper products or objects displaying Sallman's art. Because it is so closely associated with Sallman, Warner Press is very careful about who it allows to reproduce the images. In the 1990s it gave the statuary company of Enesco—a secular company—a license to use Sallman images in its Gifts of Faith line. In its publicity catalogues, Enesco carefully places the classic *Head of Christ* next to the other, less well known images. The other paintings cannot stand by themselves; they need to tap into the power of the classic image in order to be appealing to the consumer. Enesco also positions Catholic imagery next to what some have come to understand as a Protestant icon. By laying a rosary next to the *Head of Christ* and a photograph of a family member, it visually links Catholicism to a generic Christianity—connecting both to the sacred family. Warner Press's granting of a license to Enesco is thus a return to the situation of the nineteenth century: secular companies sell religious goods because religious goods sell. Just as the nineteenth-century statuary company offered Protestant and Catholic images because members of both groups bought them, a twentieth-century statuary company offers Protestant, Catholic, and now Jewish figurines to American consumers. To be modern in the 1990s means to be old-fashioned. Businesses, both secular and religious, respond by creating nostalgia. Fashion, family, and faith continue to provide the ingredients for the commercial religious economy.

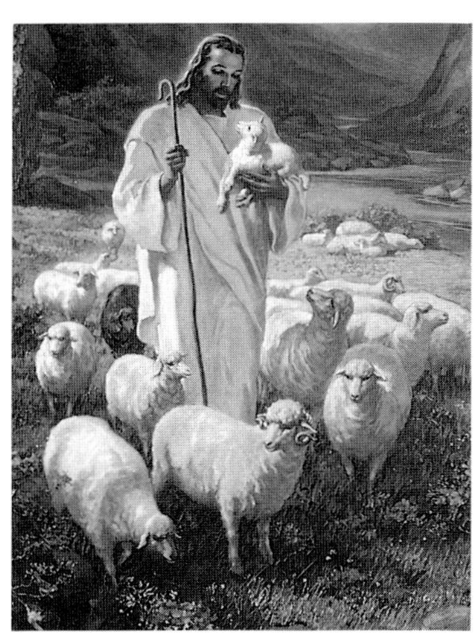

The Ministry of Christian Art

Evangelicals and the Art of Warner Sallman, 1942–1960

BETTY A. DEBERG

4

In 1958 Carl F. H. Henry, a member of the faculty of Fuller Theological Seminary, founding editor of *Christianity Today,* and an acknowledged leader of a new generation of conservative Protestants who called themselves evangelicals, dedicated one of his editorials to Warner Sallman and his art. It is a masterpiece of ambivalence. Acknowledging that Sallman's *Head of Christ* is "perhaps the most widely known and loved pictorial presentation of Christ" and that the work has "inspirational qualities founded in evangelical piety," he nevertheless asked, *"Does the work represent authentic Christian art?"* Although he was aware that the painting had been attacked even by some evangelicals as a copy of another artist's work (see Lhermitte, *Friend of the Humble,* fig. i.4), as showing a too human or too feminine Christ, and as expressing superficial and commercialized spirituality, Henry was unable to reject it. He ended the editorial with a warning that evangelical artists should be careful not to move into more abstract forms of painting because "art is moving [again] toward content and subject matter."[1]

Henry's ambivalence stems from the predicament of the second generation of fundamentalists, who came of age in the 1940s (throughout this chapter I shall call them neo-evangelicals). The neo-evangelical establishment they constructed consisted of the National Association of Evangelicals, founded by Harold John Ockenga in 1942; the Billy Graham Evangelistic Association; Youth for Christ; Campus Crusade for Christ; and such institutions of higher education as Wheaton College (which was called the Evangelical Harvard), Trinity Evangelical Divinity School, Gordon-Conwell Theological Seminary, Asbury Theological Seminary, and Fuller Theological Seminary. The empire included several publishers: Eerdmans, Zondervan, Baker, and Word. Its biweekly magazine, *Christianity Today,* according to one evangelical scholar was *"the* periodical voice" of neo-evangelical intellectuals—an evangelical counterpart to *Christian Century.*[2]

Neo-evangelicals placed high priority on sound scholarship, academic credentials, social respectability, and cultural refinement.[3] They were embarrassed by the "obscurantism, anti-intellectualism and bad manners so characteristic of what Fundamentalism had been up until then."[4] Gordon H. Clark, who taught philosophy to some of these neo-evangelicals at Wheaton College, was disdainful of the "hill-billy evangelism" of earlier fundamentalism.[5] Henry himself, in a book tellingly titled *Evangelicals in Search of Identity,* wrote that his movement, which he called the "growing evangelical mainstream," was distressed by the "fundamentalist far right" because of its "personal legalisms, suspicion of advanced education, disdain for biblical criticism per se, polemical orientation of theological discussion, judgmental attitudes toward those in ecumenically related denominations, and an uncritical political conservatism . . . that, while politicizing the gospel on the right, deplored politicizing it on the left."[6]

Seeking respectability in the world beyond the fundamentalist subculture, many in this generation received advanced degrees from prestigious research universities; seventeen of them did graduate work in theological disciplines at Harvard in the 1940s.[7] They were proud of advances in neo-evangelical higher education which made their colleges and theological schools look more like their distinguished counterparts in the larger culture. Among trends in contemporary evangelical education highlighted by Frank E. Gaebelein (neo-evangelical son of Arno C. Gaebelein, one of the most radical and militant fundamentalists of his generation) were an "increased consciousness of the value of higher intellectual standards," a "new consciousness of the relation of Christianity to culture," a "penetration of isolationism . . . through the recognition of values in the educational philosophy and practice of other Christian groups not commonly associated with evangelicalism," and a "growing drive toward a more articulate and competent scholarship, especially on the graduate and seminary levels." When Gaebelein discussed in more detail how neo-evangelicalism could relate to culture, he rejected fundamentalism's tendency to shun culture and instead advocated a "conversation with culture in which evangelicalism stands firmly within 'the Biblical landscape of reality.'" He pointed proudly to the "revival of good music" on neo-evangelical campuses. "To be sure," he admitted, "a good deal of second-rate music too often associated with evangelicalism remains with us. Yet notable progress has been made."[8]

"The Biblical landscape of reality" is an ironic phrase in the context of the neo-evangelicals' quest for respect and acceptance from the cultured despisers of fundamentalism. Although they strove mightily to distance themselves from the militancy, isolationism, and anti-intellectualism of their fundamentalist parents and childhood churches, and were quite successful, they refused to abandon most of the theological positions of fundamentalism. Consequently, although they may have believed Sallman's work to be second-rate art, it was virtually impossible for them to reject it or to encourage other evangelicals to do so, especially if it meant embracing instead the abstract art that was all the rage in high-culture circles and among the liberal mainstream theological elites. Their theological inheritance from fundamentalism would keep them outside the world of art museums and galleries.

The National Association of Evangelicals met in Chicago for its second annual convention in 1943 with about a thousand delegates from fifty denominations. They unanimously passed a statement of faith, a "minimal statement—the common denominator of united evangelical action." The seven points of the statement reiterated the theological fundamentals around which fundamentalists rallied in the second and third decades of the twentieth century. The first principle was the inspiration and infallibility of the Bible. The third affirmed the historicity of Jesus, the virgin birth, the miracles, vicarious sacrificial atonement, the bodily resurrection, heavenly ascension, and second coming of Christ. Although there were disagreements in the neo-evangelical camp on the fine points of regeneration, or new birth, theology, all present were able to affirm that regeneration was absolutely essential for salvation.[9]

Neo-evangelicals, like their fundamentalist forebears and contemporaries, saw in contemporary culture the ongoing spread of humanistic skepticism and atheism, which denied the historicity of biblical accounts of Jesus and which posited, in place of the concrete events and facts of Jesus, human reason and experience as authoritative for religion and morals. Harvard-trained neo-evangelical Harold B. Kuhn harkened back to J. Gresham Machen, a first-generation fundamentalist intellectual at Princeton Theological Seminary, to insist again in the 1950s that "theology rests upon facts; its truth is of a kind with the truth which forms the basis for scientific endeavor." Because historical facts do not change, Christian truth need not—indeed should not—be reinterpreted for each generation. Rather, each generation must learn to conform to the biblical truths that, neo-evangelicals believed, were outlined so clearly in the Bible and in such simple propositional statements of faith as the one adopted in Chicago in 1943. Truth is not elusive, subjective, or changeable. A commonsense reading of the Bible reveals eternal, unchanging truth clearly and objectively.[10] And like fundamentalists before them, neo-evangelicals understood that one of their most important purposes was "engaging in the defense of the Bible."[11]

New Testament scholarship in Europe and in the prestigious

theological schools in the United States at the time was dominated by Rudolph Bultmann, who perhaps represented Christian existentialism in one of its purest forms. Bultmann rejected the historicity of the supernatural or miraculous elements in biblical accounts of Jesus, even and especially the resurrection, and offered instead an existentialist "encounter" interpretation of the resurrection. The body of Jesus was not literally raised from the dead; rather, *Christ* was raised in the *experience* or consciousness of the disciples, and continues to be raised in the experience of people everywhere who hear the *kerygma,* the message of Christianity preached in an authentic and life-changing way. Bultmann transformed the resurrection of Jesus from a historical event in the past to an experience in the present.[12]

Neo-evangelical scholars attacked Bultmann for giving up the one sure, unchanging *fact* of Christian salvation, the literal resurrection of Jesus in Palestine during the first half of the first century of the Common Era. According to J. Marcellus Kik, Bultmann attempted to pour biblical revelation into an "existential mold." Therefore, the "miracles become extraneous as does all that is judged mythical. The inflexible mold excludes among other teachings the incarnation and resurrection of Jesus, the vicarious atonement and justification by faith. The final product . . . is a pitiful human figure poorly adorned with existential wisdom and bearing the inscription: *created by Bultmann.*"[13]

Also criticized by neo-evangelicals was the Christian realism of Reinhold Niebuhr, which emphasized the reality of human sinfulness but did not support the fundamentalist or neo-evangelical view of the historicity of all parts of the New Testament. Edward Carnell, president of Fuller Theological Seminary, discerned the problem that Niebuhr shared with much contemporary theology. Although Niebuhr's Christian realism contained a "concrete view of sin," Carnell admitted, it "converts to an abstract view of salvation" because "Niebuhr does not speak about Christ's literal cross and resurrection at all. He speaks, at most, of the 'symbols' of the cross and resurrection."[14] The conservative scholar, in contrast, uses only the "knowledge of grammar and the facts of history to determine his exposition. . . . The evangelical restrains his imagination in dealing with the problems of age, authorship and sources."[15] The "genuine pathos" of theological liberalism was, according to Ned B. Stonehouse, dean of Westminster Theological Seminary in 1957, that "many a modern inquirer" finds the "Jesus of the Gospels unacceptable" and "more or less unconsciously refashions the portrait to conform Jesus to his own presuppositions or predilections."[16] Neo-evangelical James I. Packer concluded, "Only when we abandon the liberal view that Scripture is no more than fallible human witness, needing correction by us, and put in its place the biblical conviction that Scripture is in its nature revealed truth in writing, an authoritative norm for human thought about God, can we in principle vindicate the Christian knowledge of God from the charge of being the incorrigibly arbitrary product of our own subjective fancy."[17] Carl Henry, speaking of the "dialectical-existential" theology of liberal theologians, complained that it "championed the 'kerygmatic Christ' to the neglect of the historical Jesus": "The 'witness of faith' thus replaced interest in the 'facts of history'; existential experience rather than objective history became the pivot of divine revelation. . . . Present-day Christian theology can be rescued from this costly development only by a full rehabilitation of the historical realities of the Gospel."[18] For evangelicals of every stripe, "Christ of the Bible and Christ of personal experience must be the same." One's idea or image of Christ cannot stray from the biblical accounts without losing Christ himself.[19]

Just as neo-evangelicals rejected Rudolph Bultmann's attempt to free the essence or truth of Christianity from the mythological form and content of the biblical accounts of Jesus, so too did they express alarm at modern art that attempted to free Christian essence or truth from the historical person of Jesus and the historical facts of his life, death, resurrection, and ascension as they believed these facts were described precisely in biblical texts. Just as they rejected the existentialist theologians' emphasis on personal predicament and subjective experience, so too were they uneasy with the lack of representational or figurative content in modern abstract art, which seemed to allow meaning, even about subjects as central as Jesus, to remain unfixed and completely subjective. In their view, just as no true Christian is free to live apart from belief in the facticity of Christ and salvation in Christ, so does no true Christian art stray from that content. Christian art expresses Christ, not the self. One evangelical scholar in 1958 complained that the dominating spirit in the contemporary world of high-culture art was the "frantic attempt to express the deeper realities of the soul by means of unconventional and chaotic abstraction." The heresy of abstract art was that "instead of holding up a mirror to nature, the artist today deliberately distorts nature in order that he may mirror the human soul." Such artists as Piet Mondrian, Mark Rothko, Paul Klee, Willem de Kooning, and Jackson Pollock were guilty of "Gnosticism," of "shattering all norms of painting in the interest of an antinomian expression. But all alike have despaired of this world, and at the expense of communicability they have run to a mystic realm of the soul . . . where conversation is limited to the coterie who have the esoteric gnosis." The *Christian* artist should not give in to the spirit of this age, full of the excess of existential despair: "Painting, which is not in the service of the spirit of this age but of Christ, must convey more than the fragmentization of this world. . . . It must bear Christ in passionate Incarnation and triumphant Resurrection, in suffering witness in this age and confident hope in the coming age."[20]

In 1956, *Christianity Today* carried a review of Salvador Dali's *The Sacrament of the Lord's Supper*. The reviewer was bothered by the surrealistic aspects of the painting, fearing that it did not "reach beyond the subjective impression to the historical realities at the center of the Christian faith." In Dali's painting, the reviewer asked, "has the transition really been made from the subconscious and beyond the consciously subjective to the historical and rational, without which the central events and doctrines of the Christian revelation vanish into nebulous subjective mysticism?" What seems to have mattered most to this neo-evangelical art critic was, in the end, whether the canvas "represent[s] the Last Supper as an historical event."[21]

Kriebel and Bates, the merchandiser of Sallman's art, recognized evangelical misgivings about modern art and played to them in its advertising: "Amidst all the ugly things that modern society has been promoting in the name of advancement and culture, such as unrealistic art objects and paintings, featuring the extreme in art, music, speech, conduct, and dress; it is gratifying to people of Christian culture to know that we still have for our choosing things that are true, beautiful and good. There are still millions of people who have not 'bowed the knee to Baal.'"[22]

Kriebel and Bates, perhaps to discourage subjectivism in the interpretation of the Bible and of art that represented biblical subjects, published detailed interpretations of most of Sallman's major paintings.[23] In them, Sallman's art was repeatedly praised for its realistic portrayals of the natural landscape of Palestine. These materials imply that realism in portraying the natural environment of Jesus means a realistic—that is, historically accurate—presentation of Jesus himself and the events of his life or afterlife that are the subjects of the paintings. In a brief interpretation of *Christ in Gethsemane* (pl. II), Fred Bates praised the painting for giving us the "complete story in a panoramic view of the Garden at the foot of the Mount of Olives, which lies just east of the wall of Jerusalem and across the brook Kidron, *all in true perspective*" (emphasis mine).[24] The painting was also interpreted in the *1947 Annual* of the North American Baptist General Conference, in which Sallman's careful representation of the Palestinian landscape is linked to a strict historical interpretation of Luke 22:41–42:

> Sallman's "Gethsemane," as do all of his paintings, vividly makes clear the Scripture account. . . . His pictures are true and accurate, even in geographical detail. This painting . . . was based on the Scripture, "And he was withdrawn from them a stone's cast, and kneeled down and prayed, saying, 'Father, if thou be willing, remove this cup from me; nevertheless not my will, but thine be done.'"[25]

Published interpretations of *The Lord Is My Shepherd* (see pl. V) contain references to both the accuracy with which Sallman re-created the Palestinian landscape and the accuracy of Sallman's portrayal of first-century Palestinian shepherding:

> In the early spring the Judean hill country is ablaze with the color of wild flowers . . . though the land is burned brown as toast for much of the rest of the year. It is this springtime that Sallman pictures. . . . The Shepherd in this picture has led his sheep through the dark shadows of the canyon into the sunlit pasture lands in the foreground. Six miles northwest of Jerusalem is a narrow gorge, "The Valley of the Shadow of Death." In ravines such as this lurk marauding robbers and wild beasts of prey. . . . The finest watering place in that section is just beyond this valley, and the sheep follow the shepherd as he leads the way thither, walking quietly, confidently at his side. . . . The herdsman of the East never drives his sheep; they are always led. . . . guided only by the voice of the shepherd and the tapping of his staff as he goes ahead.[26]

The interpretive pamphlet published to accompany Sallman's *The Road to Emmaus* (fig. 4.1) also emphasizes the factual basis of the

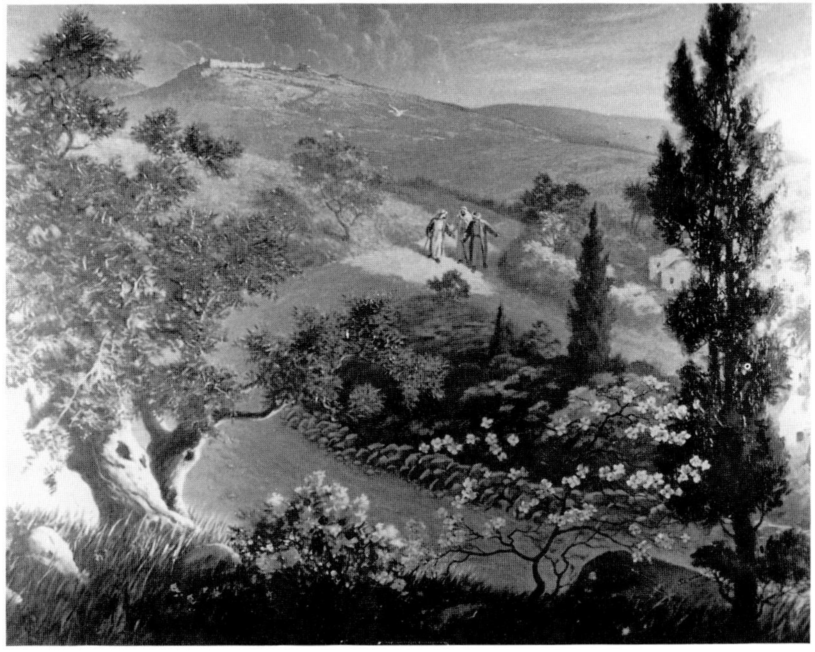

4.1. Warner Sallman, *The Road to Emmaus,* 1961, oil on canvas, 32 × 39¾". Courtesy Jessie C. Wilson Galleries, Anderson University.

landscape and contrasts it with a purely imaginative rendering of this resurrection narrative:

> The "Road to Emmaus" by Sallman is not just a landscape from the artist's imagination with the three Biblical figures added; but instead, it is an authentic landscape of the Holy Land taken from sketches made many years ago before the modern changes of today. The mountain, hills, flowers and trees complete the setting as it could have been in Jesus' days. . . . The city of Jerusalem, with its walls and its gates, is shown as it actually was. . . . The roads, the trees and flowers are authentic. Emmaus was six or eight miles northwest of Jerusalem on the road to Joppa which was about twenty-seven miles from Jerusalem. Viewing Jerusalem in the background, the observer is looking southeast. Jerusalem was nearly 3,000 feet above sea level and naturally visible at a distance of many miles.[27]

Biblical or historical accuracy seems stretched to the breaking point in the painting *Teach Me Thy Way* (pl. VIII), in that it portrays a scene that cannot be found in any of the gospel narratives—Jesus in conversation with a young boy. Yet, again, the interpreter appealed to the realism of the landscape in order to defend the entire scene as realistic and historical: "Warner Sallman once again has drawn aside the curtain which veils events of long ago and has given to us another magnificent view into the life of our Lord. In fact, the artist has depicted on the canvas a picture so radiantly warm and realistic that without difficulty we let our imaginations carry us back over the span of the centuries to become a part of the scene." This imaginary event is related as if it were biblical; the narrative, however, is Sylvia E. Peterson's, who by including allusions to actual New Testament material gave her interpretation of the painting a biblical tone:

> On the occasion here portrayed, Christ had found a brief respite from the throngs in this lovely spot. . . . While he was resting he had caught sight of a young boy, gaily dressed in a red robe and cap, standing along the near-by roadside and gazing as if transfixed at the city in the distance. . . .
>
> "Come here, my young friend," the Master had called.
>
> The disciples resting a distance beyond had heard this and rebuked Jesus.
>
> "Why bother with the child? You are much too tired. Why not rest?"
>
> "Rest?" Jesus must have answered. "Wist ye not that I must be about my Father's business?" . . .
>
> How easy it was to talk to Jesus, the boy discovered.
>
> . . . He is the most wonderful person I have ever met. How can I become like Jesus?
>
> "Master," he exclaims, "teach me thy way!"[28]

Consumers and potential consumers of Sallman's art were encouraged to recognize Sallman as an expert in the geography and landscape of Palestine. The published interpretations of his paintings thus denied the imaginative aspects of Sallman's work and created instead a tradition of interpretation which claimed that Sallman's paintings were accurate portrayals of Jesus and of certain events in his life recounted in New Testament texts.

Some of Sallman's evangelical interpreters went so far as to ascribe the same kind of divine inspiration to his *Head of Christ* that they believed lay behind the inerrant biblical text. Dorothy C. Haskin, in a Zondervan book, *Christians You Would Like to Know,* quoted Sallman as insisting that "whatever I have done is not of myself but of the Spirit of Christ which has been with me throughout the years." The *Link,* a Protestant journal for armed forces personnel, published Glenn D. Everett's story of Sallman's painting. Everett told of a conversation between Sallman and Charles Ray Goff, minister of the Methodist Temple in Chicago and one of Sallman's spiritual mentors. Sallman told Goff that his lectures at the YMCA had inspired the picture, saying, "I didn't paint it, you did." Goff replied, "I didn't paint it either, Warner. . . . I just read the New Testament in those Bible classes. . . . Warner, if I didn't paint it, and you didn't paint it, . . . it must be that God painted it, using us as his human agencies."[29]

Sallman's paintings were thus interpreted by and for evangelicals as the visual-art equivalent of a theology based on facts, as recorded in the Bible, rather than on human imagination, speculation, or experience—as the visual equivalent of verbal inerrancy. The strength of this commonsense theology and art was that they appealed to the "common man." As neo-evangelical L. Nelson Bell surmised, the "ordinary layman—the man in the office, in the shop, in the everyday pressures of work—needs a Christian faith which is vital but simple, concise but accurate, factual but practical."[30] Both Carl Henry and Edward Carnell, two of neo-evangelicalism's most respected intellectuals, wrote essays comparing Billy Graham to two giants of non-evangelical theology, Karl Barth and Reinhold Niebuhr. In an editorial in 1956 Henry expressed some ambivalence about Billy Graham—perhaps his preaching is simplistic; he "sketches the picture in too broad strokes." Nevertheless, Henry decided to publish in *Christianity Today* an article by Graham on biblical authority in evangelism, and Henry's editorial in that issue defended his decision to an audience that he knew would be skeptical of Graham's status as an intellectual. According to Henry, Graham had none of the "half-hearted confidence in the reliability and authority of Scripture" characteristic of Barth: "Nobody has profounder right than Mr. Graham to a hearing on the subject of the authority of the Bible in evangelistic preaching. He has earned that right theoretically, by his devout study of the Word, and pragmatically, by his passionate proclamation of it to an age of theological unbelief. . . . His ministry supplies the theological enterprise with a graphic reminder that the mysteries of higher criticism are unnecessary for grasping the essence of the biblical message . . . and also that the simple believer often stands closer to the heart than the sophisticated critic."[31]

As Billy Graham prepared for his 1957 New York evangelistic crusade, Carnell reflected about Graham's chances in that city and about New York's most prominent theologian, Reinhold Niebuhr. Carnell, like Henry, expressed ambivalence about Graham: "After Billy Graham has reviewed the plan of salvation, he has very little to add. Billy Graham has not been to seminary. He has no criteria by which to measure the shades of better and worse in the complex systems which vie for the modern mind." Yet Carnell could not dismiss Graham because of Graham's appeal to ordinary people: "Billy Graham preaches Christ in such clear and forceful language that even a bartender can find his way to the mercy seat. This is why the multitudes discover a power in Billy Graham which they miss in Reinhold Niebuhr. Billy Graham may know little about the inner technicalities of theology, but he does rest in the full and undoubted persuasion that Christ was delivered for our offenses and was raised for our justification. . . . The common man is weary of theories; he is hungry for the gospel; he craves a firm note of authority."[32] A truly "Christ-like preacher" knows how to "make the truths of God seem real and interesting to ordinary people."[33]

Their sensitivity to the tastes of everyday Christians, in art and in preaching, was another reason why the neo-evangelical elites found it impossible to dismiss Sallman's work. Henry began his editorial on Sallman with the affirmation that the *Head of Christ* "is perhaps the most widely known and loved pictorial presentation of Christ." Henry knew that artists and art critics had ridiculed the painting; nonetheless, "nearly 100 million copies of the picture have been sold the world over. Catholics and Protestants alike point to the work as a choice example of contemporary inspirational art. . . . The attending publicity made Sallman himself world-famous."[34] Another evangelical defended Sallman's paintings because of their widespread public acceptance: "Art experts . . . are not the ones responsible for its public acceptance. Rather, a picture gains prominence because of its acceptance by the average Joe Doakes on Mainstreet who knows nothing more about a picture than the fact that he likes it."[35]

Like fundamentalists of an earlier generation, neo-evangelical leaders depended on the strength of a popular movement, rather than on acceptance in such bastions of intellectual and cultural power as universities and museums. Reinhold Niebuhr could have Union Theological Seminary, Columbia University, and the Metropolitan Museum of Art; Billy Graham and Warner Sallman would take the rest of the city.[36]

I began this chapter with reference to Carl Henry's editorial about Sallman in which Henry asked, "Does the work [*Head of Christ*] represent authentic Christian art?" On that occasion, Henry's refusal to dismiss the painting as unworthy, or as bad art, was rooted primarily in his characterization of Sallman as a devout evangelical Christian. Henry quoted Sallman: "I believe everyone who has committed himself to Christ our Lord desires to serve him with whatever gifts or talents he may possess. On this premise, with Jesus Christ as my guide, it has been my goal to yield whatever abilities God has given me to his honor and glory. . . . By divine direction I was led step by step toward a ministry of Christian art. I give God the glory for whatever has been accomplished by my efforts to bring joy and happiness to people throughout the world." Henry also recounted in abbreviated form the story of the miraculous origin of the painting: Sallman, needing to meet a deadline for a magazine cover illustration, received in a dream or vision the image that he immediately sketched and which was the basis of the famous oil painting.[37]

A significant portion of evangelicals' appreciation of Sallman's creations rested on their evaluation of him as a "consecrated artist."[38] In evangelical publications, Sallman was repeatedly described as a devoted Christian who was also graced with a humble and pleasant personality. In a widely reprinted article, Sylvia E. Peterson praised Sallman's art because it "bespeaks not only artistic ability but a great soul and a beautiful Christian character. . . . Genuine friendliness, true humility, a deep concern for his fellow men and a vital interest in the progress of the kingdom of God are outstanding traits which he possesses. In his denomination as well as in his church he has held positions of leadership. His willingness to serve and his gracious spirit have won for him countless friends. One young person, after having met Warner Sallman, expressed a sentiment which all who know him share: 'Now I see how a man like that could make a painting like the *Head of Christ*.'"[39] Another admirer described Sallman in this way:

> Sallman is a tall man, brawny, of much the same proportions as his Christ. He has the solid hands of a workman.

> His strong features wear a gentle, thoughtful expression.
> His head is in the clouds, but through the clouds he sees the
> Master. . . . Sallman is not only modest but friendly. All
> his adult life he has attended the Edgewater Mission Cove-
> nant Church of Chicago. . . . He is a Christian with deep
> compassion for the lost. When one of his unsaved relatives
> was to undergo an operation, Sallman . . . spent . . . the
> night in prayer. He is an artist with an artist's lack of appre-
> ciation of the value of material possessions. He keeps him-
> self poor giving away his time and his talents.[40]

According to some of his evangelical interpreters, Sallman's piety is apparent in his artworks. "One can readily see that the artist approaches all of his work with the deepest reverence. His work cannot help but reveal a profound devotion to the Subject of his paintings."[41]

The character of the artist is a central part of neo-evangelical thinking about art. In 1966, an entire issue of *Christianity Today* was devoted to a discussion of the "Christian stake in education and the arts." Two major articles discussed visual art. One, by Gordon Kelly, a "Christian painter," contained a negative evaluation of art "used only for self-expression leading to the worship of the creature," rather than worship of God. Kelly decried some modern art for being "neurotic evidence" of "man's pathological preoccupation with himself, ending in meaninglessness and despair." The Christian artist, according to Kelly, in order to "fulfill his high calling in Christ," needs "discipline, discernment, and order." Aesthetics must be "subjected to the mind of Christ."[42]

The second article, by H. R. Rookmaaker, a Dutch art historian and close friend of evangelical leader Francis A. Schaeffer, is cast in the form of a letter to a young, recently converted woman who wants to "work as an artist—as a Christian." Happy to know of her artistic talent and her desire to use it in Christian vocation, Rookmaaker gives her advice and issues warnings. Because a Christian possesses Christian freedom, she is free "from tradition, from the feeling that everything you do has to be original, from certain fixed rules said to be necessary in art—but also from the thought that to be creative you must break all kinds of rules and standards." Christian artists, though not limited to representational art, should realize that nonrepresentational art provides no more freedom than the "most involved allegorical or storytelling art." Christian artists are free from the "sinful lust for money, from seeking man's praise, from the search for celebrity," and from the "need to slap the contemporary in the face, as some streams of art nowadays deem necessary." True Christian art is not "autonomous, and it has thousands of ties with human life and thought." Unlike modern abstract art, which has little meaning because "all ties with reality have been cut," the Christian artist makes art "while thinking of his neighbors in love, helping them, and using his talents on their behalf." Rookmaaker warned the artist about "false art theories," which have "pervaded the Christian world" from the post-Christian, anti-Christian, or humanistic world of high-culture art, and which teach, wrongly, that the artist should be an "asocial being, a non-conformist in the wrong sense, a dangerous prophet, an abnormal being who lives in an alien world."[43]

Neo-evangelicals, suspicious of the world of high-culture art and the artists that inhabit it, saw a necessary relation between the Christian faith and life of the artist and her or his art. It was virtually inconceivable that true Christian art could be produced by anyone who was not a professed evangelical. No evaluation of Christian art could be conducted without attention to the religious beliefs and character of the artist. The frequent reiteration of Sallman's credentials as a deeply pious and firmly committed evangelical layman legitimated his art and its claim to represent Christian truths. As Carl Henry concluded, "The Christian artist must paint, write, compose, or perform in the integrity of the new man in Christ," and there seemed no doubt that Warner Sallman did so.[44]

One of the most important ingredients—perhaps the most important—of evangelical piety and character is conversion. The Christian artist must be a "new man in Christ." The doctrine of regeneration, or new birth, was not an innovation of the neo-evangelicals or their fundamentalist predecessors but was part and parcel of the American Protestant experience. It was forged in Puritanism and Pietism; was central to the frontier strategy of the Methodists, Baptists, Disciples and Churches of Christ, Cumberland Presbyterians, and other denominations; and was taken to the stage by such revivalists as Charles Finney, Dwight Moody, Billy Sunday, and Billy Graham. Graham represented mainstream evangelicalism in describing conversion as a four-step process:

> First, You must recognize what God did: that He loved
> you so much He gave His Son to die on the cross. . . .
> Second, you must repent for your sins. . . .

> Third, you must receive Jesus Christ as Savior and
> Lord. . . . This means that you cease trying to save your-
> self and accept Christ as your only Lord and your only
> Savior. Trust Him completely, without reservation.
>
> Fourth, you must confess Christ publicly. This confes-
> sion is a sign that you have been converted. . . . It is ex-
> tremely important that when you receive Christ you tell
> someone else about it just as soon as possible. This gives
> you strength and courage to witness.[45]

In his study of religious conversion, Lewis R. Rambo identified two types of conversion operative in evangelical circles. The first is affiliation, in which an individual with no religious commitment moves to full involvement with a religious group. The second type, intensification, is a revitalization of a religious faith with which the convert has had some previous affiliation. "It occurs when nominal members of a religious institution make their commitment a central focus of their lives."[46] Although evangelicals raised millions of dollars and devoted thousands of lives to bringing Christ to the unchurched, they were also fully aware that many within the church stood in need of conversion, of an intensification of faith and commitment in a born-again experience. Billy Graham preached that neither a Christian upbringing nor church membership makes a Christian: "You must come under the Lordship of Christ. You must be born again. You must repent of sin. You must be converted. You must have a personal relationship with Christ. . . . And it is a daily experience."[47] Evangelicals, therefore, were called to a ministry both beyond and within the churches. Salvation was impossible without regeneration.

With regard to conversion, published materials about Sallman emphasized two things. First, Sallman himself had had a conversion experience. In one account of the event, Sallman wrote, "As I survey my 60 years of life, there is but one pivotal spiritual experience which embraces all the others that preceded or followed it. As a lad of 16, in the midst of all the mental and emotional conflicts of adolescent years, my personal crisis was resolved at an evangelistic meeting in a Chicago church. My burden of sin and guilt was removed, and I shall never forget the thrilling joy of that moment of experiencing God's redeeming grace. Since that time my life has been based on that experience, and has been directed toward serving God in every way."[48] Another account of Sallman's conversion was written by Dorothy Haskin: "About that time, Wilbur Chapman and Charles Alexander were holding city-wide revival campaigns in Chicago. The church Sallman attended co-operated by having an evangelist preach. He was a stout man named Munro. The young artist listened, was moved. When the invitation to come forward was given, his fair face flushed, but he was too embarrassed even to hold up his hand. He knelt in the pew, and in faltering sentences, told God he believed in the Lord Jesus Christ as his Savior. Shortly afterwards Sallman made public confession of his faith and sang in the Chapman-Alexander choir."[49]

Second, Sallman's art was interpreted by his evangelical admirers and by his merchandisers not only in the context of Sallman's own piety and conversion experience but also as the appropriate outcome of such conversion. The converted are, after all, supposed to respond to their new birth by telling others about it, by becoming witnesses to the saving power of Jesus. Sallman's motivations as an artist were regularly described as evangelistic. He was quoted in one Sunday school periodical as saying, "I'm not in this for myself. . . . I believe the Lord has given me a job to do—of pointing people to Christ through the medium of art."[50] In another context, Sallman was quoted as referring to his painting as preaching, as a "means of proclaiming a message about this Friend who was his personal Savior."[51] Just as a good evangelistic sermon "brings a group . . . face to face with Jesus Christ,"[52] so Sallman expressed the hope that he could "succeed in helping men to see Christ."[53]

The manufacturers of mass-produced Christian art encouraged their evangelical audience to believe that putting these images in public places could work regeneration within the unconverted. An ad for Best Seller Publicity of Chicago carried the headline "Let This Famous Christian Artist Help You Win the Unconverted" and informed readers that "alert Christians are taking advantage of this possibility for a great Gospel ministry—by putting these posters in street cars, buses, schools, other public buildings."[54]

Sometimes Kriebel and Bates published short worship services or program ideas emphasizing conversion and taking Sallman's paintings as their points of departure. A "plan for service of unveiling" was published in the interpretive brochure accompanying the painting *Follow*

Thou Me in 1949 (fig. 4.2). Each follower of Christ was asked to bring a friend to a service at which the picture would be "unveiled and discussed." Six people were to prepare short statements ahead of time, each describing the "deciding factor . . . that caused him to leave all to follow Christ." Six others were to be selected at random during the service and each asked to offer "three special benefits derived . . . from having made his decision to follow Christ." After a discussion of the topic "follow thou me," the reading of John 21:15–22, and the reading of the interpretation of the painting from the pamphlet, the service was to be concluded with the singing of a favorite hymn.[55]

Besides the production of the original art from which the mass reproductions were made, Sallman's major evangelistic activities were "chalk talks" (see fig. 1.4). At these talks Sallman would deliver an inspirational message to an audience before, during, and after reproducing in pastels the *Head of Christ.* A newspaper account of a chalk talk in 1960 estimated that Sallman had delivered about five hundred of these talks. The same account reported that the most moving part of Sallman's presentation was his recounting of the vision on that sleepless night in 1924 that led to the initial sketch of Jesus (see the *Son of Man,* fig. i.6), which was later to become the oil painting. Sallman's narration was particularly intense because he began the pastel reproduction of his painting with the "first sketches of the face which represented the thumbnail work Sallman had done after his vision." A member of the audience, a "father . . . sitting quietly with his sleeping baby, commented that at this point 'tears came into my eyes. It was the most beautiful thing I have ever seen.'"[56]

Sallman's chalk talks, and others by Christian artists, were understood as a particularly effective extension of the ministry of Christian art, which was primarily to elicit conversions from audience members. In a series on chalk talks and how to execute them successfully that appeared in a Moody Bible Institute magazine in the 1940s, readers were reminded that "these articles are written, not to help young people to become better artists, but to make available to them one more means of presenting the truth as it is in Christ Jesus."[57] An article on Sallman in an evangelical magazine in 1959 contained examples of individuals converted by his chalk talks.[58] A short film, co-sponsored by North Park College and Theological Seminary in 1954, presented the story of a young man's conversion during a Sallman chalk talk.[59] Sallman's self-

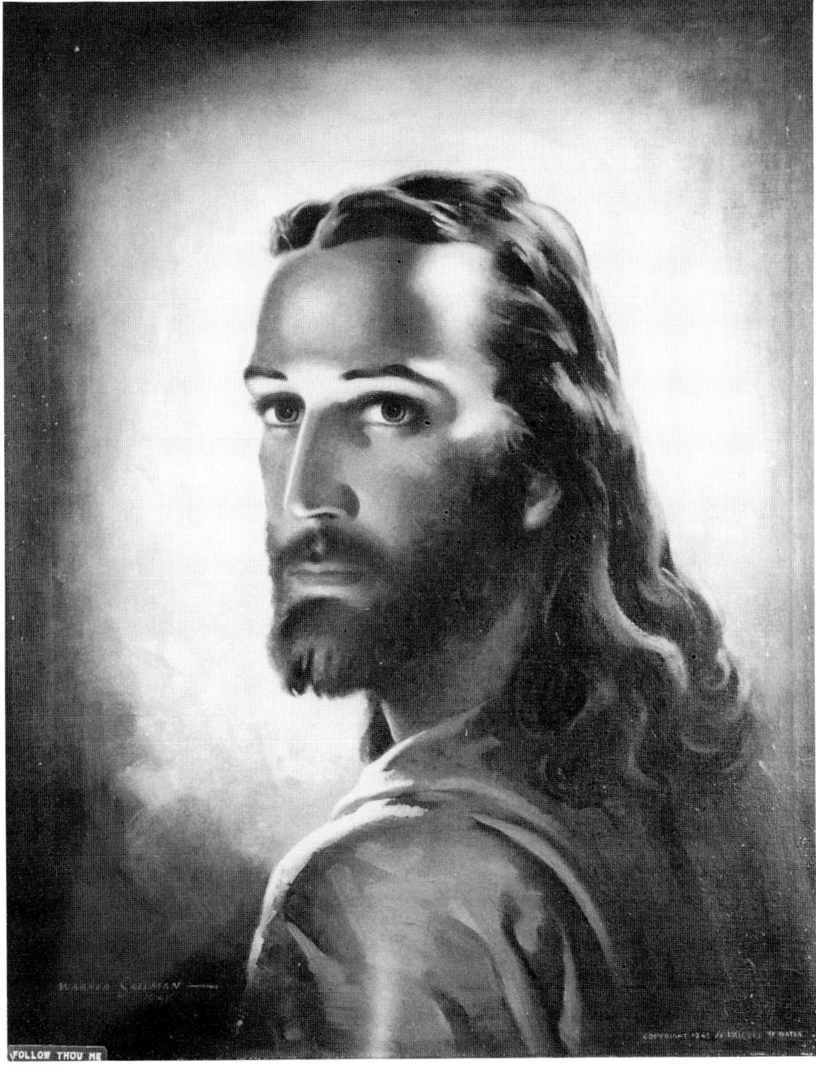

4.2. Warner Sallman, *Follow Thou Me*, 1948, oil on canvas, 28 × 22". Courtesy Jessie C. Wilson Galleries, Anderson University.

perception and public activities were in that way completely consistent with general evangelical emphasis on conversion, and the association of Sallman and his art with conversion experiences was a strategy that both church leaders and commercial publishers used to legitimate his art in evangelical circles. It would have been difficult for even the most cultured neo-evangelicals to have dismissed such an effective form of evangelism.

Sallman's art was used frequently to evangelize those who most concerned the neo-evangelical establishment, high-school- and college-age youth. Evangelical Christians had given special attention to adolescents since the late nineteenth century, when influential American psychologist G. Stanley Hall claimed that adolescence was almost exclusively the time of religious conversion. (Sallman's conversion narrative, above, supports this statement.)[60] The neo-evangelicals of the 1950s worried not only about the conversion of normal young people during this especially sensitive time of their religious lives but also about what they believed was the dangerous and unprecedented wave of juvenile delinquency. Several major articles about juvenile delinquency appeared in the first three volumes of *Christianity Today*. Noting that "blighted neighborhoods have no monopoly on delinquency," Henry Rische worried about the misbehavior of young people in suburban communities. To blame, he charged, were "adult dereliction of duty, divorce, drunkenness, and debauchery." The only solution was the "Gospel of our Lord Jesus Christ."[61] Another writer blamed the disease of juvenile delinquency on pornography, which leads young people into "too early and too erratic sexual life, . . . the cult of cynicism, vandalism, and sterile rebellion of our Beatniks."[62] Three other neo-evangelical writers placed the blame for juvenile delinquency on broken homes, working mothers, and irresponsible fathers. "It may sound old-fashioned, but . . . if our parents would have in their homes family prayer and Bible reading, they would by precept and example instill in their offspring at an early age an abiding respect for God's laws and man's laws."[63]

Neo-evangelical leaders proposed only one solution to the delinquency problem: the conversion of young people to evangelicalism. To that end they vigorously supported two major components of the evangelical empire, Youth for Christ and Campus Crusade for Christ (see fig. 1.16). Carl Henry believed that such evangelistic and educational programs as vacation Bible schools, when they brought in and saved unchurched youth from the community at large, were a "decisive factor in combatting juvenile delinquency."[64]

Because many evangelicals believed that delinquency was the result of inadequate religious training in the home, many advocated renewed attention to family life. They did so at a time when the divorce rate was skyrocketing owing to the dissolution of wartime marriages and the stress on marriages caused by the war.[65] In response, they preached that the Christian home "is the most important agency of the Kingdom on earth" and that a "Christian home means first of all that Christ is the Lord of the home and that he has pre-eminence in the lives of those who live there."[66] Men and women were regularly admonished to seek reconciliation rather than divorce. Billy Graham often preached that the practical outcome of evangelical conversion was the renewed health of troubled marriages.[67] And intact marriages could save society from dangerous delinquents.

Evangelical parents and Sunday school teachers were also given regular advice about how better to instill a Christian spirit in children and adolescents, and they were told specifically of the spiritual benefits of pictures. As early as 1928 Albert W. Beaven published a book on family life that became popular among evangelicals, *Fireside Talks for the Family Circle.* "A picture," he said, "has the ability to teach through the eye and to support the teaching that comes through the ear." He recommended that Christian parents purchase reproductions from such organizations as the Perry Picture Company so that their children could make Bible scrapbooks, and that larger prints be hung on the walls. He suggested such pictures as Hofmann's *Christ in the Temple* (fig. 4.3) and Eichstaedt's *The Infant Samuel.*[68]

The ongoing professionalization of Christian educators meant that they became even more open to various visual media, not least of which were reproductions of religious paintings. "Specialists in the field of Christian education have come to see the value of audio-visual methods and materials. . . . Fifty years ago specialists were demonstrating that a child learns more through 'the eye gate' than 'the ear gate,' through blackboard illustrations, maps, charts and diagrams. . . . Reproductions of biblical art in full color made lasting educational impressions."[69] An evangelical minister claimed that "nothing is more important in the experience of youth than the kind of pictures they habitually see." He recommended Sallman's *Head of Christ* because "just to look at that noble countenance, which expresses character, sympathy, consecration, courage, composure, devotion, strengthens my spirit and purifies my soul."[70]

Sallman and his art were associated with evangelical concern for young people in other ways, too. Many narratives of Sallman's life

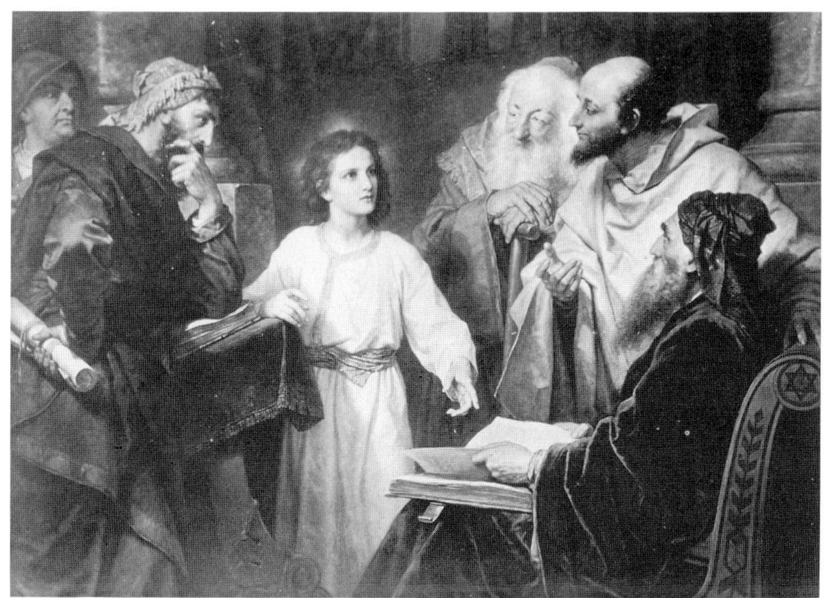

4.3. Heinrich Hofmann, *Christ in the Temple*, 1882, oil on canvas, size unknown.
Courtesy The Riverside Church, New York.

contain reference to his childhood in a Christian home and his early memories of being intrigued by Bible pictures: "As might be expected, Mr. Sallman came from a Christian home. Early in life he was stimulated by the Bible pictures he saw in Sunday School."[71] Sallman, on at least one publicized occasion, explained that the production of a picture of Christ "that would be a personal challenge to young people" was his main objective as he began thinking about the fateful 1924 magazine cover illustration.[72] In one published account, North Park College students were given credit for being the first to suggest that Sallman paint in color his cover sketch, which they had seen him produce in a chalk talk. He agreed, and produced the *Head of Christ* as we all know it today.[73]

Many of Sallman's paintings were created and marketed especially for children and youths, and for the adults who gave them gifts. One of the most striking examples is a painting of a youthful Christ called *Youth-in-Spiration*. An advertisement for the painting features two boldfaced subheads: "Christian Parent!" and "For Sunday Schools and Homes—all should have this picture." The painting was intended for the bedrooms of boys and girls and would "inspire them to live nobly." This

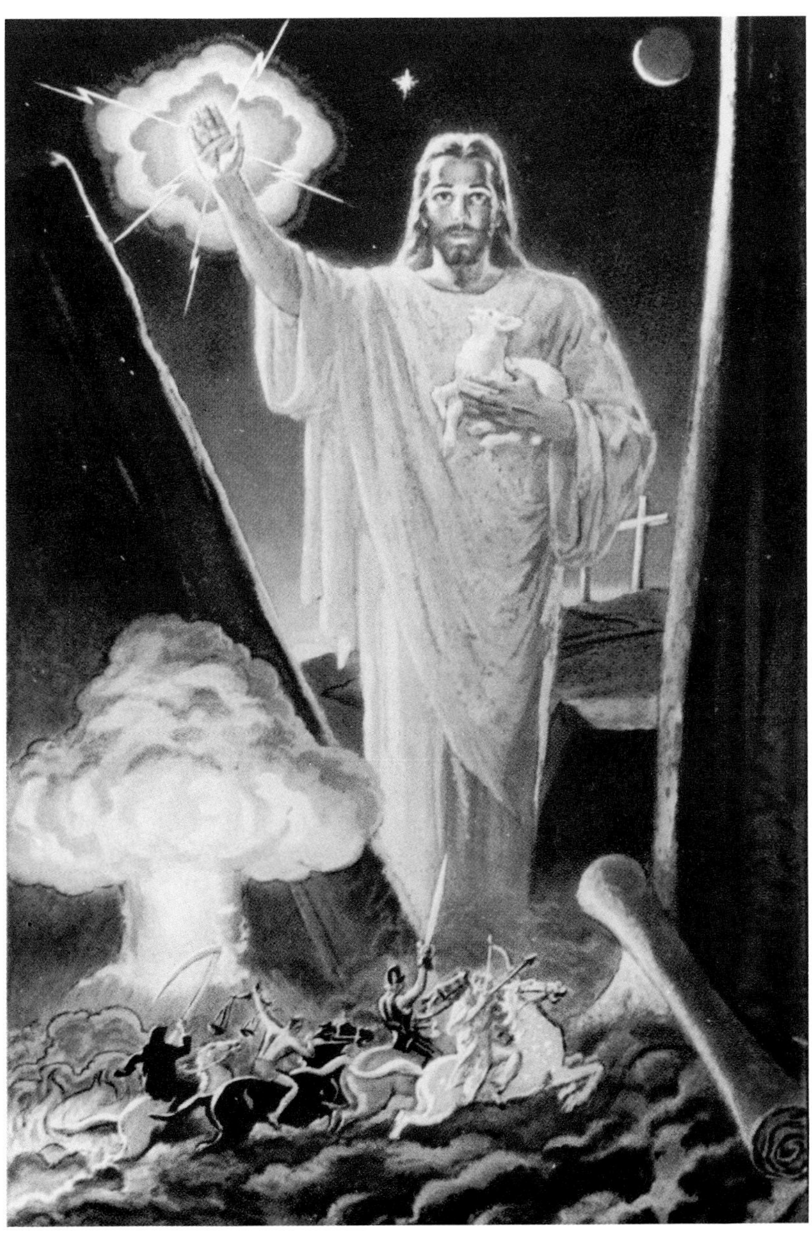

4.4. Warner Sallman, *Thine Is the Power*, 1951, oil on canvas, 72 × 48". Courtesy Covenant Archives and Historical Library, Chicago.

young Christ of the picture is the "great 'elder brother,'" a "real hero for boy or girl."[74]

Sallman's art was indeed extremely popular with young evangelicals. The Luther League of the American Lutheran Church commissioned *Thine Is the Power* for its tenth international convention, held at Michigan State College in 1951 (fig. 4.4). The Florida Conference Methodist Youth Fellowship (MYF), accustomed to using Sallman reproductions each year on its program cover, ran out of Sallman paintings in

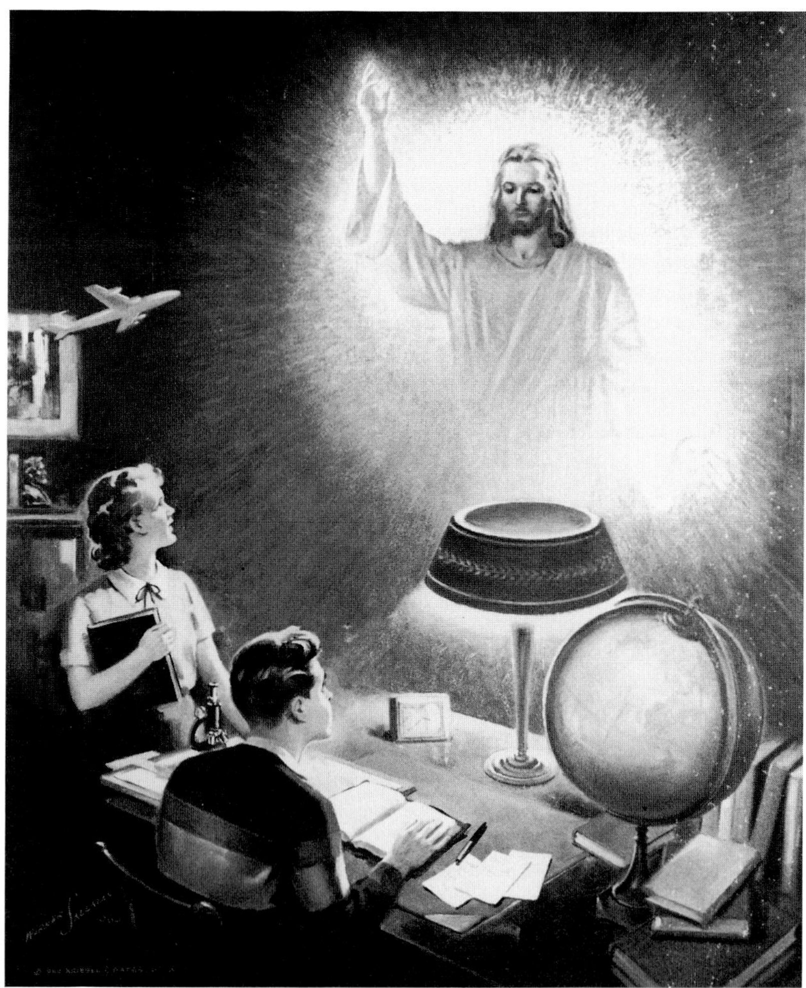

4.5. Warner Sallman, *Study to Show Thyself Approved*, 1960, oil on canvas, 36 × 30". Courtesy Jessie C. Wilson Galleries, Anderson University.

1960. The MYF therefore suggested a theme to Sallman, *Study to Show Thyself Approved,* and he created a painting of the same name that was used on the cover of the MYF program (fig. 4.5). In 1942, the Baptist Youth Fellowship of the Northern Baptist Convention used the *Head of Christ* on its recruitment poster. A Sallman chalk talk was the climax of the convention of Evangelical Covenant youth in 1958.[75] The Philadelphia central chapter of the YMCA began distributing wallet-sized reproductions of the *Head of Christ.* "In this manner we have found a very simple and unobtrusive way of emphasizing the 'c' in the Y.M.C.A," chapter leaders said.[76] Many individuals can testify to the presence of Sallman's art in their childhood homes, and to the reception of Sallman's art as gifts, during important times of transition as young people.[77]

Small wonder that Carl Henry and other neo-evangelical establishment leaders were ambivalent about Sallman's art. Although they were educated well enough to be aware of the wide chasm between Sallman's work and the modern religious art that was popular in high-culture circles, they recognized Sallman's vast appeal. His painting on biblical themes supported an understanding of the nature of biblical revelation that they preached and defended in scholarly circles. Sallman's art, like Billy Graham's preaching, while lacking a certain refinement and sophistication, helped define and promote evangelical sensibilities. Sallman, the faithful Christian, lived his religious vocation with purity of heart and a desire to bring others, especially young people, to Christ and into the evangelical fold. The evangelical establishment needed Sallman's ministry of Christian art.

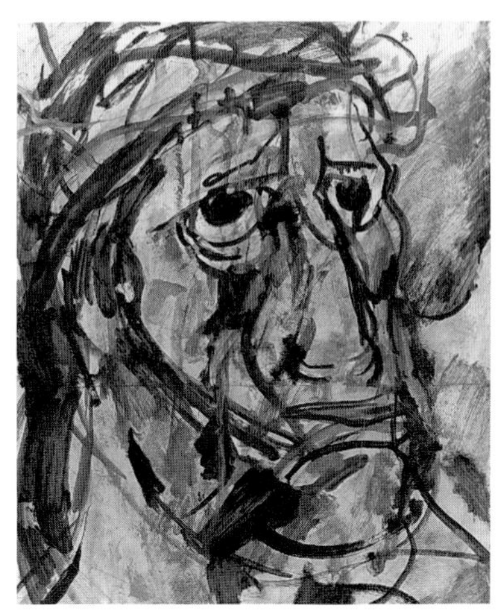

Interchangeable Art

Warner Sallman and the Critics of Mass Culture

SALLY M. PROMEY

5

In the 1980s and 1990s scholars in several disciplines have paid increasing attention to the social construction of cultural hierarchy in general and to popular culture in particular.[1] Art historians, however, have been rather slow to join conversations about the manufacture of aesthetic and cultural categories. Within this discipline, "high" or "elite" culture continues to enjoy almost exclusive privilege. For historians of American art, especially, the hesitation to expand the parameters of the discipline is unfortunate. In a national context where cultural categories remained relatively fluid until the late nineteenth and early twentieth centuries, a more elastic sense of visual culture seems appropriate.[2] The rising interest in the reception of art is an encouraging sign; if we look at the contexts in which art is viewed as well as the contexts in which it is created, a somewhat different picture comes into focus. This approach reveals not only the assumptions behind aesthetic categorization and hierarchy and the ways in which both are subject to change over time and place, but also the complex and equally changeable interrelations that govern traffic between different aesthetic or cultural worlds.[3]

This book considers a number of different publics, most of them appreciative, for the popular religious imagery of Warner Sallman. The authors' principal intention has been to understand the sorts of power invested in the images by those who actually used them, by a largely evangelical and certainly churchgoing public. But Sallman's imagery had another audience as well—an audience that, by the very vehemence of its negative reaction, acknowledged power in these images too. For this public, Sallman's *Head of Christ* (pl. I) was the most frequently cited example of the "terrible taste of Protestantism."[4] In an effort to understand the urgency of the negative response (why, for example, didn't these critics just ignore Sallman?), I focus in this chapter on Sallman's detractors, a group characterized by liberal theological and modernist aesthetic views. On both sides of the debate, participants viewed the engagement as one of serious, even ultimate, concern. To understand the values exercised and the judgments made by Sallman's critics, and to place those values and judgments within a meaningful historical context, is my goal.[5]

SALLMAN AND THE LIBERAL
PROTESTANT INTELLIGENTSIA

Simply to juxtapose an appreciative evangelical religious public with a dismissive liberal religious public would be to misconstrue the nature and strength of Sallman's appeal. Many of those for whom Sallman represented meaningful Christian devotion sat in the pews of liberal parishes. But, although exceptions on both liberal and evangelical sides certainly existed, the liberal clergy, and especially those on liberal seminary faculties and the editorial staffs of the liberal Protestant journals, generally rejected Sallman outright, whereas the evangelical clergy, seminary faculties, and press generally promoted Sallman's art as confidently as the liberals rejected it.[6]

Liberal church leaders framed their rejection of Sallman's work in the crisis rhetoric of the vigorous and public debate over the impact of mass culture on society. In the words of Tom F. Driver, scholar of religious drama and literature from Union Theological Seminary and contributing editor and drama critic for the liberal *Christian Century,*

> It is not only the fine arts which reveal the life of the times, but also the various forms of mass culture. A film such as *The Ten Commandments* reveals much about the religious taste of the populace. Here is exposed its love of the spectacular, its confusion of the sensational and the sensitive, its romantic type of hero worship, its tendency to reduce all human relations to the love-triangle, its naive, literalistic theology, and its unrealistic conception of history. Professor Tillich has suggested that to compare the photographs of Charlton Heston as Moses with the celebrated statue by Michelangelo is to observe the religious vacuity of our day. Exactly the same descent of popular taste is to be observed in popular religious "art." The sentimentalized, emasculated, super-humanized (and therefore dehumanized) Jesus who often appears is thoroughly domesticated, and therefore quite incapable of bearing an ultimate revelation.[7]

Although discussions about mass culture peaked in the United States between 1935 and 1955, in relation to Sallman's critics the specter of mass culture seemed particularly alarming throughout the decade of the 1950s.

The aesthetic and ideological preferences expressed by liberal clergy and theologians who rejected Sallman's art revealed their conviction that "authentic" religious art in the contemporary world must provide an antidote, or at least an alternative, to mass-cultural standardization, to a society built of interchangeable parts, interchangeable persons, and interchangeable art. The title of this chapter ("Interchangeable Art") places Sallman's art in the context of the means of mass production. Sallman's art was subject to the charge of standardization or interchangeability on several counts. First, Sallman adopted the conventions of mechanical reproduction even in the "original" work of art. For example, on his large paintings, he frequently *painted* the copyright and printer's mark in oil directly onto the canvas (fig. 5.1). In addition, a number of original works in ink on paper imitate the appearance of engravings or woodcuts (fig. 5.2). Second, the interchangeable or standard head appeared unmodified in numerous "different" images, as in, for example, *Ready to Go—Ready to Stay!* (pl. IX). Sometimes Sallman literally cut the head from one picture and transferred it to the next. In *Christ at Pulpit* (fig. 5.3) the change in texture from the coarser, patterned

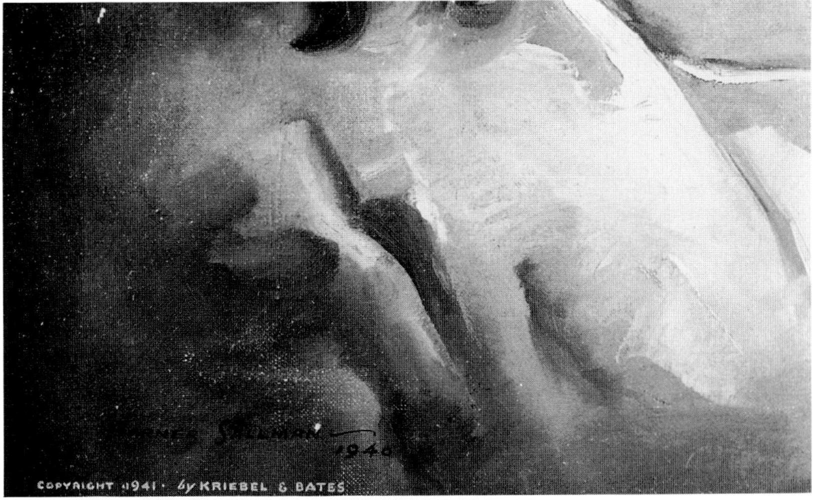

5.1. Warner Sallman, *Head of Christ,* 1940, detail of printer's mark and copyright statement. Courtesy Jessie C. Wilson Galleries, Anderson University.

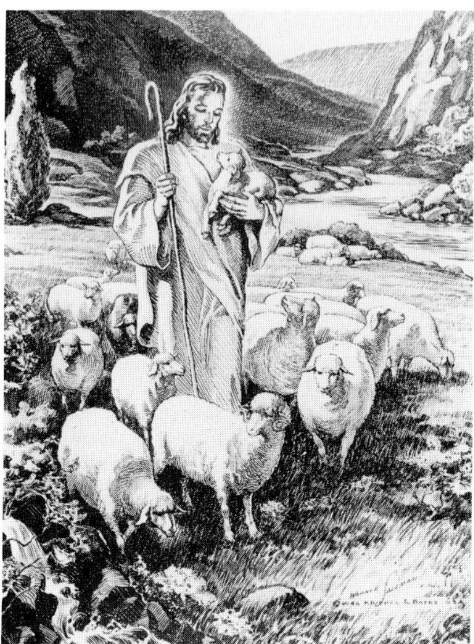

5.2. Warner Sallman, *The Lord Is My Shepherd*, 1946, ink on paper, 9⅞ × 7⅜". Courtesy Jessie C. Wilson Galleries, Anderson University.

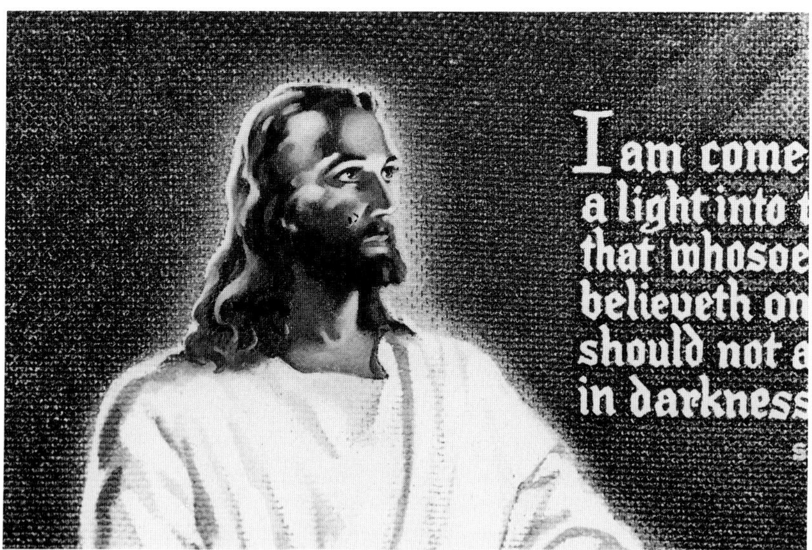

5.3. Warner Sallman, untitled (Christ at Pulpit), 1954, oil on board with collage, detail. Courtesy Jessie C. Wilson Galleries, Anderson University.

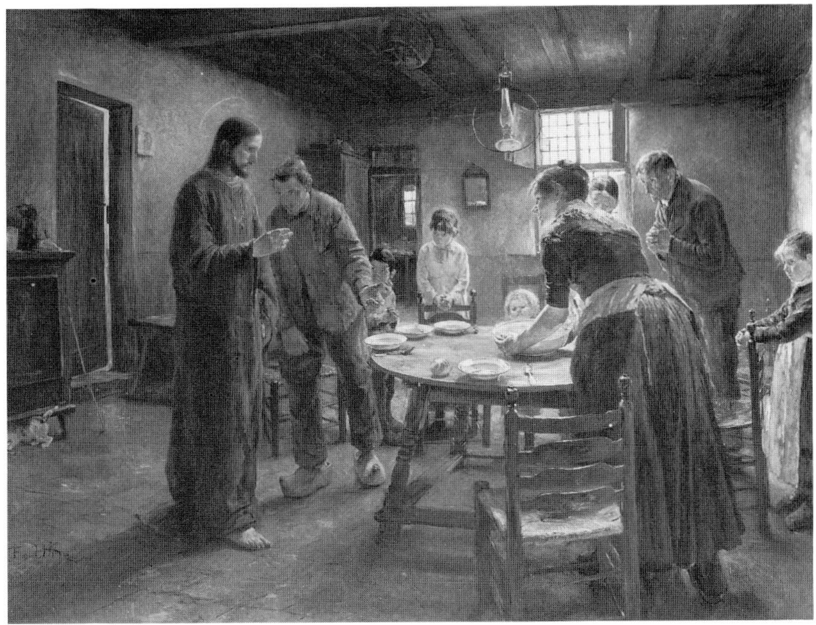

5.4. Fritz von Uhde, *Come, Lord Jesus, Be Our Guest—Table Prayer*, 1885, oil on canvas,
46 × 62". Staatliche Museen zu Berlin—Preussischer Kulturbesitz, Nationalgalerie.

pressboard support to the glossy smooth paper of the pasted head underscores Sallman's practice. Third, Sallman's liberal critics saw his work as
part of a larger genre of religious painting, almost indistinguishable by
artist, subject matter, or style.

To elaborate on the third criticism, Sallman's detractors generally perceived no essential differences between Sallman's images and
those of Heinrich Hofmann (1824–1911) or Fritz von Uhde (1848–1911),
for example; all such work they considered interchangeable and dismissed categorically (figs. 1.13 and 5.4).[8] The very fact that Sallman was
relatively infrequently named in the attacks, that his work was, rather,
described in terms of a category of despised religious "calendar art," fit
with the assumptions of the liberal perspective. According to this characterization, Sallman was not an individual creative artist but one "commercial hack" among many.[9] His was a *type* of art, interchangeable with
the work of others. To have singled him out too frequently would have
been to grant him a status that was intentionally denied, to attend to his
work and his name in a manner inappropriate to his enterprise. In their

critique the liberals allied themselves, directly and indirectly, with the era's intellectuals, people like Theodor Adorno, Dwight Macdonald, David Riesman, Erich Fromm, Lionel Trilling, C. Wright Mills, Clement Greenberg, and Paul Tillich, many of whom viewed standardized, interchangeable, homogenized mass culture as a contagion, potentially infecting and debasing all cultural activity. For both groups, liberal Protestant clergy and intellectuals, the threat of mass culture seemed very real, and both groups construed works of art like Sallman's as representative of this suspicious category.

Social fears and tensions generated by World War II intensified and exacerbated the terms of a cultural debate that, in the United States, began several decades earlier.[10] An ideologically diverse and publicly prominent group of intellectuals contributed to this anxious conversation. The refugee Frankfurt intellectuals, settling at Columbia University in 1934 and scattering more widely over the next two decades, pointed out connections they perceived between totalitarian systems in Europe and commercial culture in the United States. Mass media culture in America they characterized as a sort of "proto-fascist" phenomenon that debased sensibilities, enslaved individual minds and wills, and eradicated autonomy.[11] Different critics constructed the history of mass culture in somewhat different ways. In almost every case, however, the principal culprits were industrialization, mass production, and mass-reproductive technologies. Although obviously not limited to dictatorships, mass culture at its worst seemed to precede and characterize totalitarian states. Adorno and his colleagues Max Horkheimer and Herbert Marcuse attacked the mass "culture industry" for its promotion of a distorted or false consciousness and its production of a passively receptive, dehumanized, alienated public.[12]

United by their opposition to fascism, Soviet communism, and Western commercial culture, a whole generation of American sociologists, anthropologists, psychologists, cultural historians, art critics, philosophers, and theologians pursued their own versions of the critique of mass culture in the United States. Across a great variety of disciplines, the status of the individual in a mass society (and especially a mass democracy) gained momentum as a principal theme of a broader cultural critique. The idiom of the "mass"—undifferentiated, homogenous, mindless—reigned supreme in this literature.[13] Meaningful human identity, which presupposed both true individuality and true community, was impossible in the social constellation David Riesman characterized as the "lonely crowd."[14] In the face of authoritarian or commercial dehumanization, the liberal religious press called on religious institutions and religious individuals to oppose the "gray-flannel uniformity of the conforming culture," to be "different, separate, special, independent characters."[15] Secular and religious critics alike associated authentic individuality with freedom and democracy, both of which necessarily resisted totalitarianism and mass-cultural standardization.[16] Creativity, imagination, spontaneity, courage—precisely those qualities stifled by mass culture—characterized the free individual.

For Dwight Macdonald, and for his influential contemporary Clement Greenberg, mass culture equated with an aesthetic category that each of them called "kitsch."[17] In an essay published in *Partisan Review* in 1939, Greenberg defined the term: kitsch was "ersatz culture," a sort of pseudo-art. "Kitsch is mechanical and operates by formulas. Kitsch is vicarious experience and faked sensations. . . . Kitsch is the epitome of all that is spurious in our times. Kitsch pretends to demand nothing of its customers except their money—not even their time."[18] Because kitsch was the "faked article" and "deception," because it was "virulent" and irresistibly attractive, because it threatened the survival of "living culture," it could not just be ignored. A most troubling aspect of kitsch, for Greenberg and for Macdonald, was its effortlessness. Kitsch "predigested" art for the beholder, sparing the expenditure of energy and providing the spectator with a "shortcut to the pleasures of art that detours what is necessarily difficult in genuine art."[19] For both these intellectuals, this sort of predigestion lent itself to passive absorption, to just the nonparticipatory kind of relation with art as a commodity that the critics of mass culture decried.

Macdonald built on Greenberg's essay, stretching each set of terms, each metaphor, to accentuate the imminence of cultural crisis. According to Macdonald, kitsch was, quite simply, a "German term for 'Mass Culture.'" Mass culture and high culture relate to one another in this scenario not as leaf and branch but as caterpillar and leaf. The "parasitic," "cancerous" kitsch requires high culture as a host and ends up debasing and destroying, "extracting [high culture's] riches and putting nothing back." Unlike "folk" culture, which "grew from below," mass culture, Macdonald contended, was "imposed from above," "fabricated" by the commercial "Lords of kitsch." Ultimately, the "upper classes, who begin by using [kitsch] to make money from the crude tastes of the masses and to dominate them politically, end by finding their own culture attacked and even threatened with destruction by the instruments they have thoughtlessly employed."[20] Both Greenberg and Macdonald stated their conviction that mass culture facilitated political exploitation in fascist and communist states.

For the liberal religious critics of Sallman, although they frequently knew the work of Greenberg and Macdonald, existentialist theologian Paul Tillich established the prevailing set of alternatives for religious art in the United States in the middle of the twentieth century.[21] Explicitly invoking the critique of mass culture, Tillich, who shared much of the intellectual background and cultural experience of the Frankfurt school, drew out the connections between "authentic" art and "authentic" religion. As a public theologian, in a sense without parallel today, Tillich was widely heard and widely read. He spoke in art museums and galleries as well as in churches and seminaries. His words could be found in *Life* magazine as well as in the *Christian Century,* the *Christian Scholar, motive* magazine, and, along with Greenberg and Macdonald, in *Partisan Review*. It would be difficult to overestimate the extent of Tillich's contribution to the terms of the mass-culture debate, especially those terms employed to justify the rejection of Warner Sallman's art.

Like Greenberg and Macdonald, Tillich associated mass culture with political authoritarianism, indicting the "dehumanizing structure of the totalitarian systems in one half of the world and the dehumanizing consequences of technical mass civilization in the other half."[22] In setting out his position, Tillich reworked, while making more explicit, the underlying stylistic assumptions of Greenberg and Macdonald. Kitsch, for Tillich, was not simply a synonym for mass culture. It was, rather, principally a stylistic designation, a name for a particular sentimental mode of art-making that characterized the worst, the most dangerous, of mass-cultural representation: "I [use] the untranslatable German word *Kitsch* for a special kind of beautifying, sentimental naturalism, as it appears in disastrous quantities in ecclesiastical magazines and inside church buildings. The word *Kitsch* points not to poor art, based on the incompetence of the painter, but to a particular form of deteriorized idealism (which I like to call 'beautifying naturalism'). The necessary fight against the predominance of such art in the churches . . . leads me to the frequent use of the word *Kitsch*."[23] Greenberg and Macdonald as well as Tillich, in fact, considered vulgar and debased the academic aesthetic tradition that constituted one principal source (the other was advertising art) for Sallman's popular visual renditions (cf. figs. i.4 and i.6, and fig. 1.19 and pl. VII).[24]

That images by Uhde and Hofmann adorned German Lutheran churches in the period of their capitulation to Hitler (although both artists died in 1911) accentuated the linkage that Tillich and others perceived between beautifying naturalism and a politically dangerous mass culture. In direct response to Hitler's derision of modernism's "degeneracy," Tillich characterized beautifying naturalism as the "really degenerate art." Conflating beautifying naturalism with all forms of contemporary realism, Tillich opposed these stylistic tendencies more and more vehemently over the course of his career: "As long as we remove from our sight what we cannot help facing, we become dishonest; then that kind of art which he [Hitler] favored, that kind of beautifying realism, is what covers reality. These [modern] artists, therefore, who took away the cover from our situation, had a prophetic function in our time. I do not like all of them, either. But I know they created revealing works of art to look at which is the joy of participating in a level of reality which we otherwise can never reach."[25]

The variables used to justify the liberal Protestant dismissal of Sallman reiterated the terms of the intellectual's construction of the category of kitsch as a mass-cultural phenomenon. Nathan Scott urged the artist and the theologian to be "jointly engaged in warfare against the increasingly insidious control of the American imagination by the kitsch that is circulated in a mass society through the powerful media of the popular arts."[26] A whole set of mass-cultural associations constituted the vocabulary of the liberal religious position. Standardization, reproducibility, sentimentality, effortless absorption, commercialism, mechanization, dehumanization: these were the concerns voiced by Sallman's liberal critics.

Explicitly connecting Sallman with the mass-culture debate, one liberal religious observer expressed dismay that

> all the way from the nursery-school room to the sanctuary
> Sallman's *Head of Christ* is used in monotonous profusion,
> unrelieved by any change or freshness or difference. . . .

This has gone on until today any child of four, any grade schooler, any teen-ager or college student, any housewife, doctor, businessman, statesman, grandfather or octogenarian who is a member of a Protestant church can tell you exactly how Christ looks: like Sallman's *Head of Christ*. (One begins to doubt that he had arms and legs, so dominant is the *Head*.) But you have to admit that this mass-produced reproduction of the sentimental, effeminate face is AVAILABLE.

And in full color with special shadow-lite frame with gold leaf, or better yet, lit from behind. Or there is the handy wallet size for pocket or purse. Be a 100 percent red-blooded American Protestant . . . get a Sallman's *Head of Christ* reproduction printed on rough-textured paper to simulate the real, bona fide original oil painting. And if it isn't a Sallman, you have several other possibilities . . . equally as maudlin, sentimental, undisturbing to the spiritual consciousness, and they all leave you feeling "just great." . . . We twentieth-century Americans are nothing if not tranquilized. . . . Taste? what's *that*?[27]

In an essay in *Christian Faith and the Contemporary Arts,* Edward C. Hobbs, professor of New Testament at Church Divinity School of the Pacific, suggested that his readers contrast one of Georges Rouault's images of Christ with one of Sallman's (cf. pl. I and fig. 5.5). (Rouault was the preferred alternative for those religious liberals who insisted on some degree of figuration.) "Merely painting a culture-hero with a (blond) beard and writing the word 'Christ' beneath," Hobbs concluded, "do not make a Christian painting—the real subject still shows through (which of course accounts for the wide sale of the Sallman pictures)."[28] Like the stars of Hollywood's biblical spectaculars, Sallman's Christ was a mass-culture hero, and this status, according to Hobbs, explained the commercial success of the images. Building on this characterization, Roger Shinn maintained that "no society ever hired artists so profusely for purposes of advertising, illustration, and popular journalism. Thousands of artists make their living as priests of a commercial culture. Like Amaziah in ancient Bethel, they are employees of the kings of the culture."[29]

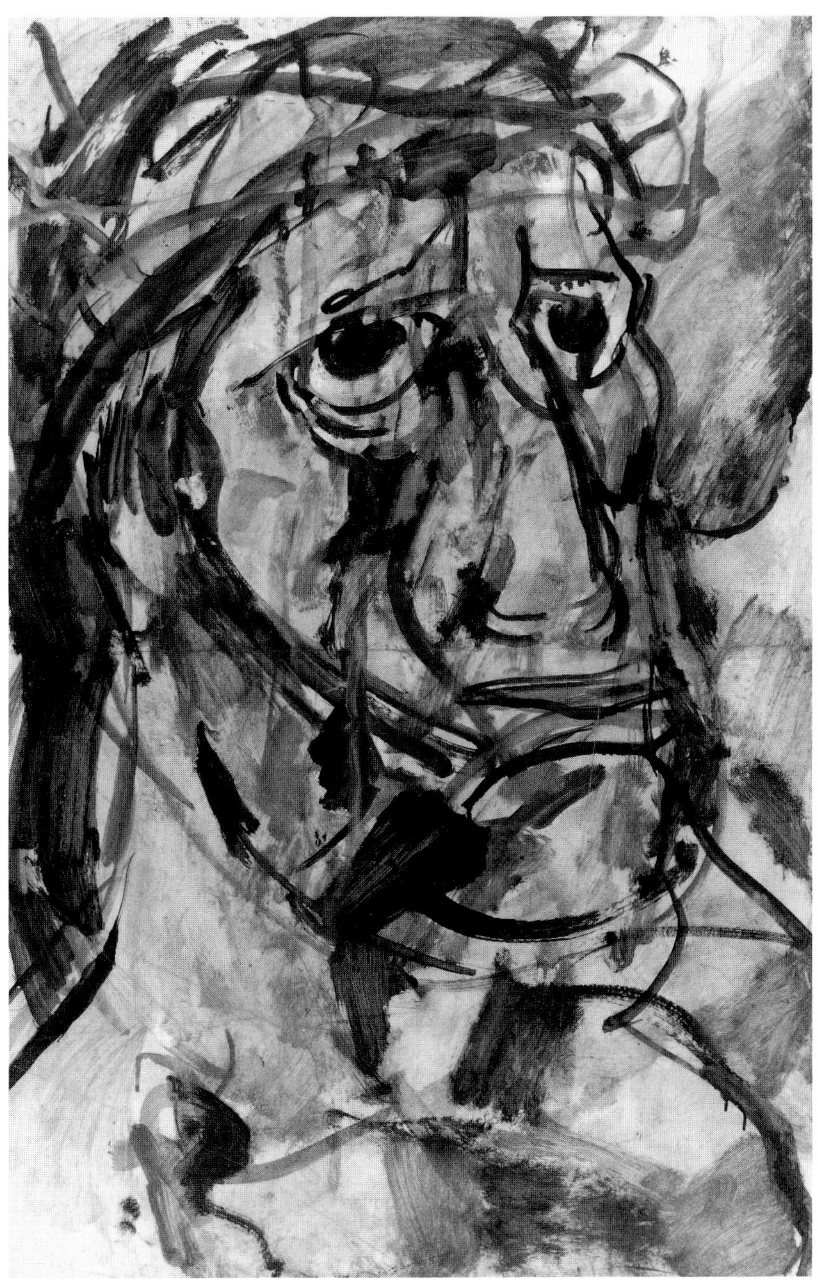

5.5. Georges Rouault, *Head of Christ,* 1905, oil on paper on canvas, 39 × 25¼″. Courtesy The Chrysler Museum, Norfolk, Virginia; gift of Walter P. Chrysler, Jr., 71.519.

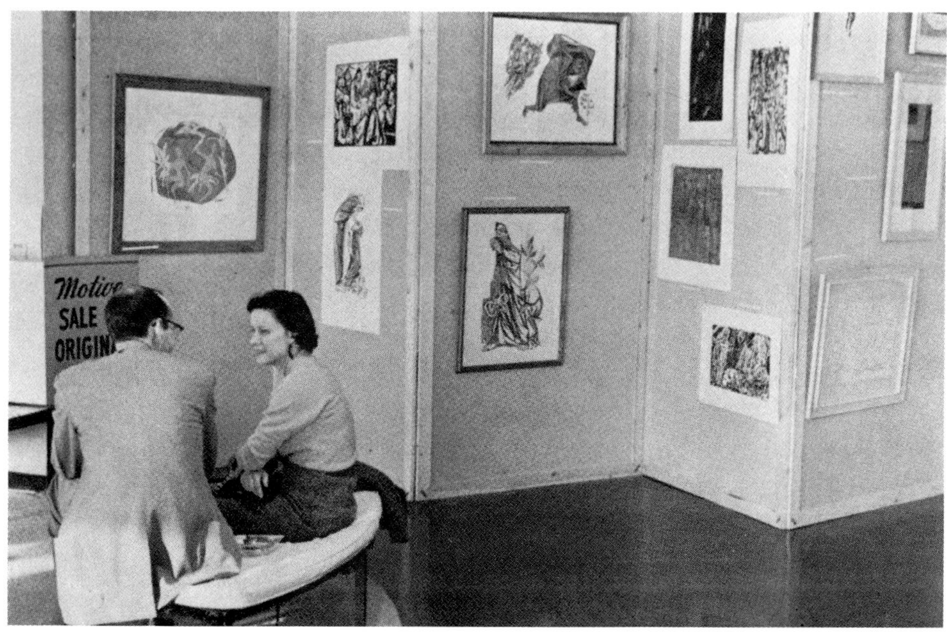

5.6. "Sale of Original Art." From *motive* magazine 18, no. 5 (February 1958), 28. Copyright 1958 by the Board of Education, the Methodist Church, Nashville, Tennessee. Used by permission.

For many, the commercial nature of Sallman's venture rendered it incapable of bearing religious or expressive sensibility.[30] Acknowledging the influence on Sallman of the visual conventions of commerce and entertainment, John Dixon maintained that "Sallman's head of Christ . . . fails even as illustration. . . . The face does no more than reproduce the fashionable and facile attraction of a movie star or an advertisement in a woman's magazine. . . . This is not the Incarnate Word but the cult hero of a culture that can think no higher than an unsexed matinee idol."[31] Sallman's training and background in advertising, the slick appearance of his work, the mode and rate of reproduction, the catalogue sales and promotion, and the mechanisms for marketing and distribution contributed to the mass-cultural assessment of his art. The Methodist *motive* magazine, a principal vehicle for negative criticism of Sallman, sponsored a sale of "ORIGINAL WORKS OF ART!" in 1958, in direct response to the "reprehensible custom of collecting art via the printing press" (fig. 5.6).[32] In the same issue of *motive,* perhaps not coincidentally featured on the opposing page, a description of a session on Christian art at the Sixth Quadrennial Conference of the Methodist Student Movement at Lawrence, Kansas, specifically placed its criticism of Sallman in the context of the commercialization of religious art. For close to an hour, two contemporary artists, Siegfried Reinhardt and Clark Fitz-Gerald, "reviewed various pieces of art that were projected on a giant screen before the audience and belted modern taste for its sentimentality and commercialism." A college student in the audience "asked what right Reinhardt had to condemn such popular works as Sallman's 'Head of Christ.' . . . Reinhardt answered: 'I condemn it on the basis that there is nothing ultimately good in it. It's cheap and fails to convey any kind of power or strength.'"[33]

Sallman's chalk talks fueled the criticism of imitation and repetition (see fig. 1.4). Here each finished product of a chalk talk was an "original," but it so closely resembled other such originals that, for the liberal critics, it hardly counted as one. Although the emphasis on the process or action of art-making was similar, the obvious parallel to the chalk talks was not the abstract expressionist who worked in solitude and isolation but the media event that drew large crowds. The analogue was popular entertainment, the amusement-park portrait rendered on the spot in pastel, not the hard-won work of the individuated creative genius. For the liberal critics, the authentic individual, like the authentic work of art, was unique, irreducible, unrepeatable. By definition, then, both authentic art and authentic individuality opposed the sort of formulaic serialization of the image represented in Sallman's work. Having trained at the School of the Art Institute of Chicago (he was enrolled in 1913 when students burned Matisse in effigy), Sallman knew the conventions of modernist high art and chose to adopt, instead, a commercial aesthetic vocabulary with roots in advertising and entertainment.

For a number of reasons, liberal Protestant intellectuals charged Sallman's *Head of Christ,* as an emblem of mass culture, with violating the standards of "true" art and "true" religion. The recurring themes of the criticism (Tillich's beautifying naturalism opposed to "modern" expressionism, sentimentality to authenticity, superficiality to depth) were never purely descriptive; they represented ethical and religious, as well as aesthetic, discernment and values.

The degree to which aesthetic, religious, and especially ethical considerations merged (inside the church and out) marks a striking feature of the debate: for example, authenticity in art was much more significant to participants than beauty. Further, to a much greater extent than might be imagined, art critic and theologian adopted similar frameworks of evaluation. That the thought and language worlds overlapped so fully is a clear indication of the alliance of Protestant intelligentsia with the secular intellectuals in the face of what each perceived as a critical challenge to their hegemony.[34] For the secular intellectuals the future of Western civilization was riding on the outcome. Liberal theologians, historians of religion, and clergy connected this "ultimate concern" regarding the Western cultural future to their own fears about the future of their faith.

For the liberal church, it was clear, Sallman's *Head* and similar mass-culturally categorized images could not represent a vital Christianity. The alternative, the art against which both mass culture and sentimental realism seemed to strive, was modernism, specifically modernist abstraction of an expressionist or abstract expressionist bent. The critique of mass culture constituted the vocabulary that validated modernism as a mainstream phenomenon in the United States. Abstraction was "vital and meaningful." It opposed a "realism hidden in the heart" to mass culture's "exterior naturalism."[35] "True" art was not representation of an illusory reality but expression of the human condition.[36]

Like their secular counterparts, many of the era's most prominent liberal religious thinkers participated in intellectualizing and idealizing not only abstract art but also its audience.[37] Abstraction, as a visual metaphor for authentic individuality, was the "thinking person's art," a serious matter that required effort to understand. While populist regionalist realism had exalted physical work in its choice of subject matter, abstract expressionism exalted the intellectual (and spiritual) work requisite to appreciation. For those steeped in the Protestant work ethic (especially its more scholarly variations), the mental ease of access to mass culture occasioned fear and discomfort.[38] That the alternative, the modern "art of alienation," generally had no direct connection to the institutional church, that it did not share with the theologian a set of orthodox (or even near-orthodox) beliefs, was not a cause for liberal concern. The very lack of institutional affiliation could be construed as an advantage when a principal fear was mind control and loss of autonomy; any "truly serious" artistic expression could be construed as religious when the prevailing liberal definition of religion was Tillich's expansive "ultimate concern for Ultimate Reality."[39]

Kitsch was both "sub-art" and "pseudo-knowledge."[40] John Dixon, in his review of Greenberg's *Art and Culture,* amplified the art critic's discussion of the "moral falsity" of kitsch: "What is the hope of true human sensibility in a society dominated by *kitsch*? To those concerned, as Mr. Greenberg is not, with the development of intelligence in the church the problem is even more acute. There is no evidence that saintliness or salvation depends on either intelligence or sensibility, but if false sensibility is seen in Mr. Greenberg's terms, not as admissible entertainment but as a lie, the moral question presses itself on us most acutely. . . . The issue is between truth and falsehood, and what is at stake is the humanness of man."[41] The opposite of kitsch, with its sentimentality and its accompanying qualities of dissemblance and disguise, was not simply "good" art, it was "honest," "genuine," "real," "true," "authentic."[42] The liberal church issued an explicit call for "aesthetic authenticity."[43] For the liberal religious as for the secular critics, modernist abstraction exemplified this key notion of authenticity as Sallman and others of his stripe exemplified sentimentality. "Perhaps no other form of religious art is more saddening and at times more nauseating than the anemic, weak, sentimentalized 'likenesses' of the Christ. Hofmann [and] Sallman . . . have portrayed a Christ that is not worthy . . . a prettified portrait for the sentimental that has no character. These portraits of Christ . . . indicate the degree to which we have weakened and sentimentalized our faith."[44]

For Sallman's critics, the "masculine" alternative to "feminine" sentimentality was surface-penetrating authenticity. Authenticity, in this context, included a number of subtly modulated variables. Authentic art should portray contemporary experience powerfully and directly: "Too many Christians have identified religious art solely in terms of subject matter, and have tried to baptize the superficial, sentimental, and commercial, meanwhile turning their backs on those who grasped and sought to portray the terrible ways in which our times and existence are out of joint."[45] For Finley Eversole, as for Scott and Dixon, the "isolation of the individual which expresses itself in themes of alienation, exile, and estrangement" accurately characterized the crisis of contemporary society. This isolation "is an illness which, portrayed in all of the modern arts, beguiles the naive into thinking that the sickness is that of art, not of man. On the contrary, the art of alienation is an interpretation of what

Gabriel Marcel calls '*our* life.'"[46] In *The Courage to Be,* a book directly
relevant to the question of authentic existence, Tillich defined the alternatives:

> Modern art is not propaganda but revelation. It shows that
> the reality of our existence is as it is. It does not cover up
> the reality in which we are living. . . . The art propagated
> by both totalitarianism and democratic conformism is dis-
> honest beautification. It is an idealized naturalism which is
> preferred because it removes every danger of art becoming
> critical and revolutionary. The creators of modern art have
> been able to see the meaninglessness of our existence; they
> participated in its despair. At the same time they have had
> the courage to face it and to express it in their pictures and
> sculptures. They have had the courage to be themselves.[47]

The artist, in the vanguard of his civilization (and I use the
masculine advisedly here), was what every authentic man should be in
the face of contemporary existence: a cultural warrior, heroic, courageous, revolutionary. By comparison with the authentic artist,

> the average man, except in momentary flashes of compre-
> hension, has not the courage to accept so large a measure of
> truth or freedom. . . . We relish a cage of conventions or
> any containment that offers a deluding sense of security.
> We prefer not to face the relentless vistas of uncertainty
> and the meaningless hazards that constantly threaten us as
> chance visitors on a strange planet.
>
> The artist, on the other hand, when courageous
> enough, will rejoice in the very situation that the rest of us
> find scarcely bearable. . . . To invent rigid and pretentious
> patterns of social behavior on the edge of the universal
> mystery, as human societies do, represents for the artist
> the building of Fort Panic at the edge of the eternal wilder-
> ness. Without uncertainties, he reveals, neither truth nor
> freedom could exist.[48]

The trope of the sublime—retrieved, recast, and gendered masculine to
reinforce the dichotomy between authentic modernist culture and sentimental mass culture—formed the discursive framework of liberal theol-

ogy and of abstract expressionism. Eversole, elaborating on Tillich's ideas in an essay that promoted abstract expressionism, extolled the courage of modern artists in terms of the "clarity, composure, and sobriety" with which they "represented the despiritualization and consequent dehumanization of our life." "The contemporary artist then is one who begins with the presupposition of damnation, with the encounter with nothingness, and seeks to wrest from the abyss some order of meaning and being."[49] Art should express, honestly and directly, this modern character rather than the anachronistic "nightgown nightmares" and "pink and blue confections" of academic art and its mass kitsch counterpart.[50]

In addition to the notion of timeliness or honesty to its own age and to the preference for "surface penetration," psychological insights delineated a related sense of authenticity. In this rendition, Sallman's art was a mass-cultural defense against the underlying anxiety of the age. But this defensive strategy could be accomplished only by avoiding the confrontation or encounter, by covering over the conflict as with false sentiment and ultimately by repressing the depth issue, sedating oneself and one's visual capacities so as not to see the truth. Here indeed was a case of religious image as opiate, as "tranquilizer." Authentic art, honest art, did not dissemble; rather, it confronted head-on the depths of the conflict and the anxiety of human existence.

What did the ideology of modernism, explicitly understood as an adversary to the mass commercialism of Sallman, gain for intellectuals in the liberal church in the 1950s? Clearly, Sallman's *Head of Christ* targeted a "cultural pressure point" for the liberal Protestant church.[51] Most important, what one religious intellectual and promoter of modernism called the "recent engagement of religion and art" offered a definitive rebuttal to the specter of mass culture, which the liberal religious associated not only with Sallman's tremendously popular *Head* but also with the evangelical religious tradition that produced and promoted such images.[52] The fit of the second association was enhanced by the evangelicals' rapid and successful exploitation of mass-cultural media as part of their twentieth-century religious agenda.[53] The threat of mass culture, however, was all the greater because appreciation of Sallman did not confine itself to evangelical pews but infiltrated liberal congregations as well. The terms of the mass-culture wars, as waged by intellectuals within and without the church, provided the perfect frame for liberal

Protestant efforts to describe and reinforce the boundaries between liberal and evangelical Christianity, to aesthetically purify their own congregations, and to elevate and promote an alternate vision.[54]

In large part, the swell of interest in art and religion that emerged in the 1950s from the liberal religious side of the equation can be accounted for in art's provision of what liberal religious intellectuals and their followers deemed lacking in American mass society in general and, more specifically, among the "masses" in the pews.[55] That is to say, the very values that "mass" religious taste seemed to "dilute" and "contaminate," Sallman's critics saw defiantly restored in modern abstraction. The association of liberal religion with "authentic" art offered to reinstate the individuality, creativity, variety, imagination, and humanity that contemporary commercial life sapped. In the hyperbolic language characteristic of the debate, modern art represented, for its liberal religious promoters, a "momentous struggle in the modern soul to recover depth and wholeness, to reaffirm personal responsibility in the face of dehumanization, to find a true order beneath our modern anarchy, a true ground for human freedom and creativeness in a culture marked by impersonal tyrannies, and so to prepare the way for renewed human community."[56]

The hyperbole of the liberal religious debate was largely the product of the conviction that both authentic democracy, with its emphasis on the unique individual as political agent, and authentic Christianity, with its emphasis on individual response and responsibility, were, in some almost absolute sense, incompatible with standardization and the idiom of the mass. This incompatibility fueled the culture wars and pinpointed a major source of threat and danger: the anti-intellectual mass-cultural mentality and coercive authoritarianism were inextricably linked—and the first, it was feared, could slide easily into the second.

LIBERAL RELIGION AND HIGH ART

To a large extent I have allowed the liberal Protestant criticism of Sallman to constitute the frame for my research. As ideas found in my sources began to cohere, however, it was obvious that the criticism of Sallman introduces key issues in a major cultural contest of the mid-twentieth century. The insistent opposition of mass and high culture that forms the backbone of this contest was explicitly pursued and expanded

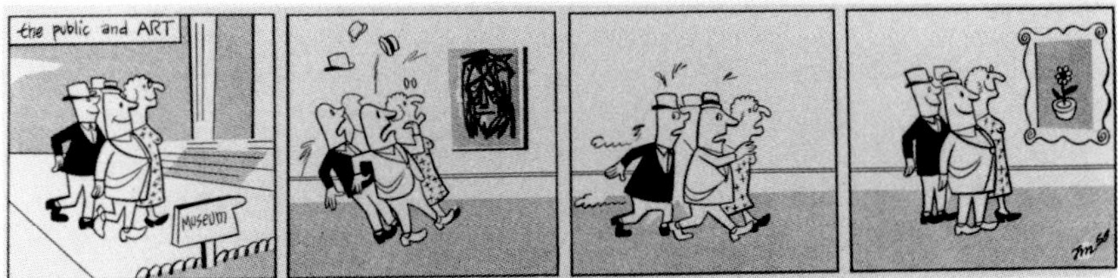

5.7. "The Public and Art." From *motive* magazine 19, no. 9 (May 1959). Copyright 1959 by the Board of Education, the Methodist Church, Nashville, Tennessee. Used by permission.

by the liberal church and the secular intellectual. As high culture had experienced a process of sacralization in the late nineteenth and early twentieth centuries in the United States, the reputation of religion had suffered numerous blows.[57] The sacralization of high culture and the secularization of modern life proceeded hand in hand. By mid-century, liberal religion heard its own language in the sacralizing vocabulary of high art, *and* liberal religion desired to increase its own "cultural capital" by associating itself with elite culture and distinguishing itself from the "anti-intellectual" and "commercial" religious culture of evangelicalism.[58] Thus liberal Protestant intellectuals, and leaders of many of the denominations they represented, claimed a status divorced from the mass or popular and associated with a culturally elevated elite.

Deliberately countering mass culture with their own notion of an intellectual and artistic "vanguard" (a reworking, perhaps, of the biblical tradition of the saving "remnant"), liberal Protestants asserted a different taste world, parallel to high culture's avant-garde, as an alternative to the evangelical competition and to alarming trends they observed in their own congregations (fig. 5.7). The liberal vanguard achieved its classic expression in a study document titled "The Church, the Arts, and Contemporary Culture," adopted by the Department of Worship and the Arts of the National Council of Churches on September 12, 1955, and approved a month later for circulation to member churches and their seminaries. "The Church should have a vanguard," the document maintained,

> of men and women qualified to interpret the significance
> of contemporary art for the believer and able to make
> contact with the influential movements of our time in art,
> architecture, music, literature and criticism. To identify

and encourage such a vanguard, to foster its common understanding of the problems involved, to build bridges of
conversation for it with the appropriate secular groups, to
open channels for its witness and impact in the life of the
churches as well as in society at large—all this requires
considered planning and organization. . . . The desired
vanguard must be mobilized, its members brought into
productive relationship not only with one another but
with various groups both within and without the Church.
The terms of the discourse cannot be confined to the arts in
any narrow sense but must involve the wider problems
having to do with the symbols and values of our society
and the vehicles of communication in our culture.[59]

Underscoring the notion of the intellectual and aesthetic gap between the
"majority of Christians" and art "in the best sense," between "predigested" mass religious culture and high religious culture, Harry Garvin,
the editor of the *Bucknell Review*, highlighted the attraction of the elite
constellation for the educated readers of his article on art and religion in
the *Christian Scholar:* "It is admirable that among the leaders of the new
movement the main tendency now is to develop a sense of the best. . . .
elsewhere [outside the universities and seminaries] everyone is more
subject to mass tastes."[60]

Liberal Protestant intellectuals did not choose to engage art at
some random moment in art's American history; rather, liberal religion
became attentive to high art just as its American star was ascending, just
as the center of the Western art world was shifting from Paris to New
York. In a society they judged to be increasingly secular, increasingly
commercial, liberal Protestant intellectuals discerned in contemporary
high culture an avenue to cultural legitimation. Harold Ehrensperger
expressed his conviction that the "religious leader is discovering that
without good art he cannot communicate what he feels is imperative for
his generation in ways that influence man's destiny and give his life
purpose."[61] Extending the terms of the mass-culture contest and especially the rhetoric of the abstract expressionist alternative, liberal Christians claimed both universality and cultural relevance—for genuine (that
is, abstract) art and for genuine (that is, liberal) religion. "The arts of a
rationalized society have celebrated technological man—a kind of propa-

gandistic art—or offered themselves as a private solace or (as all too often in the modern mass media) as vehicles of sensationalism for anonymous multitudes seeking a vicarious substitute for genuine personal life. . . . When it is recognized that genuine art is not didactic, moralistic, propagandistic, inspirational—and in this connection, not representational—*then its proper universality and cultural relevance are reestablished. . . . this same law holds for the Gospel and the arts of the Church"* (emphasis mine).[62] Because of the association of contemporary American art (abstract expressionism) with the triumph of a new global culture in the free world, the association of religion with art at just this moment implied an opportunity to culturally reconfigure Christianity as a modern, universal faith, characteristic of the free individual in the free world.[63]

From the liberal religious perspective, high culture did not surrender (as evangelical religion had) to the contaminating forces of commerce. Religious intellectuals treated high culture as self-authenticating; in the liberal religious literature, high culture shared with authentic religion a language of ultimacy and heroic subjectivity. "Good art, like all creative activity . . . even while depicting the commonplace, . . . carries [the beholder] into another, transfigured world." "Tawdry art" (and this is a telling quotation) has "made religion look tawdry and inconsequential for everyday life." As Sallman was the repository of all things despised, high art was the repository of all the values that liberal Protestant intellectuals wished to promote. The best of high art (like the best of religion) was revelatory of ultimate reality: "Art at its best and religion in its finest expression have the same end. They are not escapes from reality: they are means by which reality is given significance."[64] Mass (religious) culture, as represented chiefly in the parishes and literature of the competition but also and even more dangerously in liberal Protestant pews, threatened to dilute and contaminate high culture. Desperate to prevent further slippage, liberal Protestant intellectuals involved themselves publicly and deliberately in a larger project of boundary reinforcement and cultural mapping.

So art and religion came together not quiescently, as some have suggested, not because a decade of peace provided an opportunity for the two to become reacquainted, but because an individual and cultural identity crisis brought religion in search of art. It was not postwar prosperity and tranquillity that accounted for the rapprochement but a vital concern for the future of human culture. Impressive numbers of Protestant intellectuals (from both the religion side and the art side of the equation) understood themselves to be responding to the needs of the times by reclaiming a mode of expression and communication too long forsaken.[65]

In the 1950s the institutional Protestant church, apprehensive that it was coming late to the game and with a sense of abdicated opportunity, tried to discern a way to construct for itself a significant role in the patronage, criticism, and promotion of the arts.[66] "The church should resume its ancient and proper responsibility and productivity with reference to all the arts. It could well begin by purging its own arts, educating its own members, developing standards of perception and evaluation, making clear the theological considerations that are crucial, and at all times insisting on the wholeness of the arts in the sense that they must speak to the whole man and not to some isolated sentiment or moral intention. Even those arts of the Church which derive from the great tradition have been falsified in the modern situation and become insipid or precious or esoteric or sentimental."[67] For many religious leaders who involved themselves in the critique of mass culture, art-making itself (or, rather, fine-art-making) became a spiritual enterprise. Direct contact with art not only could provide a satisfying aesthetic experience but also increased the beholder's "capacity . . . for spiritual experience."[68] Abstract expressionists obliged by using similar terminology to define their own activity. Amos Wilder, Hollis Professor of Divinity at Harvard University and brother of Thornton Wilder, expressed feelings shared rather widely among Protestant intellectuals when he posited art as an extra-institutional custodian of religion in the modern era.[69] Writing for the *Christian Scholar,* another liberal religious academic recorded his guarded hope that the "transformation of aesthetic sensibility" would lead to a new golden age of Christianity: "If Tillich and his adherents can maintain some pre-eminence in Protestant theology, can transform the aesthetic sensibilities of the majority of Christians, and can deepen their concern in individual and social living, then the heroic age in Christian sensibility and perhaps a new golden age of Christianity will have come."[70]

In 1956 Harold Ehrensperger claimed that "no sign of the times is more evident than the awakened interest in the relationship between the arts and religion."[71] The church advanced its efforts to "heal the breach" between art and religion on multiple fronts.[72] Paul Tillich lectured on art and religion not only in churches and seminaries but also in

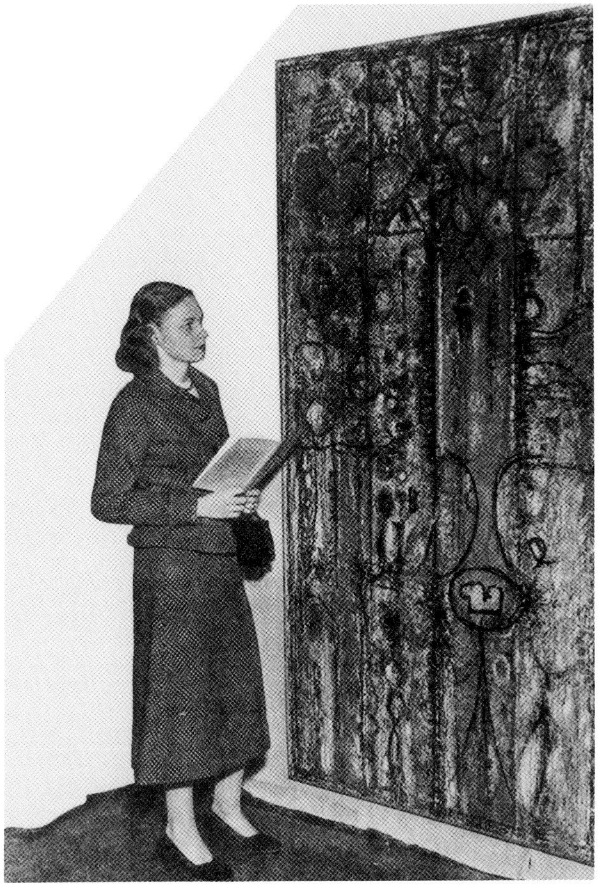

5.8. *Union Exhibition of Contemporary Religious Art*. From *motive*
magazine 13, no. 6 (March 1953). Copyright 1953 by the
Board of Education, the Methodist Church, Nashville, Tennessee.
Used by permission.

major institutions of art, including the Minneapolis Institute, the Museum of Modern Art, and the National Gallery of Art in Washington, D.C. Various liberal denominations and their seminaries held art exhibitions and festivals, often in conjunction with annual or biennial synods and conferences that attracted large numbers of people (fig. 5.8). In 1954 when the World Council of Churches met in Evanston, Illinois, the Art Institute of Chicago hosted an exhibition of religious painting and sculpture. Tillich and Yale University's Theodore Greene collaborated on the catalogue essay, "Authentic Religious Art," described in liberal religious periodicals as a definitive statement on religion and art.[73] The National Council of Churches' Department of Worship and the Arts, headed by Marvin Halverson, played a critical role in the liberal religious engagement of art. Its six commissions (architecture, art, literature, drama, music, worship) studied and promoted the relation of contemporary faith and contemporary aesthetics.[74] In addition, such major liberal seminaries as the Divinity School of the University of Chicago, Union Theological Seminary, and Boston University School of Theology instituted programs in religion and the arts.[75] And influential churches—New York's Judson Memorial Church, for example—defined their ministries in such a way as to focus considerable attention on art and artists.[76]

What comes as something of a surprise in this literature is that art's engagement of liberal religion was only somewhat more cautious than liberal religion's embrace of art. The story of art's involvement in this conversation is much more impressive than has been previously recognized. Alfred H. Barr, Jr., Charles Rufus Morey, George Heard Hamilton, Perry T. Rathbone, David E. Finley, and Duncan Phillips figure among those who promoted a modern abstract aesthetic for liberal religion in opposition to the realist styles of "godless" communism and commercial culture.[77]

I will expand on the role of just one of these individuals. Alfred Barr, founding director of the Museum of Modern Art and director of museum collections from 1947 to 1967, was the believing son and grandson of Presbyterian ministers, and a member of the Brick Presbyterian Church.[78] A large primary literature concerns Barr's efforts to set aesthetic standards for Protestant Christianity; the secondary literature does not even mention this aspect of his life.[79] As early as 1941, Barr proposed an exhibition on art and religion at the Museum of Modern Art. As he envisioned it, *The Religious Spirit in Contemporary Art* would include examples of "good" and "bad" religious art, "with a few additions such as Christmas cards and other objects which are sold and which pretend to be religious art."[80]

Beginning in 1954, Barr headed the Commission on Art formed under the auspices of the National Council of Churches' Department of Worship and the Arts (1950).[81] When, in 1955, Barr constituted the small commission subcommittee responsible for selecting Christian images for an article in *Life* magazine, he had no difficulty persuading three prominent art professionals (a museum director and two academic art historians), Perry T. Rathbone, George Heard Hamilton, and Charles Rufus Morey, to serve. The commission charged the subcommittee, of which Paul Tillich was the fifth and final member, with compiling for *Life* a list of "works of the highest artistic and religious quality which . . . would serve as an initial attack upon the banality and saccharine vulgarity of most Christian art, particularly protestant Christian art in this country."[82] The *Life* article would be designed to reach "not only several million laymen, but also tens of thousands of protestant clergy," constituencies that Barr and his committee believed to be crucial if change was to be effected. In a letter of March 21, 1955, to Rathbone, Barr noted his inclination to include a "page with small reproductions of typically bad Christian art now being used by protestant churches as illustrations for children's Bibles, church calendars, church papers and Sunday school magazines, reproductions on the walls of parish houses, etc., perhaps also Christmas and Easter cards."[83]

In a report to the Executive Board of the Division of Christian Life and Work on behalf of the Department of Worship and the Arts, Barr delivered what is perhaps his most direct criticism of his own denomination and of the National Council's other member churches:

> In the arts of painting, sculpture and book illustration our churches and churchmen seem, generally speaking, both ignorant and blind.
>
> Our churches do of course use art—but what art! Consider the vulgarity and banality of the pictures of Christ now in general use. "Gentle Jesus, meek and mild" is translated into art on the level of cosmetic and tonic advertisements. Yet these saccharine and effeminate images are distributed by millions with the tolerance and often the well-intentioned blessing of our churches. They look up at us from bulletins and calendars and Sunday school magazines and down at us from the walls of church houses and parsonages. They corrupt the religious feelings of children and nourish the complacency and sentimentality of their elders. They call for iconoclasm.[84]

In addition to his significant work with the National Council of Churches, Barr was the first president of the Foundation for Art, Religion, and Culture (ARC, incorporated in 1961), which included as corporate members, for example, Robert Motherwell, Lee Ault, Agnes Mongan, Perry Rathbone, Ad Reinhardt, and Wolfgang Stechow, as well as distinguished religious leaders.[85] Further, Barr and his colleague Peter Selz gave Tillich numerous opportunities to make his views on art and religion known in the established art context of museum lectures and catalogues.[86]

CULTURAL ANALYSIS AND SHIFTING VISUAL ARRANGEMENTS

How Sallman was seen and judged by liberal Protestants in the 1950s was a product not only of aesthetic and religious categories but, very importantly, of the broader cultural associations that adhered to those aesthetic and religious categories. When scholars examine the environments of reception—the "culture worlds" that attend a particular image—radically different "fictions" (different stories, different interpretations, different standards of evaluation) for a single image may emerge. One might justifiably say that beauty is in the culture of the beholder, for reception certainly depends on the culture of the audience. The characterizations that led liberals to reject Sallman must not be confused with the attributes valued by his supporters; on most dimensions, the different understandings of these images did not reflect simply a set of polar oppositions. Supporters of Sallman, in contrast to the liberals' focus on the *de*humanizing potential of the images, reported highly individual and personalized responses to reproductions of Sallman's paintings. The two audiences saw two different sets of issues raised in Sallman's art, and they exercised different sets of expectations in relation to those issues. What both promoters and detractors shared in Sallman's case, however, was the conviction that it was possible to produce and determine a "legitimate" religious image, or at least a legitimate sort of image, and that the process of selection was itself crucial. Spokespersons on both sides of the debate believed that art exercised a power to influence, to liberate, or to corrupt; art had a significant moral dimension. Good taste really mattered.[87]

The decisive factor in terms of the liberal Protestant reaction to Sallman was the association of his art with a homogenous mass culture, at best bland, unthinking, and uninspiring, at worst parasitic, demonic, and cancerous. I have confined the focus of this chapter to the decade of the 1950s for a reason. Although the categories of high culture and mass culture seemed to find some new degree of definition in the late nineteenth and early twentieth centuries, and modernism in the United States assumed a solid place in the high-cultural hierarchy by the 1940s, the relation between mass culture and high culture remained fluid; perhaps most fluid was the assessment of the *value* of mass culture in relation to high culture. The particular disposition of categorical relations that characterized the 1950s no longer pertained a decade later. In the 1960s, significant shifts along a number of cultural variables modified high-cultural reactions to mass culture in general and Sallman in particular. The advent of pop art represented only the most obvious high-cultural manifestation of such changes.

Scholarly exploration of some of the dynamics examined in a preliminary fashion in this chapter promises to illuminate further the mechanics of arranging visual culture in the United States. Even when such cultural categories as fine, popular, and folk obscure more than they disclose in relation to particular images, the historical construction of such aesthetic classes, in terms of the constellations of characteristics that adhere to the classifications in different times and places, can be revealing. In the 1940s and 1950s critics connected certain kinds of art to a larger humanistic vision, a vision that other images appeared to thwart. The intellectuals' rather indiscriminate association of all forms of realism with proto-fascist and communist systems produced an exaggerated attachment to abstraction.[88] The anti-intellectual assaults on modern art from the political Right, led by Joseph McCarthy and George Dondero, served only to prove the point. As aesthetic hierarchy on this side of the Atlantic crystallized and, simultaneously, as the fledgling discipline of American art history took shape, this new field, even as it revered folk culture as a chronologically distant but native source for the twentieth-century abstractions of American high culture, expressed a strong aversion to popular culture, especially in its contemporary mass forms.[89]

As Adorno, Macdonald, Greenberg, Tillich, and their followers construed mass culture, the mass object or image became the historical agent encoding meanings prescribed by the managers of mass production and acting on, manipulating, a passive inert beholder. According to Adorno and his colleague Leo Lowenthal, the development of taste was no longer a possibility in mass culture, because aesthetic preferences were imposed from without instead of generated from within the individual.[90] The perception of a reified mass-cultural entity as aggressor left the audience no recourse, no opportunity to intervene, redirect, or reshape the ideas and meanings that mass culture transmitted. This view of mass culture provided the perfect foil for an opposing notion of individuated agency in audiences for abstract art. Not surprisingly, as an alternative to mass culture, its critics promoted images that creative individuals (artists and beholders) controlled, not images that appeared to control individuals.

The 1960s produced a revolt against the cultural pessimism of the intellectuals of the 1950s. "Cultural populists" reactivated the audiences of mass culture.[91] In the process, they retrieved for their subject the label *popular* culture and asserted their conviction of its subversive and therefore potentially liberating possibilities.[92] In an age of pervasive mass media involvement in the day-to-day visual terrain and of multiculturalism's challenges to current arrangements of the visual field, however, neither the pessimism of the mass-culture critique nor the optimism of the New Left and the counterculturalists can suffice. Both these approaches rested on preconceptions of the political and social allegiances of entire classes of artistic production. Looking to opposite ends of the cultural spectrum, both asserted their own commitment to authentically democratic art.[93]

Reading contemporary mass culture (by virtue of its supposed authoritarian imposition from above) as the antithesis of democracy, the 1950s intellectuals found what they desired in modernist high culture, with its accent on subjectivity and individual creative agency. The New Left and the counterculturalists, in contrast, branded 1950s high culture as establishment, elitist, and overly self-involved. These 1960s groups discerned in contemporary popular culture (by virtue of its perceived status as a subversive grassroots phenomenon) the fullest expression of authentic democracy. Cultural critics in both decades assumed that one class of images was, as a class, more democratic than another; for both, the a priori argument instructed the uses and meanings of images. Because the arguments were motivated by issues that were often external to the images themselves, much of the debate was ultimately literary. Texts responded to texts with little consideration of specific images and specific audiences. Although these texts were certainly an important part of the relevant cultural fabric, the critical preconceptions that motivated aesthetic assessment made close examination of images and the visual dynamics of their reception unlikely. For example, the critics of mass culture could reject Sallman on the basis of similarities perceived with Soviet realism only if the basis for comparison was not principally visual; Sallman did not look like Soviet realism, but (in print) one realism sounded like another. One of the great ironies of the mass-culture critique was the failure of the liberal proponents of complexity and depth to recognize any degree of variation among the multiplicity of realisms they opposed.[94]

What is needed is not a middle ground between cultural pessimism and cultural populism but a move to an altogether different ground in order to provide a basis for investigation that does not proceed from the assumption that certain categories of images always operate uniformly. A case-by-case, as opposed to class-by-class, analysis might illuminate the multivalent capacities of images, with reference to meaning and function, at the levels of both production and consumption; such an approach might uncover diversity within classes of images and even within a single image. (Sallman's *Head of Christ* certainly demonstrates that the same image can operate in different ways for different audiences.) Finally, because different visual cultures often intersect in a single image, beginning with the images rather than the classifications might encourage examination of the seams of visual culture in the United States, the places where high culture and popular culture (or high culture and folk culture) meet, accentuating the character and self-understandings of each.

This chapter is motivated by an interest in cultural hierarchy and categorization; it is, even more important, powered by a fascination with the relation between American art and American religion. This fascination is not unrelated to the fact that, in the United States, religion acts, disproportionately, as a crucible for conflict between different visual cultures. In the religious arena, these conflicts are played out with special clarity and with high stakes; a religious and ethical overlay adheres to aesthetic judgments. Even when religious issues are not overt, they often act in some latent capacity. The debates of the 1990s surrounding the National Endowment for the Arts reflect both explicit and implicit levels of engagement. For the religious critics of mass culture in the 1950s, issues of eternal values and ultimate reality magnified and complicated an already intense secular debate. The future of God as well as the future of humanity seemed to hang in the balance.

By 1962, according to one relieved liberal observer at the *Chris-*

tian Century, Warner Sallman's *Head of Christ* and Van Gogh *reproductions* were "out," while Rembrandt, Chagall, and *motive* magazine were "in." In a demonstration of the sort of cultural categorical slippage described earlier by Russell Lynes (fig. 5.9), Rouault seemed by this time to be "so far in as to be almost out."[95] While the *Christian Century* observer's selections reflected a distinct preference for high culture, in the 1960s the *fear* of mass culture dissipated. Sallman's work was still associated with a kind of homogenized mass culture, but a differently nuanced complaint against the sameness of this religious mass culture emerged. As the ideology of consensus developed more cracks, the critics of consensus and unification theories pointed out the tendencies of mass culture to obliterate desirable subcultural distinctions. In the 1960s and 1970s a new argument against Sallman was posed by Americans eager to assert the ethnicity of Jesus as other than the Nordic blond Sallman painted. The

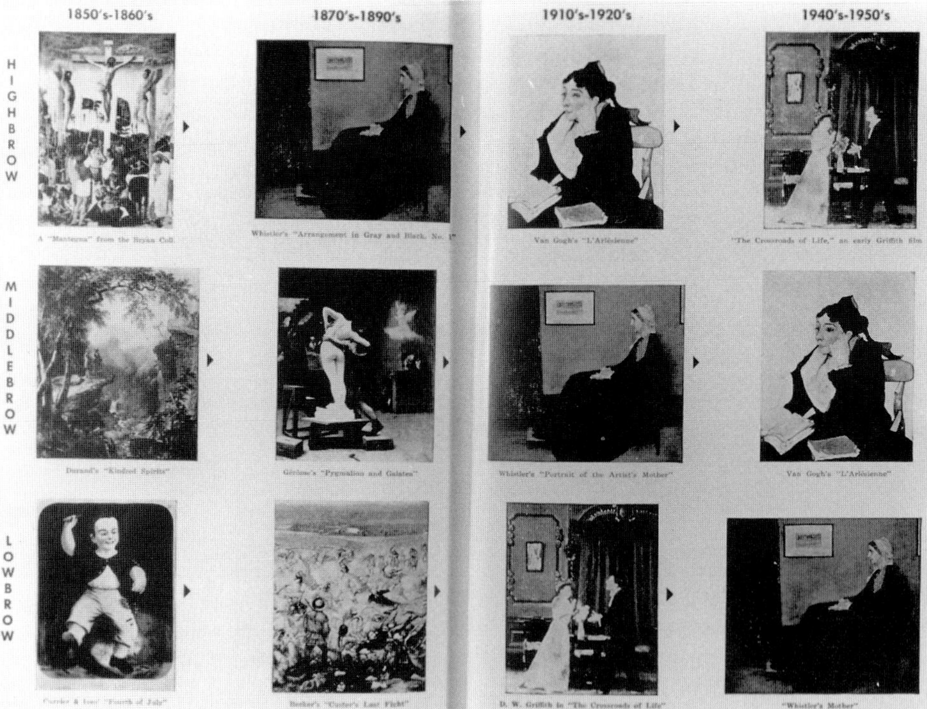

5.9. "Highbrow, Middlebrow, Lowbrow." From Russell Lynes, *The Tastemakers* (New York: Harper and Brothers, 1954). Reprinted by permission of the Estate of Russell Lynes.

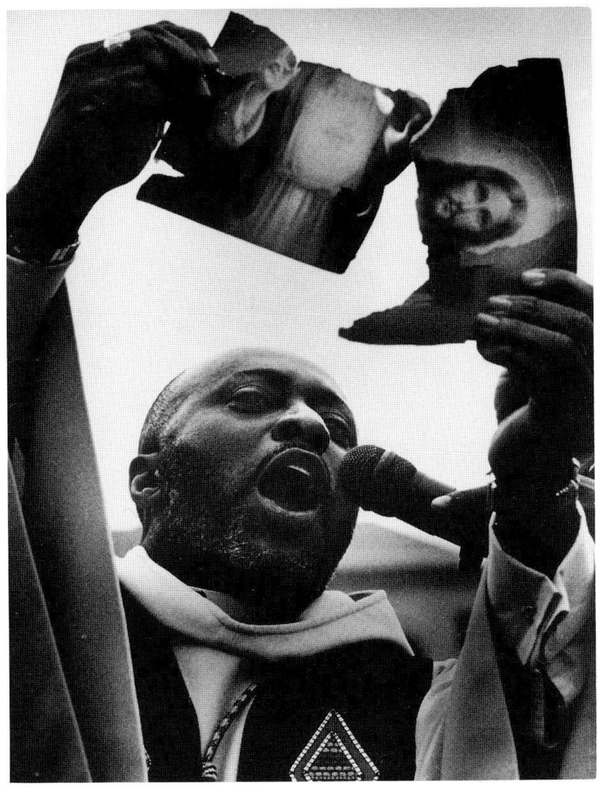

5.10. "Stallings Campaign Targets White Depictions of Jesus,"
Washington Post (April 10, 1993), B1, B4. Courtesy *Washington Post,*
photo by Bill O'Leary.

1950s debate was not only predominantly male but also almost exclusively white. The critique that emerged in the 1960s and 1970s, and
continues in the 1990s (fig. 5.10), challenged the primacy of that constit-
uency. What made Sallman problematic from the African-American
perspective, especially, was not simply the "kitschy" "beautifying naturalism" of an appropriated European academic style but the necessity for
an African-American alternative that more closely approximated the
"Jesus of history."[96] By comparison with the 1950s, the 1960s criticism
of Sallman thus engaged different culture worlds. At issue was not only
the relation of high culture to popular culture; competing popular cultures participated in charting this visual terrain. The *Christian Century*
notwithstanding, Rouault, from this vantage point, was almost as much

the transgressor as Sallman. No longer necessarily privileging expressio-
nisms (German or abstract), this new constellation of critics rejected both
Sallman and Rouault on grounds of racial exclusivity. The *Heads* that to
1950s observers had seemed to represent such dramatically different sets
of possibilities came to share over the next two decades the predicament
of racial type: both were white Jesuses in an era of public sensitivity to
racial diversity and racial identity.

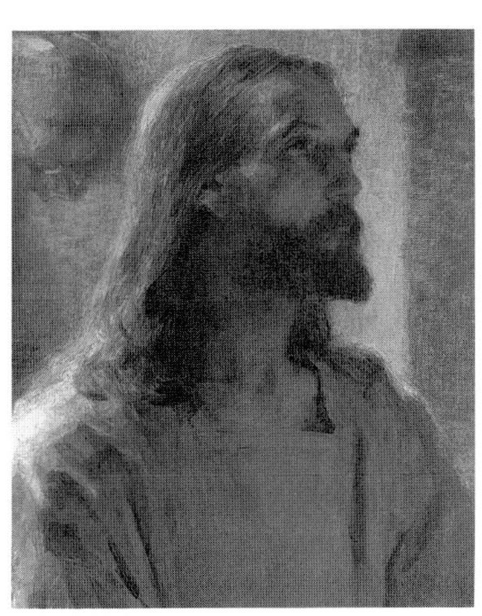

"Would Jesus Have Sat for a Portrait?"

The Likeness of Christ in the
Popular Reception of Sallman's Art

DAVID MORGAN

6

> "Don't you know who it is?" he cried in anguish.
>
> "No, who is it?" Sarah Ruth said. "It ain't anybody I
> know."
>
> "It's him," Parker said.
>
> "Him who?"
>
> "God!" Parker cried.
>
> "God? God don't look like that!"
>
> "What do you know how he looks?" Parker moaned.
> "You ain't seen him."
>
> "He don't *look*," Sarah Ruth said. "He's a spirit. No man
> shall see his face."
>
> —Flannery O'Connor, "Parker's Back"

In "Parker's Back," Flannery O'Connor joins two extremes in an antag-
onized marriage. Sarah Ruth's radical iconoclasm, mirrored in her own
"plain" appearance and schooled in her father's ministry of "Straight
Gospel" preaching, collides violently with her husband's worldly and
playful self-indulgence. When Parker is led to tattoo a Byzantine Christ
in the middle of his back, his wife responds in dismay, then angrily
accuses him of idolatry.[1] The exchange quoted here encapsulates a peren-
nial issue in popular piety: does God have a likeness to portray?

For many people the appeal of Sallman's picture of Jesus (pl. I)
resides in its *likeness* to its prototype. But if likeness means visual resemblance to an original from which an image is taken, then, as Parker's
objection to his wife suggests, no one is in the position to object unless he
or she has seen the historical Jesus face-to-face. Because most people
make no such claim, to say that a picture looks like Jesus is therefore
deceptively simple. By focusing on the assertion of likeness, in this
chapter I analyze what people have had in mind when they respond to
Sallman's picture as in some sense bearing the likeness of Jesus. I rely on
two groups of data: first, a body of letters solicited in 1993 from Sallman's admirers and detractors; and second, letters to Sallman and his
publishers, and articles about his work that appeared in the popular
religious press from approximately 1940 to 1960.[2] I also consider what
detractors of Sallman's image find *unlike* Christ about it. By examining
likeness and unlikeness, it is possible to trace the rudimentary features of
popular response to Sallman's art. In the end, response to Sallman's art

may be understood as part of a cultural system that has shaped Protestant devotion in North America during the twentieth century.

LIKENESS: RE-PRESENTING JESUS

Nearly everyone who admires Sallman's depictions of Christ, all of which are based on the original drawing of 1924 and its 1940 rendition in oil, says that these pictures look *like* Jesus (see fig. i.6 and pl. I). But the claim for such a likeness is more complex than it may appear. What does it mean to say that a picture looks like Jesus, when no one can have any visual experience on which to make such a claim? Although a small number of respondents report that they have seen Jesus and that he resembles Sallman's rendition of him, most qualify in some way the assertion of a simple resemblance. Yet many seem quite assured that this picture looks like Jesus. The record of correspondence and documents in the popular religious press since the 1940s suggests at least three major categories of likeness in the reception of Sallman's art. I have designated these varieties optical-historical, virtual, and ideological-psychological likeness. These terms represent three different but interrelated interpretations of how those who admire Sallman's pictures of Jesus consider the images to represent their subject.

The most obvious definition of likeness in the reception of Sallman's imagery is the optical-historical. A direct statement of this mode of likeness came from a woman in Arkansas, who wrote, "To me, looking at this picture brings me a peace of mind. It's hard to explain why I like it so much. I guess I picture Christ to look just as he does in this picture" (333).[3] For a great number of respondents, Sallman's *Head of Christ* is an optically correct or accurate image of the historical individual, Jesus of Nazareth. One person went so far as to say that for her the "picture is a true photo of Jesus" (292). Some respondents stressed historical accuracy to validate the authority of the picture. One writer contended that the picture was "very much like [how] Josephus, the [ancient Jewish] historian, describes Jesus" (101). No physical description of Christ exists in Josephus; however, the writer may have been thinking of a medieval Latin text ascribed to a fictitious Publius Lentulus, said to be a Roman authority in Judaea just before or after Pontius Pilate.[4] Addressed to Caesar, the letter describes the appearance of Jesus of Nazareth, which has provided some corroboration of Sallman's likeness of Christ. In a 1948 article in *Christian Life* a translation of the description was favorably compared to the *Head of Christ*.[5] The text, which preserved the condensed, anachronistic style of the medieval Latin, envisioned a "very reverent countenance" with shoulder-length hair parted in the middle and the "color of chestnuts full ripe." The forehead was said to be "plain and very delicate; his face without spot or wrinkle." The nose and mouth were "formed as nothing can be represented," while the beard was "thickish, in color like his hair, not very long forked." One respondent sent along an English version of the Latin text, which added, significantly, that Christ's eyes were blue (289).

Each of these features accords nicely with Sallman's image and therefore helps us understand how another Anglo-Saxon respondent could write, "I have seen many pictures of Jesus, but I always believed that Sallman's portrait of Jesus was the one that looked most like Jesus really looked when here on earth" (213). Others wait for the afterlife to confirm their expectation of the picture's accuracy: "There are now contemporary pictures of Christ, but for me I believe I will see the face that is in Sallman's 'Head of Christ' when He calls me home" (242; 241 makes a similar point). In either case, seeing a veritable reproduction of Jesus' features in Sallman's art was both stimulated and affirmed by the marketing of Sallman's publisher, Kriebel and Bates. In a small booklet illustrated by Sallman, written by Fred Bates, and published in 1961 to promote Sallman's oil painting *The Road to Emmaus* (see fig. 4.1), a prefatory note asserted the historical and botanical accuracy of the painting.[6] Sallman never traveled to the Holy Land and apparently copied the features of the landscape from one of many popular books of prints or photos.[7]

Several writers ascribed the accuracy or authenticity of the *Head of Christ* to the picture's visionary origin. Published accounts of the event vary, and versions passed on by respondents vary wildly. My concern is not to reconstruct a factual account of the original event. Instead, I will examine the reception of the incident in popular religious magazines and in letters, insofar as the narrative was understood to authenticate Sallman's images as a genuine representation, even a literal transcription, of Christ's appearance.

The earliest publication of the event known to me appeared in a

1943 issue of the Methodist weekly *Christian Advocate,* in which Sallman was quoted as asserting that a "visual picturization" came to him in the night: "I could almost see it on the paper. I immediately went up to my studio and made a small thumbnail sketch of the head of Christ, completed it just in time for the deadline."[8] An account published in a Methodist youth magazine in December 1943 quoted Sallman as saying, "I saw the head as clearly as though it had been put on paper" and concluded the narration with a comment on the finished charcoal drawing: "Strangely enough, it was almost precisely what I had seen in my dream. All I did was to reproduce as faithfully as I could what I had seen in my dream."[9] An article published in the North American Baptist *Annual* of 1947 refers to the "dream [that] came to him in which he received his vision."[10] In 1956 Sallman's publisher issued a folder containing a suite of images depicting scenes from the life of Christ. A biographical statement included the following quotation from Sallman: "Suddenly there flashed to my mind's eye a picture of the Christ just as if it were on my drawing board. But what was most amazing to me were the features. They were utterly different from anything I had ever conceived before."[11] The claim in this statement was that the image was completely unprecedented, that it came from beyond Sallman's imagination and previous visual experience, that he *received* it rather than created it. Once again, however, this was likely a marketing strategy of the publisher, Fred Bates. Bates, who wrote virtually all the advertising copy for the firm, inserted this quotation, and several others, into the narrative.[12] By 1956, several religious publishers had entered the marketplace with images of Jesus that competed with Sallman's, and public criticism of Sallman's picture, even allegations that it was plagiarized, had entered the popular religious press.[13]

In 1958, a Protestant journal for the armed forces published yet another variation, which stressed Sallman's piety and the masculine character of the subject of his vision:

> He had been reading the Bible before retiring and once again there flashed in his mind the picture of the vigorous young Christ [from a contemporary Bible class at the YMCA].
>
> Sallman has said subsequently that it didn't come to him quite as a dream, but as a sort of inspiration which began to

flood him as he lay in bed with his eyes shut, trying to quiet
the strange turmoil that he felt within him.

Suddenly, there was Christ visualized before him, not
as an ascetic "holy man," but as a robust young man of
perfectly normal, healthy appearance.[14]

A variation published in 1963 was pieced together from earlier accounts
in such a way as to underscore the revelatory, divine origin of the image:

He agonized in prayer but with no immediate answer.

At midnight he surrendered to apparent failure and
threw himself on his bed. Finally he fell into a heavy sleep.

Then the miracle happened:

"In the early hours of the morning before dawn there
emerged, in one illuminous moment, a visual picturization
of Jesus, so clear and definite. And it appeared to me that I
was seated at the drawing board with the completed drawing before me," says Sallman.

So real was the picturization that Sallman was soon
wide awake.

Hastily he went upstairs to his studio and made a
thumbnail sketch before the image disappeared from his
mind's eye.[15]

Sallman, whose first-person testimony usually appeared in these accounts, was gripped in this passage by a vision of himself making the
image, as if its origin were truly visionary. This "miracle" followed
prayer and surrender, which signified the artist's passive role in the
origin of the image.

These published versions and others have in turn generated variations set down in letters from the project's respondents.[16] One such
letter related that Sallman "dreamed very clearly a vision of Christ, His
face in every detail just what he felt in his heart" (143). A second writer
reported that she shared Sallman's vision, about which she read in a
booklet telling the story of Sallman's *Head of Christ*.[17] After praying
"more sincerely than I ever had before," she glimpsed the head of Christ,
although others in the room with her did not see it. Her letter concludes
with emphatic insistence, "I know exactly how Jesus looked" (262).

Another respondent, an amateur artist, copied the painting after reading about its origin.

> I have always felt confident . . . that it is an exact likeness
> of our Lord Jesus Christ. The story was that Sallman had
> been commissioned to do a painting of "how he felt Jesus
> looked." As he struggled for an image of Christ, it became
> evident to him, he was at a complete loss as to what Christ
> actually looked like. In anguish, he summoned his wife to
> come join him in prayer for an answer. The midnight
> deadline was approaching as they knelt at their bedside and
> began to pour out their hearts to God for the Image he
> needed. Suddenly, there was a flash of light and the image
> was there! Immediately he was able to complete the
> commission—the Sallman's Head of Christ we see today.
> What a vision! What a blessing! (51)

The *Head of Christ* (which the writer confused with the 1924 charcoal entitled *Son of Man*) was called an exact likeness because it was not the fabrication of Sallman's imagination but a revelation from God, piously beseeched in prayer. Whether glimpsed in a vision, based on pseudo-historical documents, or regarded as a photographic likeness of the person to be encountered one day in heaven, Sallman's image is authentic for many because of its optical-historical likeness. To look at the picture is to see the actual Christ. The art historian David Freedberg has pointed out that the same notion of optical verity or verisimilitude legitimated Orthodox icons of Christ and the Virgin. Christ's actual features had been preserved and handed down by such devices as Veronica's veil and the cloth of King Abgar.[18] In each instance, as with Sallman, the images of Christ were acheiropoetic, that is, not made with human hands. The same notion survives into the modern period in the West in a variety of sources, including the writings of the German Romantic author Heinrich Wackenroder, whose fictional *Effusions of an Art-Loving Monk* of 1796 portrayed Raphael as acquiring his characteristic portrait of the Virgin in a revelatory dream.[19]

The second genre of likeness, which I have called virtual likeness, comes close to transforming representation into presence—hence the term *virtual*. Images of Christ by Sallman cease looking *like* Christ and virtually *become* him, as Sallman illustrated in his Sunday bulletin cover entitled *Let's Go to Church* (pl. VI). In this mode of response, viewers encounter the image as more than a pictorial sign. On a few occasions the image speaks and moves as Christ himself. More typically, however, the image is addressed as if it were Christ, or a special avenue to Christ, or a sacred substitute that deserves a special degree of reverence.

Occasionally this mode of presence is fashioned by the collocation of the image in an interior space. For instance, a woman described the deployment of a Sallman image as a trompe l'oeil, the illusionistic device of fooling the eye: "I grew up in a church where the focal point was a beautiful large picture of Christ in Gethsemane surrounded by velvet drapes. It was made to look as though you were looking through a window right to the outdoors where one could actually see Christ alone in the garden" (141).

Even without the optical illusion, however, the *Head of Christ* has established a metapictorial presence of Christ for viewers. An often repeated story tells of a thief who held up a woman at gunpoint as she opened her front door. The thief "looked behind the woman where there was a picture of Warner Sallman's head of Christ, and he said to her, 'Lady, I can't do it, not with him behind you'" (10).[20] A 1947 *Newsweek* article reported that the *Head of Christ* was appearing throughout businesses in Richmond, Virginia, with the salutary effect of inducing better behavior in the workplace. One employee pointed out, "No one has cursed in my office since the picture has been on my desk."[21] A respondent indicated that she felt that the image had exerted a "big influence on the conversation and activities in our home" (293). It also provided a moral influence and suasive presence in the childhood of a Methodist clergywoman, who wrote that she spent her time as a youth "contemplating the image—wondering what Jesus was like—and felt that if the picture was with me, Jesus was too. I used to talk and pray to him via the picture. The image reminded me what was right and wrong, rather like a conscience. If I had done something I knew God didn't approve of, the picture was a gentle reproof. When I stopped going to church as a teenager, I put the picture away, as if I could avoid God!" (93). The son of a Lutheran Free Church pastor related that in his childhood, after committing an offense, he was ritually compelled by his mother to "tell Jesus you're sorry" while standing before Sallman's painting in the living room (360).

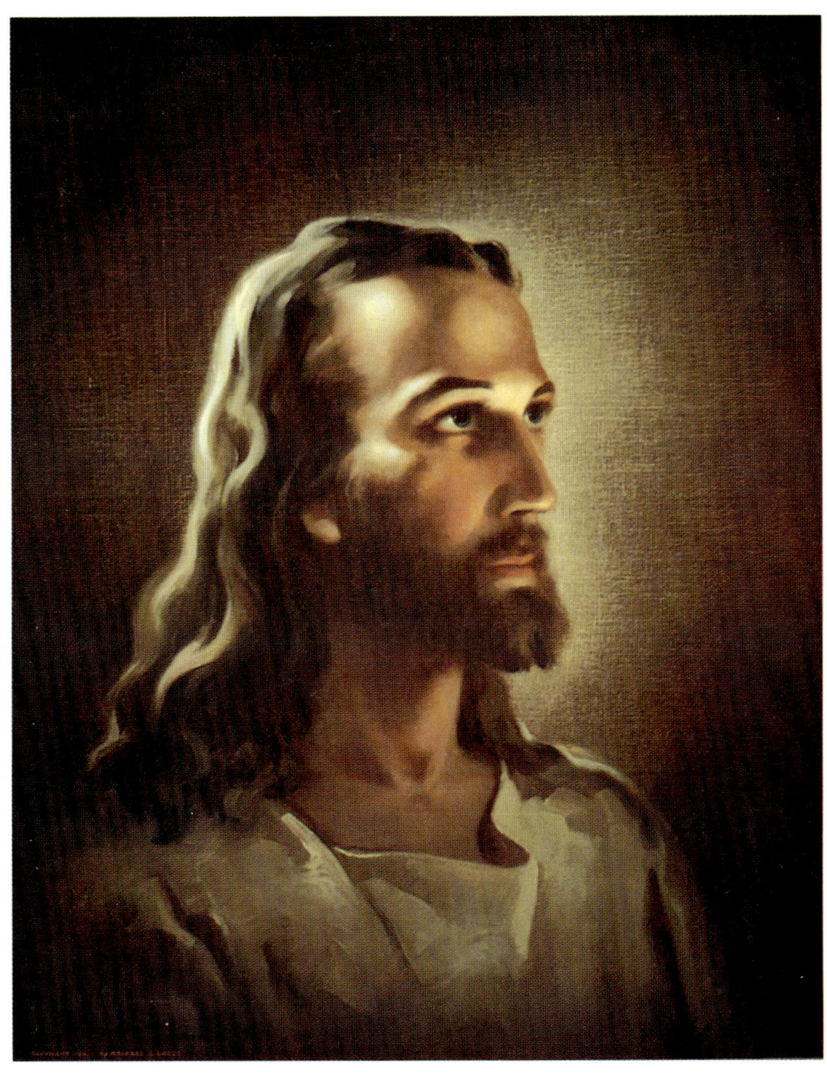

I. Warner Sallman, *Head of Christ,* 1940, oil on canvas, 28¼ × 22⅛".
Courtesy Jessie C. Wilson Galleries, Anderson University.

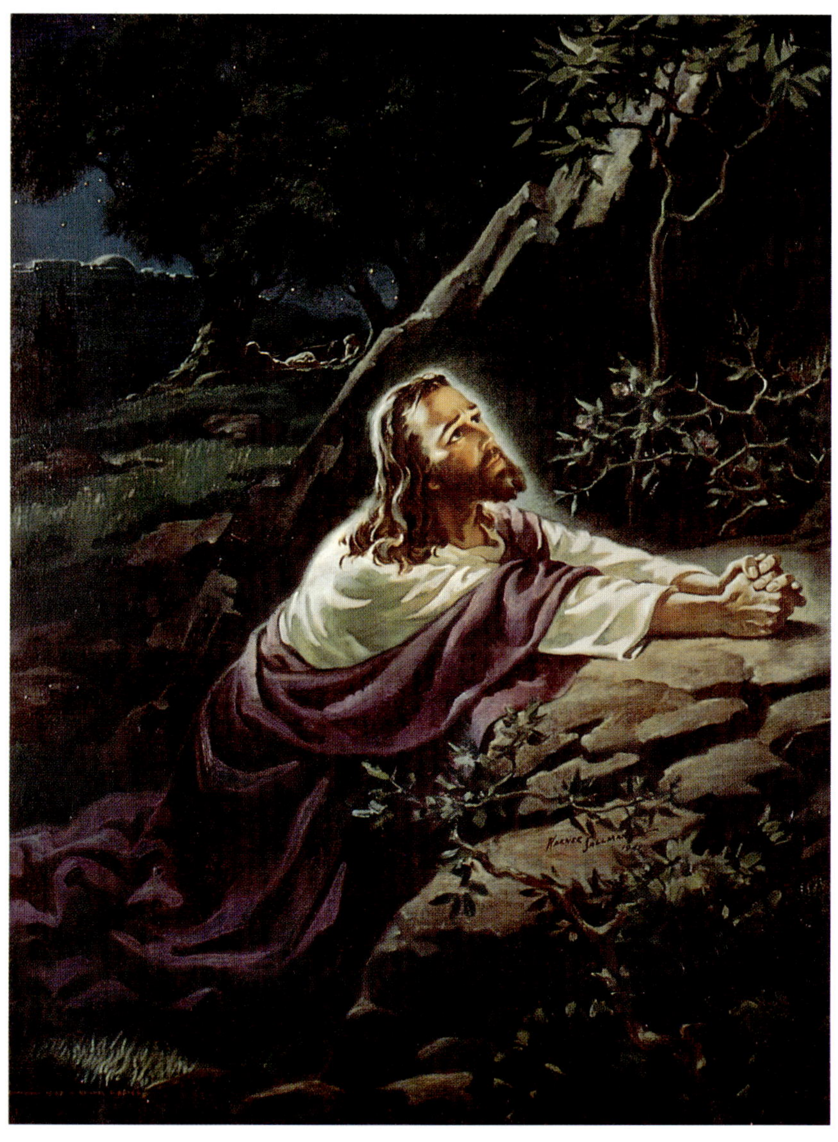

II. Warner Sallman, *Christ in Gethsemane*, 1941, oil on canvas,
40 × 30". Courtesy Jessie C. Wilson Galleries, Anderson University.

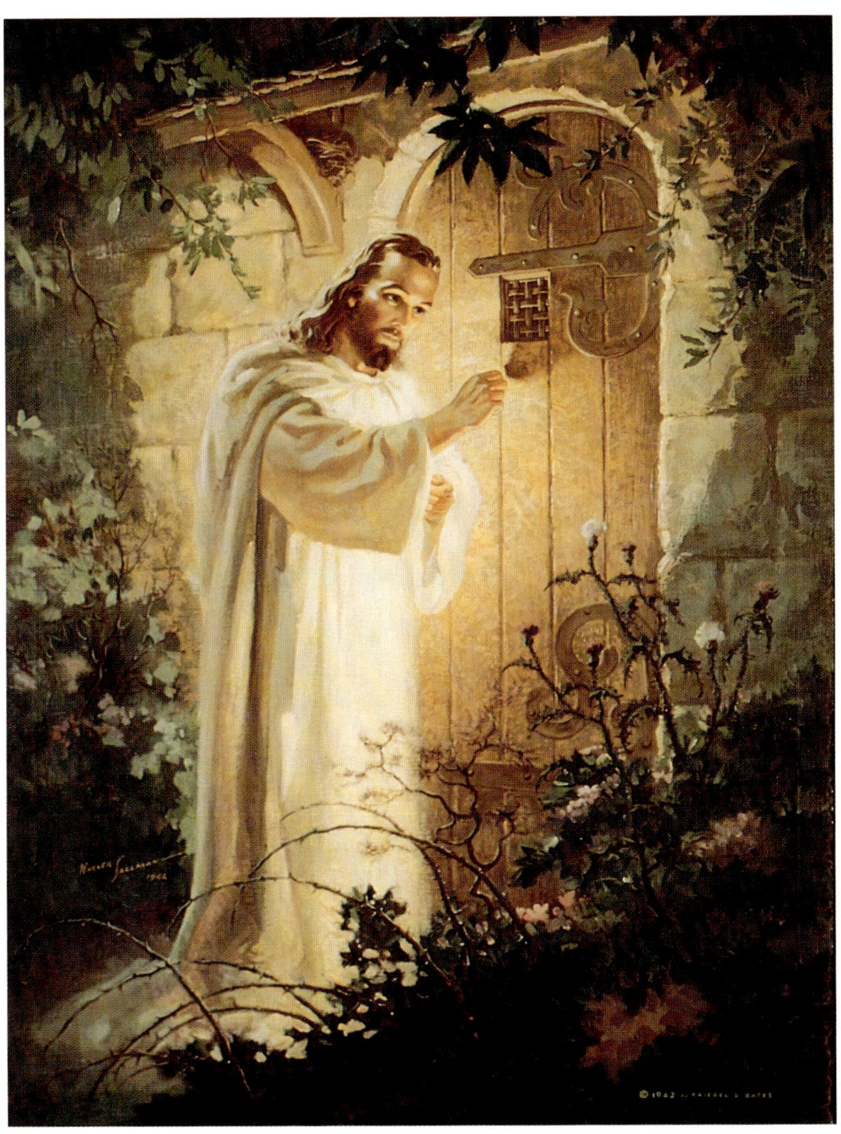

III. Warner Sallman, *Christ at Heart's Door*, 1942, oil on canvas,
40 × 30". Courtesy Jessie C. Wilson Galleries, Anderson University.

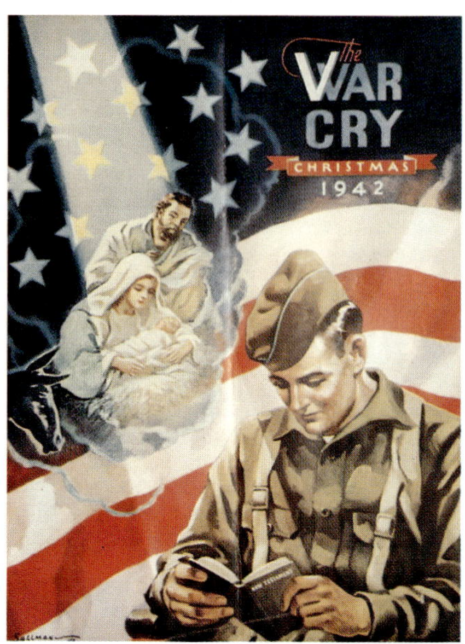

IV. Warner Sallman, *The Christmas Story*, 1942.
From *War Cry* (Christmas 1942), cover.
Courtesy The Salvation Army War Cry.

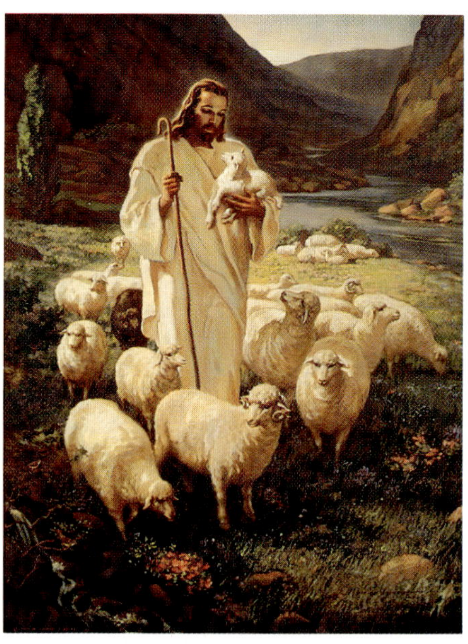

V. Warner Sallman, *The Lord Is My Shepherd*, 1943,
oil on canvas, 40 × 30".
Courtesy Jessie C. Wilson Galleries, Anderson University.

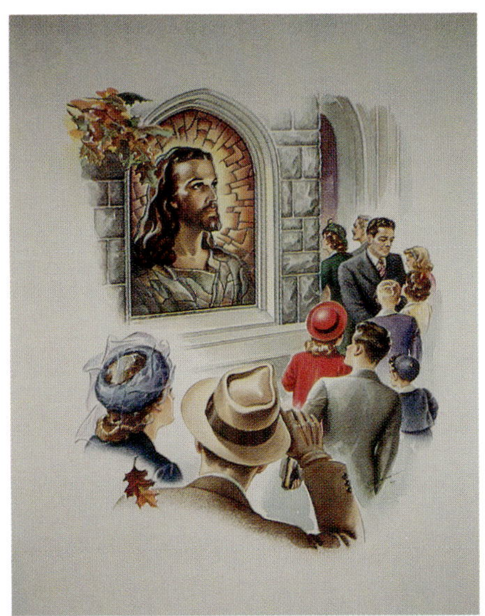

VI. Warner Sallman, *Let's Go to Church,* 1947,
watercolor, 29½ × 21½".
Courtesy Jessie C. Wilson Galleries, Anderson University.

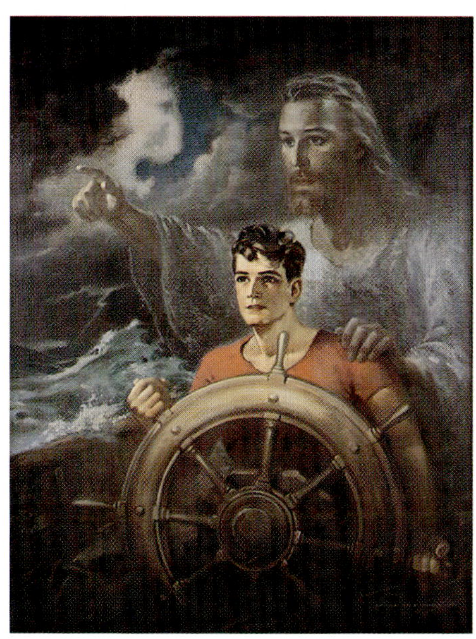

VII. Warner Sallman, *Christ Our Pilot,* 1950,
oil on canvas, 40 × 30".
Courtesy Jessie C. Wilson Galleries, Anderson University.

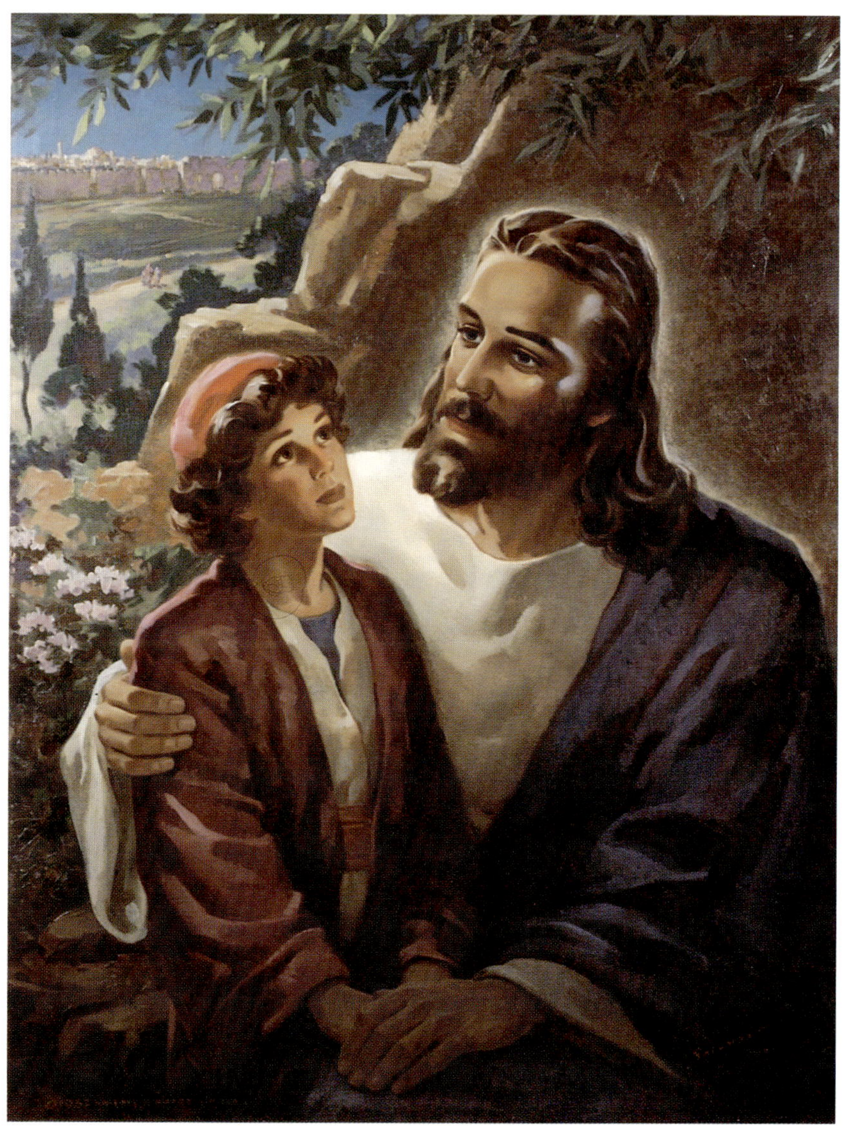

VIII. Warner Sallman, *Teach Me Thy Way*, 1951, oil on canvas,
40 × 30". Courtesy Jessie C. Wilson Galleries, Anderson University.

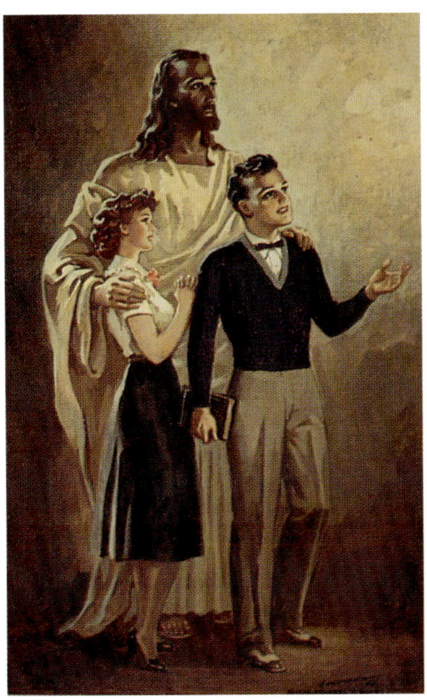

IX. Warner Sallman, *Ready to Go—Ready to Stay!*
1954, oil and collage on paper on board,
12¾ × 7⅞". Courtesy Jessie C. Wilson Galleries,
Anderson University.

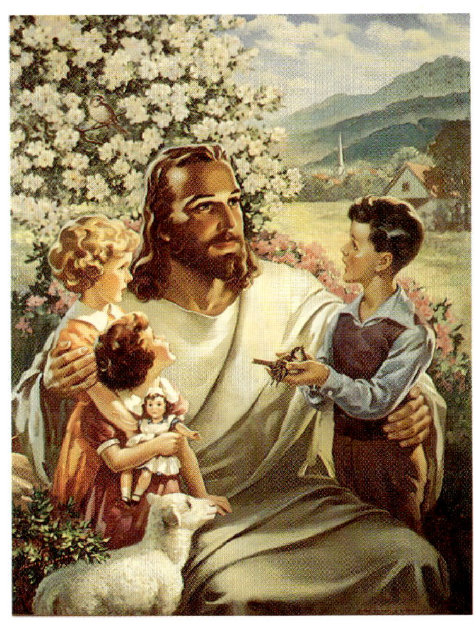

X. Warner Sallman, *He Careth for You*, 1954,
oil on canvas, 49¼ × 38". Courtesy
Jessie C. Wilson Galleries, Anderson University

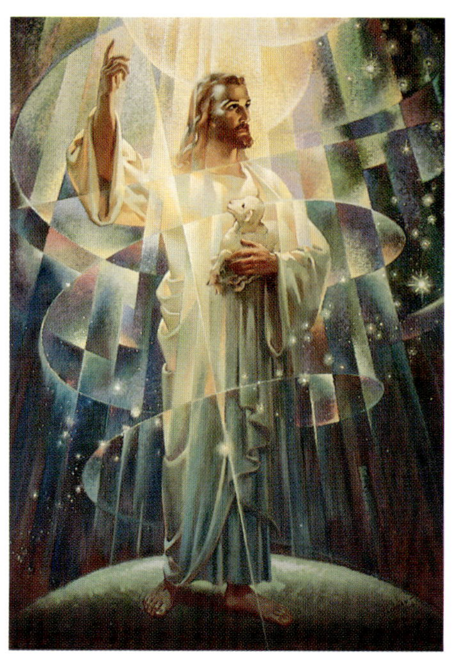

XI. Warner Sallman, *Power and Glory*, 1957,
oil on canvas, 83 1/3 × 55 1/2 ". Courtesy
Jessie C. Wilson Galleries, Anderson University.

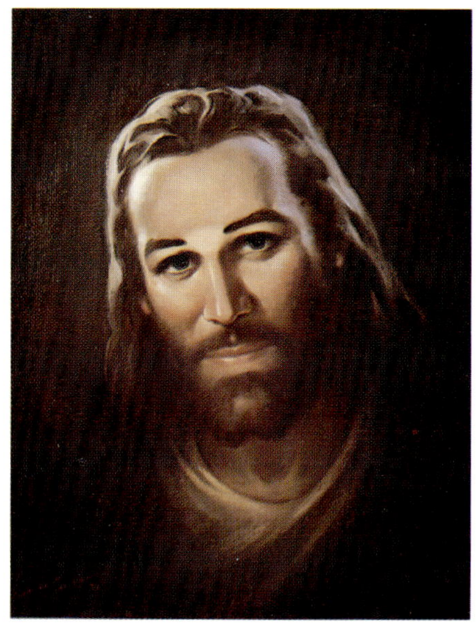

XII. Warner Sallman, *Portrait of Jesus*, 1966,
oil on canvas, 20 1/4 × 16 1/4". Courtesy
Jessie C. Wilson Galleries, Anderson University.

An unusual response from another member of the clergy represents an instance in which the image embodied the virtual presence of Jesus. Sharing a testimony of his call to the ministry, a Methodist preacher from Texas related that as a young man he attended a communion service one evening during Holy Week with two friends. The young man prayed to God for guidance in his life:

> LORD, THERE IS SOMETHING THAT YOU WANT ME TO DO, AND I CAN'T UNDERSTAND IT. PLEASE REVEAL IT TO ME. After we went and received the Communion I motion to the boys to go back into the pew. As I set there I looked at the picture [hanging in the church], if you notice the head and eyes are looking away from you. The head turn enough that the eyes looked straight at me and said, I WANT YOU TO BE MY MESSENGER. I WANT YOU TO BE FISHER OF MEN. LET GO AND I WILL DIRECT YOUR *HANDS, FEET, AND MOUTH.* YOU WILL BE MY WITNESS. It turn back just as we see it now never to turn again. We left the church and went our own ways. I did not tell my friends my experience that night. (78)[22]

This is comparable to an instance in 1993 when the image appeared to be more than an image. In Houston, an inexpensive reproduction of Sallman's *Head of Christ* allegedly secreted copious amounts of clear oil, an event that was documented on a television program called *Miracles and Other Wonders.* The image belongs to the family of a Coptic Christian boy who was miraculously cured of a form of leukemia at the same time that the picture in his bedroom began to seep oil.[23]

The final variety of likeness that characterizes a good deal of response to Sallman's art is what I call ideological-psychological likeness. By this I mean the tendency of the image of Jesus to corroborate or objectify the ideological expectation or the psychological need of a viewer.[24] Viewers find such an expectation or need fulfilled by the physical appearance of Christ in the picture. This is a subtle imaginative process, whereby physical likeness is transformed by an individual's or group's particular requirements. The effect is one of appropriation, or making an image of Jesus one's own: a correspondence is discerned between the picture and a mental image. This correspondence acts as a kind of corroboration, eliciting such comments as "This is the Christ as I have always wanted to see him" (67) or "the face of Christ as it should be!"[25] Such a Christ conforms to what he is ideologically presupposed to be or psychologically needed to be.[26]

Many people have found Sallman's Christ to look like Christ because they have needed at some moment to feel the benevolent presence of God in their lives. Many respondents recalled incidents from their childhood, which ranged from the mundane to the traumatic, during which Sallman's pictures provided comfort. One woman remembered the importance of the image for her when, as a seven-year-old, she was sleeping in a relative's home, alone in the room: "I would look at the picture and ask Jesus to keep me safe" (40). A mother related that a *Head of Christ* placed in the bedroom of her daughter helped the girl overcome the fear that the house might catch fire (32).[27] Another woman recalled the role that *Christ at Heart's Door* (pl. III) played in grim moments of her childhood: "It was a source of hope and peace in a home of alcoholism and abuse my mother received from a hurting, lost alcoholic man, my father. It hung in our dining room which I could see from my bedroom and [I] looked out on it often as I lay trying to go to sleep" (259). A woman who suffered repeated sexual abuse as a child related that the *Head of Christ* "helped to keep me sane in a world that felt very unsafe to me. After I spent hours praying for all the people who I was told would be hurt or killed if I told my secret, this picture would be the very last thing that I would look at before I closed my eyes. . . . Then I would dissociate out of my body and into the ceiling but somehow I felt that I could at least internalize the image of Jesus and that He, as I saw Him in the picture, was on the ceiling with me" (410). Others reported relying on the picture for protection and "leaning on" the image to "get me through a troubled time in my life" (323; 105). The apotropaic power of the image has been noted in natural and military perils. A man from southern California, for instance, believed that his Sallman painting conveyed God's benevolence when, during each of two earthquakes, the picture fell from the wall and landed upright without its glass cover having broken. "I've been truly blessed by that picture!" he concluded (193).

The image becomes an "authentic" likeness of Christ when it is adapted to the circumstances of those who require Christ's presence—either in solution to a crisis or, more commonly, as a formative force in their lives. The power of the image in the formation of Christian character—to make believers behave *like* Christ—has always been assumed by parents and educators in the church, who find a special place for the image among youth. Many have asserted that Sallman's image proactively shapes one's inner life into the likeness of Christ. In an article of 1947, Maurice Trimmer, a Baptist clergyman, argued that "we tend to grow like the pictures we live with; every person should have a worthy hero, an ideal in the flesh, someone whom he admires, looks up to, wants to be like."[28] Images have a persuasive consequence that is stronger than the "reason or the will." The reader is encouraged to place images in his or her environment that will produce proper "mental images." Trimmer's choice was Sallman's picture: "Just above my desk in my study is Sallman's magnificent picture, 'Head of Christ.' Its appeal to my imagination day by day refines, cleanses, edifies. Just to look at that noble countenance, which expresses character, sympathy, consecration, courage, composure, [and] devotion strengthens my spirit and purifies my soul" (p. 51). The ideal image that Christ represents for the faithful thus exhibits these characteristics in his very features. According to one respondent, the visual features of Sallman's Christ emit a "Holy radiance" and portray a similar list of desirable qualities: "righteousness, strength, power, reverence, respect, fairness, faithfulness, love, compassion" (274). In particular, these attributes are thought to be conveyed in the "way the hair in the image is highlighted in the back and [in the] highlights around the front of the head and face."

Sallman's picture of Christ acquires the theological or ideological commitments of the viewer in order to make a personal ideal visual. The image objectifies this ideal so that it might be encountered as objective and then internalized. A woman from Ohio remarked that the *Head of Christ* "is a constant reminder that my performance better be 'in line with' the picture's" (326). Like Trimmer, many people believe that images exert an autonomous influence on their viewers: "The pictures at which a person habitually looks play a prominent part in the formation of his concepts, in the molding of his character, and in the determination of his conduct. . . . Nothing is more important in the experience of youth than the kind of pictures they habitually see."[29] Children exposed to obscenity will be adversely affected: "Foul pictures pollute the minds, debauch the morals, and corrupt the characters of youth" and ultimately incite misconduct.

This search for Christ's likeness and the belief that suitable images imprint *like* attitudes and encourage appropriate behaviors suggest that for many the power of Sallman's image has consisted of its ability to cancel the difference that separates oneself from Christ. Believers feel that they are able to draw close to the Jesus who is portrayed. Yet this propensity goes beyond personal assimilation by seeking to cancel whatever differentiates *others*—one's children, one's fellows, or anyone outside of one's class, race, or nation—from oneself. The popular reception of Sallman's work reflected this concern for likeness and difference in the early 1960s, a time in American life when relations between the dominant culture, represented by white male Protestants, and all others became particularly divisive on such issues as race, gender, international relations, and countercultural and youth movements. Each of these posed a special threat of divisiveness to many conservative Protestants. Articles published in popular religious magazines during this time gathered together in an obviously didactic way several anecdotes concerning the power of Sallman's picture among nonwhites, non-Christians, and those exhibiting unacceptable behavior. We read of a white businessman, for instance, in a remote jungle, assaulted by a vicious group of headhunters who demand that he remove his clothes. In going through his billfold, they discover a small reproduction of Sallman's Christ, quickly apologize, then vanish "into the jungle without inflicting further harm."[30] A second article relates the story of the thief who aborted his misdeed when he saw the *Head of Christ* on a living room wall. Another tells of the conversion of a Jewish woman on her deathbed, when a hospital chaplain shows her Sallman's picture.[31] A Christian comic book depicts two American soldiers who befriended their Japanese captors by showing them a copy of the *Head of Christ*.[32] A second version of this story suggests that the American prisoners were able to convince the Japanese guards to surrender in part because of the salutary effect of the picture of Christ that had been sent to the Japanese from the United States before the war.[33]

The message in all such accounts was that Christ, visualized by Sallman, was the key to overcoming otherness. Jesus was everyone's friend and Lord, at work throughout the world, ultimately recognized by all. This was an important message in the context of international contention following World War II. The pocket version of the *Head of Christ* served as the principal icon in conservative political propaganda from evangelical quarters. Carl H. Duning, an Indiana businessman, pitted what he called card-carrying Christians against "card-carrying Communists." In a 1948 tract publicizing his Christ in Every Purse campaign of sending reproductions of the *Head of Christ* to U.S. soldiers, Duning called for an end to violence and a "turn to moral values."[34] "Peace," he wrote, "can come to us individually, to our communities, and to our national life by a recognition of the supremacy of moral force." The substitution of moral for military force, Duning claimed, would bring an end to the confusion caused by the war. The picture of Jesus would inspire a "closer communion with the Captain of our Salvation." Military rhetoric remained, reappropriated in the service of the Cold War ideal of a moral presence around the world.

The capacity of images to police the boundaries of difference, even to overwhelm them with the forces of good, is evident in *Power and Glory* (pl. XI), which represents the response of Sallman and his publisher to the Soviet threat of Sputnik in 1957. *Power and Glory,* dubbed Sputnik by employees of the publishing firm, shows a Caucasian Christ (the head of Jesus reproduced exactly from the 1940 portrait) posed like Caesar on top of the world.[35] Christ remains triumphant in a world of modern technology and Soviet achievement. Sallman mimicked modernist techniques of painting (futurist lines of force and the faceted geometry of cubism) to signify a space-age Jesus still very much in charge of the universe.

THE PRESENCE OF THE PERSONAL JESUS

The image's power among Protestants to shape likeness to Christ clearly contradicts the common assertion that images serve no purpose in Protestant piety. It also reveals that the strength of Sallman's *Head of Christ* for many Protestants (and non-Protestants) lies in its capacity to make visual, and therefore in some sense to embody, the personal savior, who "saves, comforts, and defends" them, to borrow a catechetical phrase. The image has allowed many to gaze on what they believe Jesus is like, not just physically but spiritually. Physical appearance becomes countenance, a manifestation of personality in the face. In this manner, Christ's personal significance for one's life is made visual: the face that one sees belongs to the divinity who cares *personally* for one's welfare. This visual personification of Christ clearly serves the evangelical imperative of a personal relationship with Jesus. Christ is encountered face-to-face.

Evidence of this encounter between viewer and picture and of what it means for individuals' piety abounds in the letters. "There is a warmth," a Lutheran pastor wrote, "and yet an enigmatic intensity about this portrayal of Christ which has always moved me. This is a 'person' I want to know" (20). Another writer discussed the interpersonal relations of the image: "I have studied the face many times. It is the softness of the eyes and the face. I picture what it would be like to talk to this person. I feel he would understand anything you would say to him and would answer in kindness and understanding. He would also be firm. I study this picture many times when I am troubled" (39). A member of the Methodist clergy noted how he and a friend in boot camp during World War II were struck by the *Head of Christ,* particularly by "its beauty and its meaning and its power to attract our attention" (22). Many found that the image commanded their attention in a way that required a personal response: "More than once I was completely captivated by the painting. Seems I could sit and look at it for the longest [time]" (71). A woman who "gave [her] life to Christ" while watching Sallman create his image at a chalk talk said, "When I look at it . . . I am reminded that Jesus Christ is my Lord and Savior. He died for me. Am I able to give my life for Him?" (63). Another woman wrote that the images "bring me close to my Saviour and Friend" (92). Many respondents found the notion of a friendly Christ important. As one man put it, "It's the Jesus that I love and know above all things, he's my friend. I can walk and talk with him. I know he cares for me and my family. And best of all he's real and alive" (216). In this passage occurs a phrase that probably derives from a well-known folk song cited by at least two respondents who found Sallman's image repugnant for the very reason that this man considered the image so meaningful: it evoked a sentimental intimacy with Jesus (2; 298). Written in 1912, *In the Garden* expresses the personal, indeed, even privatistic relation that American evangelical Christianity has made the center of its piety. Consider the first verse and refrain:

> I come to the garden alone
> While the dew is still on the roses;
> And the voice I hear,
> Falling on my ear;
> The Son of God discloses.
>
> And He walks with me,
> And He talks with me,

> And He tells me I am His own,
>
> And the joy we share as we tarry there,
>
> None other has ever known.[36]

The hymn evokes an intimate space in an enclosed garden in the early morning when no one else is about. This sequestered space is visualized in Sallman's work by the placement of Christ in garden settings and enclosures (see pls. II, III, VIII, and X and my discussion in Chapter 1), and serves as the site of Jesus' private revelation to the soul. Such appropriation of Jesus appeals directly to the individual by offering something that "none other has ever known." Robert Orsi reports the same response in Roman Catholic devotion to St. Jude: one informant told him that "in enjoying friendship with Saint Jude you feel an intimate personal feeling, almost like you are the only one praying to him."[37] Knowledge of the saint's favors is generally passed from person to person among friends and family members. Yet unlike the Catholic devotion to St. Jude—which includes an essential public component of visiting the shrine and writing votive letters to the shrine's magazine, *The Voice of St. Jude,* where they were often published—the Protestant veneration of Sallman's Christ often includes no public expression.[38]

Personal Protestantism, for lack of a better term, seems to rest on an intimate relation between the individual and the deity, a close, private, unique fit between one's need and God's power to fulfill that need. Likeness in this sense means assimilation, or the inclination of both viewer and image toward one another. This likeness can be conceived as optical, as in the case of one writer who noted a resemblance between Sallman's Christ and photographs of her father as a young man (24), or it can consist of the feeling of affection toward the image: people like it, in other words, because of how it makes them feel. "It gives me a sense of peace and calmness whenever I look at it, and a feeling of someone protecting me and a person I can talk to anytime of the day" (105). A Lutheran woman explained it this way: "Being able to have some kind of image of Christ makes it much easier to pray to Him, feel a kindred spirit with Him, and turn to Him in times of trouble. This face also makes Christ look calm and ever-patient, strong of will and determined. It takes away the 'abstract' and substitutes a 'tangible'" (254). Another Lutheran was thankful that a "picture of my Lord helped me have a more personal relationship with Him, with God" (24). Yet another respondent related that the *Head of Christ* was the "first image in my memory associated with Jesus as a person. . . . That image was a personification to me of someone who was otherwise an abstract being" (230). Most people experience this personal presence as a comforting, reassuring feeling of God's concern for their lives. A Methodist church worker from North Carolina stated that the Christ of Sallman's picture "appears to be so very human and such an excellent listener as well as a very compassionate person" (146). The emphasis placed on friendship with Christ by many of Sallman's admirers characterizes the Christian faith as a relationship with Jesus that serves as an ever-present source of solace and encouragement. Sallman's picture visualizes the evangelical cult of friendship with Jesus, praised by generations of believers in a well-known nineteenth-century hymn:

> What a Friend we have in Jesus,
> All our sins and griefs to bear!
> What a privilege to carry
> Everything to God in prayer!
> O what peace we often forfeit,
> O what needless pain we bear,
> All because we do not carry
> Everything to God in prayer![39]

Viewers see in the image of Jesus what they need to find there. They are able to personalize the image in a number of ways. This process involves speaking or praying to it, meditating on it, carrying it with them daily, even displaying it prominently in the home or workplace in order to be able to talk to others about Jesus. And when they do, they often address the picture as Jesus rather than as an image of him. This slippage between sign and referent is precisely what brings the image to life for the individual. The measure of Christ's personal friendship is his constant presence, something made more palpable in the image itself.

NEGATIVE RESPONSE AND THE CASE AGAINST LIKENESS: ICONOPHOBIA, ICONOCLASM, AND THE MASCULINITY OF JESUS

Although many see in Sallman's *Head of Christ* a reflection of their own experience or likeness, others have summarily dismissed the image for the difference they see separating the Christ they espouse from the one they find visualized in Sallman's pictures. Current and long-standing objections to the Sallman corpus, particularly to the *Head of Christ,* fall into six general categories and echo objections to Sallman's work that have appeared in the religious and secular press since the late 1940s. Respondents found the work offensive because it was (1) ethnically and culturally inaccurate; (2) theologically misinformed or scripturally proscribed; (3) racist; (4) effeminate; (5) homoerotic; or (6) any one or several of the following: sweet, weak, soft, anemic, sentimental, or syrupy. For some writers the last three categories (effeminate, homoerotic, and sweet, etc.) were synonymous. Each of these kinds of response stresses explicitly how *unlike* the image is to a respondent's ideological, theological, or psychological expectations of who Jesus was and what he looked like.

A large number of negative responses came from those who regarded Sallman's image of Jesus as ethnically inaccurate. Most considered the image inappropriately Caucasian, even Anglo-Saxon or Nordic (2, 170, 179). These writers insisted that Jesus be depicted as a Jewish man in ancient Palestine or in a way that conformed to their ideological view of Jesus. One woman, a member of the United Church of Christ, expressed a strong preference for an alternative to Sallman's picture: In the early 1980s, "there was a picture in the kids' books of Jesus—a dark-complexion man with black curly hair (short) and beard, wearing knee-length shorts and a simple T-shirt and sandals. Immediately I had to acknowledge that this image of Jesus was a more accurate portrayal of him than the well-known Sallman head of Christ—a pale, soft wavy-haired likeness of any handsome European man or a white American" (29). Likeness here was conceived as conformity to a preference for contemporary appearances, a Christ made relevant to children by virtue of the fashion of current youth culture. The likeness of Christ was determined by rhetorical style. The assumption seems to be that a Christ who relates directly to children by means of dress and appearance is more Christ-like. This mother, however, could not locate a copy of this image of Jesus, so she replaced her Sallman with a picture she described as "akin to an African-American." This was not, as she called it, the "exact answer" but would suffice until she found something like the Christ she had seen in her children's books.

For many viewers Sallman's depiction is baldfaced ethnocentrism. One writer objected strongly to what she saw as "just one more tragic example of the ethnocentricity of many Christians. How many people of color can relate to this picture? Jesus himself was a Jew and not a fair-skinned, blue-eyed person in all likelihood. Let's tell it like it is!" (160). Indeed, respondents who indicated their race as of African descent were unambiguously opposed to the image on racial grounds (77, 167, 373, 420, 451).[40] One such writer insisted that "All Africans in America" should remove the Sallman image from their places of worship (167), a move that the Reverend George Stallings provocatively undertook with his public destruction of pictures of an Anglo Jesus (see fig. 5.10), including a copy of Sallman's *Head of Christ*. In 1994 and 1995 African-Americans, among others in Charlotte, North Carolina, publicly objected to the display of Sallman's painting in local YMCAs on the grounds that the image failed to depict Christ as a person of color. YMCA officials replied that Sallman's *Head of Christ* hung in churches with members of many races, but they proposed to display with the image at each site a statement acknowledging that Christ was a "dark-skinned man of Jewish descent."[41] Yet, among respondents to my query, those whose names indicated Hispanic or East Indian background admired the image (41, 33, 19). But these samples were extremely small and therefore of no statistical significance.

For other writers ethnocentricity became idolatry. Because Jesus was a Jew, one Lutheran man reasoned, an artist should "consider portraying him as a Jew lest we . . . end up falling into the error of creating a graven image because we want to praise our own national and racial bias over and against praising" the savior of humanity (280). Another writer objected to the extreme popularity of Sallman's Anglo-Saxon Christ. When one image becomes so dominant, she argued, the impression arises "that it is an accurate, literal picture of Jesus, like a photograph" (170). She considered this dangerous because it focused on the historical Jesus at the expense of the universal, timeless Christ. "In effect," she concluded, "we make this portrayal of Jesus into an idol." The false likeness created by the ubiquity of Sallman's picture is photographic and therefore idolatrous: the picture becomes the veritable image, the true icon that raises a particular view to universal status.

The greatest number of complaints about Sallman's image were theological. Idolatry was the most frequent charge—either because of an implicit ethnocentric claim of Anglo superiority or because Scripture proscribes the creation and use of images of God in worship, prayer, or devotion. These two claims of idolatry generally were made by people who fall into two opposing theological camps: conservative and fundamentalist Protestants who reject images per se, and more liberal Protestants who regard Sallman's images as an instance of cultural accommodation. Both acknowledged the power of images to form character and direct worship, and therefore approached the use of images with great seriousness. A Lutheran woman wrote that "Christ is in our heart, not visions" (240). She insisted that "no images of Christ anywhere [are] authentic." She further contended that visual images are especially misleading to children and recalled an incident from her own youth when she was frightened by a reproduction of Sallman's *Christ at Heart's Door* in her family's Bible: "Since I couldn't read I thought he was the devil trying to carry me off if he got in." Without the anchor of the accompanying text, the image could be made into whatever the child wanted. Many Protestants believe that this power of images to generate meanings, in a way that textual codes preempt by virtue of their specificity, must be controlled. Such iconophobia is certainly implicit in the stark contrast that many Protestant respondents drew between biblical word and visual image. Many stressed that Sallman's picture was "only an artist's conception" and could not bear any direct relation to the appearance of the historical Jesus. Many went so far as to quote, misquote, or paraphrase a variety of scriptural texts that they believed demonstrated the unrepresentability of Christ: 2 Corinthians 5:7: "For we walk by faith, not by sight" (303); John 4:24: "God is a Spirit: and they that worship Him must worship Him in spirit and truth" (211); 1 John 4:12: "No one has ever seen God for he is a spirit" (180); Galatians 3:28: "There is neither Jew nor Greek, slave nor free, male nor female (black nor white), for you are all one in Christ Jesus" (280). In contrast to the claims for the historical accuracy of Sallman's image, other respondents found the picture inaccurate when judged from scriptural evidence: Isaiah 53:2, understood as a prophetic description of the messiah, states that "he . . . had no beauty that we should desire him" (303) and 1 Corinthians 11:14 states that it is degrading for a man to have long hair (303, 278, 433).

Citation of the second commandment (Exodus 20:4–5) among respondents followed the traditional exegeses of Luther and Calvin, who split on their explanation of the Exodus text. Luther took the proscription of all images in the fourth verse to be modified by the fifth verse's specific application of any image to worship. Therefore, depictions of Christ or God the Father were acceptable as long as they were not worshiped. Calvin, in contrast, read the biblical text as a strict proscription of any image of the deity.[42] Accordingly, respondents could cite the second commandment against any image of God whatsoever (211) or against only the idolatrous use of images: "To my understanding, the picture 'Head of Christ,' when placed where people look at it when praying or worshipping God, is a graven image and we are doing or encouraging what we are told in the commandment NOT to do" (202). Other letter writers insisted that Sallman's picture remained a "work of art" and a "good wall picture" (211, 180). As art, it posed no danger. Iconophobia, or the fear of images, arises in some Protestants when the image is made visible during worship or prayer and itself, as the focus of vision, is taken for the object of worship. The mind is captured by what the eye sees. To have the image present is to risk mistaking it for what it only represents.

"Would JESUS have sat for a portrait?" one respondent asked (65). "I don't think HE would have. HE wasn't vain, HE was without sin." The assertion that the use of images is vanity, the product of human pride, links this modern Methodist man with the Reformation heritage of iconoclasm. As I discussed in the Introduction, Calvin attributed the use of pictures in churches to human hubris and argued that it was an insult to God, "corporeal images" being unworthy of divine majesty.[43] God must remain free of the human mind, that "perpetual forge of idols," radically other, exalted, transcendent, sublime—visually unrepresentable.[44] God is like no other. To suggest otherwise by making him appear in the likeness of a human being is to insult the majesty and glory of God. This accommodation to human needs creates idols by removing the vaunted distance between God and humanity. Humanity's submission as impotent, fearful, and unworthy before God is exchanged for one of power over God. For this reason, Calvin asserted that images "diminish reverential fear and encourage error."[45]

Opponents of Sallman's images will certainly find abundant evidence of the psychological accommodation of Christ in the responses that we have previously examined. A great deal of the Protestant critique of culture from Calvin to H. Richard Niebuhr represents an attempt to secure theology from such accommodation. But those who respond negatively to Sallman's work exhibit their own rhetorical configuration of divinity, which must be included in our analysis if we are to arrive at a fuller understanding of the anatomy of response.

Prominent in the negative reception is a rhetoric of the sublime deity that reveals a gendered conception of God. The record of negative response to Sallman's art is clear that the sublime, untouchable, unrepresentable, disembodied, impersonal, and universal God of Calvin and latter-day Protestant iconoclasts is unambiguously male. Favorite epithets for Sallman's depictions of Christ are *pretty, sweet, weak, soft, anemic, sentimental, syrupy,* and *effeminate.* All these contrast markedly with the masculine rhetoric of the sublime that many used to denounce Sallman's work. A clergyman wrote that this "namby-pamby Christ" was not equal to the prophetic tradition of social justice in the Jewish Scriptures or the words of judgment found in Matthew 25, where Christ condemned to hell those who failed to love him through their service to others (43). A writer who objected that Sallman's picture of Jesus substituted "one person's impression of Jesus" for the "Christ who is timeless and omnipresent . . . and who cannot be limited to any one physical form," stated the case for most antagonists: Sallman's picture "portrays Christ as sweet, insipid, bland, passive, and pretty, rather than as a strong, active person whose earthly existence was in an earthy, primitive (by our standards) culture and whose mission was (and still is) to change the world" (170).

Occasionally the response is even more intensely gendered. In such instances revulsion at the image is directed against the emasculation of Jesus. This is the claim of one respondent, a self-described five-point Calvinist who referred to the image as effete: "This is a Jesus who would be aghast if you tied your shoes wrong. If our Lord had been anything like the man in this portrait, Galilean fishermen and publicans would have given him a sound thrashing rather than following him, which only a handful of spiritual masochists would have done" (190).[46] A United Church of Christ clergyman told a group of colleagues at a pastoral conference in Nebraska that some of his fellow clergy "couldn't have Sallman's portrait of Christ in their churches because the finely spun hair of Christ as portrayed in the painting was too much of a come-on for the homos in the parish and the community. These pastors felt Sallman had made Christ much too effeminate" (331). A Methodist clergyman also worried about gay association with the image: "With the Culture Wars heating up, and homosexuality emerging as the point issue, this Head of Christ may prove a considerable embarrassment, given the *popular* image of the homosexual" (2). Whatever that image might be, this writer was clearly worried that Sallman's picture was a compelling visualization of it, which Christians, given the picture's popularity, would find hard to explain to non-Christians and perhaps to gays who wished to be officially recognized as gay within the fellowship of the church.

Homophobia, like iconophobia, is a fear of likeness, a fear of emasculating God, of denying to the divinity the manhood that distinguishes "him" from humanity and creation. The rhetoric of the sublime seeks to preserve this difference. This view depends on the assumption, clearly laid out in Calvin's doctrine of God, that humans can revere only a divinity whose power infinitely exceeds theirs, before whom they are submissive and impotent. This notion of power, because it accommodates the patriarchy in American culture, will inevitably demand that women and homosexuals, historically the powerless or those who must conceal their difference, are not like God. Any image that suggests such a likeness will be suspect, idolatrous, and denounced as an accommodation to culture or psychology.

The image of Christ thus inevitably becomes like those whose faith it is appropriated to assist, whether they seek the comfort of a friend or maternal figure, or the inspiration of a sublime hero. Response to Sallman's imagery suggests that charges of cultural accommodation cut both ways. Negative response is motivated by a deep opposition to what these respondents consider the image to represent: the domestic Christianity of women. One critic likened the Sallman picture to the Precious Moments figurines sold in greeting-card stores (298). Such gifts are typically purchased by women for women for the purpose of display in the home.[47] Further, the frequent observation that Sallman's Christ is effeminate—a remark made largely by men, and by male clergy in particular—is revealing when we consider that Sallman's pictures are used predominantly in the home, whose decoration and daily care has traditionally been the domain of women. Significantly, female respondents to the query in this investigation outnumbered male respondents by a factor of two to one. In short, what many of Sallman's critics may resent in the image is an icon of feminine Christianity: a "sentimentalization" of a lofty Christ as the personalized, intimate Jesus of popular strains of conservative Christianity. The nurturing, "effeminate" Jesus that many see in Sallman's pictures of Christ reminds them of a religion dominated by women: their mothers, aunts, grandmothers, and most Sunday school teachers.[48] They oppose to this a sublime Christ. As undeniable as it is unsurprising, Sallman's detractors, no less than his admirers, assimilate their deity to a cultural construction. But for the many more male respondents who cherish the *Head of Christ,* men who do not discern anything effeminate about the depiction but rather see a Jesus who is both manly and accessible, it would appear that Christ as both friend and virile man makes Christianity safe for men, secures it as a domain where male power and nurturing, authority and intimacy are possible. This no doubt appeals to many wives and mothers within conservative Christianity for whom the family and the formation of youth are well served by a visual interpretation of Jesus that stresses both authority and intimacy, and does so in a way that lends itself to display and devotion in the home.

Judging from the appearance of Sallman's *Head of Christ* in the media during the 1990s, the relevance of the picture for many Christians is no longer Christ's masculinity.[49] Instead, Sallman's image of Jesus has reaffirmed two themes in its previous popular reception: deliverance from personal illnesses and deliverance from cultural ones. In tabloid print and television Sallman's and similar religious imagery has been linked to miraculous appearances and to a cure for such ailments as cancer and depression.[50] Moreover, in a much publicized court case in Michigan, in which the American Civil Liberties Union charged that a public high school violated the First Amendment's establishment clause by displaying the *Head of Christ,* the image was regarded by supporters as a symbol of political opposition to secularism and an intrusive federal government in the culture war between Left and Right.[51]

The Jesus sought by believers during the fin de siècle appears to be a healer and an icon of old-time religion. Sallman's most well known images have been issued as collectible plates, perhaps in the attempt to capitalize on the nostalgia of a graying American populace at the end of the twentieth century.[52] Given the continuities with evangelical needs earlier in the century, the *Head of Christ* seems to envision the Jesus whom many seek, which suggests that Warner Sallman's Jesus may enjoy the light of a new millennium.

APPENDIX:

SOURCE MATERIAL

Throughout 1993, seventy-three religious publications of diverse confessional and denominational affiliation or orientation were contacted with the request to advertise a query for information concerning readers' responses to the art of Warner Sallman. The sample was selected almost entirely from the listing of religious periodicals in the United States compiled in Kenneth Bedell and Alice M. Jones, eds., *Yearbook of American and Canadian Churches 1992* (Nashville: Abingdon Press, 1992), 231–42. Some of my colleagues suggested a few other periodicals. The ones that were queried broke down as follows: 2 African-American, 6 Baptist, 5 Church of God, 10 Roman Catholic, 12 Pentecostal, 4 Lutheran, 5 Methodist, 10 Fundamentalist, 1 Mormon, 1 Salvation Army, 5 Evangelical, 1 Reformed, 2 Presbyterian, 2 Nazarene, 2 Disciples of Christ, 2 Church of Christ, 1 Evangelical Free, 1 Liberal Protestant, and 1 Evangelical Covenant. At least five additional sources—one publication (Church of God in Christ) and church bulletins or newsletters (Presbyterian, Independent, Methodist, and United Church of Christ)—ran the advertisement without having been contacted. Only twenty of those contacted agreed to run the ad.

The ad consisted of a small black-and-white reproduction of Sallman's *Head of Christ* and a variation on the following text: "Do you know this picture? A group of scholars is studying the role this image and others by the artist Warner Sallman (including 'Christ at Heart's Door,' 'The Good Shepherd,' and 'Christ in Gethsemane') have played in the lives of Christians. Does Sallman's *Head of Christ* or any other of his works hang in your home, school or church? What has the imagery meant for your devotions, worship, prayer, family or friends? Please send response to David Morgan [with my address]."

A total of 531 responses were received. They have been numbered in order of receipt and deposited in the archives of the Jessie C. Wilson Galleries of Anderson University, Anderson, Indiana, where they may be consulted according to the letter number to which I refer in the text.

Approximately 20 of the 531 letters were received in response to local and national press on the Sallman project in the spring of 1994 from readers of newspapers and the audience of a Chicago radio station (WMBI,

FM 90.1). An article on the project in the *Chicago Tribune* of March 4, 1994, was placed on the Associated Press wire service and subsequently appeared in several papers around the country.

The following information will offer some analysis of the raw data, although I hasten to point out that these statistics are not intended as quantitatively rigorous. They provide general features of the responses and the respondents.

Gender of respondents: Of the 531 responses, 168 correspondents were identifiable by name or other indication as men, and 351 as women.

Positive versus negative responses: 61 respondents (11.6 percent of the respondents who expressed an opinion) expressed a negative opinion of Sallman's work. Of the unfavorable responses, 30 percent were from male clergy; none were from female clergy. Men wrote 60 percent of the unfavorable responses, and women wrote 72 percent of the favorable responses. Of the favorable responses, 15 percent came from people who identified themselves as clergy.

The average age of correspondents who identified their age or provided reliable means for doing so (such as date of graduation from high school) was 59. Among these respondents, the youngest was 17 and the oldest 93. Of the 93 respondents who indicated their age, only 14 indicated an age of less than 40, and 59 respondents indicated that their age was 55 or older. An additional 113 respondents provided enough information to determine that their age was over 50 (i.e., by indicating years of marriage, number and age of children or grandchildren, or number of years retired). Of this group, 33 appeared to be over 65. This raises the average age of the respondents into the 60s, which corresponds meaningfully to the date of Sallman's art: in the early 1940s many of the respondents would have been in their late teens or early 20s; in other words, they were the generation that fought in World War II and matured in the postwar, baby boom years.

Confessional affiliation: 128 respondents either identified themselves as Methodist or responded to the ad placed in the *United Methodist Reporter,* 99 identified themselves as Lutheran or responded to the ad in *Lutheran Witness* or *Lutheran Partners,* 20 identified themselves as Roman Catholic, 21 identified the evangelical *Christian Reader* as the source of their response, 17 identified the fundamentalist *Christian Standard* as the

source of their response, 27 identified themselves as Seventh Day Ad-
ventists or responded to the ad placed in (Adventist) *Signs of the Times,* 14
identified themselves as members of the Evangelical Covenant Church
or responded to the ad placed in the *Covenant Companion,* 14 identified
themselves as Baptist or responded to the ad placed in the (Baptist)
Beacon, 10 identified the *Christian Century* as the source of their response,
6 identified themselves as Mormon, 5 identified themselves as members
of the Church of God, 5 as members of the Church of the Nazarene, 4 as
Presbyterian, 3 as Anglican, and 2 as Disciples of Christ. I have not listed
church affiliation that only occurred once, nor have I included those who
did not identify a confessional affiliation.

Notes

Introduction

1. For a select variety of examples see the following: Paul DiMaggio, "Market Structure, the Creative Process, and Popular Culture: Toward an Organizational Reinterpretation of Mass-Culture Theory," *Journal of Popular Culture* 11, no. 2 (Fall 1977), 436–52; the many essays in *The Culture of Consumption: Critical Essays in American History, 1880–1980,* ed. Richard Wightman Fox and T. J. Jackson Lears (New York: Pantheon Books, 1983); Neil Harris, *Cultural Excursions: Marketing Appetites and Cultural Tastes in Modern America* (Chicago: University of Chicago Press, 1990); Janice A. Radway, *Reading the Romance: Women, Patriarchy, and Popular Literature* (Chapel Hill: University of North Carolina Press, 1984); Karal Ann Marling, *As Seen on TV: The Visual Culture of Everyday Life in the 1950s* (Cambridge: Harvard University Press, 1994); Patricia Anderson, *The Printed Image and the Transformation of Popular Culture, 1790–1860* (Oxford: Clarendon Press, 1991); Miriam Formanek-Brunell, *Made to Play House: Dolls and the Commercialization of American Girlhood, 1830–1930* (New Haven: Yale University Press, 1993).

2. Several studies approach religious images as part of American material culture or the history of popular culture: Colleen McDannell, *The Christian Home in Victorian America, 1840–1940* (Bloomington: Indiana University Press, 1986); James R. Curtis, "Miami's Little Havana: Yard Shrines, Cult Religion and Landscape," in *Rituals and Ceremonies in Popular Culture,* ed. Ray B. Browne (Bowling Green: Bowling Green University Popular Press, 1980), 105–19; Sally M. Promey, *Spiritual Spectacles: Vision and Image in Mid-Nineteenth-Century Shakerism* (Bloomington: Indiana University Press, 1993); David Morgan, "Imaging Protestant Piety: The Icons of Warner Sallman," *Religion and American Culture: A Journal of Interpretation* 3, no. 1 (Winter 1993), 29–47.

3. For consideration of this response see Chapter 5 of this volume.

4. See discussion in Doreen M. Rosman, *Evangelicals and Culture* (London and Canberra: Croom Helm, 1984), 147–48; and John Dillenberger, *The Visual Arts and Christianity in America: From the Colonial Period to the Present,* expanded edition (New York: Crossroad, 1989), 1–20, 39–56.

5. Karl Barth, *The Humanity of God* (Richmond: John Knox Press, 1960), 57.

6. Martin Luther, *Against the Heavenly Prophets in the Matter of Images and Sacraments* (1525), Luther's Works, American Edition, ed. Jaroslav Pelikan, vol. 40 (St. Louis: Concordia Publishing House; Philadelphia: Muhlenberg Press, 1958), 92.

7. Carl C. Christensen, *Art and the Reformation in Germany* (Athens: Ohio University Press; Detroit: Wayne State University Press, 1979), 110.

8. Luther, *Against the Heavenly Prophets,* 99, 86.

9. I depend on the excellent study of Zwingli by Charles Garside, Jr., *Zwingli and the Arts* (New Haven: Yale University Press, 1966). On hearing versus seeing in Zwingli see p. 175.

10. Ibid., 92–93.

11. Quoted in Garside, *Zwingli and the Arts,* 178.

12. Ibid., 171. On Zwingli's spiritualism in relation to his view of images see Sergiusz Michalski, *The Reformation and the Visual Arts: The Protestant Image Question in Western and Eastern Europe* (London: Routledge, 1993), 51–59.

13. John Calvin, *Institutes of the Christian Religion,* trans. Henry Beveridge (Grand Rapids, Mich.: Eerdmans, 1962), chap. 11, 90–103.

14. Ibid., 94; cf. Barth, *Humanity of God.*

15. For an instructive discussion of depictions of God the Father from the late medieval period to William Blake and nineteenth-century Romantic painters see Adolf Krücke, "Der Protestantismus und die bildliche Darstellung Gottes," *Zeitschrift für Kunstwissenschaft* 12 (1958), 59–90.

16. Calvin, *Institutes,* 100.

17. Plato, *The Republic of Plato,* trans. Francis Macdonald Cornford (London: Oxford University Press, 1945), 10.602.

18. Calvin, *Institutes,* 94.

19. Ibid., 97.

20. Hans Belting, *Likeness and Presence: A History of the Image Before the Era of Art,* trans. Edmund Jephcott (Chicago: University of Chicago Press, 1994), 459–70.

21. Ibid., 467–68.

22. On popular use of print imagery in the Reformation see R. W. Scribner, *For the Sake of Simple Folk: Popular Propaganda for the German Reformation* (Oxford: Clarendon Press, 1981).

23. For a superb bibliography see Linda B. Parshall and Peter W. Parshall, *Art and the Reformation: An Annotated Bibliography,* Reference Publications in Art History (Boston: G. K. Hall, 1986), esp. 99–144, "Text Illustration and Printed Propaganda."

24. See *1472–1553 Lucas Cranach D. Ä. Das gesamte graphische Werk,* intro. Johannes Jahn (Herrsching, Germany: Manfred Pawlak Verlagsgesellschaft mbH, 1972), figs. 429–41, for examples of Cranach's book illustration for Luther's work.

25. For images of Luther by Cranach et al. see *1472–1553 Lucas Cranach D. Ä. Das gesamte graphische Werk,* figs. 207, 405, 442, 665–66, 670, 672, 694–95, 777. For seventeenth-century woodcut images of Luther see Dorothy Alexander with Walter L. Strauss, *The German Single-Leaf Woodcut 1600–1700: A Pictorial Catalogue* (New York: Abaris Books, 1977), 1: 135, 140, 188, 400; 2: 567, 617, 618.

26. Hans Belting, *The Image and Its Public in the Middle Ages: Form and Function of Early Paintings of the Passion,* trans. Mark Bartusis and Raymond Meyer (New Rochelle, N.Y.: Aristide D. Caratzas, 1990); for a study of the iconography of the face in non-Western popular visual culture see W. H. McLeod, *Popular Sikh Art* (Dehli: Oxford University Press, 1991).

27. Tessa Watt, *Cheap Print and Popular Piety, 1550–1640* (Cambridge: Cambridge University Press, 1991), 137.

28. Reproduced in Watt, *Cheap Print and Popular Piety,* 233.

29. For a discussion of Mede's chart and its meaning see Katharine R. Firth, *The Apocalyptic Tradition in Reformation Britain, 1530–1645* (Oxford: Oxford University Press, 1979), 213–24.

30. On the Millerites and for several examples of their visual culture see Ronald L. Numbers and Jonathan M. Butler, eds., *The Disappointed: Millerism and Millenarianism in the Nineteenth Century* (Bloomington: Indiana University Press, 1987).

31. On the Millerite aversion to pictorial representation see the brief notice "End of the World," *Signs of the Times* 5, no. 10 (May 10, 1843), 76.

32. Keith Moxey has discussed the discursivity of the sixteenth-century German woodcut in *Peasants, Warriors, and Wives: Popular Imagery in the Reformation* (Chicago: University of Chicago Press, 1989), 128–29.

33. See Alexander and Strauss, *German Single-Leaf Woodcut,* 1: 178, 162, 143; 2: 588, 621, 668.

34. See ibid. for numerous examples.

35. See Margaret T. Hills, ed., *The English Bible in America: A Bibliography of Editions of the Bible and the New Testament Published in America, 1777–1957* (New York: American Bible Society and New York Public Library, 1962).

36. Julius Schnorr von Carolsfeld, *Die Bibel in Bildern* (Leipzig: Georg Wigand Verlag, 187?).

37. *The Doré Bible Illustrations,* intro. Millicent Rose (New York: Dover, 1974).

38. Millicent Rose, "Introduction to the Dover Edition," in *Doré Bible Illustrations,* vi.

39. Rev. Ingram Cobbin, *Cobbin's Commentary on the Bible for Young and Old,* ed. Rev. E. J. Goodspeed (New York: Selmar Hess, 1876); Edward Eggleston, D.D., *Christ in Art: The Story of the Words and Acts of Jesus Christ* (New York: J. B. Ford, 1875).

40. This image is one in a long line of commemorative portraits of Luther, which show him standing resolutely, holding the Bible, gazing out, and often accompanied by a chronology of important dates in his life. See Alexander and Strauss, *German Single-Leaf Woodcut,* 1: 135, 140. For an excellent examination of nineteenth-century popular lithographs and their production and commerce see Peter C. Marzio, *The Democratic Art: Chromolithography, 1840–1900. Pictures for a Nineteenth-Century America* (Boston: David R. Godine, 1979).

41. R. Laurence Moore, *Selling God: American Religion in the Marketplace of Culture* (New York: Oxford University Press, 1994).

42. For a fascinating study of this development see Leigh Eric Schmidt, "The Commercialization of the Calendar: American Holidays and the Culture of Consumption, 1870–1930," *Journal of American History* 78, no. 3 (December 1991), 887–916, esp. 890; also T. J. Jackson Lears, "From Salvation to Self-Realization: Advertising and the Therapeutic Roots of the Consumer Culture, 1880–1930," in *The Culture of Consumption: Critical Essays in American History, 1880–1980,* ed. Richard Wightman Fox and T. J. Jackson Lears (New York: Pantheon Books, 1983), 1–38.

43. Moore, *Selling God,* 76.

44. See William Waits's discussion of the decision among Americans in the first decades of the twentieth century to substitute for more costly and useful items the inexpensive simplicity

and convenience of greeting cards as a suitable gift between friends, in *The Modern Christmas in America: A Cultural History of Gift Giving* (New York: New York University Press, 1993), 70–79.

45. Quoted in Garside, *Zwingli and the Arts,* 172.

46. Roland Barthes, "The Photographic Message" (1961), reprinted in *The Responsibility of Forms,* trans. Richard Howard (Berkeley: University of California Press, 1991), 3–20; see also "The Rhetoric of the Image," in *Responsibility of Forms,* 21–40.

47. See Chapter 6, which examines this kind of common statement in the popular reception of Sallman's *Head of Christ.*

48. In his otherwise stimulating study of sixteenth-century woodcuts, Keith Moxey has claimed that "as a sign system," the work of art is "wholly determined and shaped by the culture in which it has currency" (*Peasants, Warriors, and Wives,* 6). Not only does this insistence on determinism reintroduce the very positivism that Moxey rightly seeks to unseat, and not only does it elide "determined" and "shaped," two different modes of causation, but it also undermines what the author presently affirms, namely, that the historical perspective of interpretation shapes the historian's work (*Peasants, Warriors, and Wives,* 9). Must not the open-endedness of historical interpretation preclude any notion of strict determinism?

49. Lawrence W. Levine, *Highbrow Lowbrow: The Emergence of Cultural Hierarchy in America* (Cambridge: Harvard University Press, 1988), 33.

50. For Levine's definition of sacralized art see ibid., 120.

51. Ibid., 121–35.

52. Clifford Geertz, "Religion as a Cultural System," in *The Interpretation of Cultures* (New York: Basic Books, 1973), 87–125; I have also found helpful Stewart Elliott Guthrie's reflection on a cognitive theory of religion and his discussion of Geertz's essay: Guthrie, *Faces in the Clouds: A New Theory of Religion* (New York: Oxford University Press, 1993), 8–38, esp. 27–32.

53. See, e.g., Svetlana Alpers, *Rembrandt's Enterprise: The Studio and the Market* (Chicago: University of Chicago Press, 1988); and Michael Baxandall, *The Limewood Sculptors of Renaissance Germany* (New Haven: Yale University Press, 1980). More helpful, however, as systemic description and analysis of popular visual culture are the following insightful studies in the history of photography and prints: Elizabeth Anne McCauley, *Industrial Madness: Commercial Photography in Paris, 1848–1871* (New Haven: Yale University Press, 1994); Catherine A. Lutz and Jane L. Collins, *Reading National Geographic* (Chicago: University of Chicago Press, 1993); David E. Nye, *Image Worlds: Corporate Identities at General Electric, 1890–1930* (Cambridge: MIT Press, 1985); and Peter C. Marzio, *Democratic Art.* I have also found helpful, in this regard, work in the sociology of art: Diana Crane, *The Transformation of the Avant-Garde: The New York Art World, 1940–1985* (Chicago: University of Chicago Press, 1987); and David Halle, *Inside Culture: Art and Class in the American Home* (Chicago: University of Chicago Press, 1993).

Chapter 1
The Visual Culture of American Protestantism

1. Estimates in the media since the 1950s vary considerably, but in 1971 Kriebel and Bates indicated in sales material that "over three hundred million reproductions [of the *Head of Christ*] in many sizes have been printed and distributed" ("Warner Sallman Has Gone to His Reward but He Has Left His Message with Us!" advertising galley, Bates File, Sallman

Archives, Anderson University). When Anderson University (in Anderson, Indiana) acquired the Sallman collection in 1987, the *Muncie Evening Press* reported that an "estimated
400 million copies of the *Head of Christ* have been printed" ("Anderson College Acquires
Collection of Famous Religious Art" [May 28, 1987], 22). Charles Bates, the son of the
original publisher, Fred Bates, stated in an interview with me on July 19, 1991, that the
image had been reproduced more than 500 million times by the time Kriebel and Bates
liquidated in 1986. Jack R. Lundbom cited the same figure in his article "Warner E.
Sallman: A Centenary Tribute to a Covenant Artist," *Covenant Companion* 81, no. 7 (July
1992), 10. A 1994 appointments calendar (*Warner Sallman: Paintings of Jesus*) published by
Warner Press, current copyright holder of the Sallman corpus at Anderson University,
states in a brief biography of the artist that "so far, over 500 million prints of all sizes have
been distributed throughout the world."

2. Reported to me by Charles Bates, interview of July 19, 1991.
3. Reported to me by Lars-Birger Sponberg, interview of August 3, 1991.
4. See the typescript entitled "History of Kriebel and Bates, Publishers of Sallman's Master-
    pieces," by Fred M. Bates, written about 1945, p. 4, in the Bates File, Sallman Archives.
5. Bates, interview.
6. Letter 274, Correspondence File, Sallman Archives. I solicited letters to explore the popular
    reception of Sallman's art. Discussion of the instrument and the statistical results of this
    solicitation appears in the Appendix to Chapter 6. Letters from this sample will be referred
    to by a letter number in parentheses throughout the remainder of this book.
7. Paul Robert Roth, "Christ and the Muses," *Christianity Today* 2, no. 11 (March 3, 1958), 9.
8. Letter to Sallman, July 4, 1957, photocopy in possession of Howard W. Ellis, Greencastle,
    Indiana; quoted in David Morgan, "Imaging Protestant Piety: The Icons of Warner Sall-
    man," *Religion and American Culture: A Journal of Interpretation* 3, no. 1 (Winter 1993), 33.
9. Tom Smith, "Tiny Picture of Christ Weeps Tears of Blood," *National Enquirer* (August 21,
    1979), 29.
10. *Ladies' Home Journal* 39 (December 1922), 20.
11. Margaret Anderson, "His Subject Shaped His Life," *War Cry* (December 9, 1961), 7–8, 10.
12. "Son of Man," 16-mm film written by Dale McCulley, directed by Henry Ushijima
    (copyright North Park College and Theological Seminary, 1954); video transfer in the
    Sallman Archives.
13. Edward Barry, "Jesus of Nazareth," *Chicago Sunday Tribune* (April 10, 1949), 8, 14.
14. "Masterpieces by Warner Sallman," catalogue, Kriebel and Bates, 1981, n.p.
15. See letters 38, 107, 150, 177, 245, and 297, Correspondence File, Sallman Archives.
16. The following observations are based on an examination of yearbook class photographs
    from 1900 to 1968 in the archives of Moellering Library, Valparaiso University.
17. Because Sallman's portraiture is always somewhat anachronistic, it is worth noting that the
    high forehead was a phrenological index of intellectual power and benevolent character.
    Phrenology, a widespread nineteenth-century passion, focused on the shape of the skull as
    the visible signature of personality. According to the leading advocate of and writer on
    phrenology, Orson Fowler, the size of the forehead indicated the relative development of
    the brain organs responsible for kindness and intellectual powers of observation. See O. S.
    Fowler, *Human Science, or, Phrenology* (Philadelphia: National Publishing, 1873), 28–30.
    The literature produced by phrenologists included diagrams of the skull and dozens of
    portraits of famous men and women to illustrate the principles of reading character from
    the shape of the skull.

    By the time Sallman painted his *Portrait of Jesus,* some professional photographers no longer considered the vignette appropriate for male subjects. A trade book of the time, for instance, stated, "From the standpoint of pure photography, an artist or a jury will turn thumbs down on sight of a vignette, for the sole reason that the subject of the picture has no base, and is apparently floating in air, thereby violating a fundamental rule of accepted pictorial composition. Nevertheless, vignettes of babies and children, against white backgrounds especially, can be very lovely indeed, and can be equally attractive as treatments of older subjects." Edwin A. Falk, Sr., and Charles Abel, *Practical Portrait Photography for Home and Studio,* 2nd ed. (New York: American Photographic Book Publishing, 1967), 165.

18. From my conversation with Charles Bates, July 19, 1991.

19. An article in *Christianity Today* in 1958 reported that DeWitt Jayne, professor of art at Wheaton College, leveled the charge of plagiarism at Sallman in regard to the use of Lhermitte's painting for the *Head of Christ.* See the article with no author indicated, "Evangelical Piety and Christian Art," *Christianity Today* 2, no. 11 (March 3, 1958), 26. See also letter 118, Correspondence File, Sallman Archives, from a professor at Wesley Theological Seminary, Washington, D.C.

20. For instance, in the Chicago metropolitan area, *Christ in Gethsemane,* 1940, after Hofmann, South Chicago Evangelical Covenant Church, Chicago, Illinois. I would like to thank Jack R. Lundbom for this and additional information on four other reproductions of the Hofmann image by Sallman. A sixth copy of the image hangs in the Country Evangelical Covenant Church in Eligin, Illinois.

21. All quotes from Sylvia E. Peterson, *Story of Sallman's "Teach Me Thy Way"* (Indianapolis: Kriebel and Bates, 1952), 6–9.

22. For discussion and reproduction of two of these images, see William Vaughan, *German Romanticism and English Art* (New Haven: Yale University Press, 1979), 224–25, figs. 157 and 158.

23. Sallman collected many such books, according to Charles Bates and one of Sallman's sons. Bates, interview; James Sallman, interview with me on March 9, 1992. Several books gathered together a variety of images that could have provided sources for many of Sallman's pictures. See, for instance, Abram Elder, *The Light of the World or Our Saviour in Art* (Chicago: Elder, 1896) and William E. Barton, *Jesus of Nazareth* (Boston: Pilgrim Press, 1903). Sallman also borrowed from the work of a fellow Chicago religious illustrator, Harry Anderson, whom he knew in the mid-1940s before Anderson moved to Washington, D.C., to produce work for the Review and Herald Press of the Seventh-Day Adventist Church. Anderson's 1945 painting *What Happened to Your Hand?* was the source of Sallman's 1954 *He Careth for You.* But in the case of Sallman's *Christ at Heart's Door,* the
· influence went in the other direction: Sallman's painting was the basis for Anderson's well-known *Prince of Peace,* which shows a colossal Jesus in Manhattan, knocking at the "door" of the United Nations building. For reproductions of Anderson's paintings see Raymond H. Woolsey and Ruth Anderson, *Harry Anderson: The Man Behind the Paintings* (Washington, D.C.: Review and Herald Publishing Association, 1976), 35 and 97.

24. *A Series of Interpretations of the Sallman Religious Masterpieces* (Indianapolis: Kriebel and Bates, n.d.), which, on the basis of internal evidence, must have been published in 1955 or shortly thereafter.

25. See, e.g., Jon Pahl, *Hopes and Dreams of All: The International Walther League and Lutheran Youth in American Culture, 1893–1993* (Chicago: Wheat Ridge Ministries, 1993). On the Sunday school see Anne M. Boylan, *Sunday School: The Formation of an American Institution, 1790–1880* (New Haven: Yale University Press, 1988).

26. Annie Ward Byrd, "Vision and Duty," *Sunday School Intermediate Teacher* 3, no. 1 (January–March 1942), 58.
27. *A Series of Interpretations,* n.p.
28. "Masterpieces by Warner Sallman," n.p. The same copy is found in *A Series of Interpretations,* n.p.
29. *A Series of Interpretations,* n.p.
30. More than twenty letters refer to this imagery; see such letters as 32, 182, 200, 322, 362, 372, 391, and 494. See also Dale Francis, "Protestant Revolt Sent Religious Art into a Continuous Decline," *San Francisco Monitor* (June 1, 1956), 1.
31. *Son of Man,* charcoal, 1924, property of the artist's family; *The Christ,* pastel, 1935, copyright The Messenger Corporation; *Son of Man,* chalk, date unknown, reproduced in the Gospel Trumpet Company catalogue of 1938.
32. See, e.g., Sylvia Peterson, "Into All the World," typescript, ca. 1956, 2–3, Sallman Archives; anonymous, "He Painted Jesus' Picture," *Sunday Pix* (January 15, 1961), 1–2.
33. Quoted in Peterson, "Into All the World," 13.
34. From July 1, 1939, to July 1, 1941, the Army alone swelled from 174,000 to 1,400,000; cited in A. Russell Buchanan, *The United States and World War II* (New York: Harper & Row, 1964), 1: 120–22. The Allied assault in Sicily got under way in the summer of 1942.
35. William B. Waits, *The Modern Christmas in America: A Cultural History of Gift Giving* (New York: New York University Press, 1993), 1–6.
36. Ibid., 7–15.
37. Kriebel and Bates sales figures cited in Morgan, "Imaging Protestant Piety," 45, n. 3; sales records in possession of Charles Bates. Quotation is from *COR* 23, no. 6 (June 1951), 1. A former employee of Kriebel and Bates has indicated that the Sacred Heart was photomechanically imposed on the painting. (Bates, interview. This cannot be confirmed, however, because the location of the original painting is unknown.)
38. For further discussion of the appeal of print media to the "visual literacy" of Protestants see Morgan, "Imaging Protestant Piety," 40–44.
39. Howard W. Ellis, *Story of Sallman's "Head of Christ"* (Indianapolis: Kriebel and Bates, 1944). Sylvia E. Peterson, "The Ministry of Christian Art," *Lutheran Companion* 55, no. 14 (April 2, 1947), 10–12.
40. Charles Bates, interview.
41. Sylvia E. Peterson, telephone conversation with me, August 7, 1991.
42. Howard Ellis, *The Story of Sallman's "Good Shepherd"* (Indianapolis: Kriebel and Bates, 1944). For an instance of nineteenth-century orientalist prose on the subject of Sallman's painting see "The Good Shepherd," in *The Illustrated Family Christian Almanac for 1860* (New York: American Tract Society, 1860), 42.
43. See "Sallman's 'The Lord Is My Shepherd,' An Interpretation," in *A Series of Interpretations,* n.p.
44. Ibid., 7.
45. Ibid., 8.
46. Ibid.
47. For a discussion of this rhetoric and its relation to the market for Sallman's image see Erika Doss's discussion of Sallman as adman (Chapter 2).
48. See Gail Bederman, "'The Women Have Had Charge of the Church Work Long Enough': The Men and Religion Forward Movement of 1911–1912 and the Masculinization of Middle-Class Protestantism," *American Quarterly* 41 (1989), 432–65.

49. See Ellis, *Story of Sallman's "Head of Christ,"* 5–6. This conversation is discussed in greater detail in Chapter 2.

Chapter 2
Cultural Origins of Sallman's Imagery

1. Rev. E. O. Sellers is quoted in Howard W. Ellis, *Story of Sallman's "Head of Christ"* (Indianapolis: Kriebel and Bates, 1944), 6.

2. David Morgan notes the connections between Sallman's portrait and contemporary photography in "Imaging Protestant Piety: The Icons of Warner Sallman," *Religion and American Culture: A Journal of Interpretation* 3, no. 1 (Winter 1993), 40, and in Chapter 1 of this book. The Library and Archives at North Park College, Chicago, contains a *Head of Christ,* signed by Sallman and dating from 1940, that clearly shows how the artist simply painted over a print of the *Son of Man.* The "original," or best-known, version of the *Head of Christ* is in the Jessie C. Wilson Galleries, Anderson University.

3. John W. Cook, "Material Culture and the Visual Arts," in *Encyclopedia of the American Religious Experience,* ed. Charles H. Lippy and Peter W. Williams (New York: Charles Scribner's Sons, 1988), 3: 1364. On the *Head of Christ*'s wide-ranging appeal see Chapter 6 and its appendix, in this book.

4. Warren Susman, "Culture Heroes: Ford, Barton, Ruth," in *Culture as History: The Transformation of American Society in the Twentieth Century* (New York: Pantheon, 1984), 129; and T. J. Jackson Lears, "From Salvation to Self-Realization: Advertising and the Therapeutic Roots of the Consumer Culture, 1880–1930," in *The Culture of Consumption: Critical Essays in American History, 1880–1980,* ed. T. J. Jackson Lears and Richard Wightman Fox (New York: Pantheon, 1983), 31.

5. William McDermott, "The Miracle Picture," *Christian Life* 24, no. 11 (March 1963), 27.

6. Warner Sallman, "Two Artists Depict Christ: Warner Sallman and Birger Sponberg," *Covenant Companion* 49, no. 16 (April 15, 1960), 8.

7. Roland Marchand, *Advertising the American Dream: Making Way for Modernity, 1920–1940* (Berkeley: University of California Press, 1985), xvii. Veteran adman James R. Adams is quoted on p. 45; see also James R. Adams, *Sparks off My Anvil* (New York: Harper, 1958).

8. Sallman is quoted in Sylvia Knudson Larson, "Warner Sallman and His Ministry of Christian Art," a nonpaginated pamphlet published in conjunction with an exhibit of Sallman's art at Covenant Village, Northbrook, Illinois, 1984.

9. Sylvia E. Peterson, *The Ministry of Christian Art* (Indianapolis: Kriebel and Bates, 1947), n.p. Munkácsy's paintings also made a big impact on the young James Joyce, who wrote about the artist and the painted image of Christ in one of his first literary essays, "Ecce Homo," in September 1899. See Ellsworth Mason and Richard Ellmann, *The Critical Writings of James Joyce* (1959; Ithaca: Cornell University Press, 1989), 31–37.

10. Peterson, *Ministry of Christian Art,* n.p. For examples of nineteenth- century Christian images that Sallman may have seen, see Joseph Lewis French, *Christ in Art* (Boston: L. C. Page, 1900); William Griffith, *Great Painters and Their Famous Bible Pictures* (New York: William H. Wise, 1925); Clifton Harby, *The Bible in Art* (New York: Garden City Publishing, 1936); and Cynthia Pearl Maus, *Christ and the Fine Arts* (New York: Harper and Brothers, 1938). See also the discussion on Munkácsy and other nineteenth-century painters of religious icons in Aleksa Celebonovic, *Some Call It Kitsch: Masterpieces of Bourgeois Realism* (New York: Harry N. Abrams, 1974), 47–75. On Doré's work see Gustave

Doré, *The Bible in Pictures: The Dramatic Events of the Old and New Testaments Presented in All of Gustave Doré's Unforgettable Drawings* (New York: William H. Wise, 1934). Morgan has reported that Sallman was an "avid collector" of nineteenth- and twentieth-century Christian images and that he displayed them in his home studio; see Chapter 1.

11. Sallman quoted in Peterson, *Ministry of Christian Art*, n.p.

12. J. Gordon Melton, *The Encyclopedia of American Religions* (Wilmington, N.C.: McGrath Publishing, 1978), 1: 166–67; Vergilius Ferm, *Pictorial History of Protestantism* (New York: Philosophical Library, 1957), 320–21. For further information on the Covenant church see Karl A. Olsson, "The Evangelical Mission Covenant Church and the Free Churches of Swedish Background," in *The American Church of the Protestant Heritage,* ed. Vergilius Ferm (New York: Philosophical Library, 1953), 249–76.

13. Warner Sallman, "Put Your Hands to Work, Your Heart to God," *Covenant Companion* 44, no. 3 (January 15, 1960), 3.

14. Sallman, "Put Your Hands to Work," 3, and Sallman, "My Greatest Spiritual Experience," *Covenant Youth Today* (May 13, 1956), 6. For reference to Sallman's Prohibition work see Ben Bankson, "Happy Birthday, Mr. Sallman!" *Covenant Companion* 56, no. 8 (April 21, 1967), 26; see also Dorothy C. Haskin, "The Man Who Painted a Manly Head of Christ," in *Christians You Would Like to Know* (Grand Rapids: Zondervan, 1954), 65–72, for reference to Sallman's participation with the J. Wilbur Chapman and Charles Alexander revival campaigns in Chicago. On Protestants and Prohibition see Martin E. Marty, *Righteous Empire: The Protestant Experience in America* (New York: Dial Press, 1970), 214.

15. See Rolf Lundén, *Business and Religion in the American 1920s* (New York: Greenwood Press, 1988), 74, for a discussion of how plays and especially films were used as evangelistic appeals in Protestant churches of the 1920s; see Betty A. DeBerg, *UnGodly Women: Gender and the First Wave of American Fundamentalism* (Minneapolis: Fortress Press, 1990), 102–3, for a discussion of how conservative fundamentalists attacked plays and films on the basis of their danger to public and private morality.

16. Thanks to Jack R. Lundbom for providing much of this information; his unpublished biography of Sallman is titled "Masterpainter: Warner E. Sallman."

17. Barton is quoted in Lundén, *Business and Religion,* 105; see also Lears, "From Salvation to Self-Realization," 30–36; and Leo P. Ribuffo, "Jesus Christ as Business Statesman: Bruce Barton and the Selling of Corporate Capitalism," *American Quarterly* 33 (Summer 1981), 206–31. Barton's agency merged with the George Batten Company in 1928 to become Batten, Barton, Durstine, and Osborn. In addition to *The Man Nobody Knows* (Indianapolis: Bobbs-Merrill Company, 1924), Barton wrote many books and articles on Christ and Christianity, ranging from *A Young Man's Jesus* (1914) to *What Can a Man Believe?* (1927). On Ayer see Stephen Fox, *The Mirror Makers: A History of American Advertising and Its Creators* (New York: William Morrow, 1984), 21–22; on the Ayer agency's preference for Christian employees see Marchand, *Advertising the American Dream,* 36.

18. Olga E. Lindborg, "Another Picture of Jesus," in *Our Covenant 1942: An Illustrated Annual of the Evangelical Mission Covenant Church of America* (Chicago: Covenant Book Concern, 1942), 69–70.

19. For works by Gibson and Flagg see Susan E. Meyer, *America's Great Illustrators* (New York: Harry N. Abrams, 1978), 208–31, 256–79. Henry C. Pitz, *Two Hundred Years of American Illustration* (New York: Random House, 1977), 116, 118.

20. A comparison of Sallman's piano ads with those done for Steinway by N. W. Ayer shows

just how conservative Sallman was in terms of employing modern art styles in advertising; see Marchand, *Advertising the American Dream*, 142. See also Fox's discussion of the 1920s Steinway account in *Mirror Makers*, 131.

21. Lears, "From Salvation to Self-Realization," 3.

22. Daniel Pope, *The Making of Modern Advertising* (New York: Basic Books, 1983), 22–29, as noted in Marchand, *Advertising the American Dream*, 6.

23. Marchand, *Advertising the American Dream*, 31. On the mobilization of graphic arts into public service see Neil Harris, "Graphic Art for the Public Welfare," in *Graphic Design in America: A Visual Language History* (Minneapolis: Walker Art Center, 1989), 74–95.

24. *The Age Factor in Selling and Advertising: A Study in a New Phase of Advertising* (Chicago: Photoplay Magazine, 1922), 10, 40, 45, 55.

25. That he was allowed to sign his ads indicates Sallman's status in the industry: most commercial illustrators were prohibited from such self-expression. For no apparent reason, Sallman occasionally used the alias Elias (his middle name) to sign the drawings he made for various religious magazines in the 1920s; see "Elias," in *Our Covenant: An Illustrated Annual of the Swedish Evangelical Mission Covenant of America*, ed. Olga E. Lindborg (Chicago: Covenant Book Concern, 1929), 11–14. For more discussion on the issue of personal creativity and the use of signatures in advertising see Michele H. Bogart, *Artists, Advertising, and the Borders of Art*, esp. chap. 3, "Art Directors and the Art of Commerce" (Chicago: University of Chicago Press, 1995). On Hopper and Anderson see, respectively, Gail Levin, *Edward Hopper: The Art and the Artist* (New York: W. W. Norton, 1980), 22, and Stuart Ewen, *Captains of Consciousness: Advertising and the Social Roots of the Consumer Culture* (New York: McGraw-Hill, 1976), 66.

26. Carl F. H. Henry, "Sallman Made the Deadline," *Evangelical Beacon* 13, no. 4 (October 26, 1943), 3.

27. Lundén, *Business and Religion*, 18, 57.

28. Ibid., 69–74. Likewise, in *Babbitt*, Lewis described how Reverend John Jennison Drew made his church (Chatham Road Presbyterian) a "true community center" containing "everything but a bar." Lewis, *Babbitt* (New York: Harcourt, Brace, 1922), 205. *Elmer Gantry* was published in 1927.

29. A complete collection of these papers can be found in the North Park College and Theological Seminary Library.

30. *Forbundets Veckotidining* (June 4, 1929), 9.

31. R. Laurence Moore, *Selling God: American Religion in the Marketplace of Culture* (New York: Oxford University Press, 1994), 231–33. See also Dennis N. Voskuil, "Reaching Out: Mainline Protestantism and the Media," in *Between the Times: The Travail of the Protestant Establishment in America, 1900–1960*, ed. William R. Hutchison (New York: Cambridge University Press, 1989), 81–82.

32. These works appeared as covers in the *Covenant Companion* in June 1926, April 1929, and December 1930, respectively.

33. These works appeared in the *Covenant Weekly* (June 18, 1935), 1; the *Covenant Companion* (December 16, 1933), 6; and the *Covenant Companion* (October 1924), cover, respectively.

34. These works appeared in the *Covenant Weekly* (November 27, 1923), 1, and the *Covenant Companion* (April 1928), cover.

35. *Christian Herald* 45 (November 25, 1922), 2, noted in Lundén, *Business and Religion*, 37.

36. *Covenant Companion* (July 24, 1929), cover.

37. Much of the following discussion is indebted to material in Gail Bederman, "'The Women Have Had Charge of the Church Work Long Enough': The Men and Religion Forward

Movement of 1911–1912 and the Masculinization of Middle-Class Protestantism," *American Quarterly* 41, no. 3 (September 1989), 432–65, and DeBerg, *UnGodly Women,* 13–41.

38. Barton was far more liberal than Sallman and, as a primary exponent of the consumer culture, challenged the absolute authority of biblical doctrine in most of his books. As Bederman remarks, however, "Barton concentrated on the therapeutic ethos and the consumer economy precisely in order to show Jesus' masculinity." Bederman, "'The Women Have Had Charge,'" 464 n. 98.

39. Ibid., 438; DeBerg, *UnGodly Women,* 80, 92.

40. Bederman, "'The Women Have Had Charge,'" 432–34.

41. DeBerg, *UnGodly Women,* 90.

42. Peterson, *Ministry of Christian Art,* n.p. Sallman credited Goff's "realistic presentation of the Son of God" for a "large share of the incentive and the immediate inspiration for my 'Head of Christ.'" Sallman, "My Greatest Spiritual Experience," 6. In his September 1924 cover for the *Covenant Companion,* Sallman depicted a group of adult Bible class students and their teacher gazing at a scriptural text writ in the air: "Saved for service, study to shew thyself approved unto God, a workman that needeth not to be ashamed, rightly dividing the word of truth" (2 Timothy 2:15).

43. Olga E. Lindborg, "Choosing Pictures That Illustrate Bible Stories," *Covenant Companion, Teacher's Companion* 2, no. 4 (September 1923), 5–6.

44. Olga E. Lindborg, "Choosing Pictures That Illustrate Bible Stories," *Covenant Companion, Teacher's Companion* 2, no. 5 (October 1923), 6–7. Although it was published after Sallman made *Son of Man* in 1924, the article "Without a Halo" in the *Covenant Companion* (April 1, 1933), 3, also emphasized the construction of a realistic Jesus.

45. Warren Susman, "'Personality' and the Making of Twentieth-Century Culture," in *Culture as History,* 271–85. On the development of audiences' fascination with stars and celebrities see Neil Harris, "The Drama of Consumer Desire," in *Cultural Excursions: Marketing Appetites and Cultural Tastes in Modern America* (Chicago: University of Chicago Press, 1990), 186–87.

46. Sallman, quoted in David Morgan, "Sallman's *Head of Christ:* The History of an Image," *Christian Century* 109, no. 28 (October 7, 1992), 869.

47. For hundreds of head shots see Daniel Blum, *A Pictorial History of the Silent Screen* (New York: G. P. Putnam's Sons, 1953); on the use of color in commercial illustration see Neil Harris, "Color and Media: Some Comparisons and Speculations," in *Cultural Excursions,* 318–36.

48. See, e.g., Haskin, "The Man Who Painted a Manly Head of Christ," 65, and the repeated references to the portrait's manly qualities in the letters solicited by David Morgan. For one essay describing the picture's postwar popularity see Sylvia Peterson Knudson, "Sallman's *Head of Christ* Still Blessing," *Covenant Companion* 63, no. 1 (January 1, 1974), 3–5, 29. On gender tensions in post–World War II America see, e.g., Elaine Tyler May, *Homeward Bound: American Families in the Cold War Era* (New York: Basic Books, 1988).

49. Celeste Olalquiaga, *Megalopolis: Contemporary Cultural Sensibilities* (Minneapolis: University of Minnesota Press, 1992).

50. The present-day declension of the *Head of Christ* may further be explained, however, by the contemporary dominance of another image. Indeed, as I explore in "St. Elvis: Fans, Faith, and Sacred Objects" (manuscript), whereas the *Head of Christ* once dominated postwar domestic interiors, the devotional image that most often appears in post-Vietnam American living rooms is that of Elvis Presley. That is to say not that Elvis has supplanted Christ but that, today, *images* of Elvis seem to generate more passion and emotional response than

images of Jesus. The image of Elvis is as popular, as broadly marketed, and as contentiously critiqued as Sallman's image of Christ once was; it also is an image that is profoundly ubiquitous and mercurial. In the 1990s Elvis' "deification" has become the subject of many scholarly investigations, most of them attributing it to mass marketing and a susceptible (read "irrational") public. For a selection see Simon Hoggart, "Elvis of Nazareth," *New Statesman* 5, no. 210 (July 10, 1992), 24; Lynne Joyrich, "Elvisophilia: Knowledge, Pleasure, and the Cult of Elvis," *Differences* 5, no.1 (Spring 1993), 73–91; and Ted Harrison, *Elvis People: The Cult of the King* (New York: HarperCollins, 1992). Such accounts not only disenfranchise Elvis fans by consigning them to a low social and religious stratum but mistakenly equate Elvis veneration with Elvis worship. Moreover, they fail to explain how and why images of Elvis, unlike those of other popular contemporary figures, have taken on the dimensions of faith and devotion, viewed by believers as empowered icons and artifacts, which can fulfill wishes and desires.

51. Clifford Geertz, *The Interpretation of Cultures* (New York: Basic Books, 1973).

Chapter 3

Marketing Jesus

1. The following discussion is based on Colleen McDannell, *The Christian Home in Victorian America, 1840–1900* (Bloomington: Indiana University Press, 1986).

2. William Ranlett, *The Architect* (New York: W. H. Graham, 1847), 3.

3. Oliver Smith, *The Domestic Architect* (Buffalo: Derby, 1857), iv.

4. R. K. Hennywood, *Relief-Molded Jugs, 1820–1900* (Woodbridge, England: Antique Collectors' Club, 1984), 27–31, 51, 108, 159, 184–88, 196. See also Arlene M. Palmer, "Religion in Clay and Glass," *American Art and Antiques* 2 (1979), 80–87.

5. J. R. Miller, *Weekday Religion* (Philadelphia: Presbyterian Board of Publication, 1880), 269.

6. The Catholic story is somewhat different. American Catholics imported religious goods from Europe and sold them through stores owned by Catholics. Religious orders of priests, monks, and nuns also were active in distributing Catholic material culture. Nineteenth-century secular companies, however, also distributed Catholic images along with Protestant ones. The popularity of Warner Sallman's art in the 1940s and 1950s corresponded to the rising ecumenical spirit in the United States. As Catholics moved out of their urban ethnic enclaves and into the suburbs, they associated more with Protestants. The Liturgical movement of the same period also emphasized a more Protestant style of worship. Catholics began to accept Protestant images (reading them as Christian) in the 1950s, and, after the Second Vatican Council (1962–65), Warner Sallman's art became ubiquitous in Catholic bookstores.

7. Elsie de Wolfe, *The House in Good Taste* (1911; New York: Century, 1913). For an excellent discussion of twentieth-century design see *High Styles: Twentieth-Century American Design,* with an introduction by Lisa Phillips (New York: Whitney Museum of American Art, 1985); on the realization of such designs in middle-class housing see Candace M. Volz, "The Modern Look of the Early Twentieth-Century House: A Mirror of Changing Lifestyles," and Katherine C. Grier, "The Decline of the Memory Palace: The Parlor after 1890," both in *American Home Life, 1880–1930: A Social History of Spaces and Services,* ed. Jessica H. Foy and Thomas J. Schlereth (Knoxville: University of Tennessee Press, 1992), 25–74; Gwendolyn Wright, *Building the Dream: A Social History of Housing in America* (Cambridge: MIT Press, 1981), 158–76; and Margaret Marsh, *Suburban Lives* (New Brunswick: Rutgers University Press, 1990), 90–155.

8. Ogden Codman, *The Decoration of Houses* (New York: Charles Scribner's Sons, 1897), xix.

9. Lizabeth A. Cohen, "Embellishing a Life of Labor: An Interpretation of the Material Culture of American Working-Class Homes, 1885–1915," in Thomas J. Schlereth, *Material Culture Studies in America* (Nashville: American Association for State and Local History, 1982), 289–305. For a discussion of twentieth-century aesthetics and class see David Halle, *Inside Culture: Art and Class in the American Home* (Chicago: University of Chicago Press, 1993).

10. Robert S. Lynd and Helen Merrell Lynd, *Middletown: A Study in Contemporary American Culture* (New York: Harcourt, Brace, 1929), 100.

11. In 1898, Church of God leaders moved the publication of *Gospel Trumpet* from Grand Junction, Michigan, to Moundsville, West Virginia. They moved it again in 1906 to Anderson, Indiana, which remained the home of the periodical and Church of God headquarters. In 1957 the publication was renamed *Vital Christianity* and is still issued under that name.

12. The publishing and merchandising company became an important stabilizing force for the Church of God because founder Daniel Sydney Warner opposed all forms of ecclesiastical organization. In the Church of God, ordination is simply a recognition of the call to preach, each congregation is independent and calls its own pastor, and because the General Assembly of ministers and laypersons cannot speak for the whole movement, its resolutions are not binding. Given such a decentralized organization, the financial and theological presence of Gospel Trumpet Company was critical for the survival of the Church of God.

13. The Gospel Trumpet Company first used the name Warner Press in 1929 and registered it as a trademark in 1930. Warner Press was used during the 1940s to describe the wholesale division, and Gospel Trumpet Company referred to the total publishing and merchandise endeavor. In 1962 the name Gospel Trumpet Company was retired, and the firm became Warner Press.

14. Gospel Trumpet, "1895 Descriptive Catalogue of Books and Tracts, etc." All Gospel Trumpet and Warner Press catalogues are located at the Warner Press headquarters in Anderson, Indiana. I would like to thank Charles Herrington for so graciously sharing with me his materials and insights into the company. His historical summaries were invaluable for this research.

15. N. H. Byrum, *Familiar Names and Faces* (Moundsville, W.Va.: Gospel Trumpet, 1902), 102.

16. Ibid., 140.

17. Harold L. Phillips, *Miracle of Survival* (Anderson, Ind.: Warner Press, 1979), 198.

18. Ibid., 150.

19. Ibid., 153f.

20. Ibid., 226.

21. *1982 Warner Press Annual Report.*

22. On the social significance of mottoes see Kenneth Ames, "Words to Live By," in *Death in the Dining Room and Other Tales of Victorian Culture* (Philadelphia: Temple University Press, 1992), 97–149.

23. On the creation of Mother's Day by florists, ministers, and promoters of domesticity see Leigh Eric Schmidt, "The Commercialization of the Calendar: American Holidays and the Culture of Consumption, 1870–1930," *Journal of American History* 78 (1991), 887–916.

24. Phillips, *Miracle of Survival,* 194.

25. Gospel Trumpet, "1925–1926 Trade Catalog."

26. Roland Marchand, *Advertising the American Dream: Making Way for Modernity, 1920–1940* (Berkeley: University of California Press, 1985), 9.

27. Ibid., 118.

28. Exhibitions in 1929 of French-influenced Art Deco moderne furniture include the *Eleventh Annual Exhibition of American Industrial Art* at the Metropolitan Museum and a show organized by R. H. Macy and Company at Designer's Gallery. Phillips et al., *High Styles,* 64.

29. Marchand, *Advertising the American Dream,* 140.

30. Gospel Trumpet, "1937–1938 Gospel Trumpet Company Catalog."

31. Marchand, *Advertising the American Dream,* 264–84. The intermingling of advertising and religion started earlier. In 1906, for example, a window display used a cross and lilies to sell hats during Easter time. See Schmidt, "Commercialization of the Calendar," 896.

32. Rolf Lundén, *Business and Religion in the American 1920s* (New York: Greenwood Press, 1988), 56–88 ("Religion as Business"); see also Robert Handy, "The American Religious Depression, 1925–1935," *Church History* 24 (1960), 3–16. Handy quotes Charles Fiske's 1929 statement: "America has become almost hopelessly enamoured of a religion that is little more than a sanctified commercialism." (8).

33. "Sermons in Slogans," *Literary Digest* 73 (April 29, 1922), 31–32.

34. Gospel Trumpet, "1937–1938 Gospel Trumpet Company Catalog."

35. Gospel Trumpet, "1922–23 Religious Books for the Home Church Study."

36. Byrum, *Familiar Names and Faces,* 176.

37. Ames, *Death in the Dining Room,* 144.

38. Marchand, *Advertising the American Dream,* 360.

39. Gospel Trumpet, "1900 Catalogue of Holiness Literature."

40. See Ralph W. Hyde, "The Traveling Bible Salesman: The Good Buck from the Good Book," in *The Bible and Popular Culture in America,* ed. Allene Stuart Phy (Philadelphia: Fortress Press, 1985), 137–64.

41. Typical of the ads for religious merchandise are those for Christian Light Press of Elizabethtown, Pennsylvania, in *Christian Life* (1946), 6; Christian Company, Chicago, in *Christian Life* (1948), 53; Judson Press, Philadelphia, in *King's Business* (1924), 830; and Church Service, New York, in *Christian Advocate* (1920), 251. The ad for coats was in *King's Business* (1924), 258.

42. Phillips, *Miracle of Survival,* 246.

43. For a discussion of imagery by Sallman that predates 1924 see Chapter 2.

44. Jack R. Lundbom, "Warner E. Sallman: A Centenary Tribute to a Covenant Artist," *Covenant Companion* (July 1992), 10.

45. Charles Herrington, interview with me, June 1993.

46. Charles Bates (son of Fred Bates and a member of the Kriebel and Bates partnership), phone interview with me, January 1994.

47. Fred M. Bates, "History of Kriebel and Bates, Publishers of Sallman's Masterpieces," typescript, 1945, Sallman Archives, Wilson Galleries, Anderson University.

48. According to Fred Bates's account, "On July 8, 1943, an additional [to the original $100] payment of $1,550 was made to Warner E. Sallman to cover the four paintings, namely, 'The Head of Christ,' 'Gethsemane,' 'Christ at Heart's Door,' and 'The Lord is My Shepherd.' This special payment provided that along with preceding payments in the amount of $450 already made toward these paintings, he would be considered as having received $1,000 for his 'Head of Christ,' $250 for 'Gethsemane,' $400 for 'Christ at Heart's Door,' and $350 for the 'Lord is My Shepherd,' a grand total of $2,000 for the first four paintings.

On February 14, Kriebel and Bates paid Warner Sallman $500 for the 'Boy Christ,' then later in the year, August 3, an additional payment of $2,000 was advanced to Mr. Sallman to apply on all of the paintings. This made a total of $4,952.30 paid for the five paintings . . . thus establishing the price of about $1,000 for each painting." In the 1940s, Sallman received the following as contract royalties for reproductions: "Size 30″ × 40″, $100 per thousand; size 22″ × 28″, $50 per thousand; size 16″ × 20″, $15 per thousand; size 11″ × 14″, $10 per thousand; size 8″ × 10″, $4.50 per thousand; size 5″ × 7″, $2.50 per thousand; size 4″ × 5″, $1.00 per thousand; 2½″ × 3½″, 50¢ per thousand; size 1¼″ × 1¼″; 25¢ per thousand; on Triumphant Life Calendar backs, 50¢ per thousand, and on Bedtime Prayer Reminder Cards, 25¢ per thousand." Bates, "History of Kriebel and Bates," 4–5.

49. Ibid., 5.

50. Warner Press, "Warner Press Catalog," 1953.

51. Letter 215, Correspondence File, Sallman Archives.

52. Robert Ellwood, *One Way: The Jesus Movement and Its Meaning* (Englewood Cliffs, N.J.: Prentice Hall, 1973), 18–20. On life-style Christianity see David Harrington Watt, *A Transforming Faith: Explorations of Twentieth-Century American Evangelicalism* (New Brunswick: Rutgers University Press, 1991), 24–25; Richard Quebedeaux, *The Young Evangelicals: Revolution in Orthodoxy* (New York: Harper and Row, 1974), 40.

53. Stan Jantz, "Maranatha Village," *Bookstore Journal* (July–August 1974), 119.

54. Dana J. Lowe, "People in Progress: Suppliers Share Their Stories," *Bookstore Journal* (September 1979), 109. For discussions of Christian jewelry see Lesley Hull, "Jewelry in a Christian Bookstore? Why Not?" *Bookstore Journal* (June 1975), 9–10; Danny DeVeny, "How to Merchandise and Sell Jewelry," *Bookstore Journal* (November–December 1978), 13f.

55. On Christian retailing see Colleen McDannell, *Material Christianity: Religion and Popular Culture in America* (New Haven: Yale University Press, 1995).

56. Susan Hare, interview with me, June 1993.

Chapter 4
Evangelicals and Sallman's Art

1. Carl F. H. Henry, "Evangelical Piety and Christian Art," *Christianity Today* 2 (March 3, 1958), 26, 32. Jane W. Lauber, a Wheaton College graduate and artist, criticized Sallman's work as a cliché because it was reproduced so often and on such pedestrian objects as key chains and clocks. See Lauber, "Are We Losing Our Artistic Heritage?" *Christianity Today* 10 (September 2, 1966), 24. Robert Paul Roth, a Lutheran evangelical and New Testament scholar, called Sallman's work the "calendar art of the unsophisticated" and charged that the *Head of Christ* was a "pretty picture of a woman with a curling beard who has just come from the beauty parlor with a Halo shampoo," in "Christ and the Muses," *Christianity Today* 2 (March 3, 1958), 9.

2. Richard Quebedeaux, *Young Evangelicals: Revolution in Orthodoxy* (New York: Harper and Row, 1974), 36. I am indebted to Quebedeaux's book for my entire description of the neo-evangelical empire. See also Louis Gasper, *The Fundamentalist Movement, 1930–1956* (Grand Rapids, Mich.: Baker Book House, 1963), and George Marsden, *Reforming Fundamentalism: Fuller Seminary and the New Evangelicalism* (Grand Rapids, Mich.: William B. Eerdmans, 1987).

3. See Rudolph Nelson's biography of Edward Carnell, a neo-evanglical leader. Nelson

interpreted Carnell's fundamentalist childhood home and faith as "stigmata," an analysis based on Erving Goffman, *Stigma: Notes on the Management of Spoiled Identity* (Englewood Cliffs, N.J.: Prentice Hall, 1963). According to Nelson, Carnell and other neo-evangelicals of his generation yearned for acceptance by "normal" people outside the fundamentalist subculture: "What festered in his mind . . . was the inescapable and unendurable realization that everything his family stood for religiously was regarded by people outside the fold with indifference and often contempt." Nelson also generalized Carnell's feelings of social stigma to "thousands of people in fundamentalist churches" in the 1930s, owing to a large extent to the "debacle" of the Scopes trial in 1925, during which the national media painted a portrait of fundamentalists as ignorant and superstitious bigots. Nelson, *The Making and Unmaking of an Evangelical Mind: The Case of Edward Carnell* (Cambridge: Cambridge University Press, 1987), 16–27.

4. Quebedeaux, *Young Evangelicals,* 28.

5. Gordon H. Clark, "Apologetics," in *Contemporary Evangelical Thought,* ed. Carl F. H. Henry (Great Neck, N.Y.: Channel Press, 1957), 137.

6. Carl F. H. Henry, *Evangelicals in Search of Identity* (Waco, Tex.: Word Books, 1976), 30–31.

7. See the list in Nelson, *Making and Unmaking of an Evangelical Mind,* 55–56.

8. Frank E. Gaebelein, "Education," in Henry, *Contemporary Evangelical Thought,* 163–78.

9. Gasper, *Fundamentalist Movement,* 28–29.

10. Harold B. Kuhn, "Philosophy of Religion," in Henry, *Contemporary Evangelical Thought,* 239; see also L. Nelson Bell, "A Layman and His Faith: Simplicity in Preaching—A Plea," *Christianity Today* 2 (February 17, 1958), 19. See George M. Marsden, *Fundamentalism and American Culture* (Oxford: Oxford University Press, 1980), for a good description of the thought of Machen and of commonsense philosophy. For a helpful taxonomy of evangelical theories of biblical authority see Gabriel Fackre, "Evangelical Hermeneutics: Commonality and Diversity," *Interpretation* 43 (April 1989), 117–28.

11. Edward J. Young, "The Old Testament," in Henry, *Contemporary Evangelical Thought,* 38.

12. Alister E. McGrath does a good job of describing the basic shape and implications of Bultmann's work in *Christian Theology: An Introduction* (Oxford: Basil Blackwell, 1994).

13. J. Marcellus Kik, "Are Evangelicals Literalists?" *Christianity Today* 1 (November 12, 1956), 27.

14. Edward John Carnell, "Can Billy Graham Slay the Giant?" *Christianity Today* 1 (May 13, 1957), 4.

15. Kik, "Are Evangelicals Literalists?" 27; see also G. Brillenburg Wurth, "Theological Climate in America," *Christianity Today* 1 (February 18, 1957), 13.

16. Ned B. Stonehouse, "The Pathos of Religious Liberalism," *Christianity Today* 1 (April 29, 1957), 3; see also George Eldon Ladd, "Revelation, History, and the Bible," *Christianity Today* 1 (September 30, 1957), 7.

17. James I. Packer, "Contemporary Views of Revelation, Part II," *Christianity Today* 3 (December 8, 1958), 17.

18. Carl F. H. Henry, *Frontiers in Modern Theology* (Chicago: Moody Press, 1964), 60–61; see also Henry, *The God Who Shows Himself* (Waco, Tex.: Word Books, 1966), 22, 90.

19. L. Nelson Bell, "A Layman and His Faith: The Christ of the Bible," *Christianity Today* 1 (August 19, 1957), 19.

20. Roth, "Christ and the Muses," 9. The contrast between neo-evangelical and liberal ideas about modern art is very clear if one compares Roth to liberal Finley Eversole: "Our art is an art of anguish and guilt, of isolation and emptiness, of doubt and damnation. . . . Yet

our art has discovered, as the art of no other generation has, the meaning of freedom, of courage, of inwardness and honesty. Clearly, modern art is the child of the twentieth century!" Finley Eversole, ed., *Christian Faith and the Contemporary Arts* (Nashville: Abingdon Press, 1957), 11.

21. "Dali's Place in Religious Art," *Christianity Today* 1 (December 10, 1956), 26–27, 34.

22. From an undated ad produced after Sallman's death by Kriebel and Bates, Bates File, Sallman Archives, Anderson University.

23. Such an interpretive pamphlet of Sallman's *The Boy Christ* was advertised for twenty-five cents. "In a 12-page booklet . . . Mr. Ellis gives the background of the painting and the story to be found in it. For parents and teachers it provides an abundance of material which can be used in connection with the picture. The booklet itself is an inspiration to read." *Moody Monthly* 45, no. 9 (May 1945), 497.

24. Publicity letter by Fred M. Bates, n.d., Bates File, Sallman Archives.

25. Mrs. William Jeschke, "Sallman's Paintings of the Master: The Story of an Interview with Warner Sallman and an Interpretation of his Six Famous Paintings," *1947 Annual,* vol. 2 (Cleveland: North American Baptist General Conference, 1947), n.p.

26. Howard W. Ellis, *Story of Sallman's "Good Shepherd"* (Indianapolis: Kriebel and Bates, 1944), 6–7; see also another brief interpretation, "Sallman's 'The Lord Is My Shepherd': An Interpretation," in *A Series of Interpretations of the Sallman Religious Masterpieces* (Indianapolis: Kriebel and Bates, n.d.), n.p.

27. Fred Bates, *The Road to Emmaus* (Indianapolis: Kriebel and Bates, 1961), frontispiece, 14; see also comments on the painting *Mary and Martha with Jesus* in Elna Kenney, "Sallman's Religious Paintings," *Idaho Free Press* (December 1, 1962), 12.

28. Sylvia E. Peterson, *Story of Sallman's "Teach Me Thy Way"* (Indianapolis: Kriebel and Bates, 1952), 5–9.

29. Dorothy C. Haskin, *Christians You Would Like to Know* (Grand Rapids, Mich.: Zondervan Publishing House, 1954), 66; Glenn D. Everett, "Story of a Great Picture," *Link* 16, no. 4 (April 1958), 63.

30. Bell, "A Layman and His Faith: Simplicity in Preaching," 19.

31. Carl F. H. Henry, "Evangelism and the Sacred Book," *Christianity Today* 1 (October 15, 1956), 23. The article by Billy Graham is "Biblical Authority in Evangelism," 5–7, 17.

32. Carnell, "Can Billy Graham Slay the Giant?" 4.

33. Andrew W. Blackwood, "Marks of Great Evangelical Preaching," *Christianity Today* 1 (November 12, 1956), 5.

34. Henry, "Evangelical Piety and Christian Art," 26.

35. Bruce Baylor, "A Man's Artist," *Sunday School Promoter* 5, no. 2 (May 1943), 26.

36. See Mark A. Noll's assessment that an essential characteristic of fundamentalism was its identity as a popular movement and its preference for technique and argumentation that appealed to the general public. His study of evangelical biblical scholarship reveals how even the most scholarly evangelical leaders disengaged from the academic guild for a "marriage of convenience between conservative scholars and the revivalist tradition." Noll, *Between Faith and Criticism: Evangelicals, Scholarship, and the Bible in America* (San Francisco: Harper and Row, 1969), 47.

37. Henry, "Evangelical Piety and Christian Art," 26.

38. T. A. Stafford, "A Consecrated Artist," *Expositor and Homiletic Review* 43, no. 3 (March 1941), 142–43.

39. Sylvia E. Peterson, "The Ministry of . . . Christian Art," *Christian Digest* 12 (September

1947), 34–35. The article also appeared in *War Cry* 27, no. 1378 (May 24, 1947), 4–5, 8; *Lutheran Companion* 55, no. 14 (April 2, 1947), 10–12; and *Sunday School Herald* 11, no. 6 (April 20, 1947), 121–22.

40. Haskin, *Christians You Would Like to Know,* 66.

41. Jeschke, "Sallman's Paintings of the Master," 21.

42. Gordon Kelly, "The Mystery of Aesthetics: A Christian Painter Shares His Artistic Convictions," *Christianity Today* 10 (September 2, 1966), 27–28, 33.

43. H. R. Rookmaaker, "Letter to a Christian Artist," *Christianity Today* 10 (September 2, 1966), 25–27. Compare this statement to a liberal's description: "Artists tend to be neurotic personalities. They cannot live with themselves or adjust to others. Even if others were to conform to them, they would not be able to accept the *status quo* for long. . . . They are cursed, and at the same time blessed, with a higher tension of sensitivity. . . . Where there is no strife and tension there is not art, in a pure sense. Scribes and hacks who produce continuously are like parasites living on the ideas of others. They are men of good stability and so they bring forth nothing novel in the arts." Julius Portnoy, "Is the Creative Process Similar in the Arts?" in Eversole, *Christian Faith and the Contemporary Arts,* 60–61. On Rookmaaker's close relationship with Francis Schaeffer see Linette Martin, *Hans Rookmaaker: A Biography* (Downers Grove, Ill.: InterVarsity Press, 1979), 107–8.

44. Carl F. H. Henry, "The Christian Stake in Education and the Arts," *Christianity Today* 10 (September 2, 1966), n.p.

45. Billy Graham, *How To Be Born Again* (Waco, Tex.: Word Books, 1977), 168. See Peter Toon, *Born Again: A Biblical and Theological Study of Regeneration* (Grand Rapids, Mich.: Baker Book House, 1987), for a historical survey of the development of conversion theology.

46. Lewis R. Rambo, *Understanding Religious Conversion* (New Haven: Yale University Press, 1993), 12–16.

47. Billy Graham, *The Challenge: Sermons from Madison Square Garden* (Garden City, N.Y.: Doubleday, 1969), 112; see also Andrew W. Blackwood, "Evangelism and Preaching," in Henry, *Contemporary Evangelical Thought,* 294; Toon, *Born Again,* 175.

48. Warner Sallman, "My Greatest Spiritual Experience," *Chicago Daily News* (March 10, 1953), 30.

49. Dorothy C. Haskin, "The Man Who Painted a Manly Head of Christ," *Contact* 5, no. 5 (February 1, 1953), 4.

50. Baylor, "Man's Artist," 26.

51. T. Otto Nall, "He Preaches as He Paints," *Classmate* 50, no. 50 (December 1943), 6.

52. Blackwood, "Evangelism and Preaching," 285.

53. Nall, "He Preaches as He Paints," 7.

54. *Moody Monthly* 41, no. 6 (February 1941), 359.

55. Fred Bates, *Story of Sallman's "Follow Thou Me"* (Indianpolis: Warner Press, 1949), 10–11.

56. Hiley H. Ward, "Stern or Tender? Artist Undertakes Job of Drawing Jesus at Worship Service," clipping from an unknown newspaper, Bates File, Sallman Archives. Another newspaper account describes a similar service: see "Church to Get Picture Artist Reproduced Here," *Anderson (Ind.) Daily Bulletin* (July 21, 1961), n.p. For yet another account of the beginning of Sallman's chalk talks see Everett, "Story of a Great Picture," 12–17, 62–63.

57. James F. Harrison, "Chalk Illustration," *Moody Monthly* 47, no. 6 (February 1947), 452.

58. Haskin, "The Man Who Painted a Manly Head of Christ," 10–11. Evidence suggests that

people were converted by Sallman chalk talks; see letters 63, 75, 263, 335, 344, and 387 in the Correspondence File, Sallman Archives.

59. Dale McCulley, *Son of Man,* dir. Henry Ushijima (Chicago: North Park College and Theological Seminary, Swedish Covenant Hospital, and Evangelical Mission Covenant Church of America, 1954).

60. Joseph F. Kett, *Rites of Passage: Adolescence in America, 1790 to the Present* (New York: Basic Books, 1977), 204–7.

61. Henry Rische, "What Young People Need," *Christianity Today* 1 (July 8, 1957), 13–14.

62. Pitirim A. Sorokin, "Demoralization of Youth: Open Germs and Hidden Viruses," *Christianity Today* 3 (July 6, 1959), 3.

63. Talbot Ellis, "A Judge Speaks Out," *Christianity Today* 3 (July 6, 1959), 12; see also, in the same issue, Russell J. Fornwalt, "'For They Have Sown the Wind,'" 8–10, and J. Marcellus Kik, "Combating Juvenile Delinquency," 13–15.

64. Carl F. H. Henry, "A Christian Answer to America's Youth Problem," *Christianity Today* 3 (February 16, 1959), 21.

65. Glenda Riley, *Divorce: An American Tradition* (New York: Oxford University Press, 1991), 159.

66. Blackwood, "Evangelism and Preaching," 310; and L. Nelson Bell, "A Layman and His Faith: Building Christian Homes," *Christianity Today* 2 (March 3, 1958), 19. See David Harrington Watt's description of evangelical concerns about family life in *A Transforming Faith: Explorations of Twentieth-Century American Evangelicalism* (New Brunswick: Rutgers University Press, 1991), 61–62, 84–91.

67. See, e.g., Graham, *How to Be Born Again,* 10, 20–21.

68. Albert W. Beaven, *Fireside Talks for the Family Circle* (Philadelphia: Judson Press, 1928), 56–64.

69. "Space Age Teaching Tools," *Christianity Today* 3 (August 31, 1959), 8.

70. J. Maurice Trimmer, "The Influence of Pictures," *Religious Digest* 20, no. 141 (June 1947), 50–51.

71. Howard Ellis, *An Interpretation of Sallman's "Head of Christ" Painting* (Indianapolis: Kriebel and Bates, 1944), 5; see also Nall, "He Preaches as He Paints," 6–7; Gerard Johnson, "Friends Fete Artist on Sixtieth Birthday," *Covenant Weekly* 41 (May 16, 1952); Jennie Vimmerstedt, "Warner Sallman Given 'Upper Room' Citation," *Jamestown (N.Y.) Post-Journal* (October 10, 1957), 1; Jeschke, "Sallman's Paintings of the Master," 20; and Peterson, "Ministry of Christian Art."

72. Nall, "He Preaches as He Paints," 7.

73. Everett, "Story of a Great Picture," 16.

74. An undated ad in the Bates File, Sallman Archives.

75. See a short interpretation of *Thine Is the Power* in the Bates File, Sallman Archives, for information about the Luther League; *Tellum* 31, no. 1 (June 1960), 3, for the Methodist Youth Fellowship; a copy of the Baptist Youth Fellowship poster (Philadelphia: Judson Press, 1942) in the Bates File, Sallman Archives; news of the Evangelical Covenant Youth Rally in "Artist Who Painted Famous 'Head of Christ' to Sketch at Covenant Youth Rally Tonight," *Miami Herald* (June 21, 1958), 9-A.

76. "Philadelphia Central Uses Sallman's 'Christ' to Spread Christian Message," *National Council Bulletin* 21, no. 5 (May 1947), 10.

77. See letters 324, 325, 326, 341, 357, 363, 365, 366, 375, 383, 395, 398, 419, 422, 423, 435, 438, 443, 466, and 478 in the Correspondence File, Sallman Archives.

Chapter 5
Sallman and the Critics of Mass Culture

An Ailsa Mellon Bruce Senior Fellowship at the Center for Advanced Study in the Visual Arts at the National Gallery of Art made possible the completion of the final draft of this chapter. I gratefully acknowledge the Center's generous support.

1. See, e.g., Joan Shelley Rubin, *The Making of the Middlebrow* (Chapel Hill: University of North Carolina Press, 1992); Paul DiMaggio, "Cultural Boundaries and Structural Change: The Extension of the High Culture Model to Theatre, Opera, and the Dance, 1900–1940," in *Cultivating Differences: Symbolic Boundaries and the Making of Inequality*, ed. Michèle Lamont and Marcel Fournier (Chicago: University of Chicago Press, 1992), 21–57; Janice A. Radway, *Reading the Romance: Women, Patriarchy, and Popular Literature* (Chapel Hill: University of North Carolina Press, 1984); David Halle, *Inside Culture: Art and Class in the American Home* (Chicago: University of Chicago Press, 1993); and Lawrence W. Levine, *Highbrow/Lowbrow: The Emergence of Cultural Hierarchy in America* (Cambridge: Harvard University Press, 1988).

2. By no means do I advocate revision of the historical canon of fine art to include artists like Warner Sallman. What is called for, instead, is the serious examination of the arrangement of visual culture in the United States and art-historical consideration of extra-canonical aspects of the visual field. As a first step, this necessitates maintaining a dialectical or circular relation between understanding and evaluation, so that evaluation does not precede and truncate understanding.

3. Cf. Howard S. Becker, *Art Worlds* (Berkeley: University of California Press, 1982); and Diana Crane, "High Culture Versus Popular Culture Revisited: A Reconceptualization of Recorded Cultures," in Lamont and Fournier, *Cultivating Differences*, 58–74, esp. 60, 68.

4. Elwood Ellwood, "Return from Miltown: The Terrible Taste of Protestantism," *motive* 18, no. 1 (October 1957), 14–17.

5. For my purposes and for the period of time under consideration, William R. Hutchison's definition of the Protestant establishment and its relation to liberal religion is useful. According to Hutchison, the Protestant establishment, the "group of churches and network of leaders that appear, prima facie, to have dominated American Protestantism in the earlier twentieth century, and to have enjoyed considerable religious and cultural authority in the environing society," included seven denominations: Congregationalists, Episcopalians, Presbyterians, Baptists and Methodists (especially in the North), Disciples of Christ, and Lutherans. Acknowledging that these denominations all retained the allegiance of people who were not liberals, Hutchison suggested that "liberal" was, nevertheless, the descriptive terminology used most frequently in theological seminaries and relevant periodicals to characterize this group, the principal religious heirs of liberal ideology and its mythology of the individual. Although I am aware that the terminology precludes recognition of certain complexities, in this chapter I will follow this usage. William R. Hutchison, "Preface: From Protestant to Pluralist America," and "Protestantism as Establishment," both in *Between the Times: The Travail of the Protestant Establishment in America, 1900–1960*, ed. William R. Hutchison (Cambridge: Cambridge University Press, 1989), x, 13–16.

    In the 1950s, although the apparent hegemony of the Protestant establishment held, the move from a Protestant America to a pluralist America was well under way. Hutchison, "Preface," vii. In fact, the urgency of the liberal reaction to Sallman can be accounted for, in part, by uncertainties attending this transition.

6. This chapter is not an exhaustive examination of diversity within camps but a general consideration of the differences between two major publics—an overview of some of the recurring issues, variables, and concerns. Despite the polarizing discourse of the debate, careful analysis reveals multiple perspectives and cultures within individuals as well as between individuals.

7. Tom F. Driver, "The Arts and the Christian Evangel," *Christian Scholar* 40, no. 4 (December 1957), 334.

8. The linking of Sallman with such high-culture artists as Hofmann and Uhde demonstrates the conflation, in this literature, of mass culture and its reproductive technologies with the stylistic traits Tillich denounced.

9. Marion Junkin, "Truth in Art," *motive* 10, no. 1 (October 1949), 23.

10. See, e.g., Janice Radway, "The Scandal of the Middlebrow: The Book-of-the-Month Club, Class Fracture, and Cultural Authority," *South Atlantic Quarterly* 89, no. 4 (Fall 1990), 703–36.

11. This characterization brought Marxist sensibilities to the task of cultural criticism. From the perspective of this European-driven critique, consumption in a capitalist society reduced human beings to automatons.

12. Theodor Adorno and Max Horkheimer, "The Culture Industry: Enlightenment as Mass Deception," in *The Cultural Studies Reader,* ed. Simon During (New York: Routledge, 1993), 29–43.

13. T. J. Jackson Lears, "A Matter of Taste: Corporate Cultural Hegemony in a Mass-Consumption Society," in *Recasting America: Culture and Politics in the Age of the Cold War,* ed. Lary May (Chicago: University of Chicago Press, 1989), 38–57. Between 1944 and 1953, Dwight Macdonald revised his essay "A Theory of Popular Culture" as "A Theory of Mass Culture." Although more benign than another alternative, "mob," "mass" was also clearly more passive, more inert, less individuated than "popular." See Dwight Macdonald, "A Theory of Mass Culture," in *Mass Culture: The Popular Arts in America,* ed. Bernard Rosenberg and David Manning White (Glencoe, Ill.: Free Press, 1957), 59–73.

14. David Riesman, *The Lonely Crowd: A Study of the Changing American Character,* rev. ed. (New Haven: Yale University Press, 1970); and Macdonald, "Theory of Mass Culture," 69.

15. Editorial, "The Lonely Crowd at Prayer," *Christian Century* 73, no. 22 (May 1956), 663.

16. Radway, "Scandal of the Middlebrow," 705–6, examines the perceived incompatibility of standardization with ideal political and cultural configurations in the United States.

17. Although Dwight Macdonald modified his Marxist politics after World War II, his work in the 1950s retained elements of two earlier currents of cultural criticism: the Marxism of the Frankfurt intellectuals and the conservative defense of high culture represented in the work of T. S. Eliot and José Ortega y Gasset; see James Gilbert, *A Cycle of Outrage: America's Reaction to the Juvenile Delinquent in the 1950s* (New York: Oxford University Press, 1986), 119. Ultimately Macdonald rejected both the "conservative proposal to save culture by restoring the old class lines" and the "Marxian hope for a new democratic, classless culture" as well as the "democratic/liberal" proposal to raise the level of mass culture itself. Macdonald, "Theory of Mass Culture," 69–71.

18. Clement Greenberg, "Avant-Garde and Kitsch," in *Art and Culture* (Boston: Beacon Press, 1961), 10–12. Greenberg first published this essay in *Partisan Review* in 1939.

19. Ibid., 15.

20. Macdonald, "Theory of Mass Culture," 59; see also 60–62. Tillich sometimes translated

"kitsch" as "junk"; others rendered it "trash." See, e.g., Marvin Halverson, foreword to an issue featuring "Religious Art," *Art in America* 45, no. 3 (Fall 1957), 12.

21. Tillich became professor of philosophy at the University of Frankfurt in 1929. Because of his opposition to Nazism, he was dismissed from that institution in 1933, at the same time as Max Horkheimer and a number of other Frankfurt intellectuals. In 1934, along with other Frankfurt refugees, Tillich settled in New York as professor of philosophical theology at Union Theological Seminary with a joint appointment as professor of philosophy at Columbia University. When he retired from that position in 1955, he became university professor at Harvard, and in 1962 he accepted a special chair in theology at the University of Chicago. James C. Livingston, *Modern Christian Thought: From the Enlightenment to Vatican II* (New York: Macmillan, 1971), 356.

22. Paul Tillich, "Prefatory Note," in *New Images of Man,* by Peter Selz (New York: Museum of Modern Art, 1959), 9.

23. Paul Tillich, "Contemporary Visual Arts and the Revelatory Character of Style," in *Paul Tillich: On Art and Architecture,* ed. John Dillenberger and Jane Dillenberger (New York: Crossroad, 1987), 132–33 n. 3.

24. According to Max Horkheimer, Theodor Adorno, and Leo Lowenthal, whose work Tillich knew well, such a beautifying art of nostalgia for the past, instead of yearning for an "other" future, produced an uncritical, mesmerized, conformist audience; see Martin Jay, *The Dialectical Imagination: A History of the Frankfurt School and the Institute of Social Research, 1923–1950* (Boston: Little, Brown, 1973), 214–17. In a similar vein, Dwight Macdonald contended that mass commodification of culture could manifest itself in such "old art forms" as oil painting, as well as in the new media developed by mass culture. Thus, according to Macdonald's widely shared understanding, mass culture, while it generally relied on and conformed itself to the means of mechanical reproduction, also found stylistic expression in the traditionally nonreproducible media of fine art. Macdonald, "Theory of Mass Culture," 59.

25. Paul Tillich, "Existentialist Aspects of Modern Art," in Dillenberger and Dillenberger, *Paul Tillich,* 100–101. A large literature exists on the relation between the art of the 1940s and 1950s and the ideology of the free world. See, e.g., Annette Cox, *Art-as-Politics: The Abstract Expressionist Avant-Garde and Society* (Ann Arbor: UMI Research Press, 1982); Serge Guilbaut, *How New York Stole the Idea of Modern Art: Abstract Expressionism, Freedom, and the Cold War* (Chicago: University of Chicago Press, 1983); Eva Cockcroft, "Abstract Expressionism, Weapon of the Cold War," in *Art in Modern Culture: An Anthology of Critical Texts,* ed. Francis Frascina and Jonathan Harris (New York: Harper Collins, 1992), 82–90; Cécile Whiting, *Anti-Fascism in American Art* (New Haven: Yale University Press, 1989); Max Kozloff, "American Painting During the Cold War," *Artforum* 11 (May 1973), 43–54; and Erika Doss, *Benton, Pollock, and the Politics of Modernism: From Regionalism to Abstract Expressionism* (Chicago: University of Chicago Press, 1991).

26. Nathan A. Scott, Jr., "Art and the Renewal of Human Sensibility in Mass Society," in *Christian Faith and the Contemporary Arts,* ed. Finley Eversole (Nashville: Abingdon Press, 1957), 27. When he wrote these words, Scott was associate professor of theology and literature at the Divinity School of the University of Chicago.

27. Ellwood, "Return from Miltown," 15.

28. Edward C. Hobbs, "The Gospel in So-Called Secular Drama," in Eversole, *Christian Faith and the Contemporary Arts,* 147. In addition to his position at the Church Divinity School of the Pacific, Hobbs was a lecturer at the University of California School of Medicine.

29. Roger L. Shinn, "The Artist as Prophet-Priest of Culture," in Eversole, *Christian Faith and the Contemporary Arts,* 77. Shinn was professor of applied Christianity at Union Theological Seminary in New York.

30. Junkin, "Truth in Art," 23. Junkin criticized Sallman and Hofmann by name. The article is representative in its indication of churched resistance to certain kinds of cultural accommodation, especially to the association of the sacred with the commercial. See, e.g., H. Richard Niebuhr, *Christ and Culture* (New York: Harper and Row, 1951).

31. John Dixon, "Protestant Art and the Natural Order," *motive* 18, no. 2 (November 1956), 25. During the 1950s, John Dixon, executive secretary of the Faculty Christian Fellowship, taught at Emory University as well as at Florida Presbyterian College, where he was associate professor of art.

32. "*motive* Sales of Original Prints: A Price List," *motive* 18, no. 5 (February 1958), 28. The sale included works by Robert Hodgell; *motive* reproduced Hodgell's *Head of Christ,* as an implicit in-house alternative to Sallman's. For the first appearance of this *Head* see Robert Hodgell, "Portrait of Christ," *motive* 6, no. 3 (December 1945), 4. Hodgell provided a large number of illustrations for *motive* and served on the National Council of Churches Commission on Art. Published by the Methodist Board of Higher Education, *motive* was described by Harold Ehrensperger (scholar of religion and drama on the faculty of Boston University School of Theology and contributing editor of *motive*) as a medium "in which artists of more recent schools find sympathetic treatment"; see Harold Ehrensperger, "The Search for the Creative Image," *Christian Century* 73, no. 21 (May 23, 1956), 643. By 1958, *motive* called itself the "leading Protestant publication in the field of the arts"; see "Words into Images: *motive's* Permanent Art Collection," *motive* 18, no. 5 (February 1958), 20. The status of *motive* as a principal vehicle for negative criticism of Sallman is especially interesting given the enthusiastic support for Sallman elsewhere within Methodism.

33. "What Is 'Good' Art?" *motive* 18, no. 5 (February 1958), 29. Although the Methodists sponsored the conference, Reinhardt was a Lutheran and Fitz-Gerald an Episcopalian.

34. A particularly virulent episode of anti-intellectualism placed secular intellectuals themselves under attack from the political Right at this time.

35. Margaret Rigg, "The Art of the Byzantine Mosaics," *motive* 19, no. 6 (March 1959), 22.

36. Junkin, "Truth in Art," 23.

37. David Halle, "The Audience for Abstract Art: Class, Culture, and Power," in Lamont and Fournier, *Cultivating Differences,* 131.

38. See Ellwood, "Return from Miltown," 15, for rejection of "art you don't even have to look at."

39. Paul Tillich and Theodore M. Greene, "Authentic Religious Art," in *Masterpieces of Religious Art,* the catalogue of an exhibition held in connection with the second assembly of the World Council of Churches, July 15 to August 31, 1954, Art Institute of Chicago, 9.

40. Bernard Rosenberg, "Mass Culture in America," in Rosenberg and White, *Mass Culture,* 9.

41. John W. Dixon, Jr., "History and Morality in Art," *Christian Scholar* 45 (1962), 155–56. This article adopts specific metaphoric constructions from Macdonald in reviewing Greenberg, demonstrating that Dixon was familiar with the work of both critics.

42. When Sallman's liberal critics castigated his art for its sentimentality, which they did with considerable frequency, they meant to attack its "falsehood" and "dishonesty." In this context, the critics conceived of sentimentality as a subcategory of both beautifying naturalism and mass culture; they desired "no sweetly sentimental or slickly streamlined versions of religious themes." Catherine Linder, "Something New Between Art and Protes-

tant Theology," *motive* 13, no. 6 (March 1953), 28. The despised quality of sentimentality combined a sort of false and overinflated emotion or sentiment with a sort of superficial and debased beauty.

43. Martin E. Marty, "The Test of the Tastemakers," *Christian Century* 75, no. 8 (February 19, 1958), 228.

44. Junkin, "Truth in Art," 22.

45. Keith Irwin, "Symbolism and the Loss of Meaning," *motive* 19, no. 8 (May 1959), 23. Irwin recommended Rouault on these terms.

46. Finley Eversole, "The Brave New World of the Modern Artist," in Eversole, *Christian Faith and the Contemporary Arts,* 49–50, emphasis in original. Eversole, a staff member of the National Council of Churches, was also director of the Committee for the Interseminary Movement of the National Student Christian Federation.

47. Paul Tillich, *The Courage to Be* (New Haven: Yale University Press, 1952), 147–48; see also Tillich and Greene, "Authentic Religious Art," 9.

48. Gordon Bailey Washburn, "Claims of the Artist," *motive* 19, no. 8 (May 1959), 16. Washburn was director of Fine Arts at the Carnegie Institute.

49. Eversole, "Brave New World," 46.

50. Ehrensperger, "Search for the Creative Image," 644; Dixon, "Protestant Art and the Natural Order," 25.

51. Cf. Michael Leja, *Reframing Abstract Expressionism: Subjectivity and Painting in the 1940s* (New Haven: Yale University Press, 1993), 2.

52. Harry R. Garvin, "Religion and the Arts: The Coming Dangers," *Christian Scholar* 42 (1959), 275–83. Evangelicals saw evidence of secularization in the (liberal) definition of religion as ultimate concern for ultimate reality; liberals saw evidence of secularization in the commercialization of (evangelical) religious culture.

53. See, for example, Dennis N. Voskuil, "Reaching Out: Mainline Protestantism and the Media," in Hutchison, *Between the Times,* 72–92, esp. 89.

54. The National Council's Commission on Art enumerated explicitly the last pair of these aims in its statement of purpose. The commission should encourage churches to "purge themselves of those forms of commercialized art [labeled elsewhere in the document as feeble, saccharine, and vulgar] which are an affront to the Christian faith" and should "foster an active relationship between contemporary artists and the churches." "Statement of Purpose and Aims," Department of Worship and the Arts, National Council of Churches (the document includes statements for all six commissions of the department), the Museum of Modern Art Archives: Alfred H. Barr, Jr., Papers [AAA: 2184; 1263].

55. In a note of October 3, 1955, urging Mrs. John D. Rockefeller III to serve on the National Council's Commission on Art, the commission's chair, Alfred Barr, expressed his passionate interest in addressing the "deplorably ill-informed and uncultivated attitude toward the use of art on the part of the vast majority of clergy and church people in this country." MoMA Archives: AHB Papers [AAA: 2184; 1199].

56. [Amos Wilder], "Christianity and the Arts: The Church, the Arts, and Contemporary Culture" [hereafter NCC Study Document], MoMA Archives: AHB Papers [AAA: 3148; 588].

57. Paradoxically, at the same time that religion became interested in high art, many American intellectuals seemed to be considering the possibility that religion might fill a number of cultural voids created by the mechanics of mass culture. Overall, however, a 1950 *Partisan Review* symposium concluded that religion functioned in an essentially escapist fashion. The same conclusion was drawn by many observers of religion's demographic "revival" in the 1950s. Increases were understood to be largely deceptive, indicating the attraction of

looking to the certainties of the past for strength in time of difficulty and threat. See, for example, Editorial, "The Lonely Crowd at Prayer," 662–63.

58. Describing a process of cultural sacralization in the late nineteenth and early twentieth centuries, Paul DiMaggio asserts the linkage, in the United States, of the "high culture model" and the "trustee-governed non-profit enterprise." According to DiMaggio, this connection facilitated the separation of culture from the sphere of commerce; DiMaggio, "Cultural Boundaries and Structural Change," 22. Liberal Protestants and secular intellectuals alike wanted to separate the "sacred" (defined as religion, high culture, or some combination of the two) from the commercial.

59. NCC Study Document, MoMA Archives: AHB Papers [AAA: 3148; 584, 589]. Cf. the National Council's 1957 "Study Proposal" on "The Popular Arts and Contemporary Religious Life," MoMA Archives: AHB Papers [AAA: 2184; 1306–8]. See also the editorial "The Heavies and the Heroes," *Christian Century* 75, no. 2 (January 8, 1958), 38.

60. Garvin, "Religion and the Arts," 280.

61. Ehrensperger, "Search for the Creative Image," 643.

62. NCC Study Document, MoMA Archives: AHB Papers [AAA: 3148; 588]. On the particular appeal of abstract expressionism for liberal Protestant intellectuals see Eversole, "Brave New World," 45–55.

63. From this perspective, and in the context of the Cold War, abstract expressionism represented a global culture of American origin, evidence of what the free world could produce.

64. Ehrensperger, in "Search for the Creative Image," 644, explicitly mentions the "familiar sentimental and insipid paintings of Jesus." Many believed that the United States, in the 1950s, was approaching classlessness. In 1949 Russell Lynes, editor of *Harper's,* asserted the obsolescence of economic class and its replacement by "taste cultures"; Russell Lynes, "Highbrow, Lowbrow, Middlebrow," *Life* (April 11, 1949), 99–102. Paintings like the ones just described as familiar and insipid clarified the threat that, for many liberal intellectuals, accompanied the promise of the demise of class. Paul Tillich feared that the emerging classless society would too closely resemble the "vulgar materialism" of the middle class. Dwight Macdonald voiced a similar concern that the high and low would be swallowed by the middle.

65. The sense of past discontinuity between art and religion in the Protestant tradition was widely shared even though, in the United States especially, art and religion had a long-standing and rather intimate (albeit generally non-institutional) relationship.

66. On February 12, 1954, Marvin Halverson wrote to Alfred Barr regarding Barr's appointment as chair of the National Council's Commission on Art: "The Commission on Art is crucial, for Protestantism's failure to reckon with the visual arts represents a serious cultural lag"; MoMA Archives: AHB Papers [AAA: 2180; 458]. By the late 1950s and early 1960s, the evangelicals too were generally convinced of the efficacy of this enterprise, the only difference being that they looked at different art and with different criteria of evaluation in mind. See, for instance, Robert Paul Roth, "Christ and the Muses," *Christianity Today* 2, no. 11 (March 3, 1958), 9.

67. NCC Study Document, MoMA Archives: AHB Papers [AAA: 3148; 587].

68. Junkin, "Truth in Art," 23.

69. Amos Wilder, quoted in Nathan A. Scott, Jr., "Poetry, Religion, and the Modern Mind," *Journal of Religion* 33, no. 3 (July 1953), 196. The gravitation of both art and religion toward the discursive framework of the sublime refined the fit of this characterization. Art could, in fact, be construed as an avenue for divine encounter, a window onto ultimate reality and ultimate concern.

70. Garvin, "Religion and the Arts," 280.

71. Ehrensperger, "Search for the Creative Image," 643.

72. NCC Study Document, MoMA Archives: AHB Papers [AAA: 3148; 588].

73. Tillich and Greene, "Authentic Religious Art."

74. Marvin Halverson, "Two Experiments in Correlation: Department of Worship and the Arts," *Christian Scholar* 40, no. 4 (December 1957), 345–52.

75. Preston Roberts, "Two Experiments in Correlation: The Field of Religion and Art at Chicago," *Christian Scholar* 40, no. 4 (December 1957), 339–45.

76. See Wilson Yates, *The Arts in Theological Education* (Atlanta: Scholar's Press, 1987), 1–3.

77. See Halverson to Barr, May 20, 1955, MoMA Archives: AHB Papers [AAA: 2148; 1203], regarding the recommendations of the nominating committee of the National Council of Churches' Commission on Art. It is illuminating to recall that not until the mid-1950s did the words "under God" find their way into the Pledge of Allegiance; if the enemy was *"atheistic"* communism, then religion became a patriotic duty. Alfred Barr was an active participant in this conversation in terms of both religion and politics (although his political commitments are better known). For discussion of Barr's convictions regarding individual freedom and abstraction, especially as reflected in *What Is Modern Painting?* (in its 1943, 1952, and 1956 editions), see Patricia Hills, "The Modern Corporate State, the Rhetoric of Freedom, and the Emergence of Modernism in the United States: The Mediation of Language in Critical Practice," in *Art Criticism since 1900,* ed. Malcolm Gee (Manchester, England: Manchester University Press, 1993), 143–63.

78. Editorial introduction to *Presbyterian Life* 8, no. 25 (December 24, 1955), 2. This issue includes an article by Barr, "Unto You Is Born This Day a Savior: Paintings of the Nativity."

79. In spite of the occasional dissension surrounding his position at the Museum of Modern Art, Barr was uniquely placed as a principal arbiter of modernism to the wider American public. As a popularizer, Barr had at least one foot in the middle range despised by Macdonald (who characterized Barr's conduct in regard to MoMA as a "nine ring circus"); overall, however, the tone of the manuscript for Macdonald's *New Yorker* profile of Barr is one of admiration; MoMA Archives: AHB Papers [AAA: 2180; 678–760, quotation from 696]. Barr wrote to Macdonald in 1954, criticizing his mass-culture piece for its "rather hopeless attitude toward the cultural potentialities of the democracy"; MoMA Archives, AHB Papers [AAA: 2180; 769].

80. "The Religious Spirit in Contemporary Art," MoMA Archives: AHB Papers [AAA: 3145; 1296].

81. In 1952 Barr accepted an appointment to the Commission on Art; in 1953 he participated in identifying possible candidates for the chair, recommending consideration of John Nicolas Brown, Perry Rathbone, and Wolfgang Stechow. In 1954 he agreed to assume the position of chair himself. Earlier Barr had also accepted appointment as vice-chair of the National Council's larger Department of Worship and the Arts. See MoMA Archives: AHB Papers [AAA: 2180; 345 and 460–65].

82. Barr to Rathbone, March 21, 1955, MoMA Archives: AHB Papers [AAA: 2180; 329].

83. Ibid., MoMA Archives: AHB Papers [AAA: 2180; 330]. The article, "The Life of Christ as Seen by Great Artists," appeared in a special issue of *Life* devoted to the subject of Christianity, dated December 26, 1955.

84. MoMA Archives: AHB Papers [AAA: 2184; 1148].

85. Halverson, who resigned from the National Council in 1962 in frustration over what he perceived as the institutional church's hesitation to take appropriate advantage of what

artists, historians, and museum personnel had to offer, involved Barr and Tillich in forming "ARC"; see MoMA Archives: AHB Papers [AAA: 3148; 563–71]. In November 1993, ARC met in New Harmony, Indiana, the site of Tillich's grave. This organization is now called the Society for the Arts, Religion, and Contemporary Culture.

86. E.g., Selz's *New Images of Man,* 1959, for which Tillich wrote a prefatory note. In addition, in 1957 *Art in America* issued a special feature on religion and art in the United States. The Renaissance Society at the University of Chicago organized an exhibition and symposium, *The Conditions of Modern Man,* on contemporary art and religion, which ran from January 6 to February 2, 1957. Speakers at the symposium included members of the graduate faculties in both art history and religion; "University of Chicago Offers Religious Art Exhibit," *Christian Century* 74, no. 13 (March 27, 1957), 398. A memo from Halverson to Barr of May 20, 1955, noted the nomination of David E. Finley, George Heard Hamilton, Duncan Phillips, Robert Motherwell, and Mrs. John D. Rockefeller III to the National Council's Commission on Art; MoMA Archives: AHB Papers [AAA: 2184; 1203]. In 1956, on the occasion of the National Cathedral's fiftieth anniversary, Finley assisted with the cathedral's exhibition of "modern American religious art"; David E. Finley Papers, Box 47, "Washington Cathedral Fiftieth Anniversary Exhibition," Archives of the National Gallery of Art. The advisory committee for Union Theological Seminary's 1952 exhibition of contemporary religious art consisted of Lloyd Goodrich, Meyer Schapiro, and Eloise Spaeth, as well as Paul Tillich; see Linder, "Something New," 24–29.

87. Junkin, "Truth in Art," 23.

88. If, following Clifford Geertz, culture is a meaning-making enterprise and, following John Clarke, culture can be delineated as a "social field of meaning production," then the size of the "sample" expands or contracts based on the particular social field identified as the object of study. Different culture worlds constitute different social fields for the production of meaning. See Clifford Geertz, *The Interpretation of Cultures* (New York: Basic Books, 1973); and John Clarke, "Pessimism Versus Populism: The Problematic Politics of Popular Culture," in *For Fun and Profit: The Transformation of Leisure into Consumption,* ed. Richard Butsch (Philadelphia: Temple University Press, 1990), 28–44, esp. 28.

    Although this chapter focuses on the Protestant situation, Catholic intellectuals of the period also engaged the modernist aesthetic. They, too, opposed "realism," but on somewhat different grounds. Although they shared some of the premises of the mass-culture complaint, the key issue for American Catholics was the divinity of Christ. Catholics found realism suspect because it seemed to suggest the priority of the earthly, literal image. See, e.g., Richard Charles Muehlberger, "Sacred Art: A Critique on the Contemporary Situation," *Liturgical Arts* 28, no. 3 (May 1960), 69–72. (Although Muehlberger was a high-church Lutheran, he was profoundly influenced in his theology of art by the Catholic Art Forum. His words are representative of a widely shared Catholic perspective, and his article criticizes Sallman for "preach[ing] the gospel of the Unitarians" [70].)

89. See Roland Marchand, "Visions of Classlessness, Quests for Dominion: American Popular Culture, 1945–1960," in *Reshaping America: Society and Institutions, 1945–1960,* ed. Robert H. Bremner and Gary W. Reichard (Columbus: Ohio State University Press, 1982), 163–90. The Frankfurt School generally used popular and mass terminologies synonymously. All popular or mass culture, exhibiting a strong connection to commerce and reflecting the culture of the majority of people, was presumably imposed from above. This imposition constituted the principal distinction between popular and folk, which was understood to emerge from the people and to describe the products of specific, usually somehow isolated, groups with strong connections to tradition. During this period, the bias for folk and

against mass led to the salvage operation of casting some "desirable" popular American forms as folk in order to render them acceptable. For a variety of reasons, having principally to do with imprecision and inaccuracy in definition, the terms *folk* and *popular* have themselves problematized the study of cultural (and especially aesthetic) production in the United States.

90. Jay, *Dialectical Imagination,* 178.

91. The terminology of cultural pessimism and populism is Clarke's, "Pessimism Versus Populism," 28–44.

92. The cultural criticism of Susan Sontag and Marshall McLuhan figured prominently in this revaluation of popular culture; see Ronald Edsforth, "Popular Culture and Politics in Modern America: An Introduction," in *Popular Culture and Political Change in Modern America,* ed. Ronald Edsforth and Larry Bennett (Albany: State University of New York Press, 1991), 3–6.

93. These critical engagements of the 1950s and 1960s represented a relatively late manifestation of the long-standing concern with reconciling notions of democracy, class, and aesthetic quality in the United States. Intellectuals of the 1950s construed democracy as the right of each individual to an opinion but greatly mistrusted the wisdom of the collective mind. Reinhold Niebuhr claimed that only individuals could be truly moral. The evil associated with collectivities was much more stubborn than the evil associated with individuals; the individual's capacity to transcend evil was more fully developed than was society's. Reinhold Niebuhr, *Moral Man, Immoral Society* (New York: Charles Scribner's Sons, 1932).

94. Given the indictment of interchangeability, another, similar irony was the promotion of *any* Rouault as the preferred alternative.

95. Russell Lynes, *The Tastemakers* (New York: Harper and Brothers, 1949), 326–27; "Pen-Ultimate: One More 'In' and 'Out,'" *Christian Century* 79, no. 23 (June 6, 1962), 731.

96. Representing one aspect of this critique as it unfolds in the last decade of the twentieth century, a front-page article titled "Religion's Changing Face: More Churches Depicting Christ as Black," in the *Washington Post* (March 28, 1994), singled out Sallman's *Head of Christ* as exemplary of a popular "mythological" type of Caucasian Jesus. The article described a liturgical performance by the Reverend George Stallings of Imani Temple in which, "in Washington's Freedom Plaza on Good Friday last year, he set fire to Warner Sallman's famous image of a white Jesus." The image that Stallings destroys in figure 5.10 (from a *Post* photo of April 10, 1993) is not a Sallman. Calling for the iconoclastic and ritual "purification" of the image of the white Christ from the African-American experience, Stallings shredded and burned reproductions of works by numerous artists. Director Spike Lee's repeated use of Sallman's images in his movies (e.g., *Jungle Fever* and *Malcolm X*) demonstrates Lee's conviction that Sallman's work can function as a visual indicator of this broader ethnic critique.

Chapter 6
The Likeness of Christ in Sallman's Art

1. Flannery O'Connor, "Parker's Back," reprinted in *The Complete Stories* (New York: Farrar, Straus and Giroux, 1981). Quotation reprinted by permission.

2. For a description of the data-gathering instrument and a characterization of the letters, see the Appendix at the end of this chapter. I construct an account of the popular reception of Sallman's imagery that combines the two groups of information (materials from 1940 to

1960 and letters from the present) because the average age of those who responded to my query was 59, indicating that most respondents belonged to the generation reaching adulthood in the late 1940s and early 1950s (born ca. 1930). Clearly, the evidence of the letters sent to me is based on memory, but those who wrote acquired images by Sallman early in life and (in most cases) still display them in their homes. I do not wish to suggest that the popular reception of Sallman's work has remained unchanged since World War II. The decline of Sallman's popularity since about 1975 certainly shows that this is not the case. Asking why people bought Sallman's images in the 1940s or 1950s is not the same as asking why many people continue to admire them today. In the 1940s and 1950s the Sallman imagery was thought to shape behavior in the home and workplace; parents and friends gave pictures of Jesus to departing soldiers in order to keep them safe; and the *Head of Christ* was widely regarded as a symbol of American values during the early Cold War era. With the rise of the youth culture in the 1960s and the challenge from other religious publishers, Sallman's pictures began their decline in popularity. Today Sallman remains popular among older generations primarily as a cherished memory of divine benevolence over the course of a person's life. Nevertheless, when properly handled, the content of memories— the answers to the questions of who gave the image as a gift, what was the occasion, where did one display the image, why one liked or disliked it—constitutes useful evidence for the historian, as it often sheds the only light available on the uses to which the imagery was put.

3. Numbers in parentheses following a quotation indicate the number of the letter in the Research Query Correspondence File in the Sallman Archives of the Jessie C. Wilson Galleries, Anderson University.

4. For the Latin original and a possibly related Greek version see John McClintock and James Strong, *Cyclopaedia of Biblical, Theological and Ecclesiastical Literature* (New York: Harper, 1891), 5: 348–50.

5. Beth Lindberg, "Did Christ Look Like This?" *Christian Life* (December 1948), 19. For Josephus' brief discussion of Christ, which scholars consider a later addition to the text in whole or in part, see *The Life and Works of Flavius Josephus,* tr. William Whiston (Philadelphia: John C. Winston, 1957), bk. 18, chap. 3, 535.

6. F. M. Bates, *The Road to Emmaus,* illustrated by Warner Sallman (Indianapolis: Kriebel and Bates, 1961), title page; available in the Sallman Archives.

7. A thorough tracing of Sallman's iconographical sources has yet to be undertaken, but he possessed a large number of books on religious art and reproductions of art as well as imagery of the Holy Land (James Sallman, in conversation with me, March 9, 1992). On December 16, 1958, he wrote a note to Fred Bates and his wife to accompany a Christmas gift of a painting called *Cedars of Lebanon.* With the note, Sallman included a copy of an engraving from Sir Charles William Wilson, ed., *Picturesque Palestine,* 4 vols. (New York: Appleton, 1881–83), 2: 237, which showed a grove of cedars in Lebanon. Sallman's painting reproduced the engraving quite faithfully. A copy of the note and image are in the Bates archival material at Anderson University.

8. William L. Bird, "Sallman and His 'Head of Christ,'" *Christian Advocate* 118, no. 10 (March 11, 1943), 300.

9. T. Otto Nall, "He Preaches as He Paints," *Classmate* 50, no. 50 (December 1943), 7.

10. Mrs. William Jeschke, "Sallman's Paintings of the Master: The Story of an Interview with Warner Sallman and an Interpretation of his Six Famous Paintings," *1947 Annual,* vol. 2 (Cleveland: North American Baptist General Conference, 1947), 21.

11. The folder in the Bates material at the Anderson archives is undated but can be firmly dated from a text in it that states how many images by Sallman the publishers had issued "in the

past fifteen years" since the first image, the *Head of Christ,* appeared in 1941. *Religious Masterpieces by Sallman,* Bates Folder, Sallman Archives.

12. Charles Bates, in a telephone interview with me on October 18, 1993, indicated that his father, Fred, wrote ad copy from the 1940s until his death in 1981. Charles Bates worked in the firm from the early 1940s until its liquidation in 1987.

13. Fred Bates may have added the new phrase to Sallman's quotation in response to charges of plagiarism. Apparently some viewers noticed a remarkable similarity between the *Head of Christ* and a painting of 1892, *The Friend of the Humble,* by Léon Lhermitte. According to an article by Carl Henry, as early as 1943 an art professor at Wheaton College named DeWitt Jayne had rejected the originality of *Head of Christ* by pointing to its resemblance to Lhermitte's painting. Henry quotes Jayne as saying, "Sallman didn't even have the draftsmanship to make a good copy of it." See Carl F. Henry, "Evangelical Piety and Christian Art," *Christianity Today* 2, no. 11 (March 3, 1958), 26. I have not been able to determine whether this is a statement on record. For further discussion of the relation between Sallman's work and Lhermitte's painting see David Morgan, "Sallman's *Head of Christ:* The History of an Image," *Christian Century* 109 (October 7, 1992), 868–70.

14. Glenn D. Everett, "Story of a Great Picture," *Link* 16, no. 4 (April 1958), 14.

15. William McDermott, "The Miracle Picture," *Christian Life* 24, no. 11 (March 1963), 27–28.

16. For other published accounts see Bruce Baylor, "A Man's Artist," *Sunday School Promoter* 5, no. 2 (May 1943), 24–29; Howard W. Ellis, *Story of Sallman's "Head of Christ"* (Indianapolis: Kriebel and Bates, 1944); William F. McDermott, "Here's How Sallman Painted It," *Together* (October 1956), 47–48; Dorothy Haskin, "The Man Who Painted a Manly Head of Christ," *Contact* 5, no. 5 (February 1, 1959), 1–11. Sallman himself also disseminated the story while reproducing his *Head of Christ* and other images at his chalk talks. Many letter writers recall attending these events. A gentleman from California remembers one such occasion when he heard Sallman recount the narrative: "He said he was to illustrate an Easter picture for the front page of the newspaper. He was having difficulty in deciding on a subject or topic and it [was] getting near the deadline. One night while sleeping he said he saw a vision of how Christ might have looked. He jumped out of bed and picked up his paint brushes and painted the vision as he remembered it" (193).

17. Possibly the version written by Howard Ellis (*Story of Sallman's "Head of Christ"*).

18. David Freedberg, *The Power of Images* (Chicago: University of Chicago Press, 1989), 205–12.

19. Wackenroder's account is similar on a number of points to a variety of versions of Sallman's testimony; see Wilhelm Heinrich Wackenroder, *Herzensergiessungen eines kunstliebenden Klosterbruders,* reprinted in *Sämtliche Schriften,* ed. Curt Grützmacher and Sybille Claus (Rowohlt, 1968), 13–14. Although Sallman certainly was not familiar with Wackenroder's story, this narrative motif likely had come to represent one dominant understanding of the intersection of artistic creation and religious belief. The piety of such artists as Fra Angelico was reported by Vasari in his *Lives of Eminent Painters and Sculptors* (see Betty Burroughs, ed., *Vasari's Lives of the Artists* [New York: Simon and Schuster, 1946], 100–101). Wackenroder wrote his work after having carefully read Vasari's *Lives.* For a discussion of Wackenroder's account of Raphael and its relation to the tradition of icons see Hans Belting, *Likeness and Presence: A History of the Image Before the Era of Art,* tr. Edmund Jephcott (Chicago: University of Chicago Press, 1994), 480–84.

20. For a published version of this account see William McDermott, "Miracle Picture," 26.

21. "His Likeness," *Newsweek* 30, no. 1 (July 7, 1947), 79.

22. For another instance of the materialization of the picture see a letter to Sallman from a woman in Clinton, Iowa, dated July 4, 1957. I have quoted and discussed this letter in "Imaging Protestant Piety: The Icons of Warner Sallman," *Religion and American Culture: A Journal of Interpretation* 3, no. 1 (Winter 1993), 33.

23. Such instances are not difficult to enumerate. In 1979 a wallet-sized version of the *Head of Christ* secreted what was determined to be human blood; see my discussion of this event in Chapter 1 and in "Imaging Protestant Piety," 33.

24. I do not restrict the term *ideology* to the radical sense of false consciousness but intend by it, more generally, the domain of ideas and signifying practices that may or may not correspond to an actual state of affairs but that are nevertheless considered by those who hold them to be an accurate explanation of, and justification for, what is taken to be social reality.

25. William F. McDermott, "Here's How Sallman Painted It," 48.

26. I resist separating ideological and psychological into separate categories of response because the formation of consciousness bridges the individual and the group. I wish to keep these two in tension because the particular content of such psychological processes as regression, repression, and projection are culturally transmitted and therefore ideologically engaged. To separate them for purposes of analysis seems unnecessarily artificial.

27. One Protestant woman wrote that a copy of the *Head of Christ* was, in fact, the only item to escape damage in her home, which was destroyed by fire. The picture hung in her parents' bedroom. "Now when I see the face of Christ I see protection. He protected my parents and siblings from the fire" (527). For a fascinating parallel in the popular history of images of Martin Luther see Robert W. Scribner, "Incombustible Luther: The Image of the Reformer in Early Modern Germany," in *Popular Culture and Popular Movements in Reformation Germany* (London: Hambledon Press, 1987), 323–53.

28. J. Maurice Trimmer, "The Influence of Pictures," *Religious Digest* 20, no. 141 (June 1947), 51; condensed from the *Watchman-Examiner* (March 13, 1947).

29. Ibid., 49–50.

30. William McDermott, "Miracle Picture," 26.

31. Ibid., 28.

32. "He Painted Jesus' Picture," *Sunday Pix* (January 15, 1961), 1.

33. McDermott, "Miracle Picture," 28. A clergyman responding to the query concerning Sallman's reception recalled an incident during World War II while he was serving as a chaplain's assistant in a prison camp for Japanese prisoners of war. His attention was caught by a young Japanese soldier who seemed to want to communicate with the American but could not. "On the impulse of the moment I pulled out my billfold and showed him the picture of Christ by Sallman. His face lighted up beautifully and he pointed his finger heavenward and said something that resembled Jesus!" (18). For further anecdotes about the power of the image to transform individual lives from a fallen state, see Dorothy Haskin, "The Man Who Painted a Manly Head of Christ," 11. See also a typescript by Sylvia Peterson for another collection of midrashim culled from various sources in 1959, entitled "Into All the World," Bates File, Sallman Archive.

34. Carl H. Duning, *Christ in Every Purse* (Richmond, Ind.: Nicholson Press, 1948), 3.

35. I was told that this image was known as Sputnik in two separate conversations: with Charles Bates, July 19, 1991, and with printer Birger Sponberg, August 3, 1991.

36. C. Austen Miles, "In the Garden," in *Christian Service Songs* (Winona Lake, Ind.: Rodeheaver, Hall-Mack, 1939), 187.

37. Robert A. Orsi, "'He Keeps Me Going': Women's Devotion to Saint Jude Thaddeus and the Dialectics of Gender in American Catholicism, 1929–1965," in *Belief in History: Innova-

tive Approaches to European and American Religion, ed. Thomas Kselman (Notre Dame: University of Notre Dame Press, 1991), 157.

38. There are, of course, important exceptions: in the 1950s several public campaigns to disseminate Sallman's image achieved media attention and took the *Head of Christ* into the public domains of courtrooms, libraries, public schools, and city halls.

39. "What a Friend We Have in Jesus," in *The Methodist Hymnal* (New York: Methodist Book Concern, 1935), 240 (courtesy Whitemore and Smith). An unidentified newspaper article of 1960 in the Sallman Archives indicates that at one Sunday morning chalk talk, the organ played "What a Friend We Have in Jesus" and "My Jesus, I Love Thee, I Know Thou Art Nigh" while Sallman re-created the *Head of Christ* in chalk. Hiley H. Ward, "Stern or Tender? Artist Undertakes Job of Drawing Jesus at Worship Service," 1960, Sallman Archives.

40. Sallman is said to have been perplexed by the charge that his Christ was not Jewish (my interview with James Sallman). Explicit denials of this charge appeared in such sympathetic articles on Sallman's work as the following, which seems to respond directly to charges of ethnocentricity: "It was not a Nordic Christ, with blond hair which many northern European artists, with naive disregard for Christ's Jewish birth, had depicted on their canvasses. It was Christ with black flowing hair and a face one could expect on a Jew from rural Galilee." Glenn D. Everett, "Story of a Great Picture," *Link* 16, no. 4 (April 1958), 14. Note that the brown hair of the picture becomes black in this attempt to argue for anthropological likeness.

41. Ken Garfield, "YMCA Panel: Keep Portrait of Pale Jesus, with Explanation," *Charlotte Observer* (May 10, 1995), 1C, 5C.

42. For Luther's and Calvin's respective discussions of images and the second commandment, see the Introduction.

43. John Calvin, *Institutes of the Christian Religion,* trans. Henry Beveridge (Grand Rapids, Mich.: Eerdmans, 1962), 1: 94–95.

44. Ibid., 97.

45. Ibid., 95.

46. The phrase "five-point Calvinist" refers to the five-point declaration adopted by the General Assembly of the Presbyterian Church in 1910. These points, considered essential for genuine belief, were the inerrancy of the Bible, the virgin birth, Christ's atonement, his resurrection, and the "miracle-working power of Christ." See Ernest R. Sandeen, *The Roots of Fundamentalism: British and American Millenarianism, 1800–1930* (Chicago: University of Chicago Press, 1970), xiv, 251.

47. An article in the *Wall Street Journal* quoted several enthusiastic collectors of sculptor Sam Butcher's Precious Moments figurines, all of whom were women; "Precious Moments Is Brilliant at Answering Its Collectors' Prayers," *Wall Street Journal* (September 14, 1993), 1, A8.

48. Those who display, cherish, exchange, and pray to, through, or with Sallman's images are more often women than men. Robert Orsi has noted the same fact in popular Catholic devotion, particularly in regard to the cult of St. Jude, in two excellent articles: "What Did Women Think They Were Doing When They Prayed to Saint Jude?" *U.S. Catholic Historian* 8, nos. 1 and 2 (Winter–Spring 1989), 67–79; and "'He Keeps Me Going,'"; see also Orsi's book *The Madonna of 115th Street: Faith and Community in Italian Harlem, 1880–1950* (New Haven: Yale University Press, 1985), 204–17.

49. Perhaps this explains why the return to a masculine Christianity among American evangelicals in the 1990s has not made a point of targeting Sallman's image as problematic. On

the return to virile evangelicalism see Kenneth L. Woodward, "The Gospel of Guyhood,"
Newsweek (August 29, 1994), 60–61.

50. See Arthur Dale, "3-D Jesus Appears on T.V., Hundreds Cured by Image of Messiah," *Sun*
(May 30, 1995), 20–21; *Miracles and Other Wonders,* produced by Paul Klein and Charles E.
Sellier, 1992; Ann Victoria, "Jesus Appears at U.N. Building!" *Weekly World News* (August
23, 1994), n.p.

51. Cris Robins, "Cover Hung over Jesus after Vigil," *Herald Palladium* (March 1, 1993), 1, 4;
Rod Smith, "Jesus Portrait Down, Not Necessarily Out," *Kalamazoo Gazette* (February
22, 1995), 1, 2; David Crumm, "Jesus Buttons Staying, Says School Board," *Detroit Free
Press* (May 17, 1995), 1A, 2A.

52. The collection, called "Portraits of Jesus," is produced by the Hamilton Collection, Jack-
sonville, Florida. Frequently advertised in Sunday newspapers in the mid-1990s, the collection includes *Christ in Gethsemane, The Lord Is My Shepherd,* and *Christ at Heart's Door.*

Contributors

BETTY A. DEBERG is the author of *Ungodly Women: Gender and the First Wave of American Fundamentalism*. She is associate professor of theology at Valparaiso University and a consulting editor for the *Dictionary of American Religious Thinkers*.

ERIKA DOSS directs American studies at the University of Colorado, Boulder. She is the author of *Benton, Pollock and the Politics of Modernism: From Regionalism to Abstract Expressionism*.

NEIL HARRIS is Preston and Sterling Morton Professor of History at the University of Chicago. Among his books is *Cultural Excursions: Marketing Appetites and Cultural Tastes in Modern America*.

COLLEEN MCDANNELL is associate professor of history and holds the Sterling McMurrin Chair in Religious Studies at the University of Utah. She is the author of *The Christian Home in Victorian America, 1840-1900, Heaven: A History* (with Bernhard Lang), and *Material Christianity: Religion and Popular Culture in America*.

DAVID MORGAN chairs the Department of Art at Valparaiso University. His publications have appeared in such journals as *Eighteenth-*

Century Studies, Religion and American Culture, Journal of the History of Ideas, and *Journal of Aesthetics and Art Criticism.*

SALLY M. PROMEY teaches art history at the University of Maryland at College Park. Her book *Spiritual Spectacles: Vision and Image in Mid-Nineteenth-Century Shakerism* was awarded the National Museum of American Art's 1994 Charles C. Eldredge Prize for Distinguished Scholarship in American Art.

Index

Page numbers in italics refer to illustrations.

Credits for Chapter-Opening Illustrations

title page: Warner Sallman, *Head of Christ,* 1940, oil on canvas, 28¼ × 22⅛″. Courtesy Jessie C. Wilson Galleries, Anderson University. (Pl. I.)

page 1: Original painting by Paul Delaroche, engraved by John G. MacRae, *Our Savior.* From Rev. Ingram Cobbin, *Cobbin's Commentary on the Bible for Young and Old,* ed. Rev. E. J. Goodspeed (New York: Selmar Press, 1876), vol. 1, frontispiece. (Fig. i.2.)

page 25: Warner Sallman, *Portrait of Jesus,* 1966, oil on canvas, 20¼ × 16¼″. Courtesy Jessie C. Wilson Galleries, Anderson University. (Pl. XII.)

page 61: Warner Sallman, *Follow Thou Me,* 1948, oil on canvas, 28 × 22″. Courtesy Jessie C. Wilson Galleries, Anderson University. (Fig. 4.2.)

page 95: Heinrich Hofmann, *Christ and the Rich Young Ruler,* 1899, detail, oil on canvas. Courtesy Riverside Church, New York. (Fig. i.3.)

page 123: Warner Sallman, *The Lord Is My Shepherd,* 1943, oil on canvas, 40 × 30″. Courtesy Jessie C. Wilson Galleries, Anderson University. (Pl. V.)

page 148: Georges Rouault, *Head of Christ,* 1905, oil on paper on canvas, 39 × 25¼″. Courtesy The Chrysler Museum, Norfolk, Virginia; gift of Walter P. Chrysler, Jr., 71.519. (Fig. 5.5.)

page 181: Léon Lhermitte, *The Friend of the Humble,* 1892, detail. Gift of J. Randolph Coolidge, courtesy Museum of Fine Arts, Boston. (Fig. i.5.)